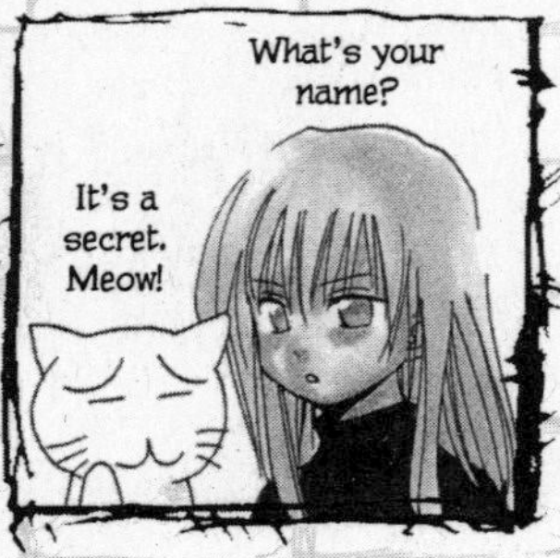
What's your name?
It's a secret. Meow!

About the cat that appears here and there... Before the serialization of ***Black Cat*** in ***Weekly Shonen Jump***, I did a one-shot story called "Stray Cat" and I kind of liked the cat, so I kept it around. In your fan letters, you've given the cat a lot of different names, and that's totally fine with me -- after all, stray cats are called by all kinds of names in all kinds of places. In fact, there's a spotted stray that wanders near my house pretty often. It has a black ring around its mouth, so I call it "Higemi" (a play on "hige," the word for beard) and I feed it sometimes.

—Kentaro Yabuki, 2001

Kentaro Yabuki made his manga debut with ***Yamato Gensoki***, a short series about a young empress destined to unite the warring states of ancient Japan and the boy sworn to protect her. His next series, ***Black Cat***, commenced serialization in the pages of ***Weekly Shonen Jump*** in 2000 and quickly developed a loyal fan following. ***Black Cat*** has also become an animated TV series, first hitting Japan's airwaves in the fall of 2005.

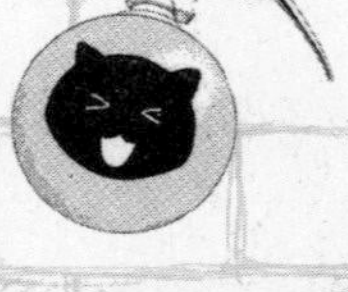

BLACK CAT VOL. 2
The SHONEN JUMP Manga Edition

STORY AND ART BY
KENTARO YABUKI

English Adaptation/Kelly Sue DeConnick
Translation/JN Productions
Touch-up Art & Lettering/Gia Cam Luc
Design/Courtney Utt
Editor/Frances E. Wall

Managing Editor/Elizabeth Kawasaki
Director of Production/Noboru Watanabe
Vice President of Publishing/Alvin Lu
Vice President & Editor in Chief/Yumi Hoashi
Sr. Director of Acquisitions/Rika Inouye
Vice President of Sales & Marketing/Liza Coppola
Publisher/Hyoe Narita

Published by VIZ Media, LLC
P.O. Box 77010
San Francisco, CA 94107

SHONEN JUMP Manga Edition
10 9 8 7 6 5 4 3 2 1
First printing, May 2006

TRAIN
HEARTNET

THE WORLD'S
MOST POPULAR MANGA

VIZ
media
www.viz.com

SHONEN JUMP
www.shonenjump.com

SHONEN JUMP MANGA EDITION

BLACK CAT™

ブラック・キャット

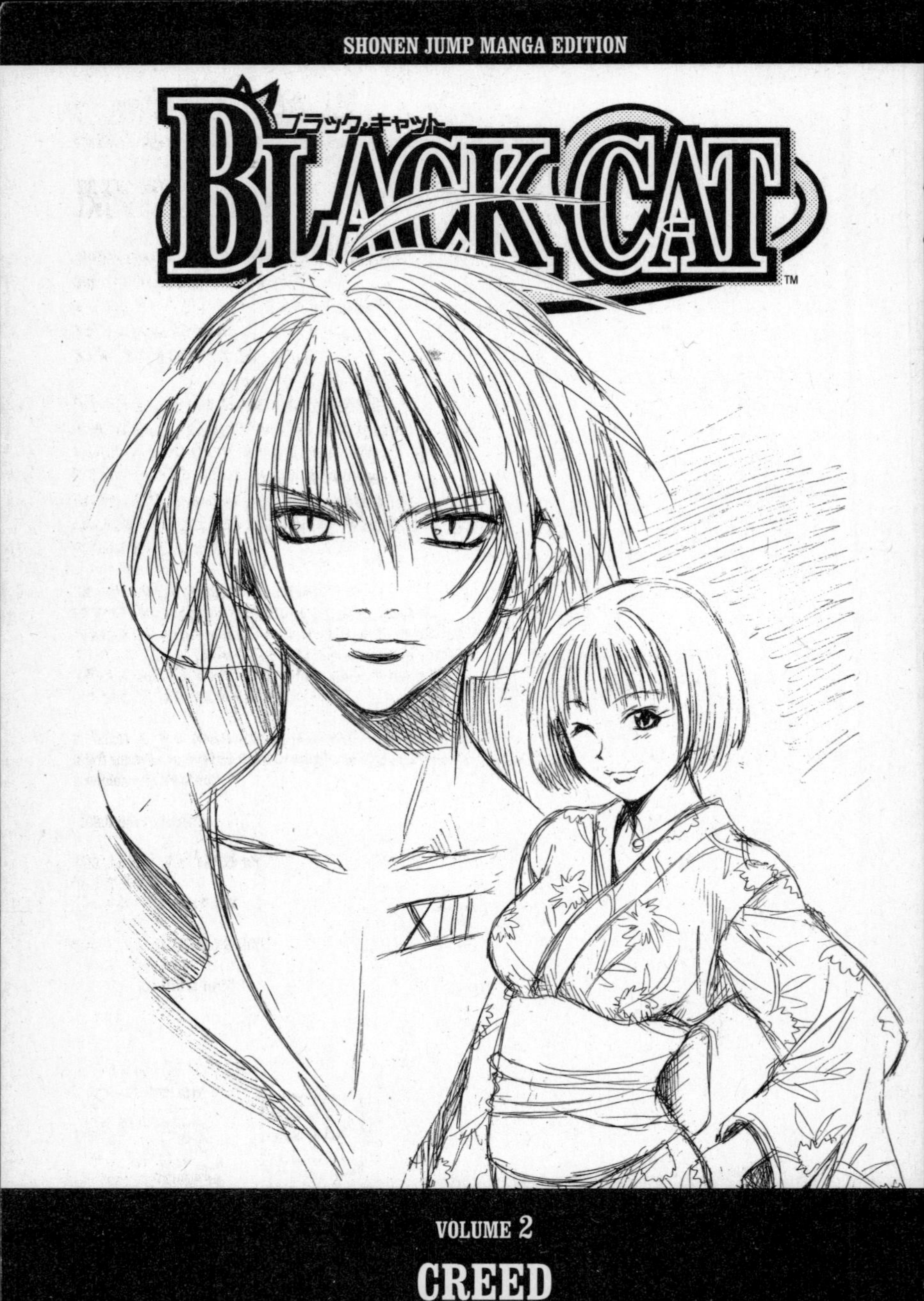
XIII

VOLUME 2

CREED

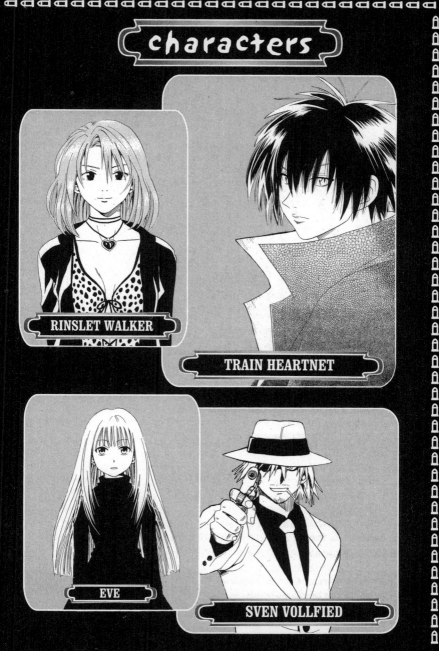

characters

TRAIN HEARTNET
RINSLET WALKER
SVEN VOLLFIED
EVE

BLACK CAT

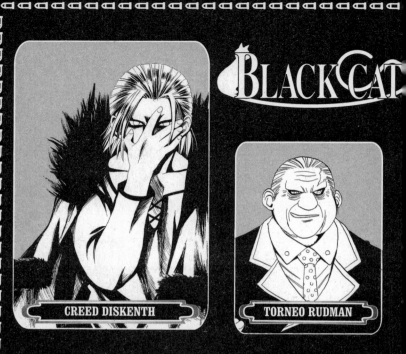

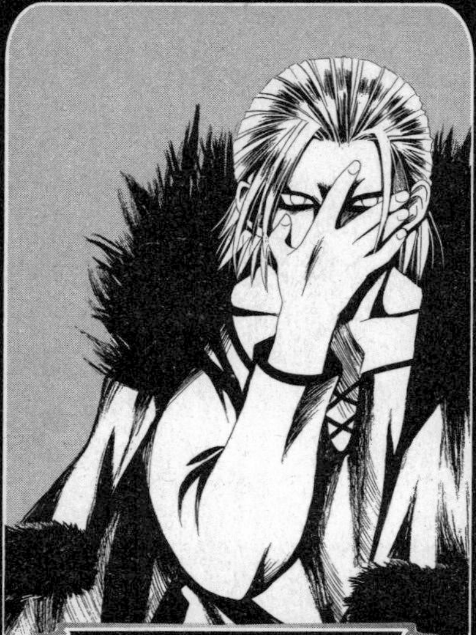
CREED DISKENTH

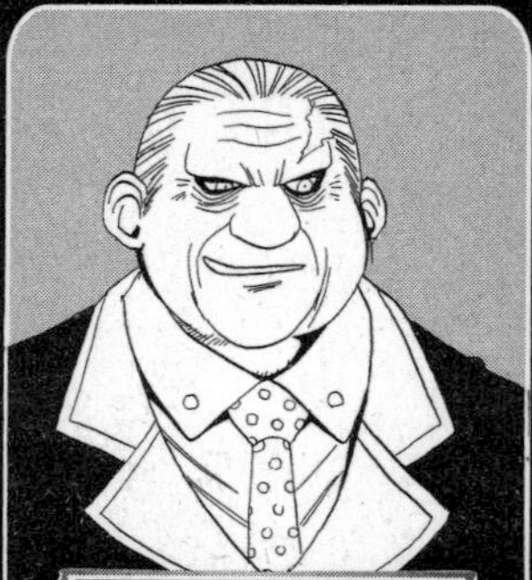
TORNEO RUDMAN

A fearless "eraser" responsible for the deaths of countless powerful men, Train "Bla Cat" Heartnet carries a pistol engraved with the Roman numeral XIII, his ag number as a member of an elite military group working under the orders of Chron a mysterious organization that secretly controls one-third of the world's economy. T years after his departure from Chronos, Train lives a carefree wanderer's life, working w his partner Sven as bounty hunters ("sweepers"), all the while pursuing a man who kill someone he cared for.

In the last volume, Train and Sven met Rinslet, a thief-for-hire who proposed an alliance the purpose of ambushing elusive crime boss Torneo Rudman. The Sweepers would bri Torneo to the authorities for a huge bounty, while Rinslet's target was Torneo's research da on the development of superhuman living weapons. Unaware of Rinslet's true motives, Tra infiltrated the Torneo Mansion alone. There he encountered a girl named Eve, a product Torneo's research. Sensing danger, Train fled. As if in pursuit, Eve also disappeared.

Sven soon happened upon Eve in town, thinking she was an innocent lost child. When Torn came looking for Eve, Sven attempted to capture him, and Eve stabbed Sven. Angry that h partner has been wounded, Train is now more determined than ever to capture Torneo…a Sven insists that he be allowed to come along so he can rescue Eve. But what dangers aw them at Torneo's mansion? Will they come face-to-face with the man who changed Trai life forever?!

BLACK CAT

VOLUME 2 CREED

CONTENTS

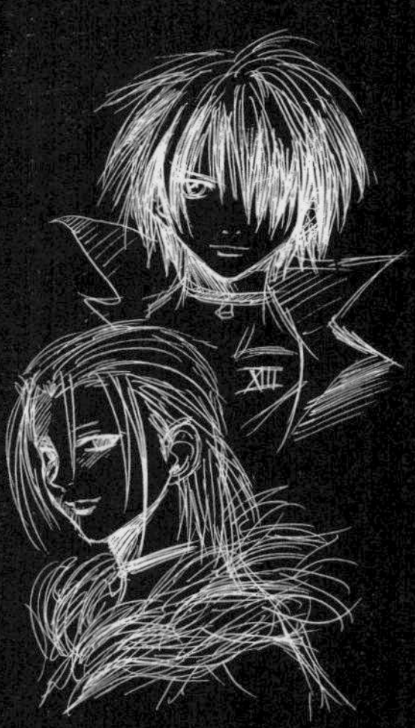

XIII

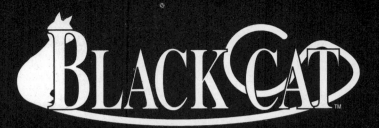

Chapter 9: Cat's Eye

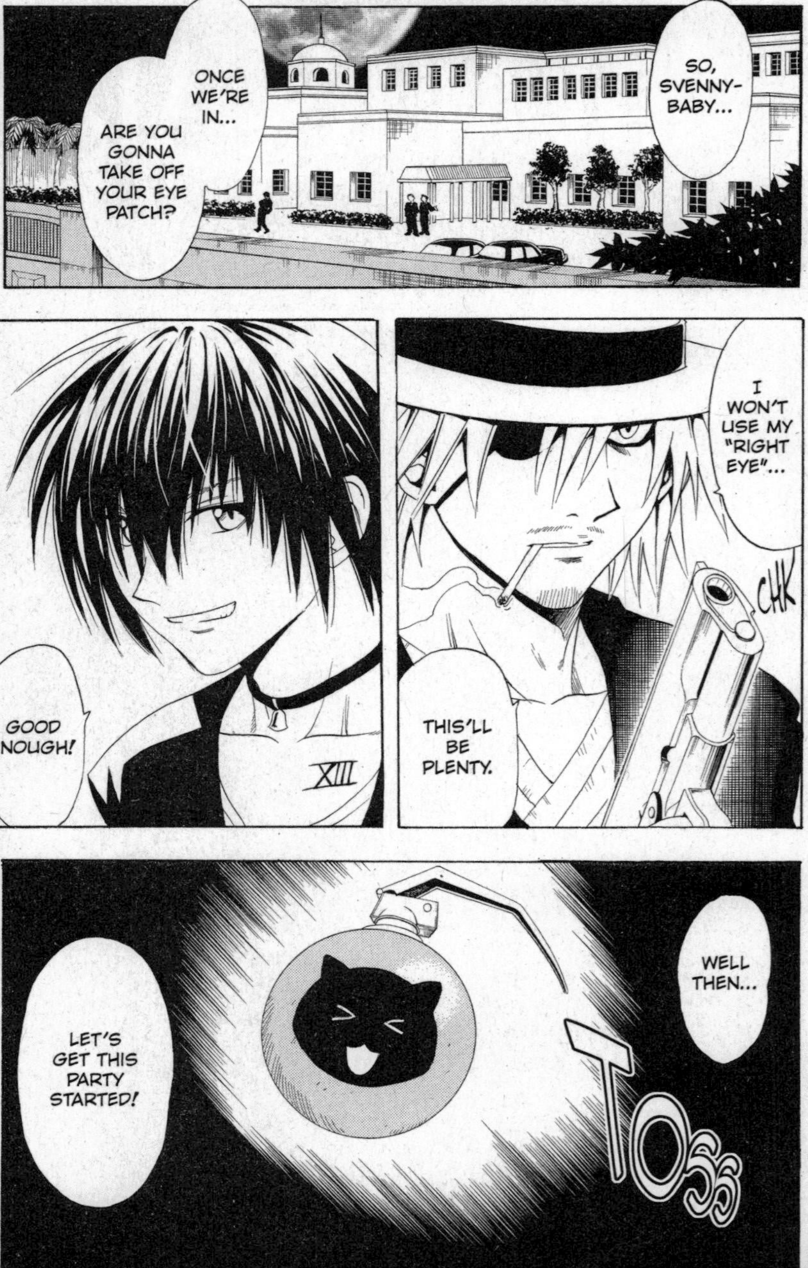
SO, SVENNY-BABY...
ONCE WE'RE IN...
ARE YOU GONNA TAKE OFF YOUR EYE PATCH?
I WON'T USE MY "RIGHT EYE"...
CHK
THIS'LL BE PLENTY.
GOOD ENOUGH!
WELL THEN...
LET'S GET THIS PARTY STARTED!
TOSS

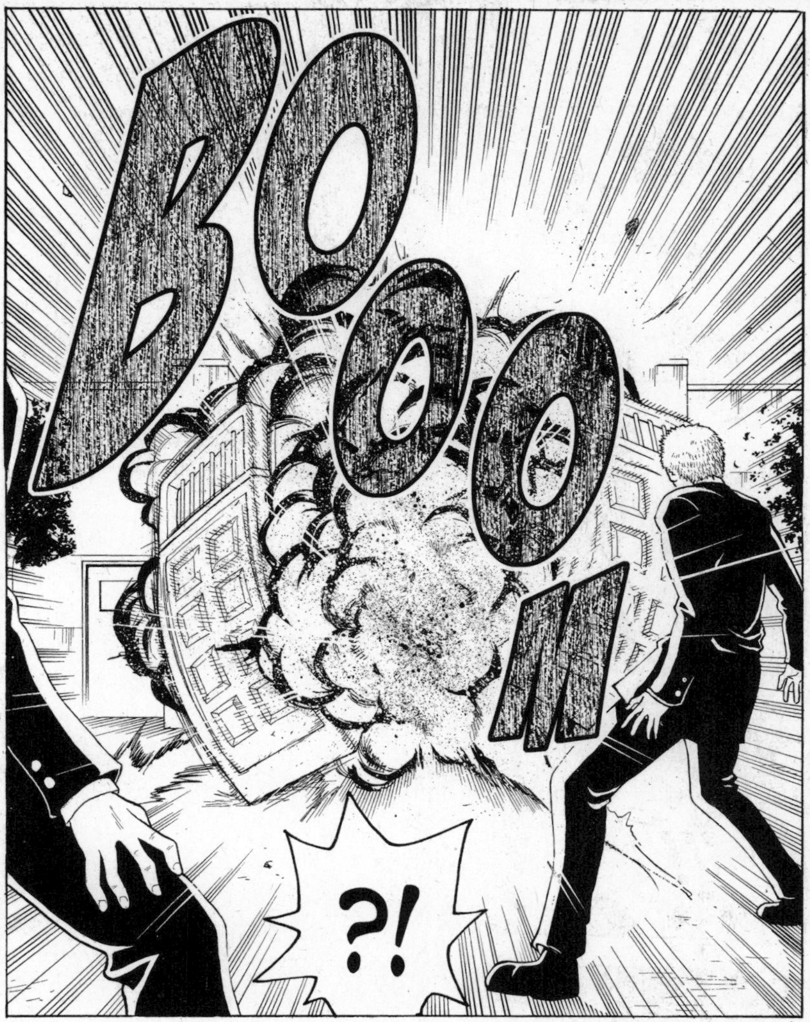
BOOOM
?!

Chapter 9: Cat's Eye

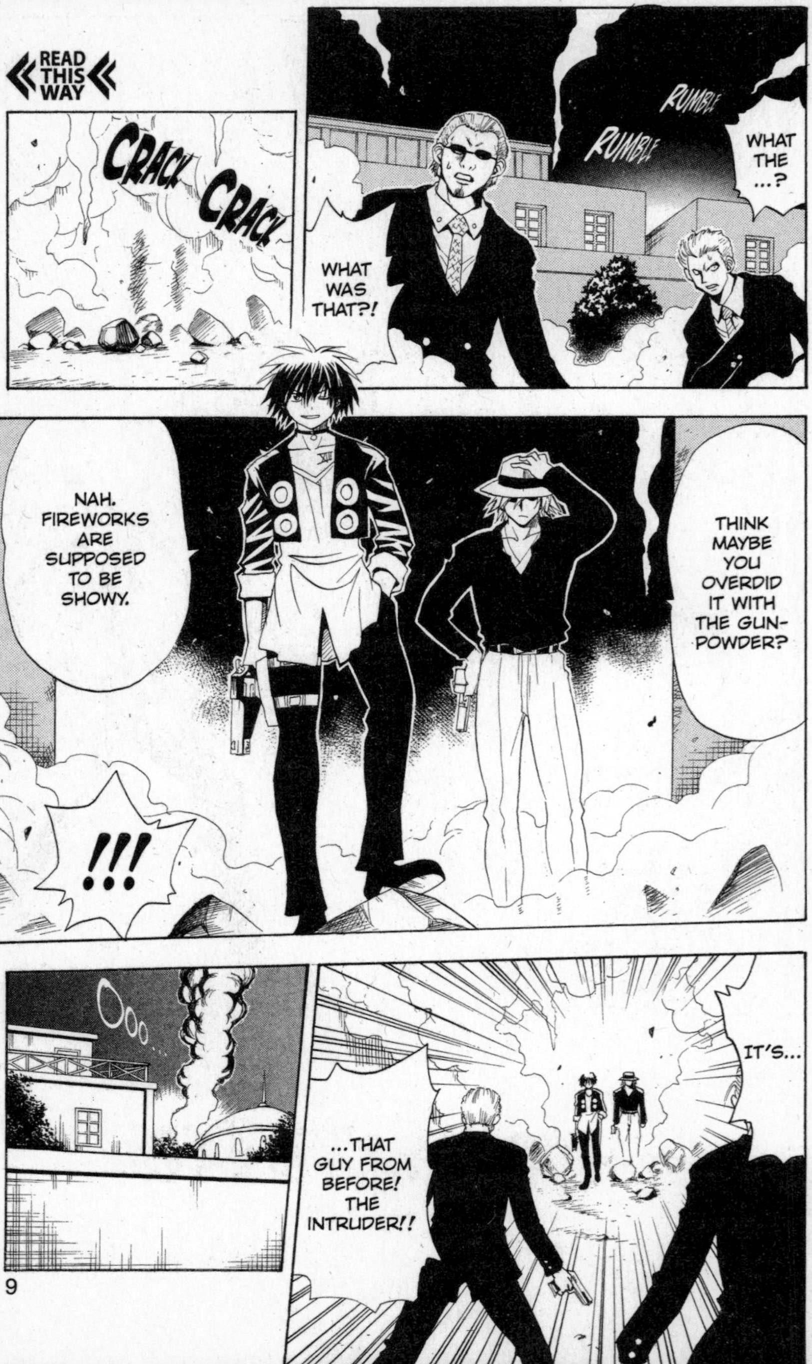
READ THIS WAY
WHAT THE ...?
RUMBLE
RUMBLE
WHAT WAS THAT?!
CRACK
CRACK
THINK MAYBE YOU OVERDID IT WITH THE GUN-POWDER?
NAH. FIREWORKS ARE SUPPOSED TO BE SHOWY.
!!!
IT'S...
...THAT GUY FROM BEFORE! THE INTRUDER!!
Ooo...

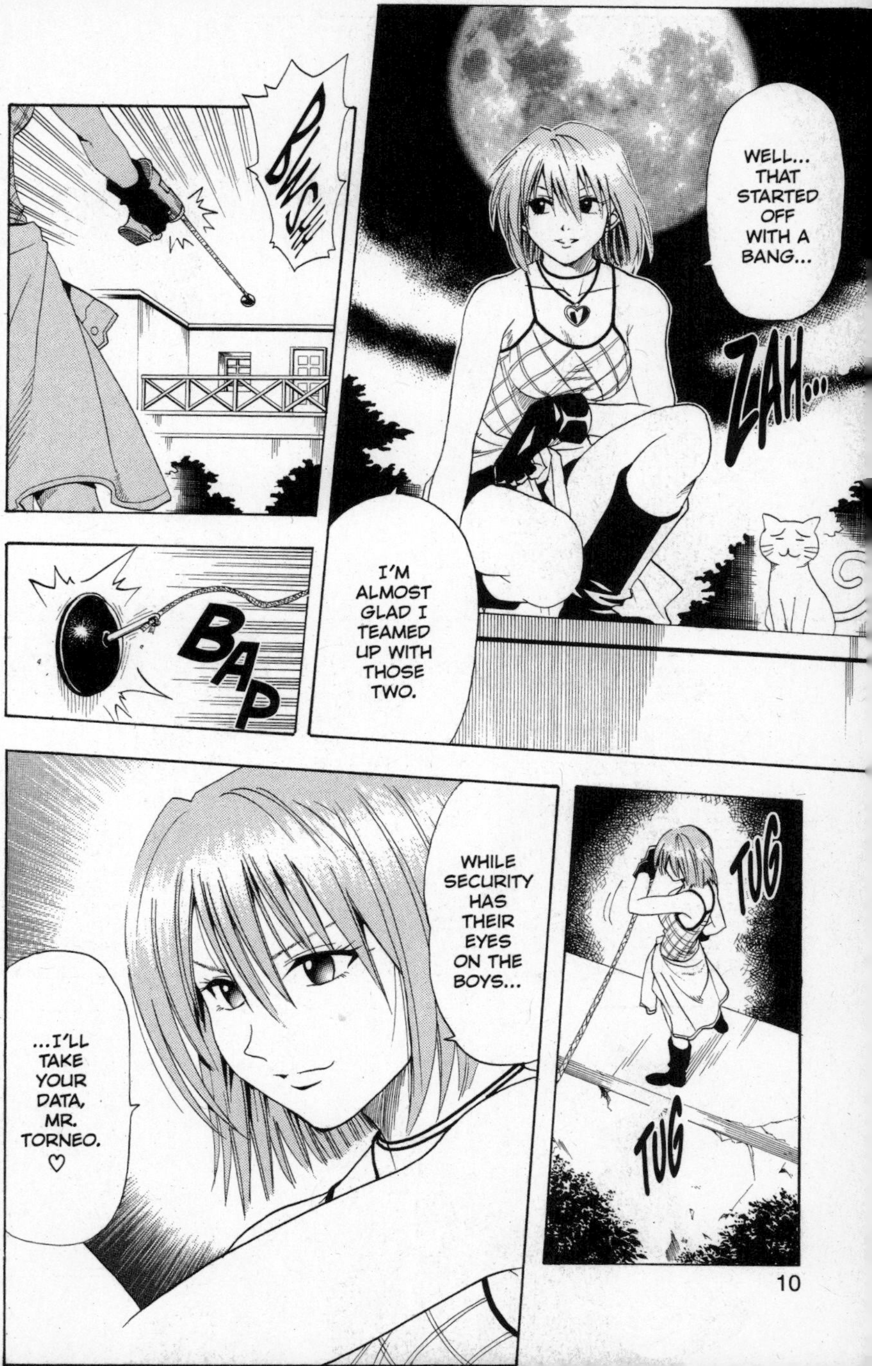

WELL... THAT STARTED OFF WITH A BANG...
ZAH...
I'M ALMOST GLAD I TEAMED UP WITH THOSE TWO.
BWSH
BAP
TUG
TUG
WHILE SECURITY HAS THEIR EYES ON THE BOYS...
...I'LL TAKE YOUR DATA, MR. TORNEO. ♡

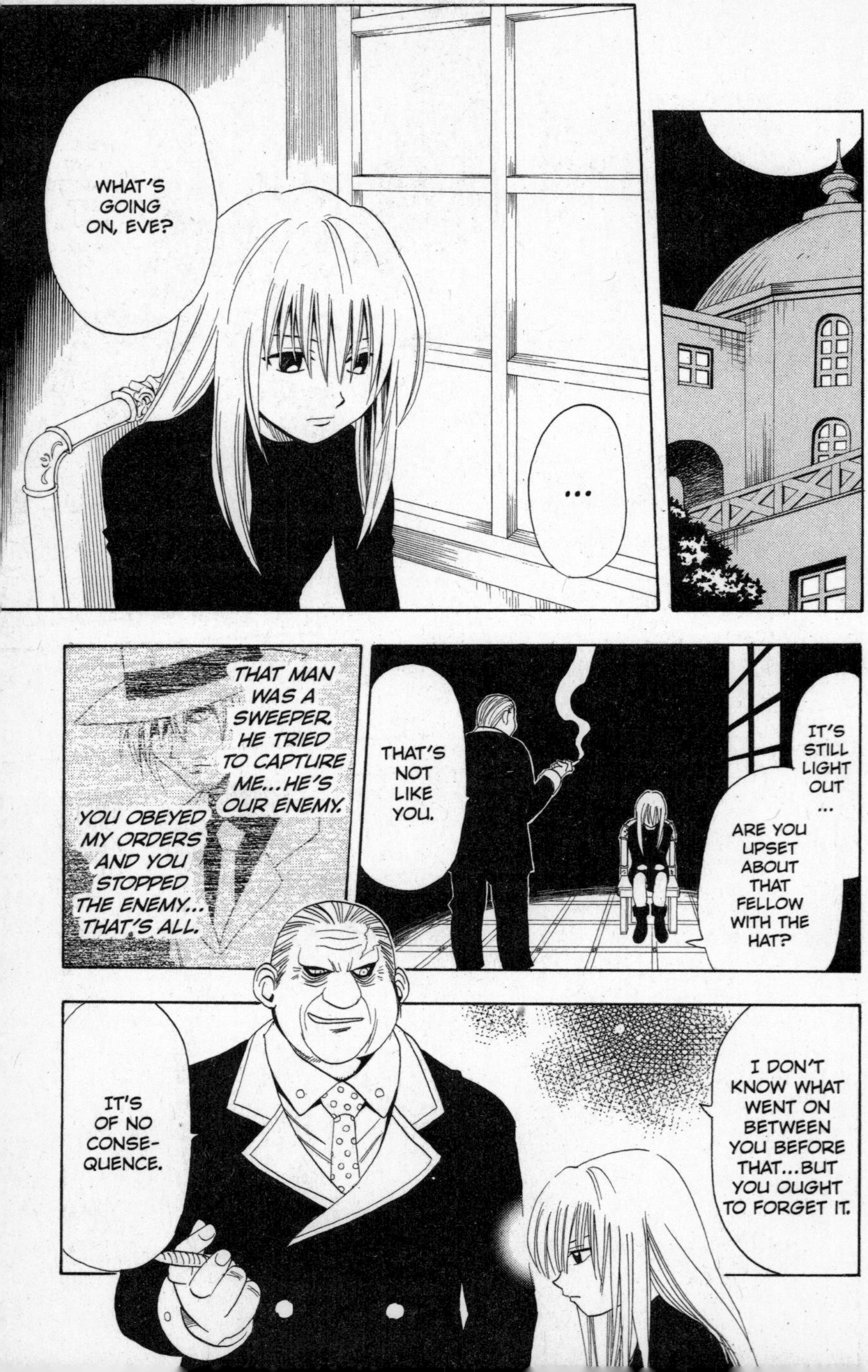
WHAT'S GOING ON, EVE?
...
IT'S STILL LIGHT OUT...
ARE YOU UPSET ABOUT THAT FELLOW WITH THE HAT?
THAT'S NOT LIKE YOU.
THAT MAN WAS A SWEEPER. HE TRIED TO CAPTURE ME...HE'S OUR ENEMY.
YOU OBEYED MY ORDERS AND YOU STOPPED THE ENEMY... THAT'S ALL.
I DON'T KNOW WHAT WENT ON BETWEEN YOU BEFORE THAT...BUT YOU OUGHT TO FORGET IT.
IT'S OF NO CONSE-QUENCE.

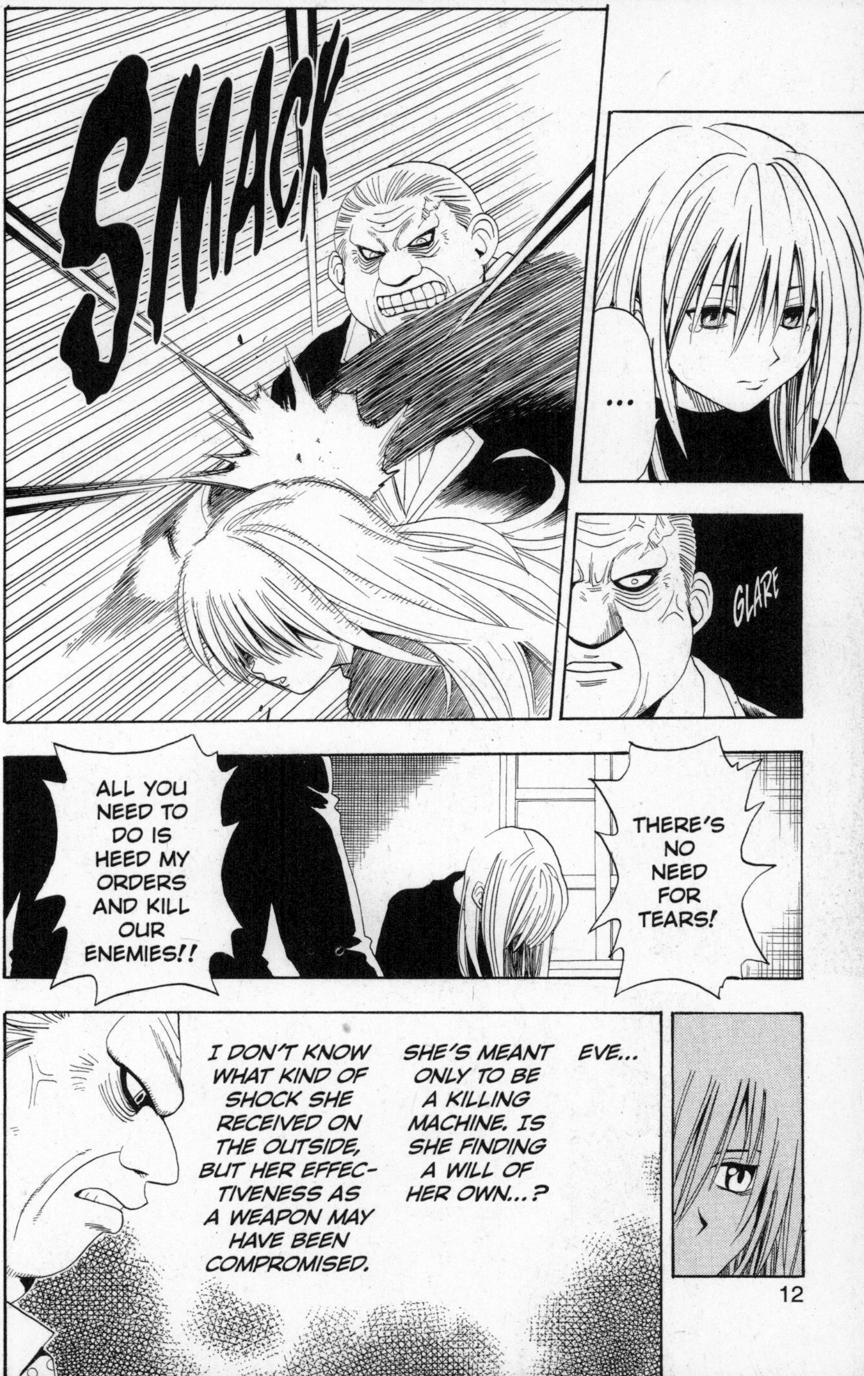
...
GLARE
SMACK
THERE'S NO NEED FOR TEARS!
ALL YOU NEED TO DO IS HEED MY ORDERS AND KILL OUR ENEMIES!!
EVE...
SHE'S MEANT ONLY TO BE A KILLING MACHINE. IS SHE FINDING A WILL OF HER OWN...?
I DON'T KNOW WHAT KIND OF SHOCK SHE RECEIVED ON THE OUTSIDE, BUT HER EFFEC-TIVENESS AS A WEAPON MAY HAVE BEEN COMPROMISED.

READ THIS WAY

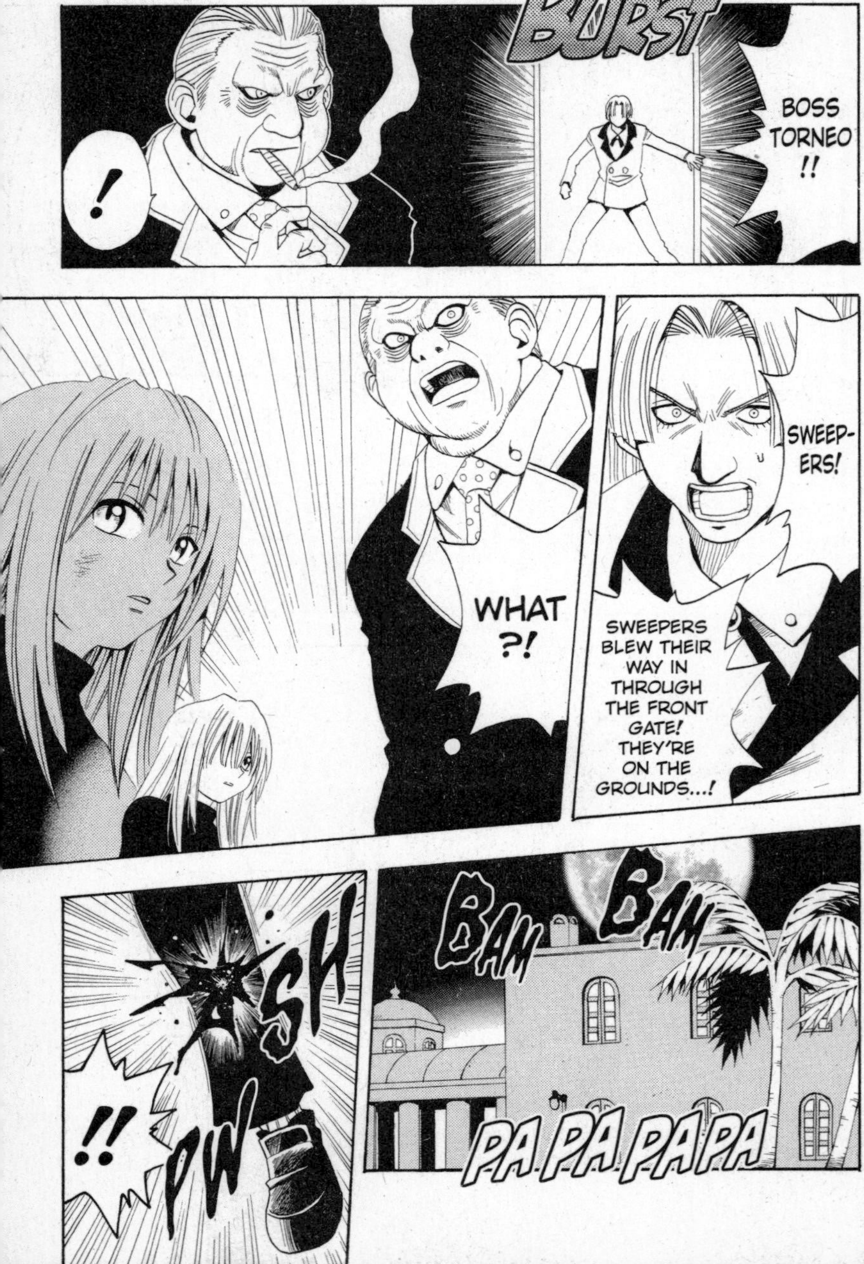

BURST
BOSS TORNEO !!
!
SWEEP-ERS!
SWEEPERS BLEW THEIR WAY IN THROUGH THE FRONT GATE! THEY'RE ON THE GROUNDS...!
WHAT ?!
BAM
BAM
PA PA PA PA PA
PWSH
!!

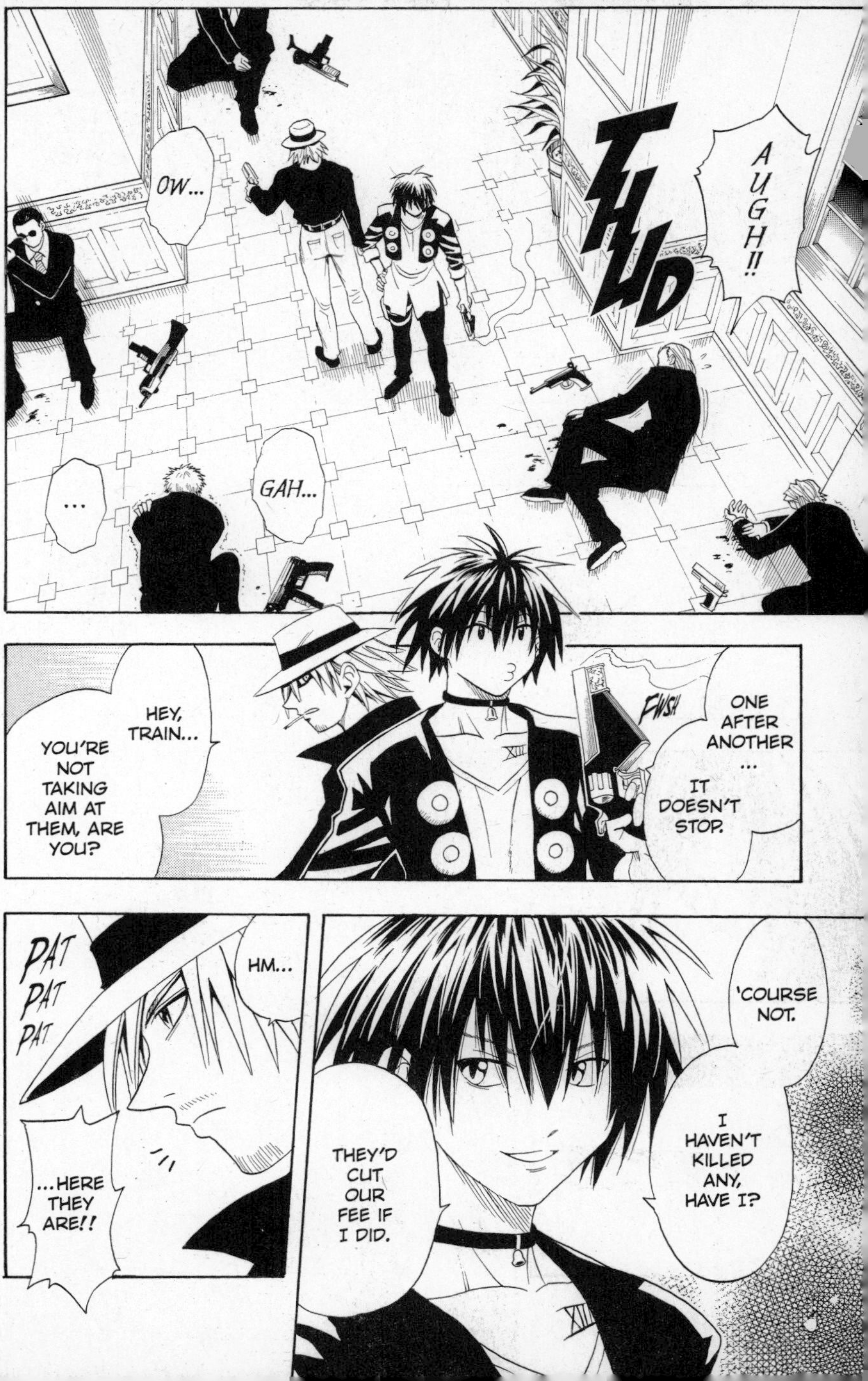
AUGH!!
THUD
OW...
GAH...
...
ONE AFTER ANOTHER... IT DOESN'T STOP.
FWSH
HEY, TRAIN... YOU'RE NOT TAKING AIM AT THEM, ARE YOU?
'COURSE NOT.
I HAVEN'T KILLED ANY, HAVE I?
THEY'D CUT OUR FEE IF I DID.
HM...
PAT PAT PAT
...HERE THEY ARE!!

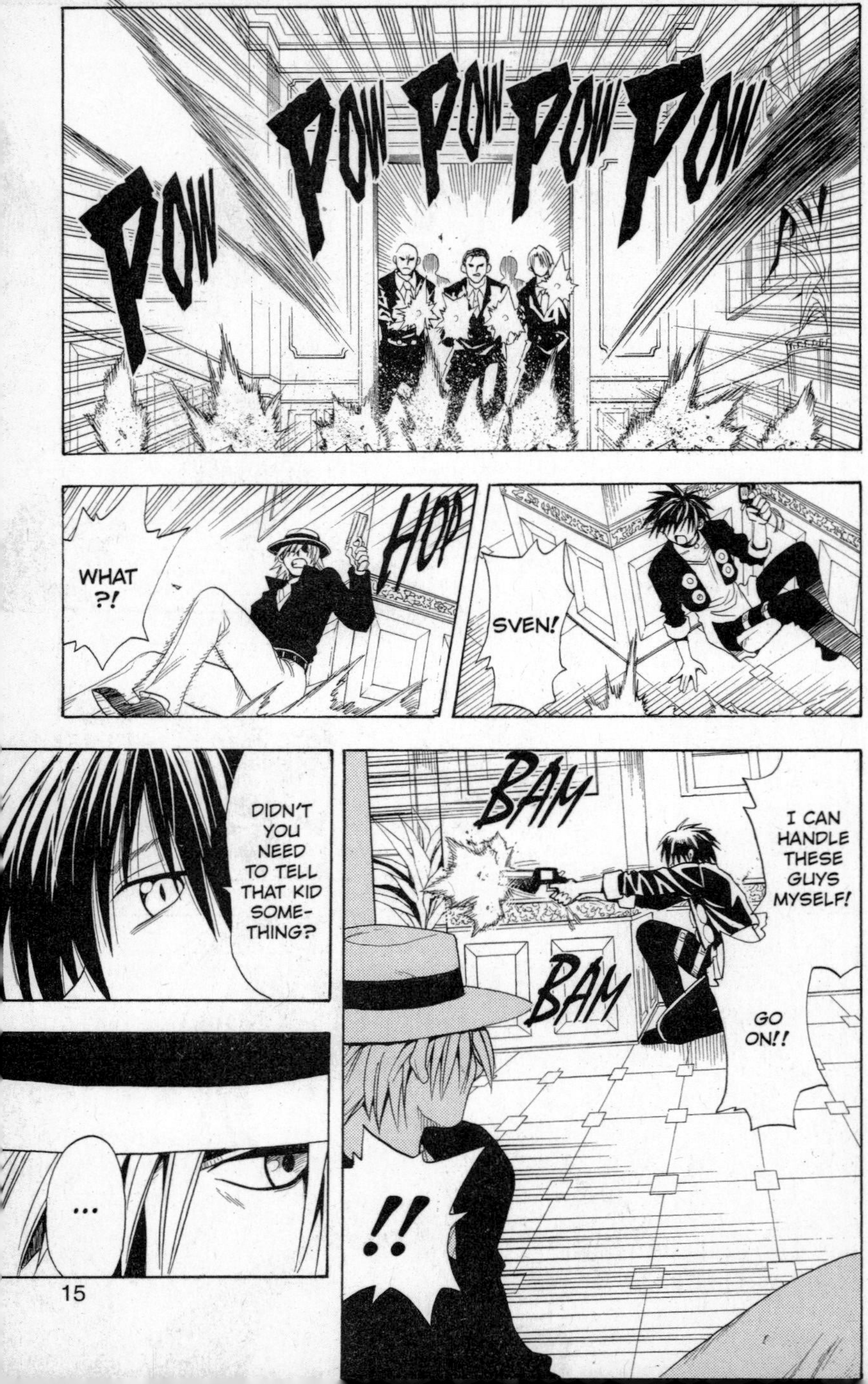
POW POW POW POW POW
SVEN!
HOP
WHAT?!
BAM
I CAN HANDLE THESE GUYS MYSELF!
BAM
GO ON!!
!!
DIDN'T YOU NEED TO TELL THAT KID SOMETHING?
...

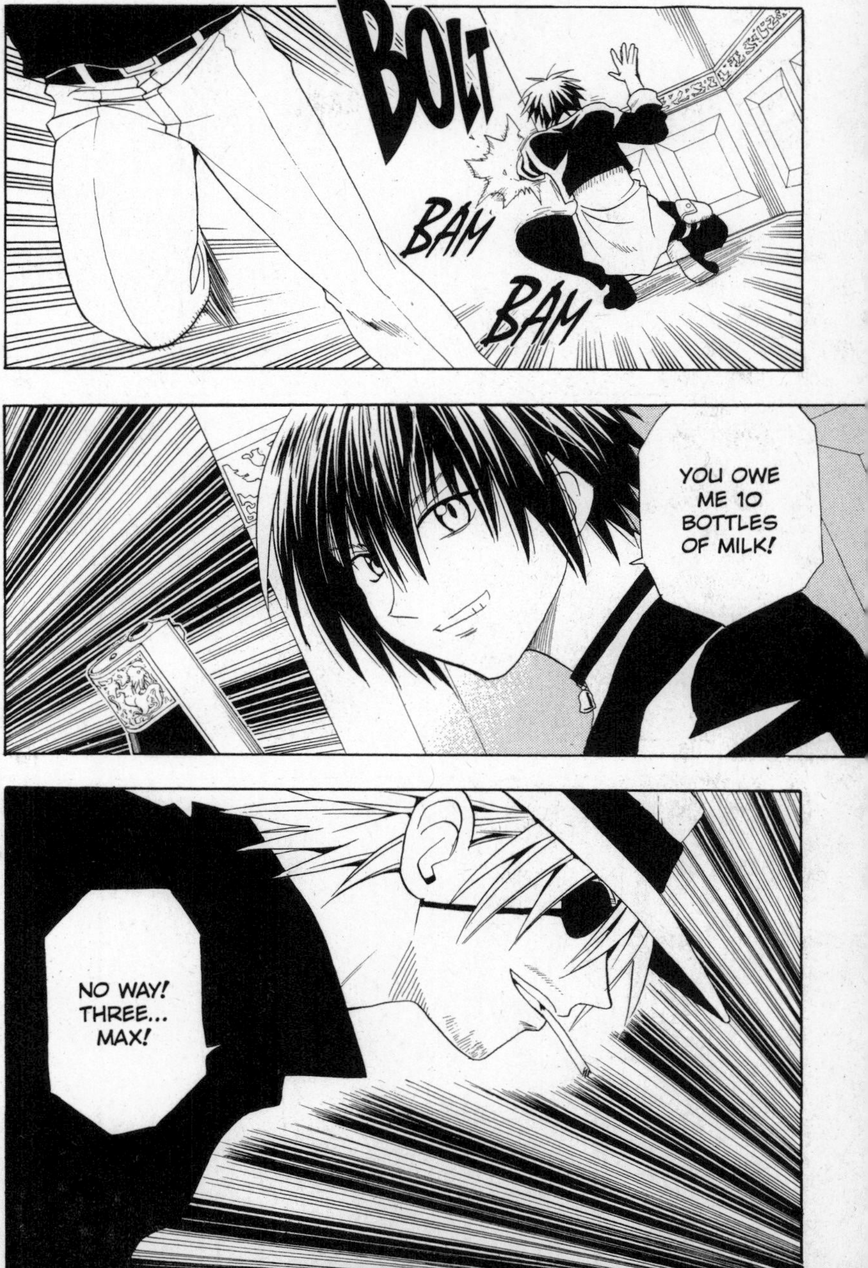
BOLT
BAM
BAM
YOU OWE ME 10 BOTTLES OF MILK!
NO WAY! THREE... MAX!

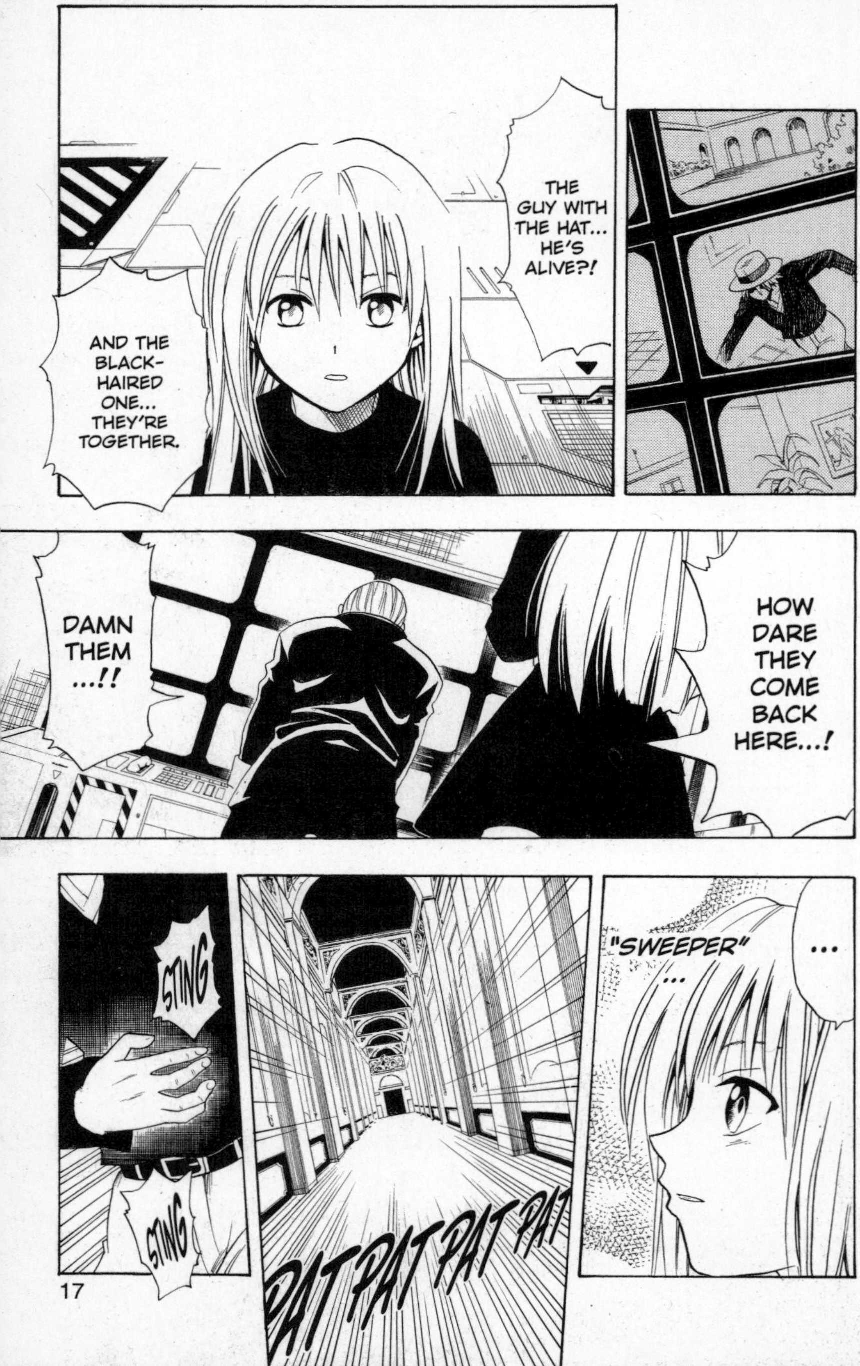
THE GUY WITH THE HAT... HE'S ALIVE?!
AND THE BLACK-HAIRED ONE... THEY'RE TOGETHER.
HOW DARE THEY COME BACK HERE...!
DAMN THEM ...!!
...
"SWEEPER" ...
PAT PAT PAT PAT
STING
STING

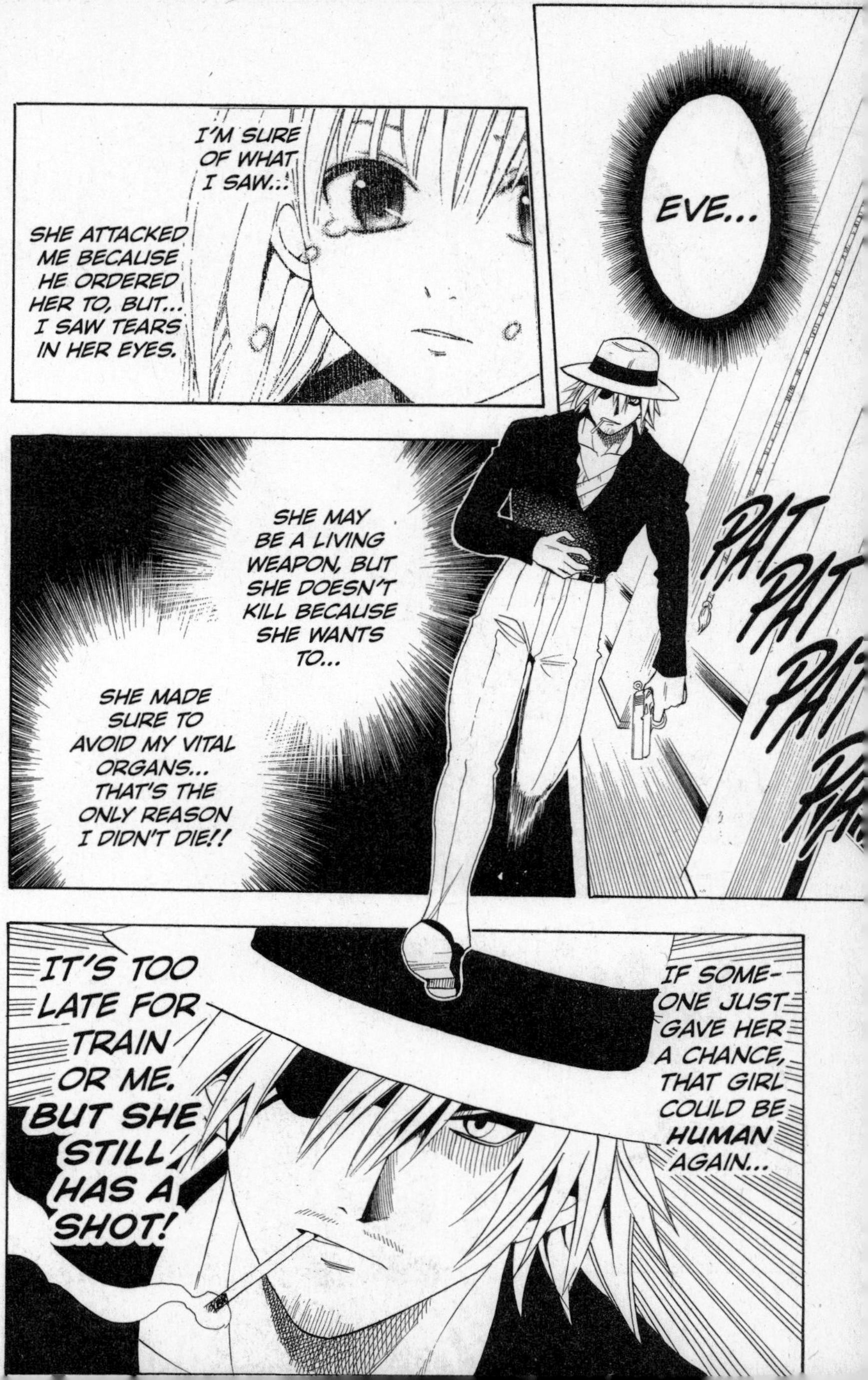
EVE...
PAT PAT PAT PAT
I'M SURE OF WHAT I SAW...
SHE ATTACKED ME BECAUSE HE ORDERED HER TO, BUT... I SAW TEARS IN HER EYES.
SHE MAY BE A LIVING WEAPON, BUT SHE DOESN'T KILL BECAUSE SHE WANTS TO...
SHE MADE SURE TO AVOID MY VITAL ORGANS... THAT'S THE ONLY REASON I DIDN'T DIE!!
IF SOMEONE JUST GAVE HER A CHANCE, THAT GIRL COULD BE HUMAN AGAIN...
IT'S TOO LATE FOR TRAIN OR ME. BUT SHE STILL HAS A SHOT!

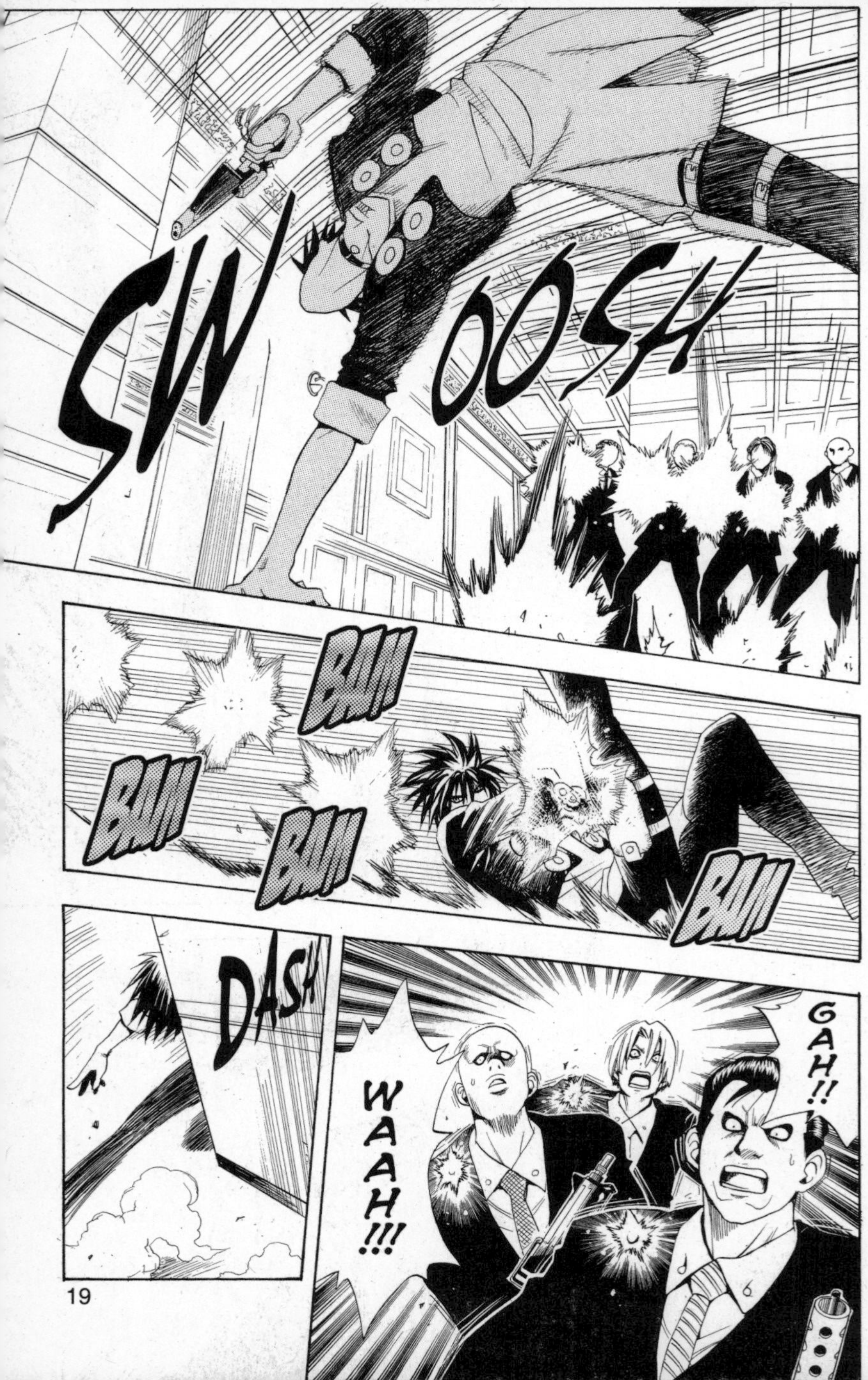
SWOOSH
BAM
BAM
BAM
BAM
GAH!!
WAAAH!!!
DASH

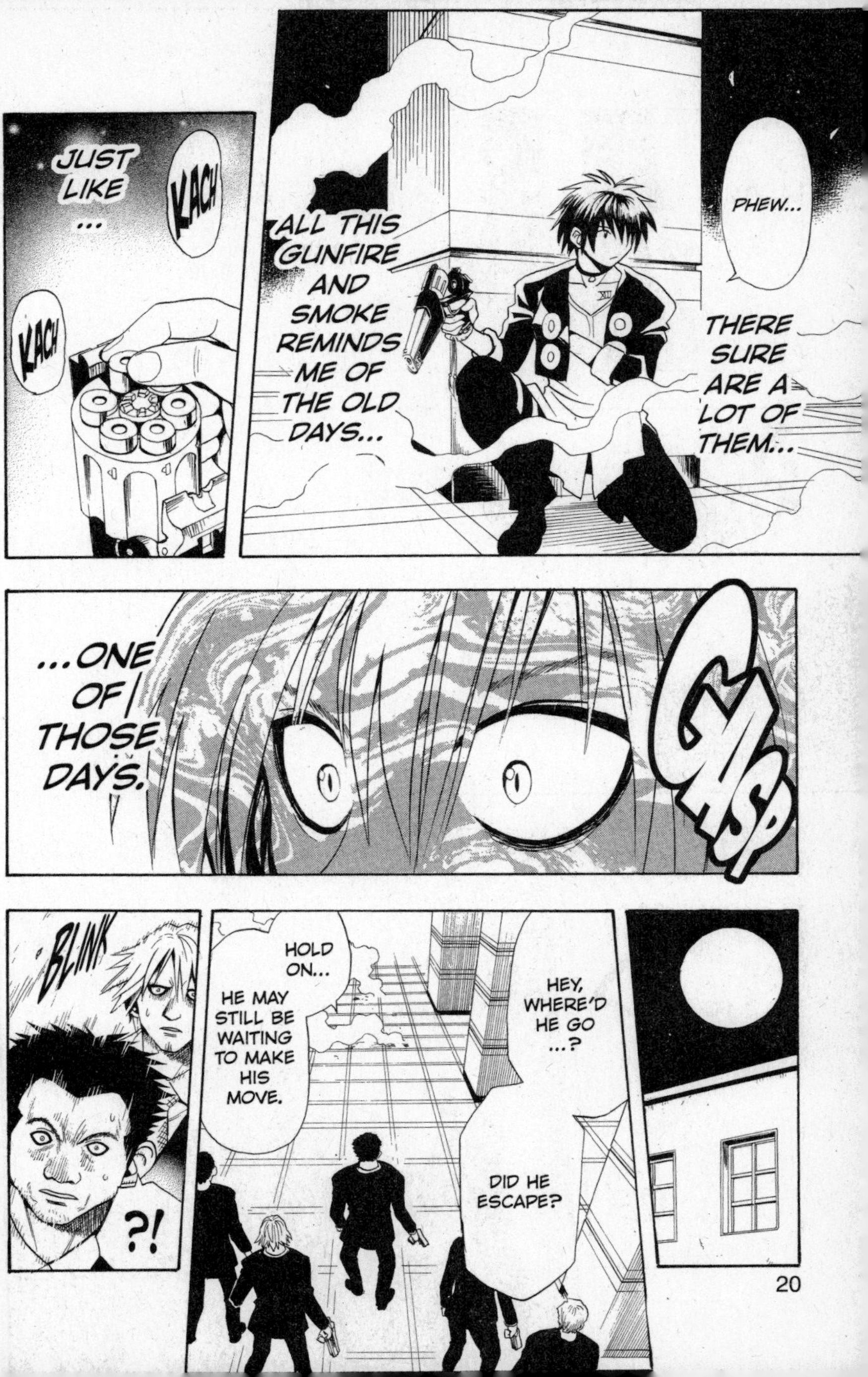
PHEW...
THERE SURE ARE A LOT OF THEM...
ALL THIS GUNFIRE AND SMOKE REMINDS ME OF THE OLD DAYS...
KACH
KACH
JUST LIKE ...
...ONE OF THOSE DAYS.
GASP
HEY, WHERE'D HE GO ...?
DID HE ESCAPE?
HOLD ON...
HE MAY STILL BE WAITING TO MAKE HIS MOVE.
BLINK
?!

READ THIS WAY

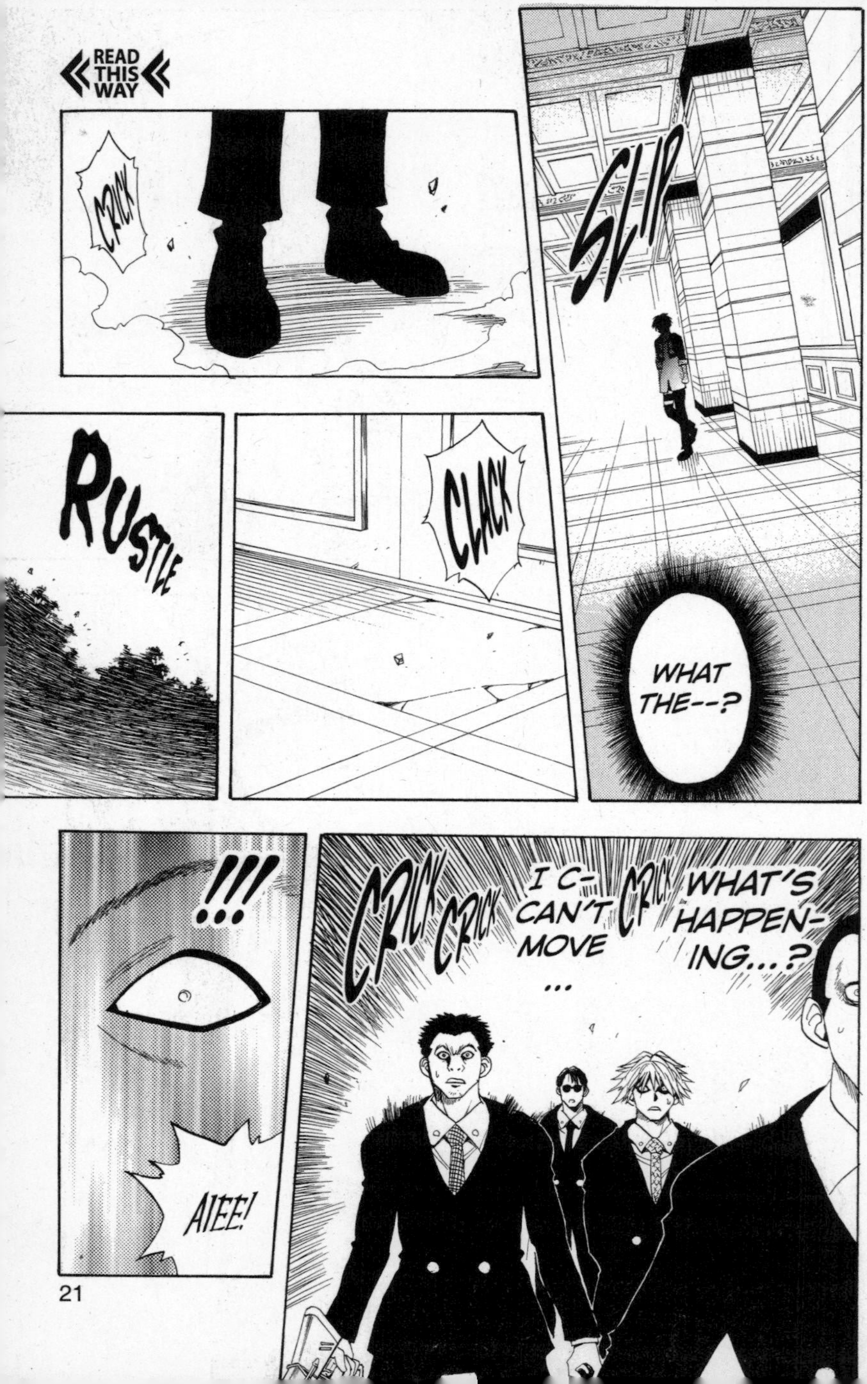

SLIP
WHAT THE--?
CRICK
CLACK
RUSTLE
WHAT'S HAPPEN-ING...?
CRICK
I C-CAN'T MOVE...
CRICK
CRICK
!!!
AIEE!

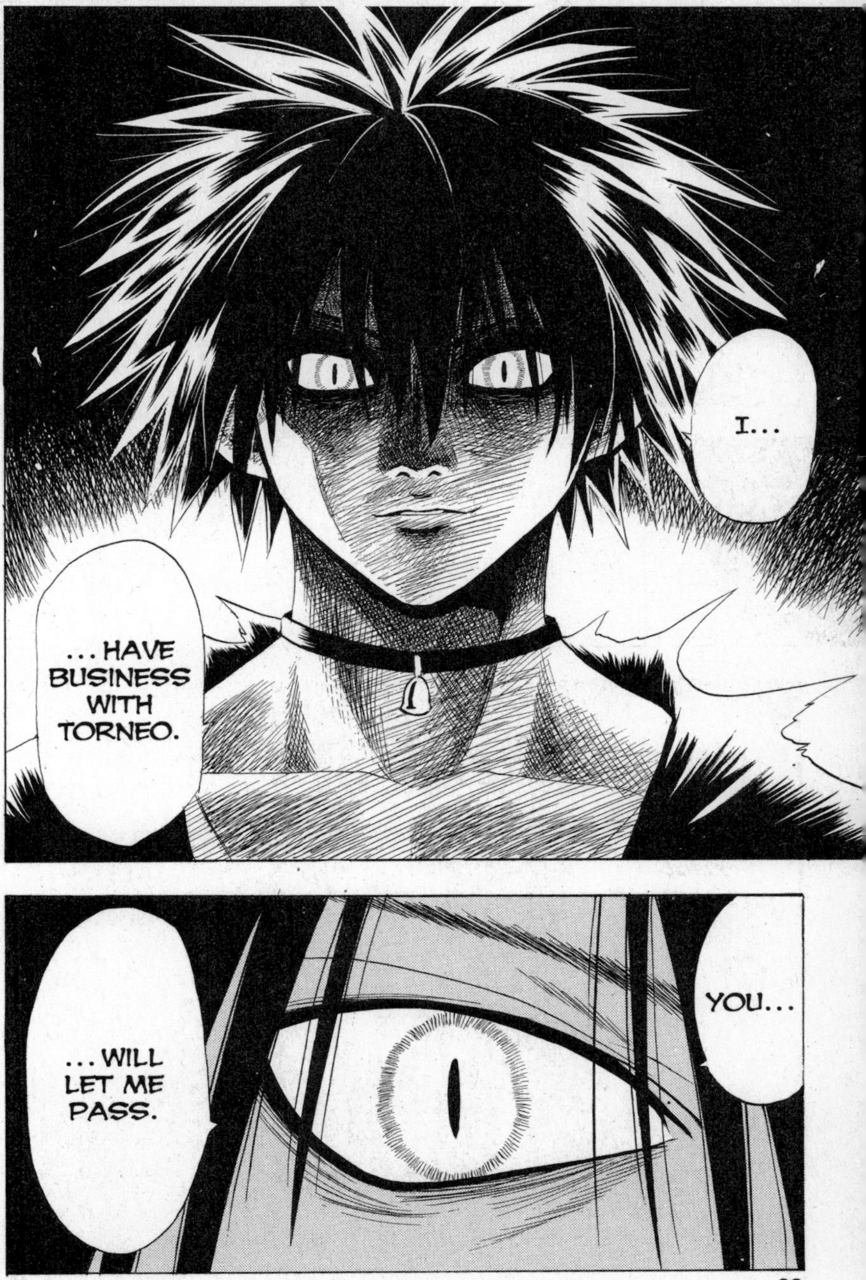
I...
...HAVE BUSINESS WITH TORNEO.
YOU...
...WILL LET ME PASS.

READ THIS WAY

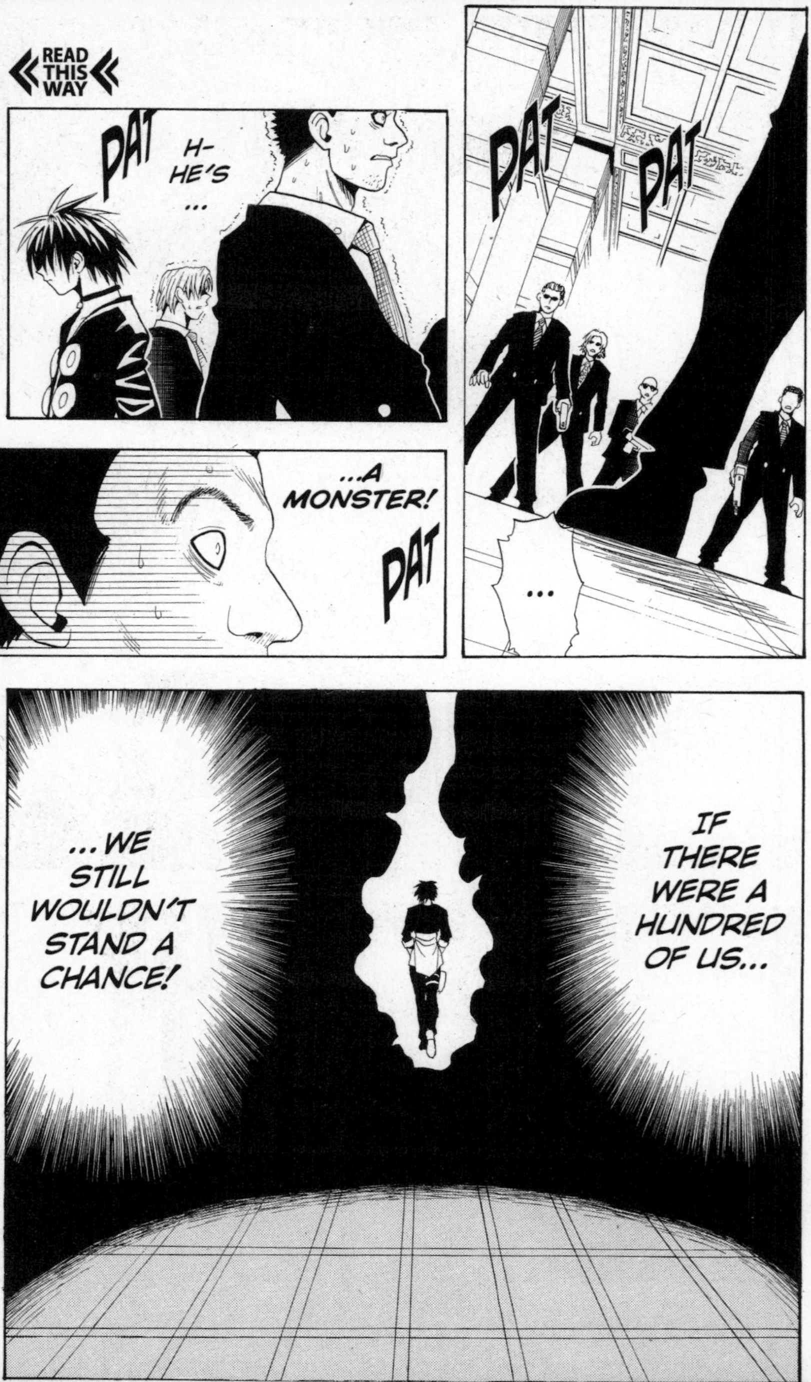
PAT
PAT
...
PAT
H- HE'S ...
...A MONSTER!
PAT
IF THERE WERE A HUNDRED OF US...
...WE STILL WOULDN'T STAND A CHANCE!

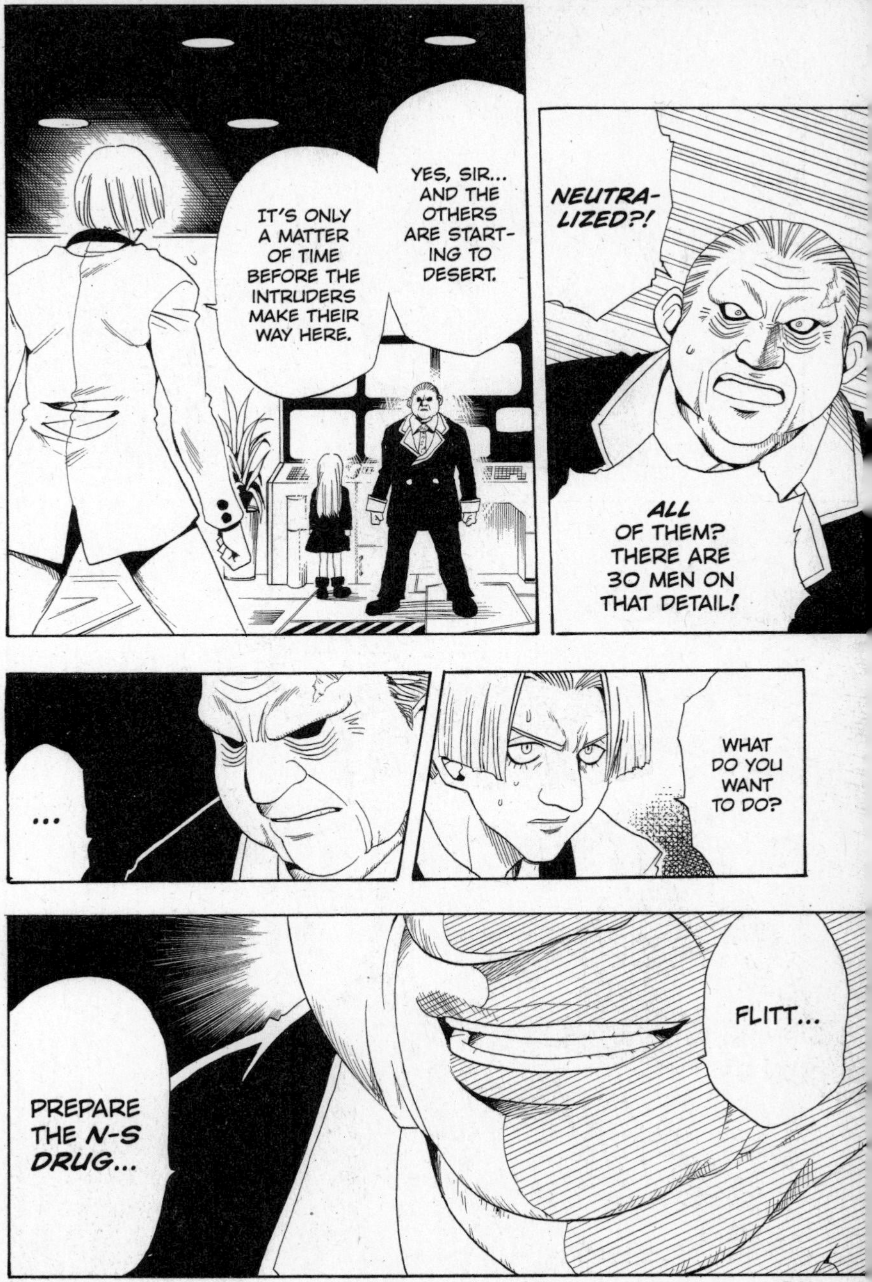
NEUTRA-LIZED?!
ALL OF THEM? THERE ARE 30 MEN ON THAT DETAIL!
YES, SIR... AND THE OTHERS ARE STARTING TO DESERT.
IT'S ONLY A MATTER OF TIME BEFORE THE INTRUDERS MAKE THEIR WAY HERE.
WHAT DO YOU WANT TO DO?
...
FLITT...
PREPARE THE N-S DRUG...

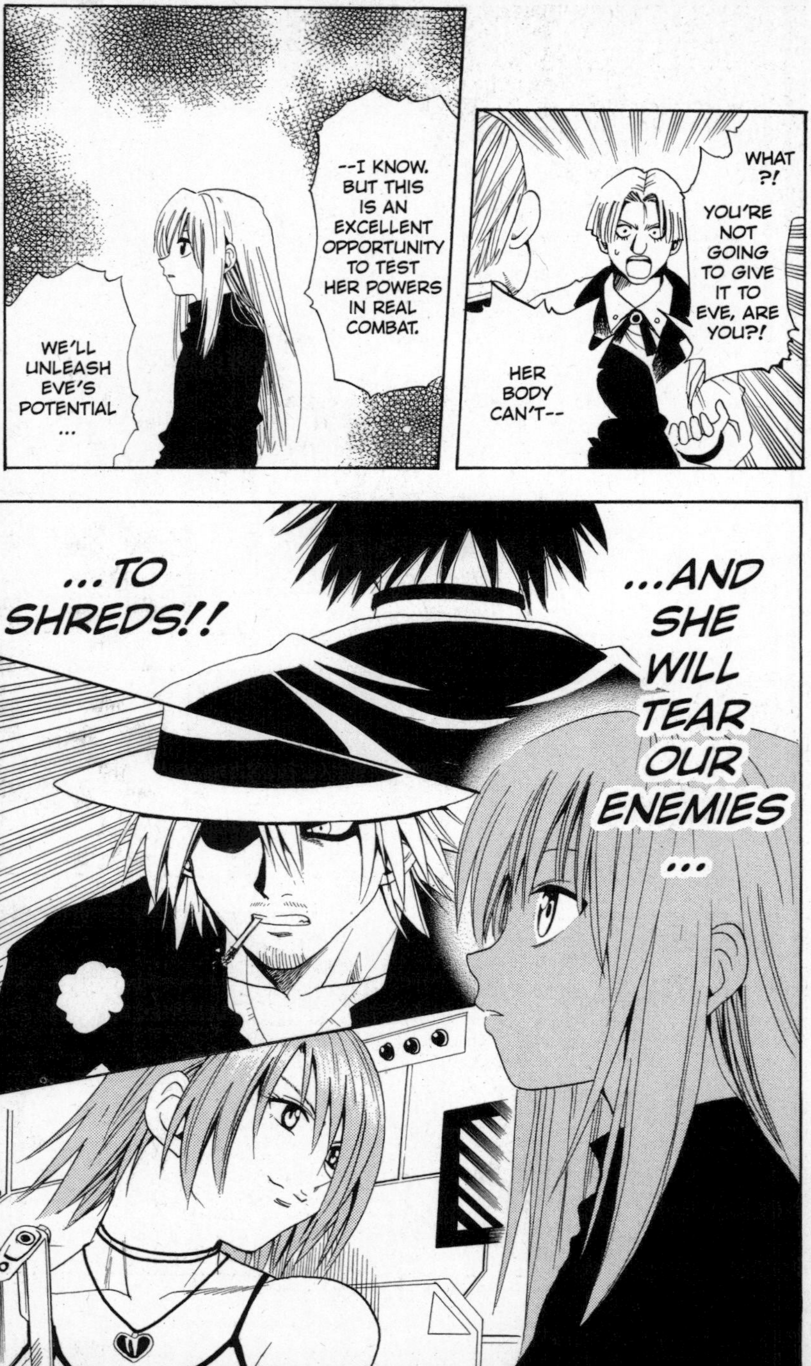
WHAT ?!
YOU'RE NOT GOING TO GIVE IT TO EVE, ARE YOU?!
HER BODY CAN'T--
--I KNOW. BUT THIS IS AN EXCELLENT OPPORTUNITY TO TEST HER POWERS IN REAL COMBAT.
WE'LL UNLEASH EVE'S POTENTIAL ...
...AND SHE WILL TEAR OUR ENEMIES ...
...TO SHREDS!!

BLACK CAT

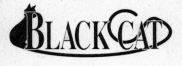

profile

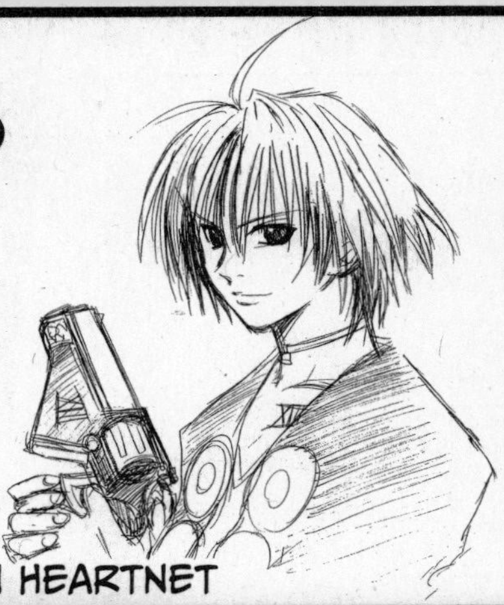

TRAIN HEARTNET

DATA	
BIRTHDAY:	APRIL 13
AGE:	23 YEARS OLD
BLOOD TYPE:	O
HEIGHT:	175 CM
WEIGHT:	65 KG
OCCUPATION:	SWEEPER
EQUIPMENT:	ENGRAVED PISTOL "HADES" (SIX CHAMBERS. WEIGHS 2.5KG. MADE FROM ORICHALCUM.)
LIKES:	MILK, SEAFOOD (NOT PICKY WHEN IT COMES TO FOOD)
DISLIKES:	CRYING WOMEN, BUGS (I.E., COCKROACHES, CENTIPEDES)
HANDEDNESS:	AMBIDEXTROUS (BORN LEFT-HANDED)
SPECIAL SKILLS:	ABLE TO SLEEP ANYWHERE. EXPERT AT DISGUISES.
COMMENTS:	HE TAKES DIRECT ACTION AND NEVER COMPROMISES HIS BELIEFS. HE WEARS HIS COLLAR AS A REMINDER THAT "YOU ARE YOUR OWN MASTER." HE HAS 20/20 VISION IN BOTH EYES.

CHAPTER 10: FREEDOM

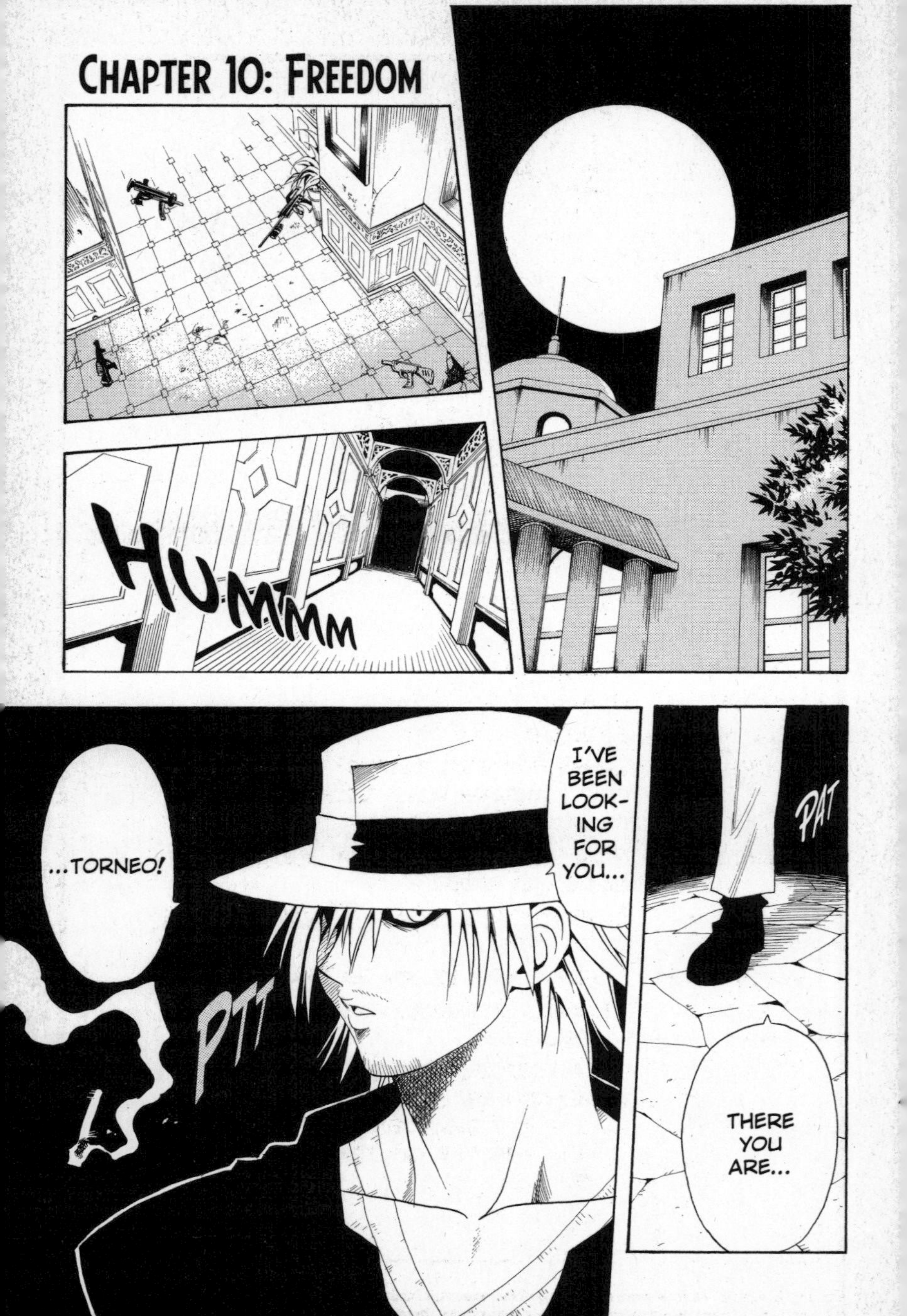
HUMMMM
PAT
THERE YOU ARE...
I'VE BEEN LOOKING-ING FOR YOU...
...TORNEO!
PTT

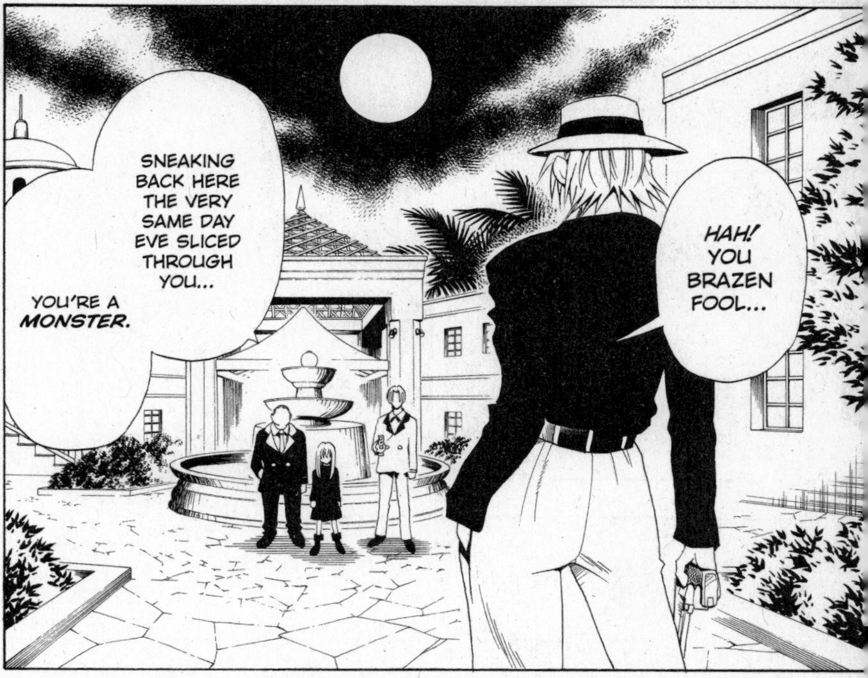
HAH! YOU BRAZEN FOOL...
SNEAKING BACK HERE THE VERY SAME DAY EVE SLICED THROUGH YOU...
YOU'RE A MONSTER.

Chapter 10: Freedom

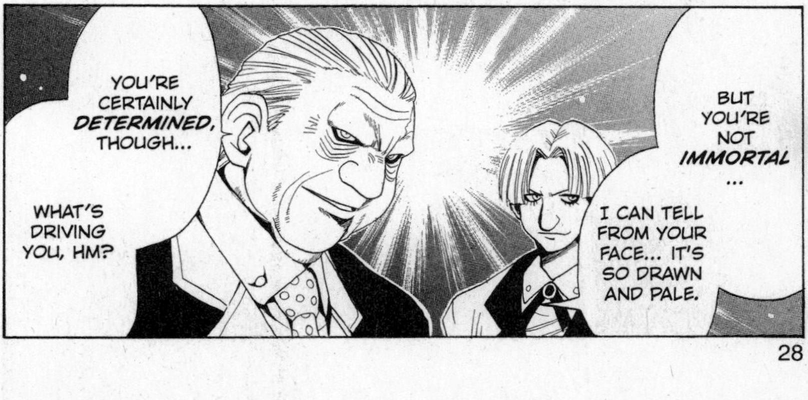
BUT YOU'RE NOT IMMORTAL ...
I CAN TELL FROM YOUR FACE... IT'S SO DRAWN AND PALE.
YOU'RE CERTAINLY DETERMINED, THOUGH...
WHAT'S DRIVING YOU, HM?

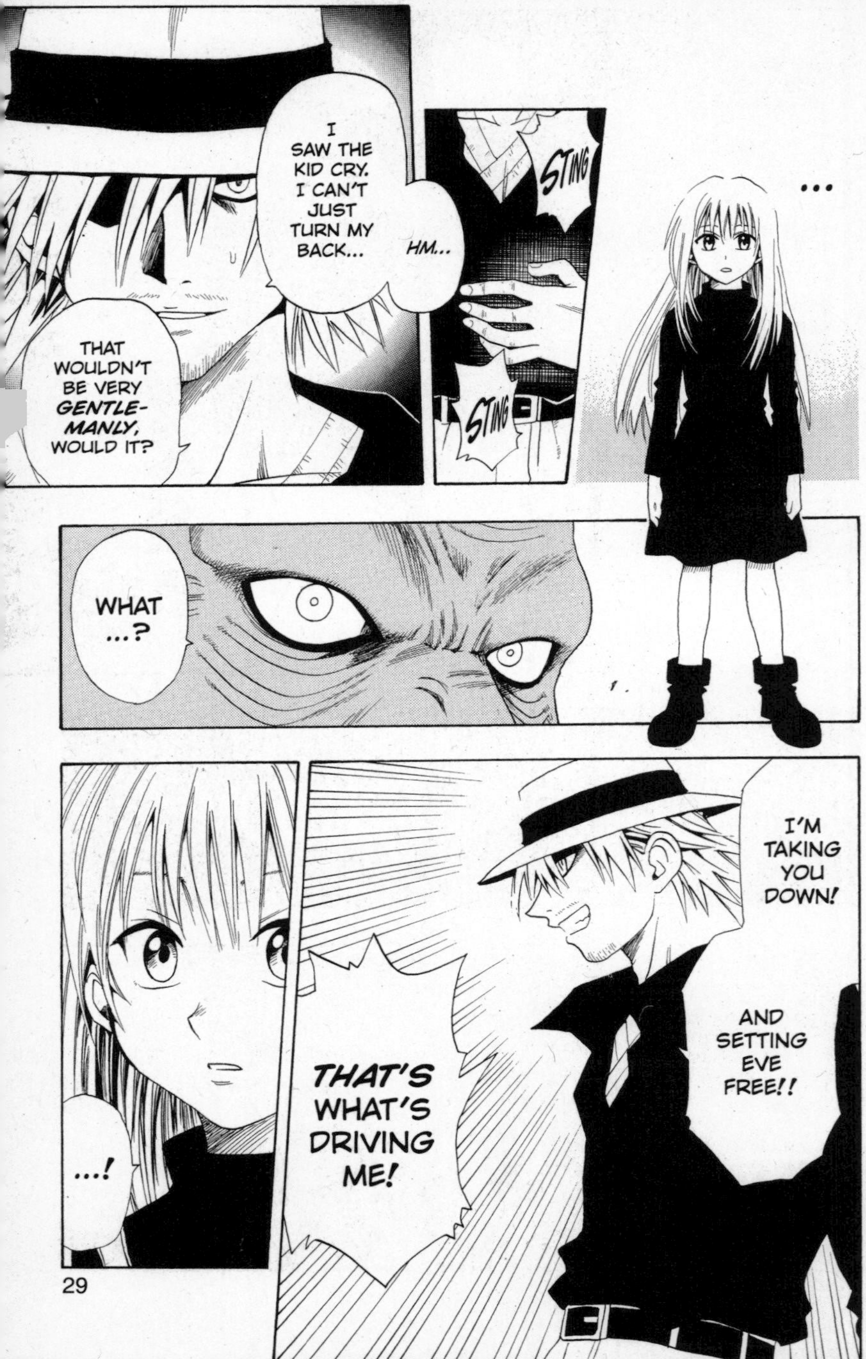
...
STING
HM...
STING
I SAW THE KID CRY. I CAN'T JUST TURN MY BACK...
THAT WOULDN'T BE VERY *GENTLEMANLY,* WOULD IT?
WHAT ...?
I'M TAKING YOU DOWN!
AND SETTING EVE FREE!!
THAT'S WHAT'S DRIVING ME!
...!

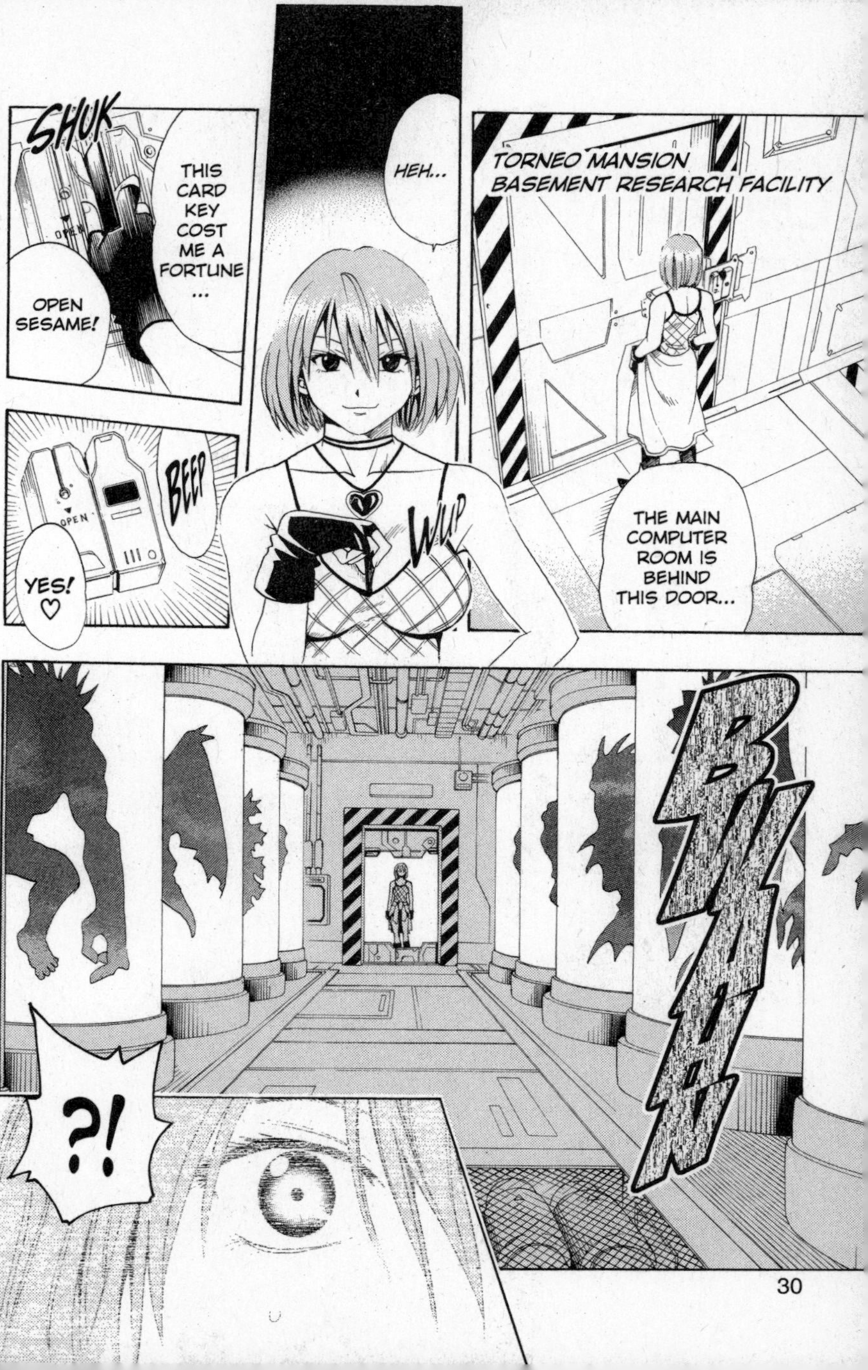
TORNEO MANSION BASEMENT RESEARCH FACILITY
THE MAIN COMPUTER ROOM IS BEHIND THIS DOOR...
HEH...
WUP
SHUK
THIS CARD KEY COST ME A FORTUNE ...
OPEN SESAME!
OPEN
BEEP
OPEN
YES! ♡
?!

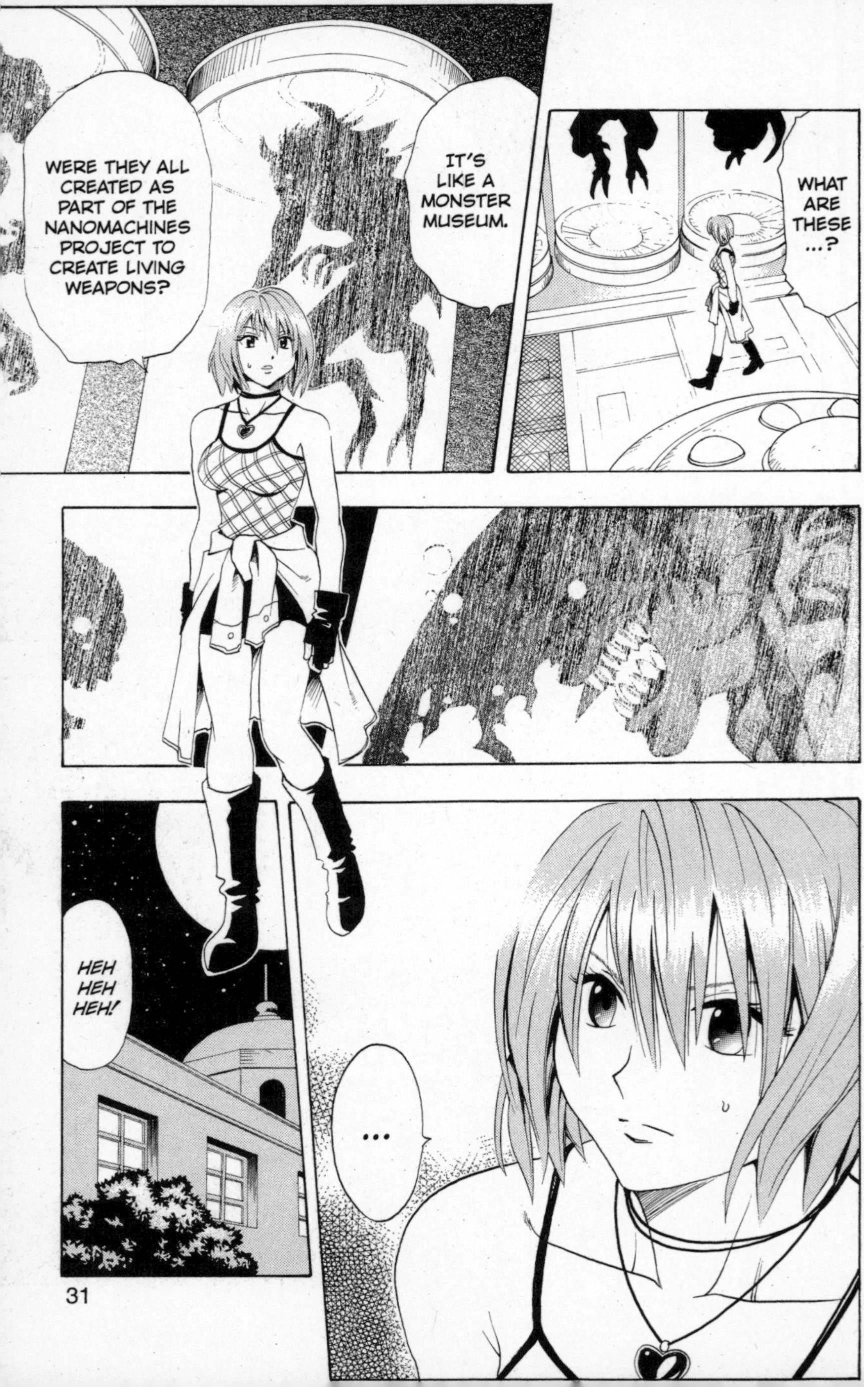
WHAT ARE THESE ...?
IT'S LIKE A MONSTER MUSEUM.
WERE THEY ALL CREATED AS PART OF THE NANOMACHINES PROJECT TO CREATE LIVING WEAPONS?
...
HEH HEH HEH!

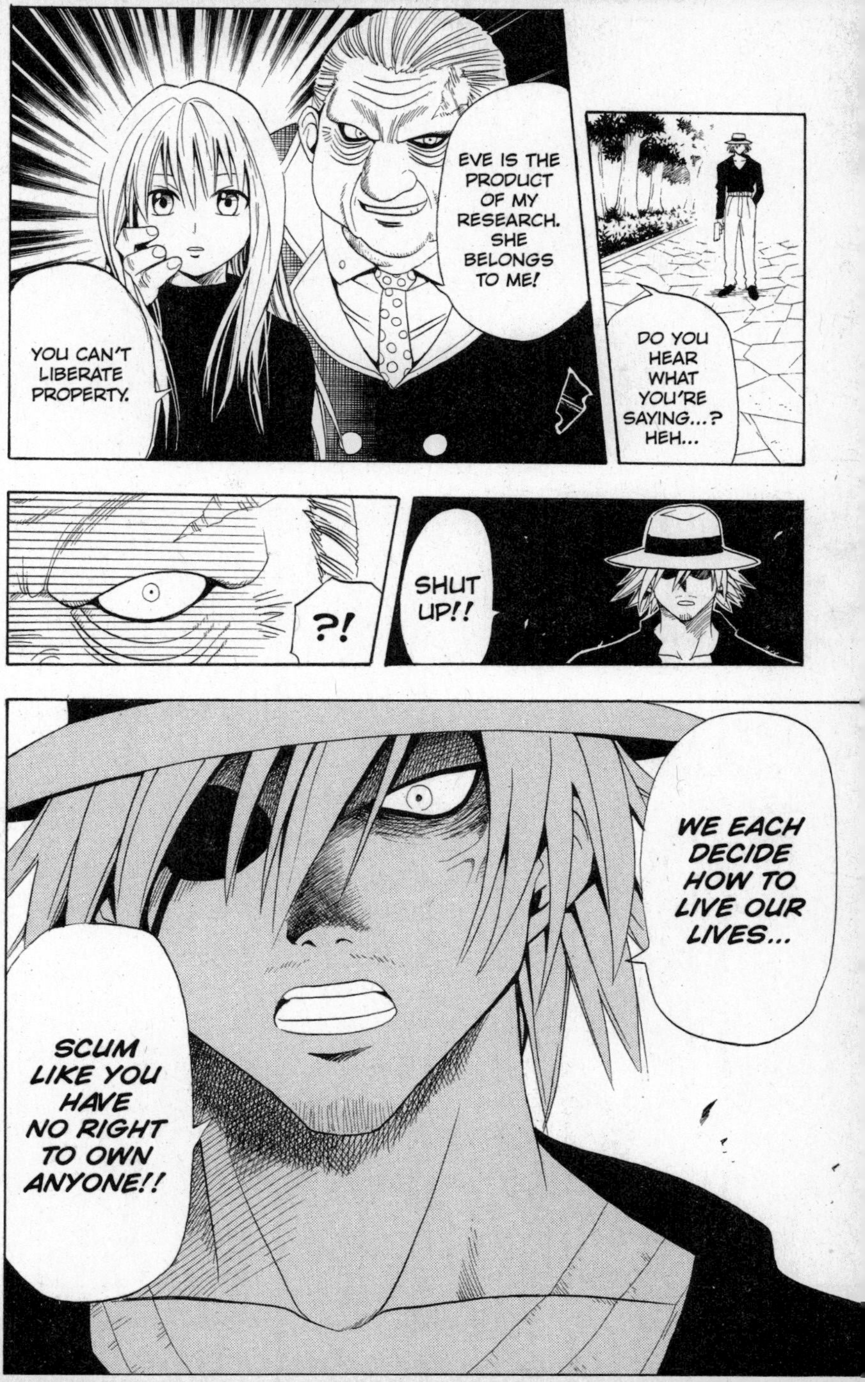
DO YOU HEAR WHAT YOU'RE SAYING...? HEH...
EVE IS THE PRODUCT OF MY RESEARCH. SHE BELONGS TO ME!
YOU CAN'T LIBERATE PROPERTY.
SHUT UP!!
?!
WE EACH DECIDE HOW TO LIVE OUR LIVES...
SCUM LIKE YOU HAVE NO RIGHT TO OWN ANYONE!!

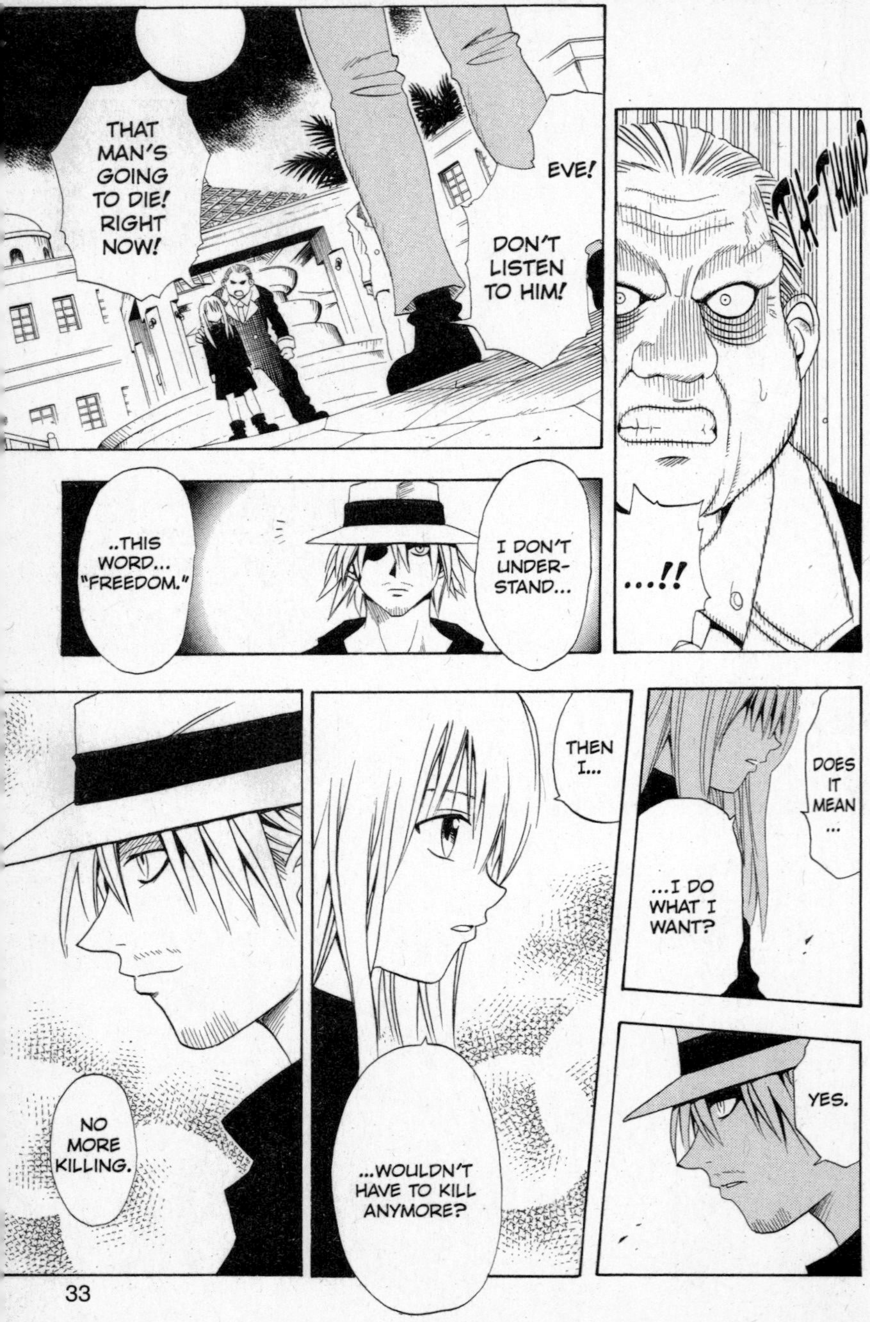

EVE!
DON'T LISTEN TO HIM!
THAT MAN'S GOING TO DIE! RIGHT NOW!
TH-THUMP
...!!
I DON'T UNDER-STAND...
..THIS WORD... "FREEDOM."
DOES IT MEAN ...
...I DO WHAT I WANT?
YES.
THEN I...
...WOULDN'T HAVE TO KILL ANYMORE?
NO MORE KILLING.

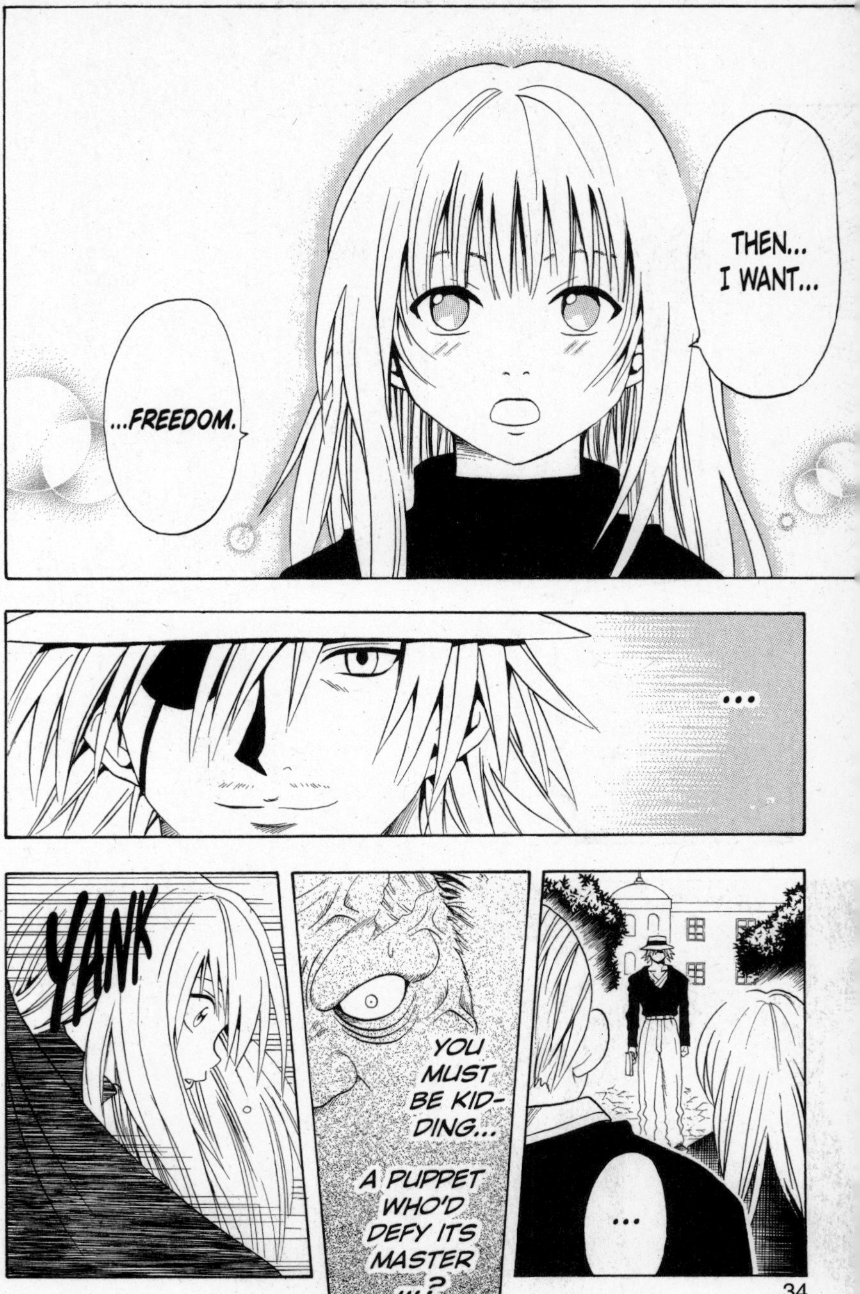
THEN... I WANT...
...FREEDOM.
...
...
YOU MUST BE KID-DING...
A PUPPET WHO'D DEFY ITS MASTER ...?
YANK

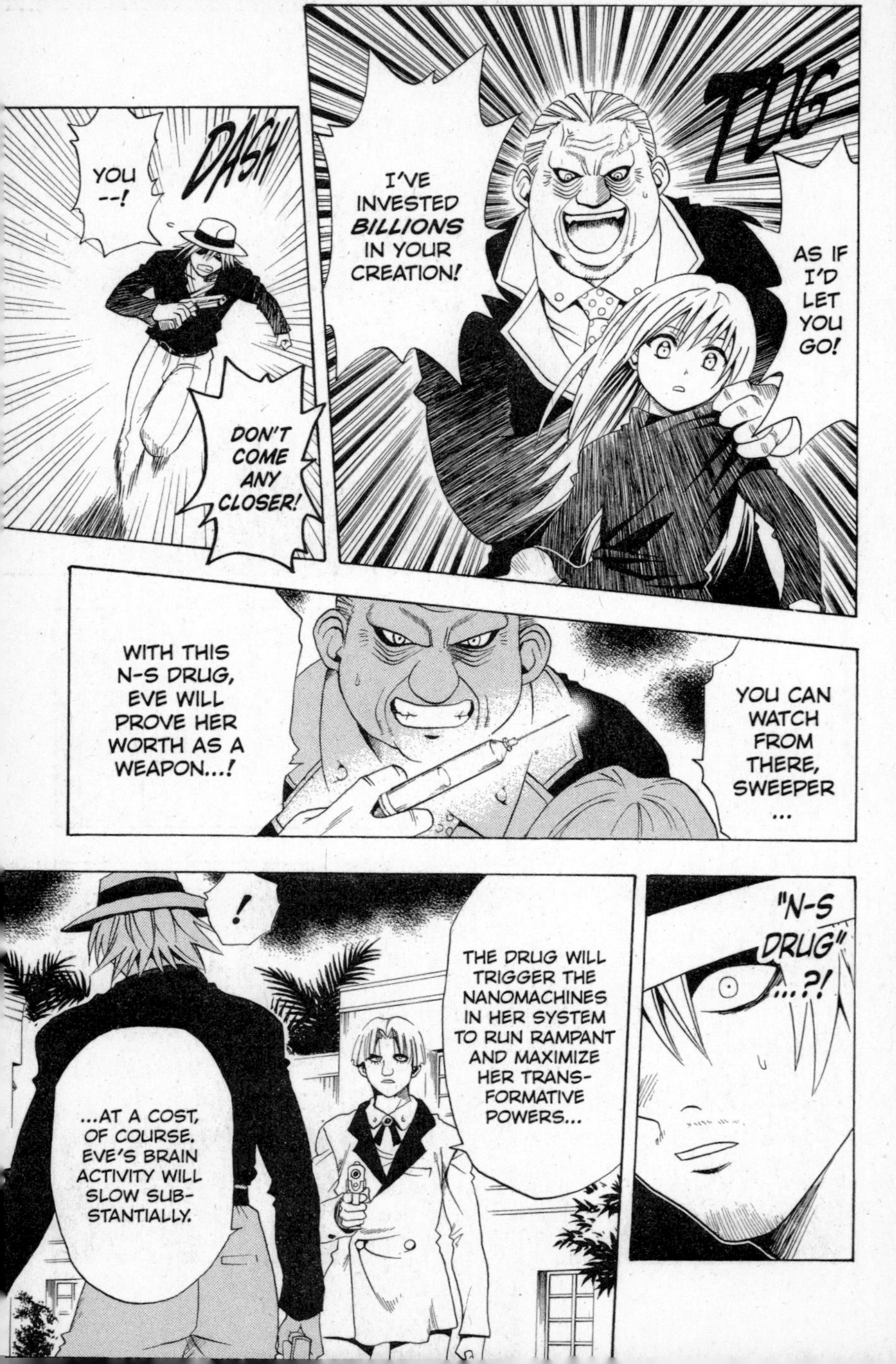
TUG
I'VE INVESTED BILLIONS IN YOUR CREATION!
AS IF I'D LET YOU GO!
DASH
YOU --!
DON'T COME ANY CLOSER!
WITH THIS N-S DRUG, EVE WILL PROVE HER WORTH AS A WEAPON...!
YOU CAN WATCH FROM THERE, SWEEPER ...
"N-S DRUG" ...?!
!
THE DRUG WILL TRIGGER THE NANOMACHINES IN HER SYSTEM TO RUN RAMPANT AND MAXIMIZE HER TRANS-FORMATIVE POWERS...
...AT A COST, OF COURSE. EVE'S BRAIN ACTIVITY WILL SLOW SUB-STANTIALLY.

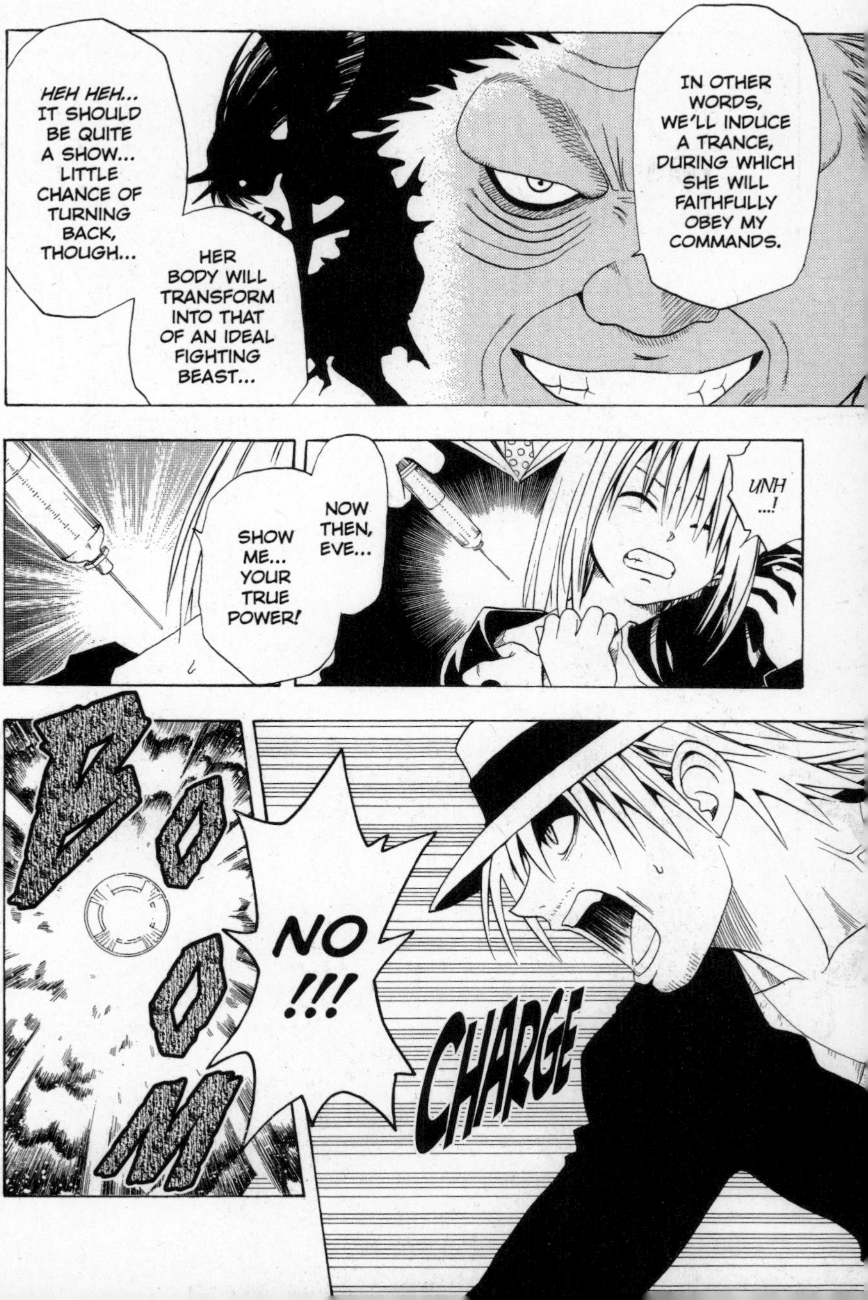
IN OTHER WORDS, WE'LL INDUCE A TRANCE, DURING WHICH SHE WILL FAITHFULLY OBEY MY COMMANDS.
HER BODY WILL TRANSFORM INTO THAT OF AN IDEAL FIGHTING BEAST...
HEH HEH... IT SHOULD BE QUITE A SHOW... LITTLE CHANCE OF TURNING BACK, THOUGH...
UNH ...!
NOW THEN, EVE...
SHOW ME... YOUR TRUE POWER!
NO !!!
CHARGE
BOOM

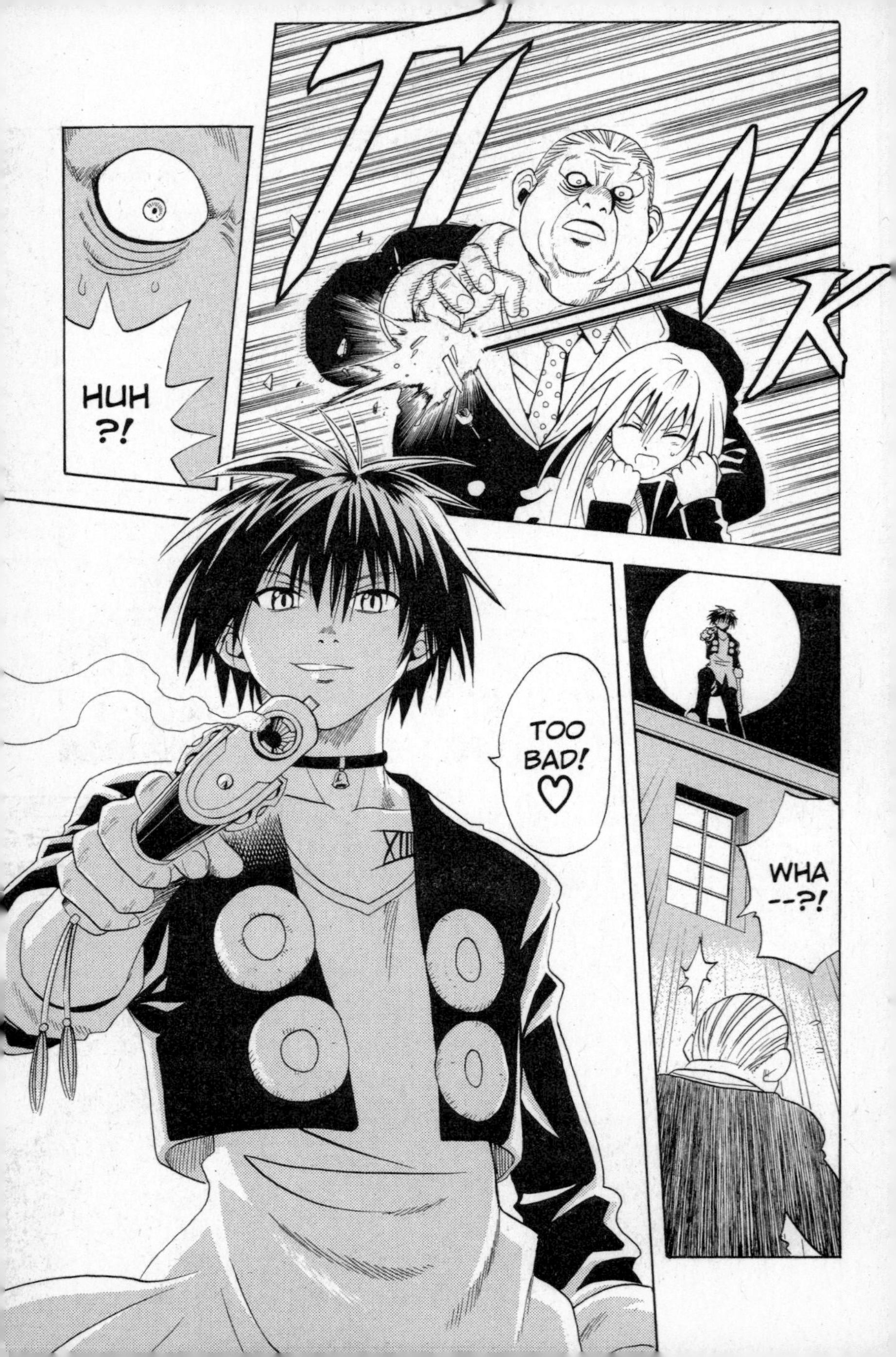
TINK
HUH ?!
WHA --?!
TOO BAD! ♥

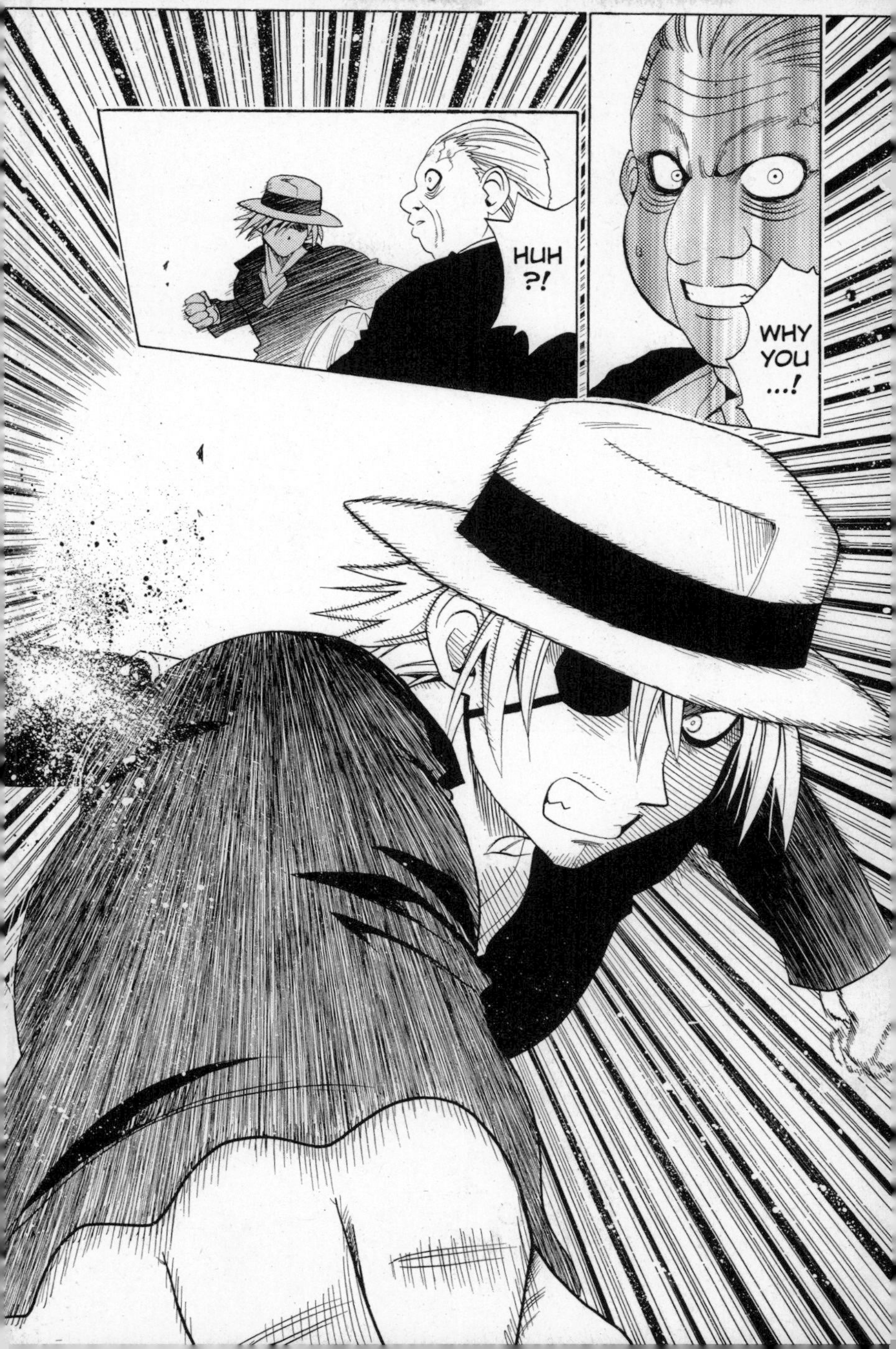
WHY YOU ...!
HUH ?!

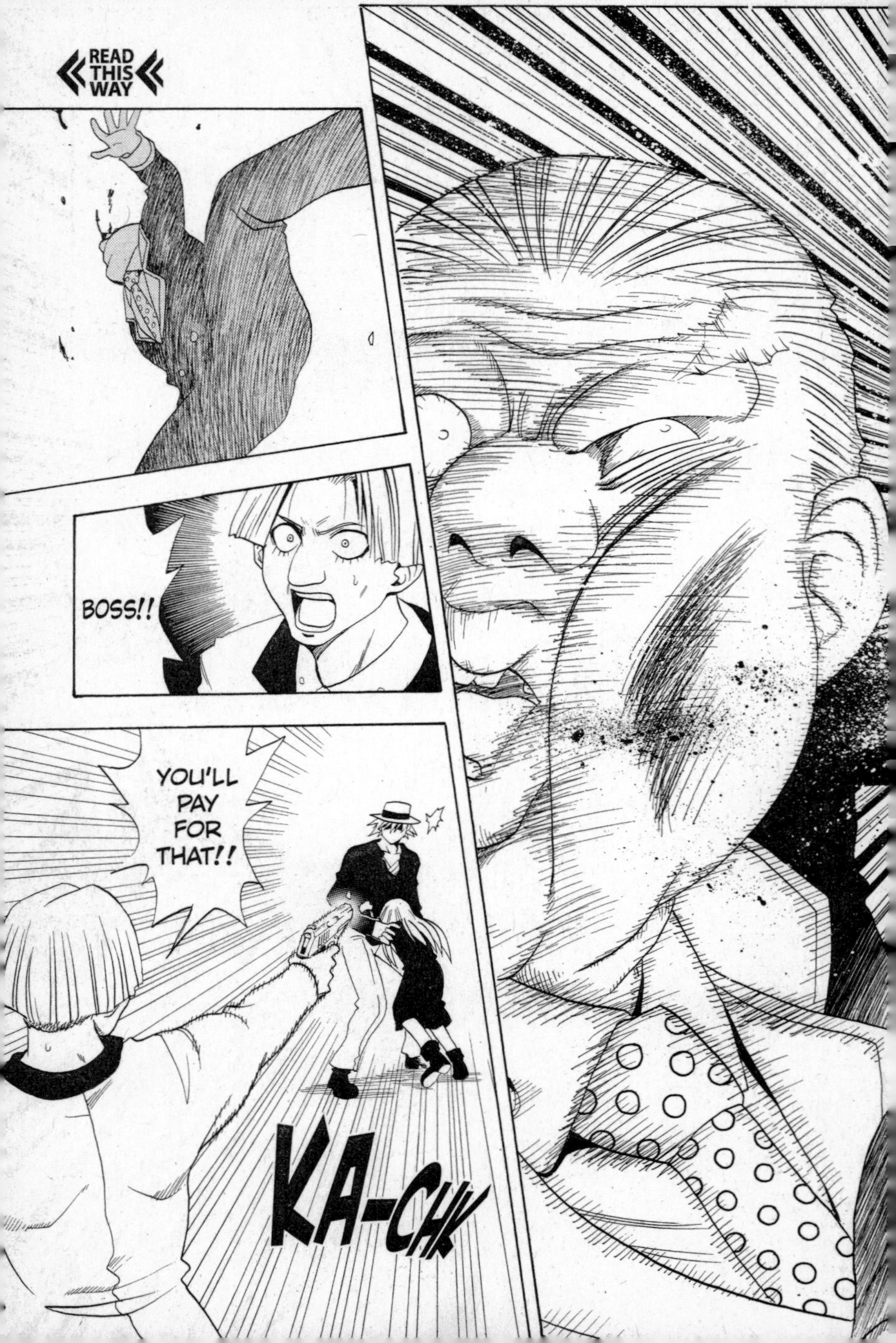
READ THIS WAY
BOSS!!
YOU'LL PAY FOR THAT!!
KA-CHK

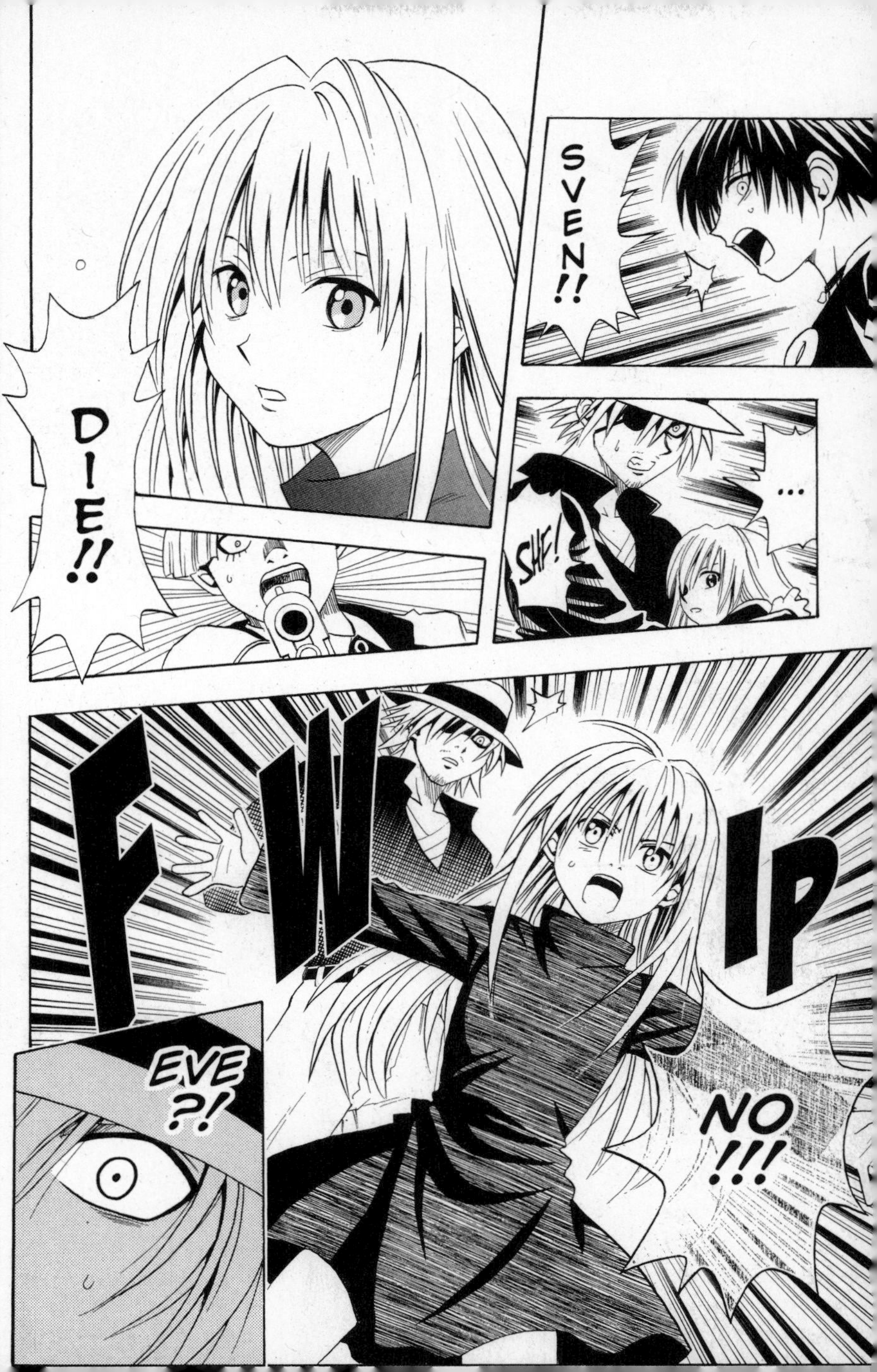

SVEN!!
...
SHF!
DIE!!
FWIP
NO!!!
EVE?!

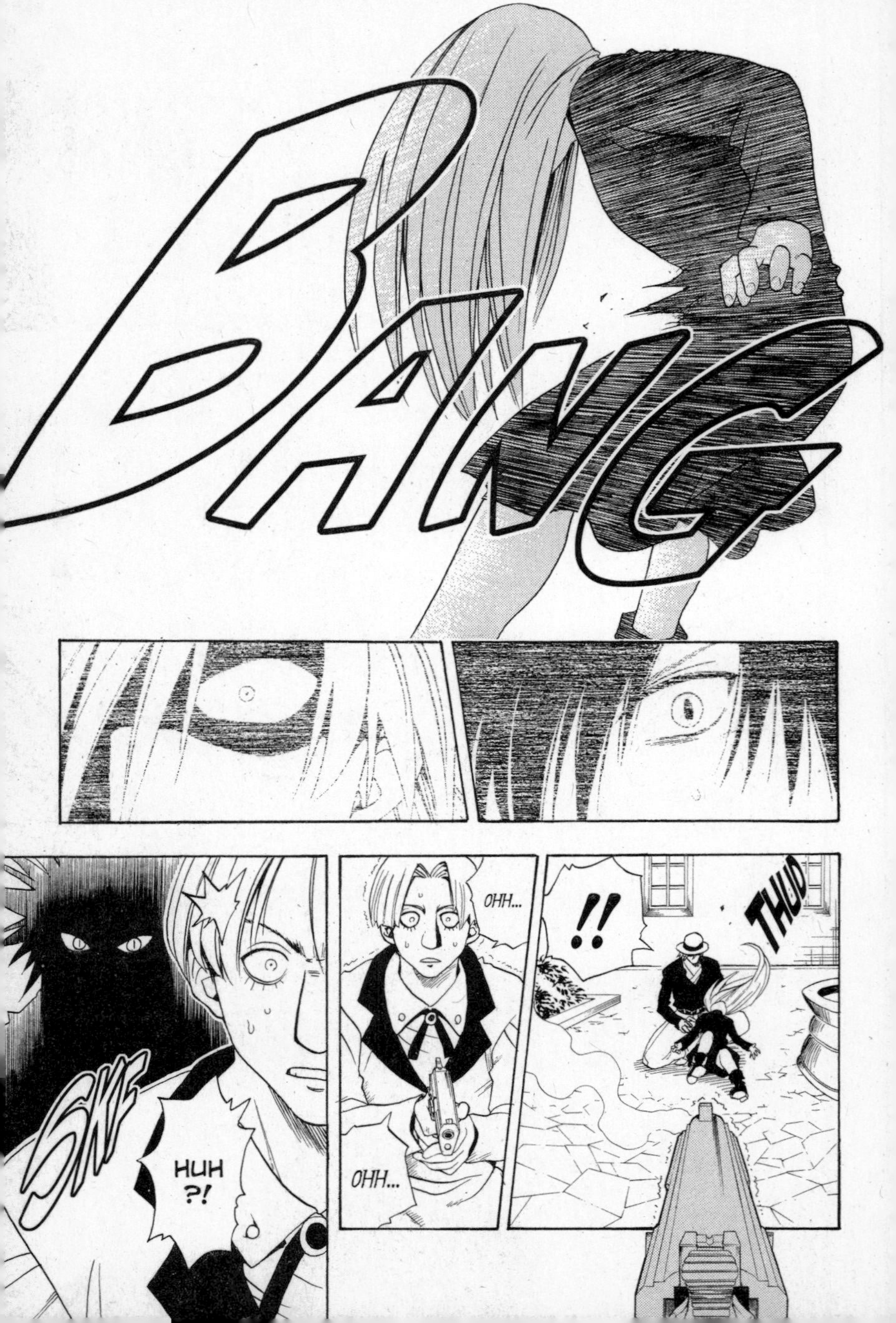
BANG
!!
THUD
OHH...
OHH...
SHF
HUH ?!

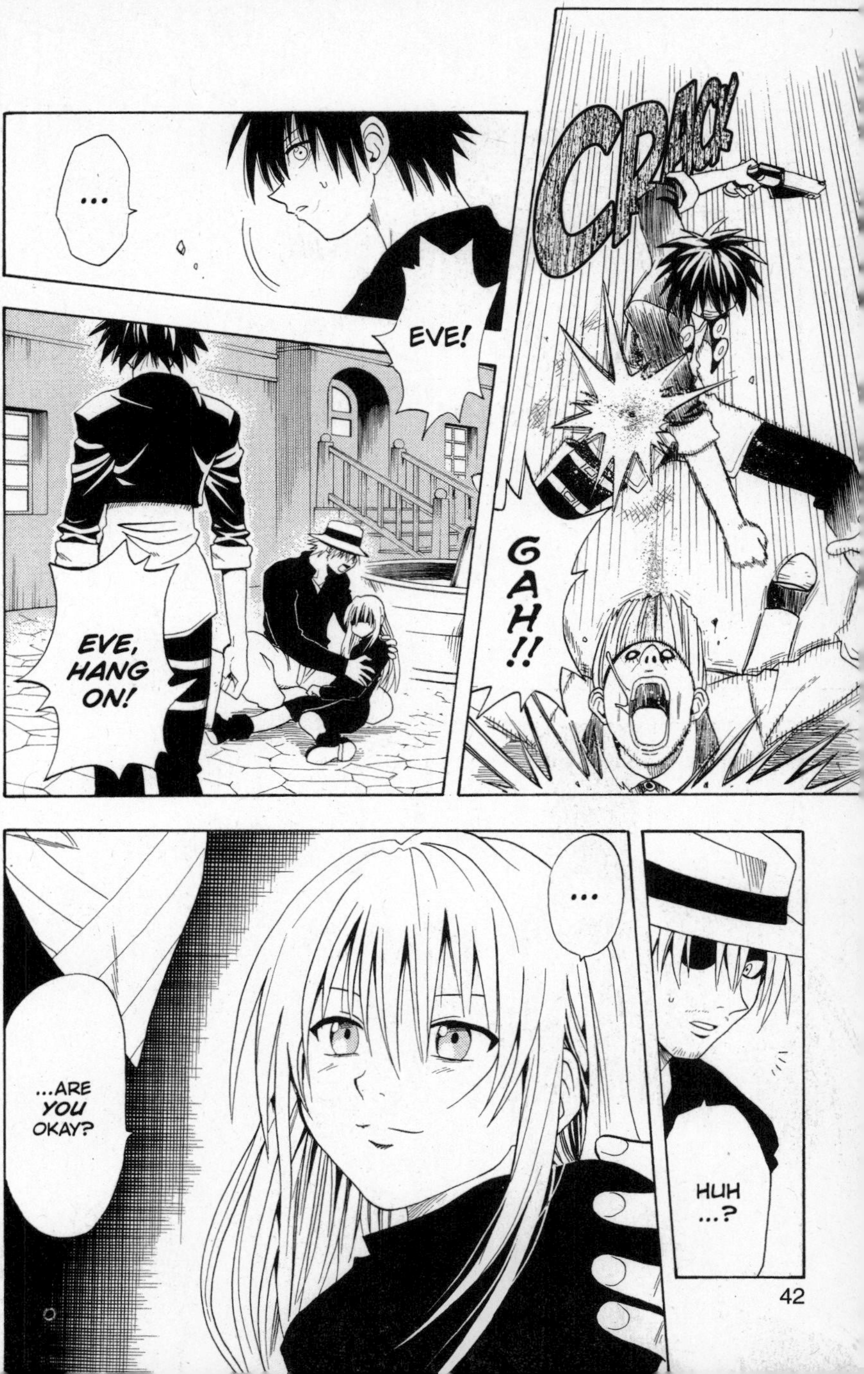

CRACK!
GAH!!
...
EVE!
EVE, HANG ON!
HUH ...?
...
...ARE YOU OKAY?

READ THIS WAY

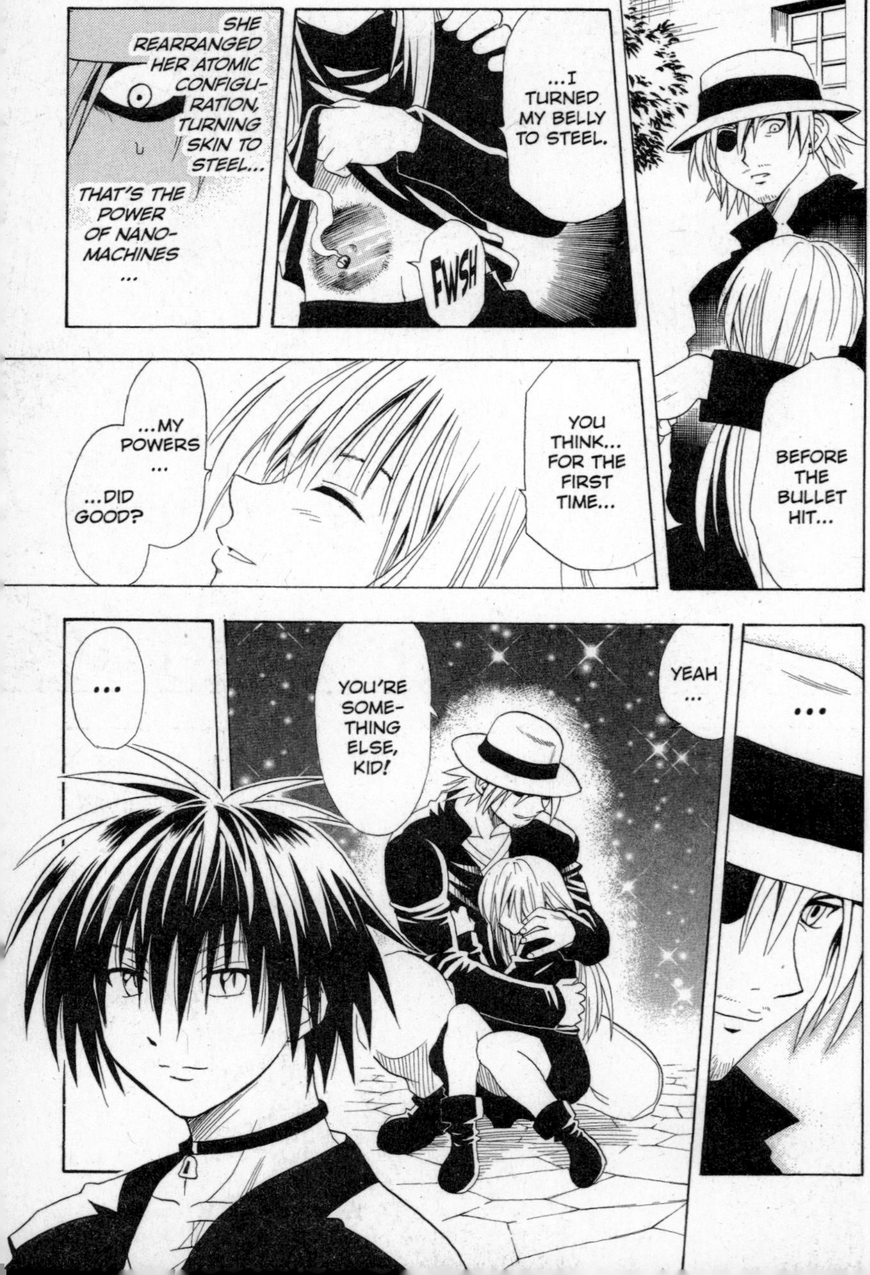

BEFORE THE BULLET HIT...
...I TURNED MY BELLY TO STEEL.
FWSH
SHE REARRANGED HER ATOMIC CONFIGURATION, TURNING SKIN TO STEEL...
THAT'S THE POWER OF NANO-MACHINES...
YOU THINK... FOR THE FIRST TIME...
...MY POWERS...
...DID GOOD?
YEAH...
...
YOU'RE SOMETHING ELSE, KID!
...

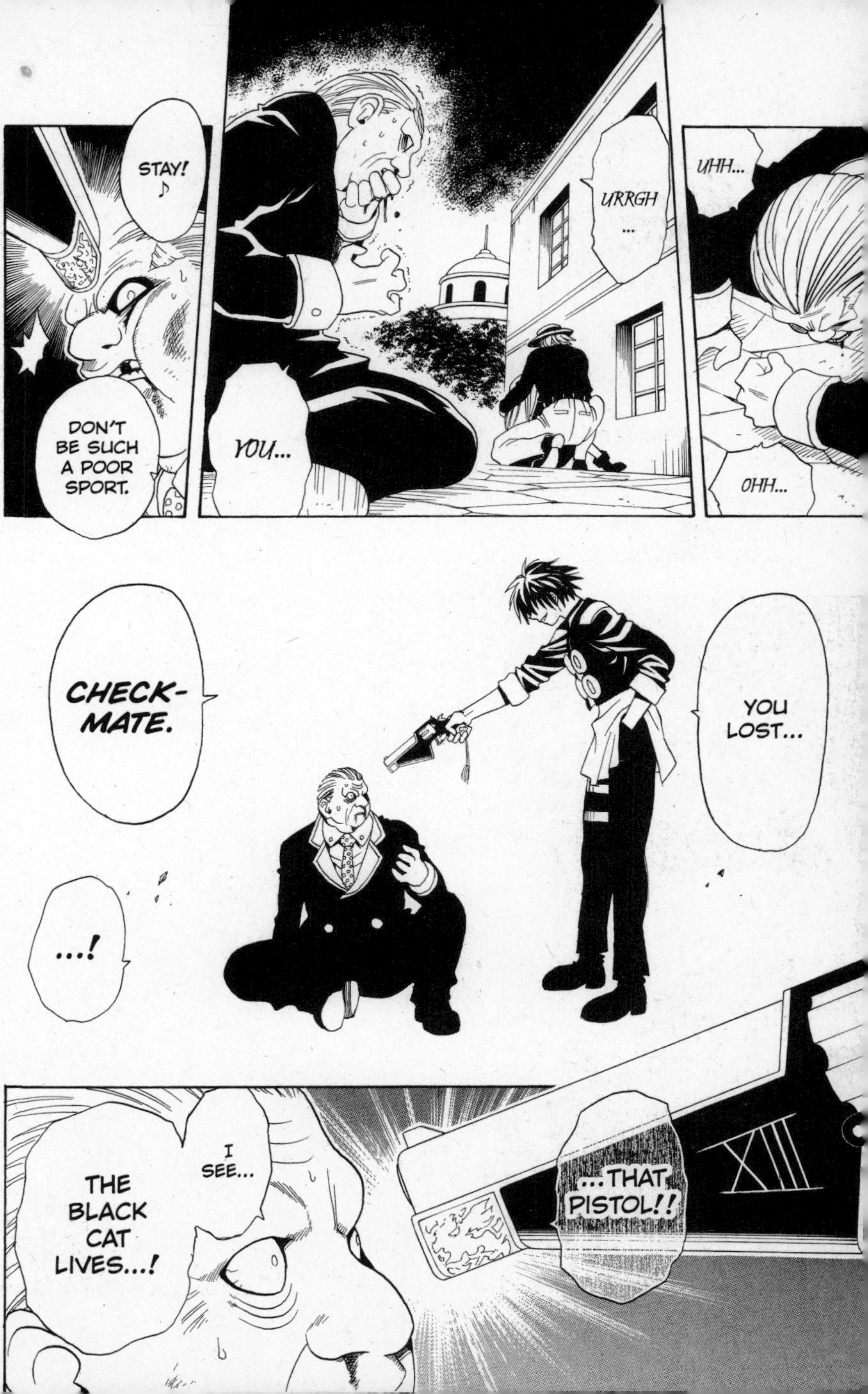
UHH...
OHH...
URRGH ...
YOU...
STAY! ♪
DON'T BE SUCH A POOR SPORT.
YOU LOST...
CHECK-MATE.
...!
...THAT PISTOL!!
I SEE...
THE BLACK CAT LIVES...!

READ THIS WAY

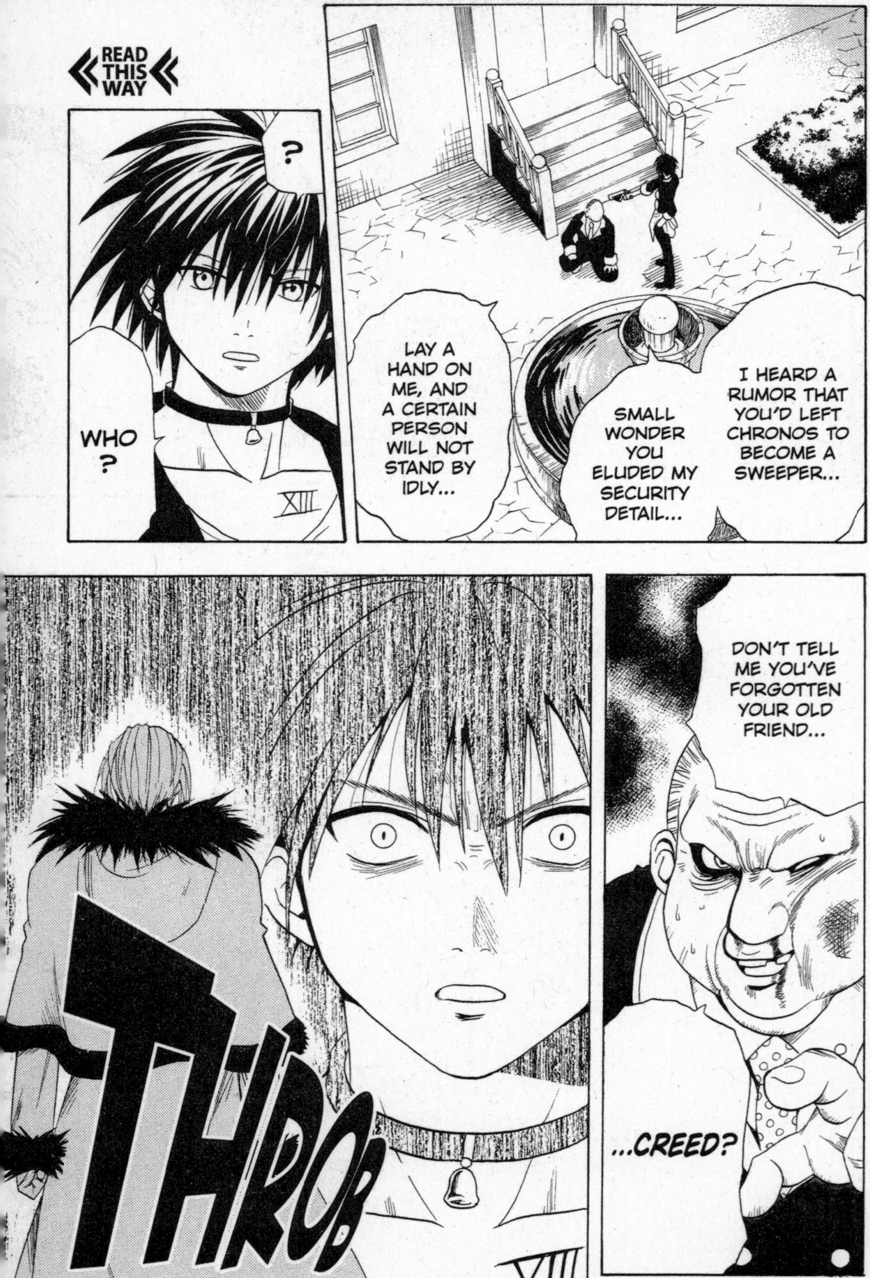
I HEARD A RUMOR THAT YOU'D LEFT CHRONOS TO BECOME A SWEEPER...
SMALL WONDER YOU ELUDED MY SECURITY DETAIL...
LAY A HAND ON ME, AND A CERTAIN PERSON WILL NOT STAND BY IDLY...
?
WHO?
XIII
DON'T TELL ME YOU'VE FORGOTTEN YOUR OLD FRIEND...
...CREED?
THROB
XIII

BLACK CAT

profile

SVEN VOLLFIED

DATA	
BIRTHDAY:	JUNE 23
AGE:	30 YEARS OLD
BLOOD TYPE:	A
HEIGHT:	180 CM
WEIGHT:	72 KG
OCCUPATION:	SWEEPER
SPECIAL SKILLS:	INVENTING TECH TOOLS, COOKING
HANDEDNESS:	RIGHT-HANDED
FAVORITE MUSIC:	JAZZ, CLASSICAL
LIKES:	LOOKING GOOD, FIXING UP CARS
COMMENTS:	SELF-STYLED LADIES MAN. HIS MOTTO IS, "BE KIND TO WOMEN, CHILDREN AND THE WEAK." "DANGEROUS WOMEN" ARE THE EXCEPTION TO HIS RULE. HIS CODE OF CHIVALRY IS HIS OWN, AND NOT THE RESULT OF HOW HE WAS RAISED. HE'S AN ESPECIALLY HEAVY SMOKER. AFTER A JOB, HE HAS TO HAVE A SMOKE.

Chapter 11: Creed

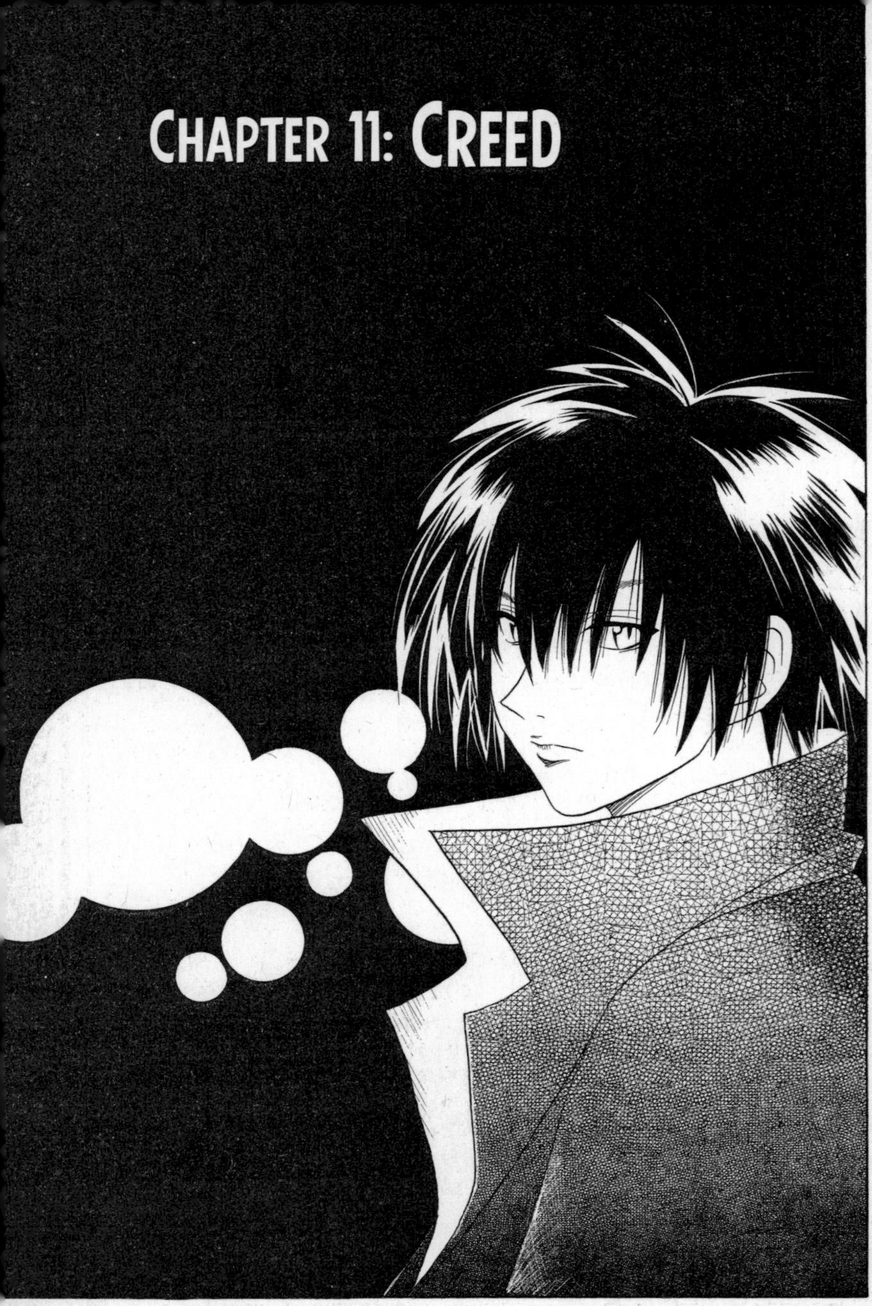

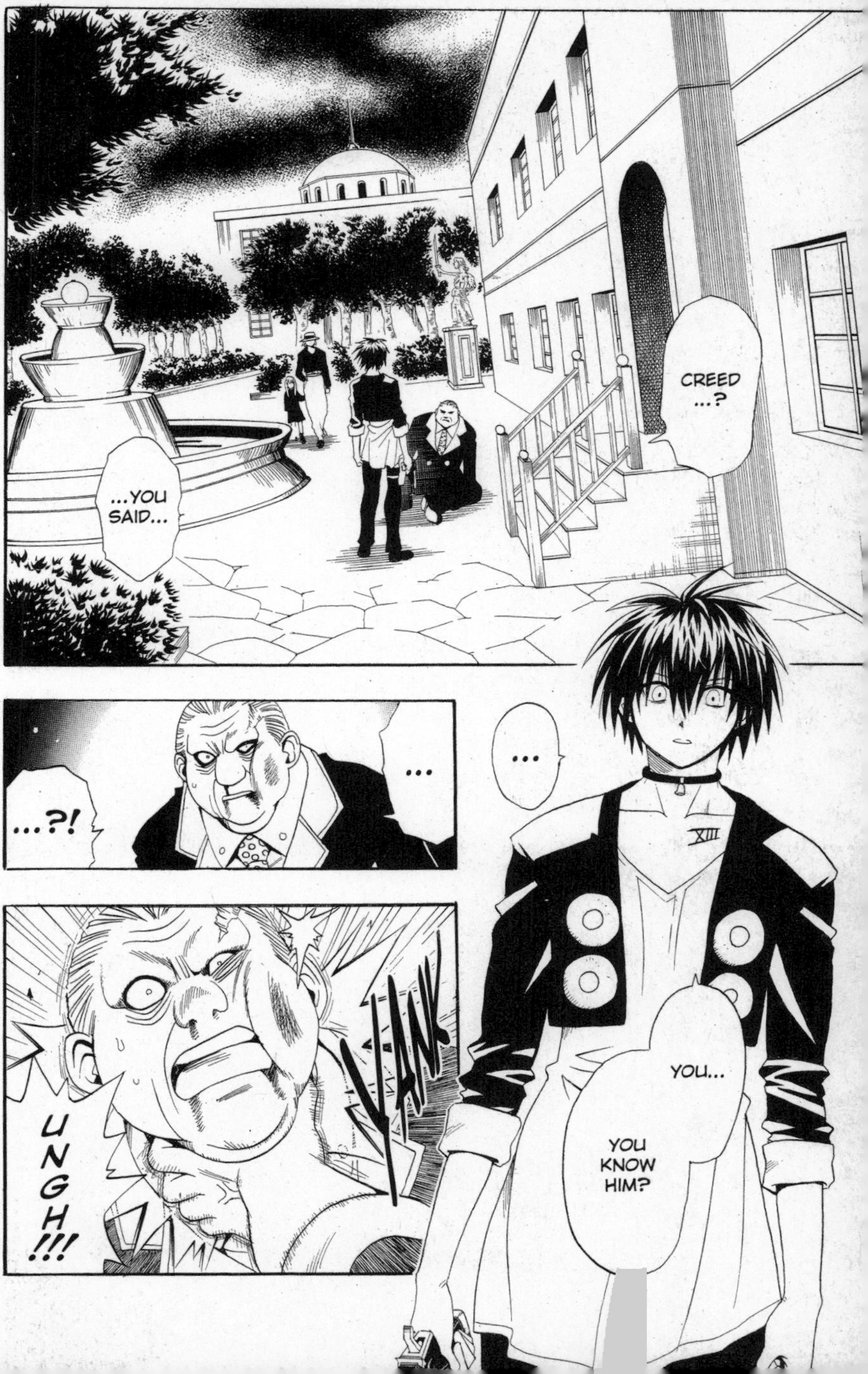
CREED ...?
...YOU SAID...
...
YOU...
YOU KNOW HIM?
...
...?!
YANK
UNGH!!!

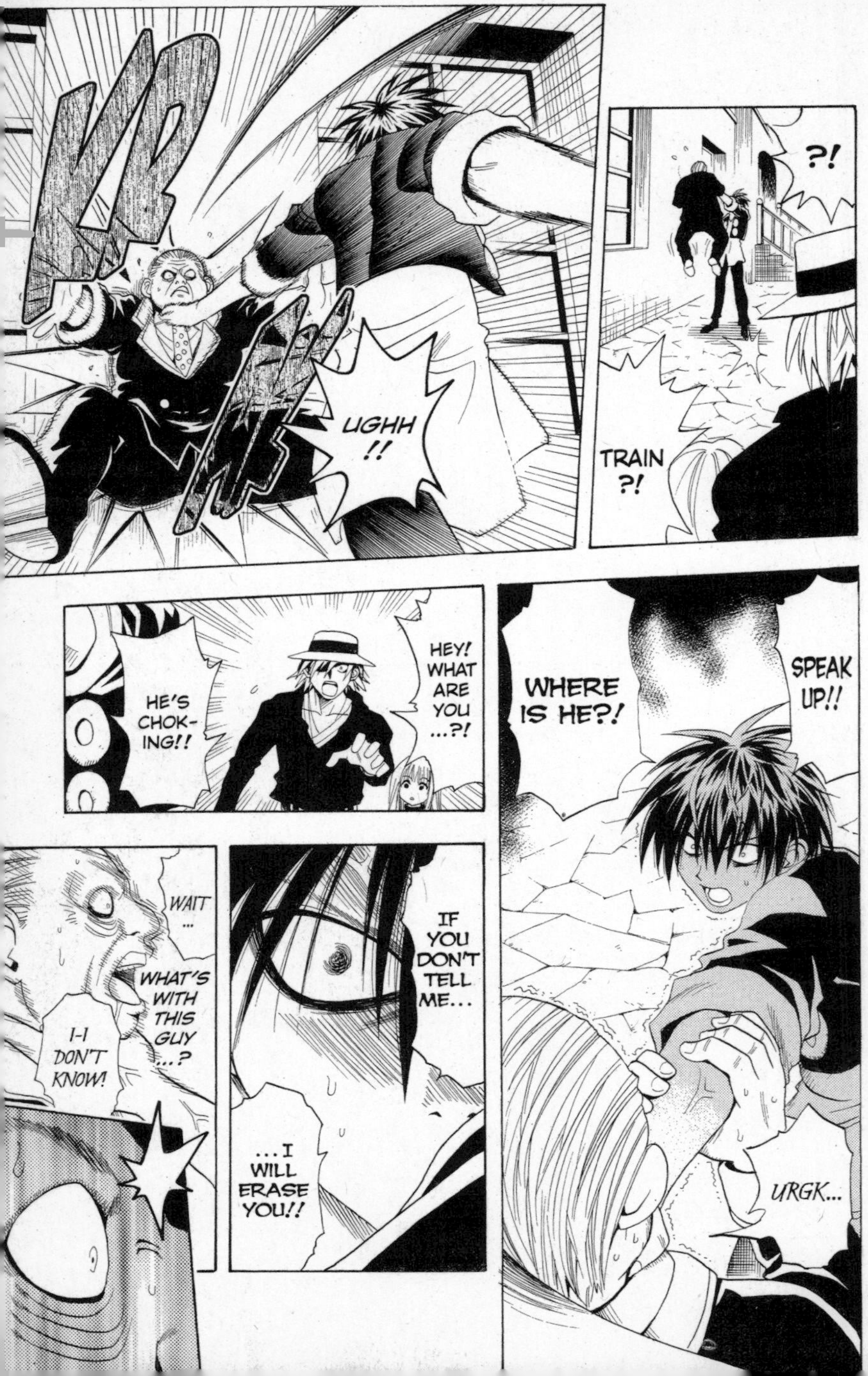
?!
TRAIN ?!
UGHH !!
SPEAK UP!!
WHERE IS HE?!
URGK...
HEY! WHAT ARE YOU ...?!
HE'S CHOK-ING!!
IF YOU DON'T TELL ME...
...I WILL ERASE YOU!!
WAIT ...
WHAT'S WITH THIS GUY ...?
I-I DON'T KNOW!

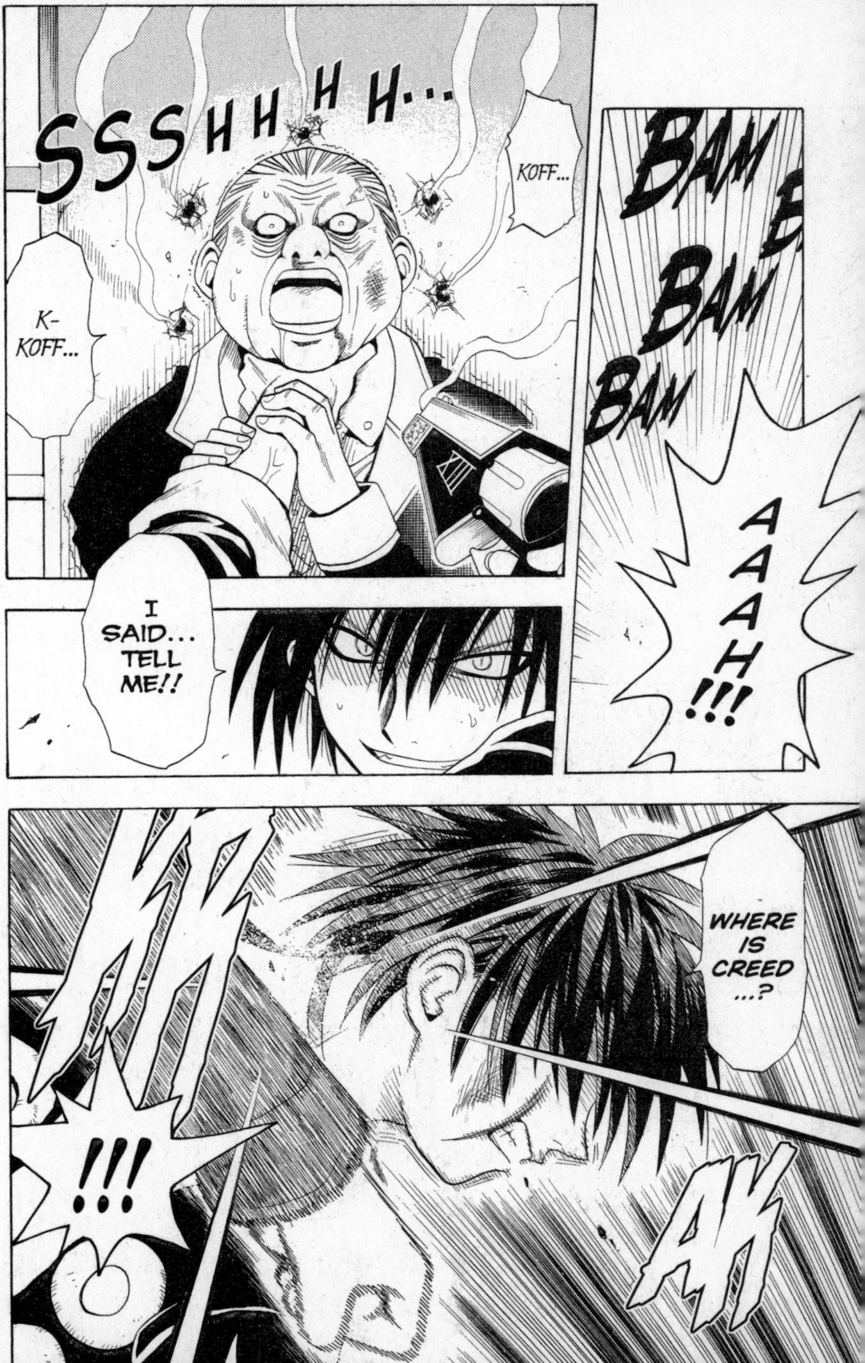
BAM BAM BAM BAM
AAAAH!!!
SSSHHHH...
KOFF...
K-KOFF...
I SAID... TELL ME!!
WHERE IS CREED ...?
AK
!!!

READ THIS WAY

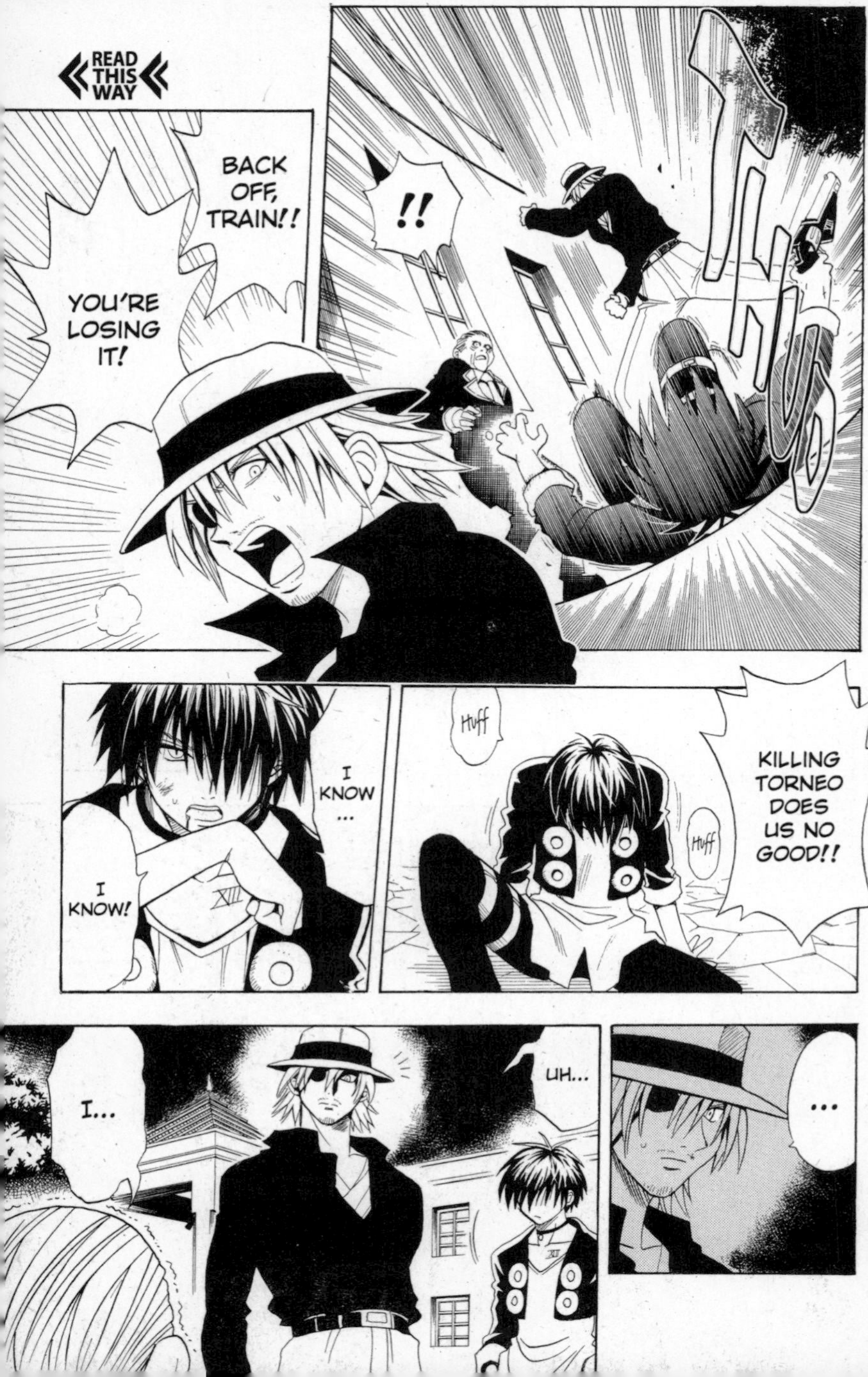
!!
BACK OFF, TRAIN!!
YOU'RE LOSING IT!
KILLING TORNEO DOES US NO GOOD!!
Huff
Huff
I KNOW...
I KNOW!
...
UH...
I...

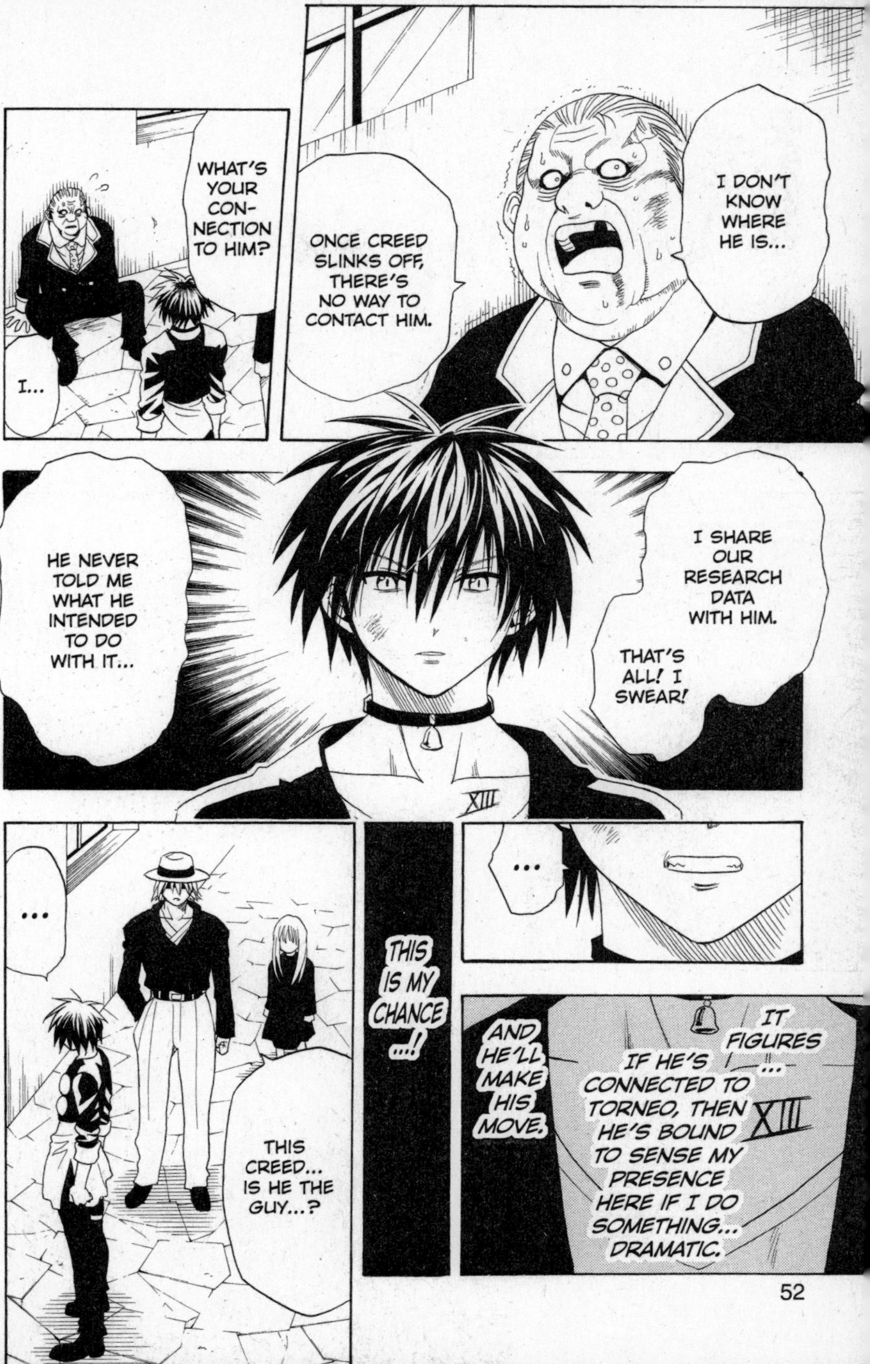
I DON'T KNOW WHERE HE IS...
ONCE CREED SLINKS OFF, THERE'S NO WAY TO CONTACT HIM.
WHAT'S YOUR CON-NECTION TO HIM?
I...
I SHARE OUR RESEARCH DATA WITH HIM.
THAT'S ALL! I SWEAR!
HE NEVER TOLD ME WHAT HE INTENDED TO DO WITH IT...
...
IT FIGURES...
IF HE'S CONNECTED TO TORNEO, THEN HE'S BOUND TO SENSE MY PRESENCE HERE IF I DO SOMETHING... DRAMATIC.
AND HE'LL MAKE HIS MOVE.
THIS IS MY CHANCE...!
...
THIS CREED... IS HE THE GUY...?

READ THIS WAY

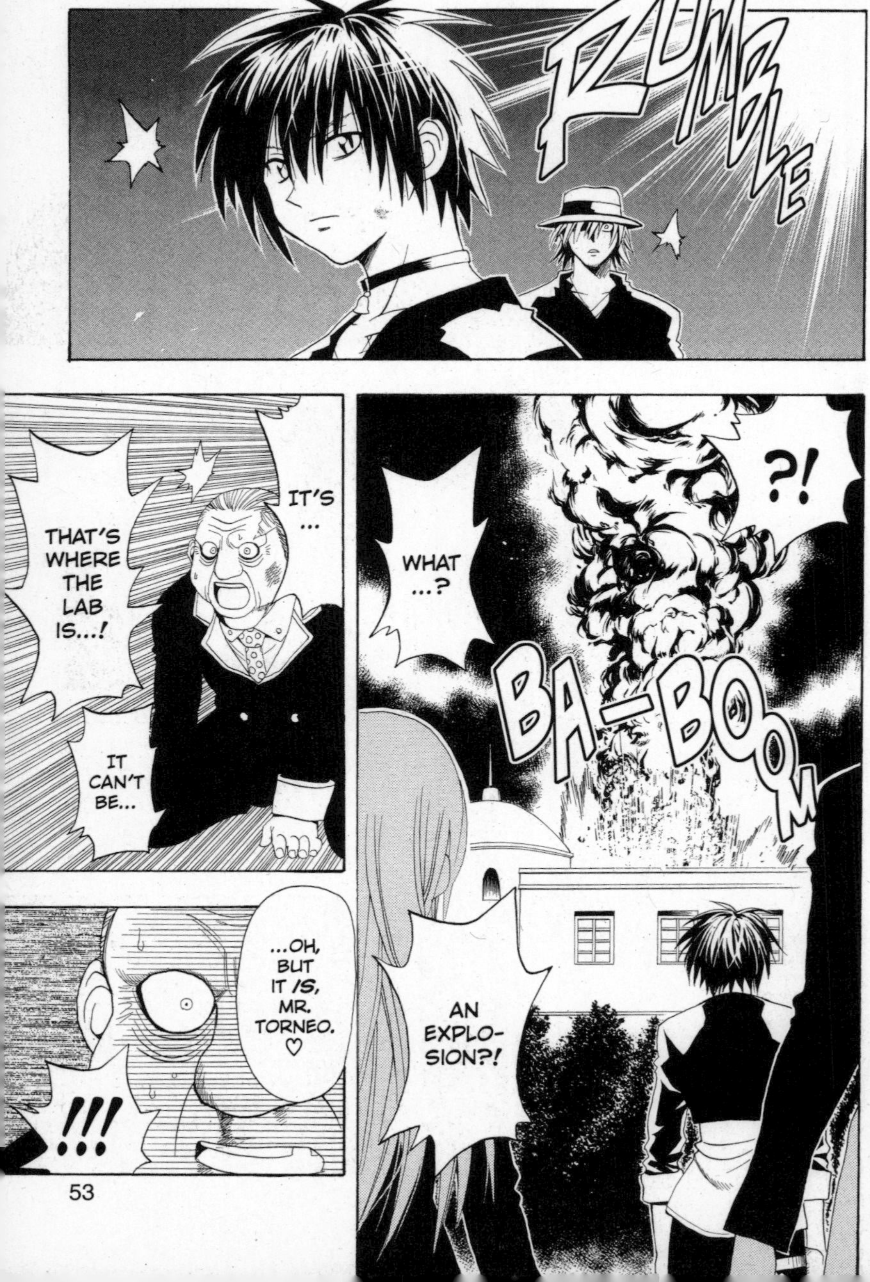
RUMBLE
?!
WHAT ...?
BA-BOOM
AN EXPLOSION?!
IT'S ...
THAT'S WHERE THE LAB IS...!
IT CAN'T BE...
...OH, BUT IT *IS*, MR. TORNEO. ♡
!!!

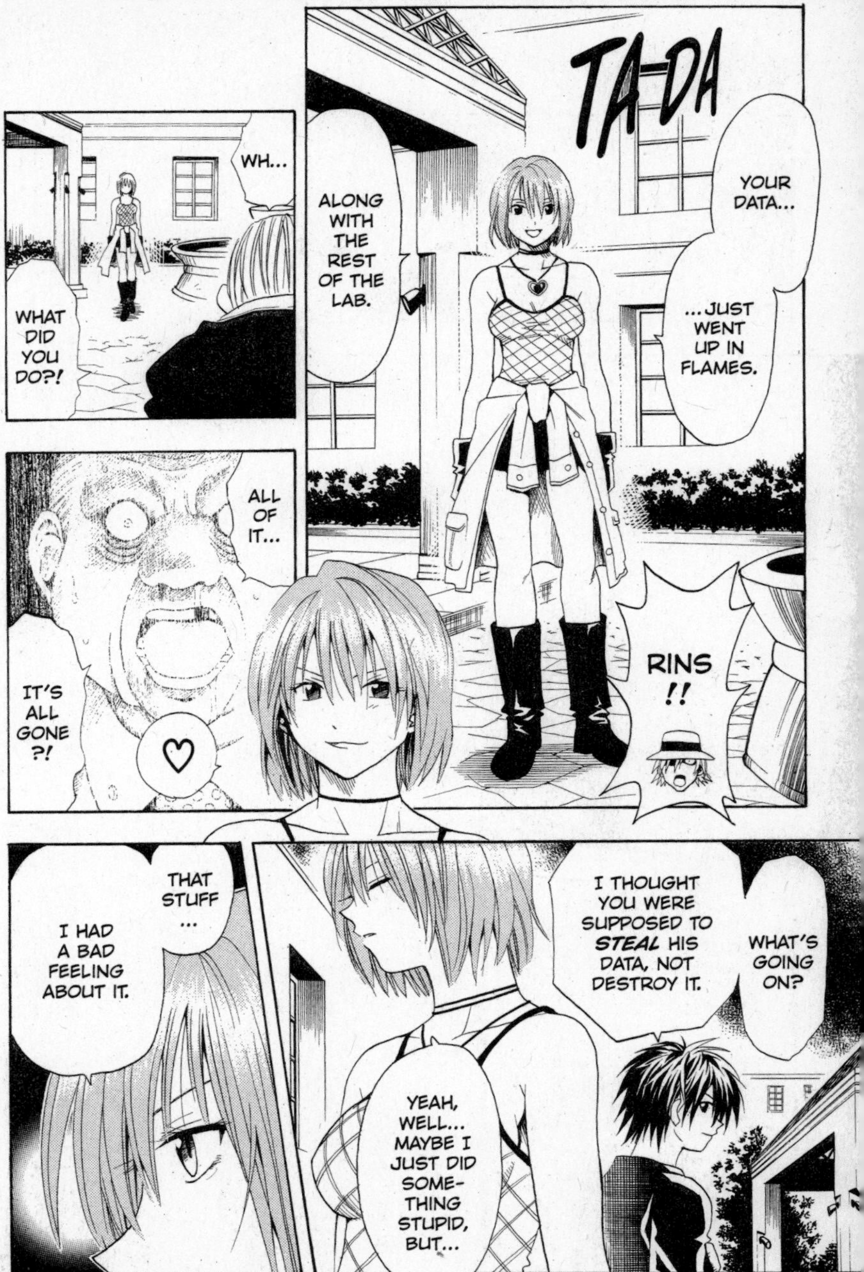
TA-DA
YOUR DATA...
...JUST WENT UP IN FLAMES.
ALONG WITH THE REST OF THE LAB.
RINS!!
WH...
WHAT DID YOU DO?!
ALL OF IT...
IT'S ALL GONE?!
♥
WHAT'S GOING ON?
I THOUGHT YOU WERE SUPPOSED TO *STEAL* HIS DATA, NOT DESTROY IT.
YEAH, WELL... MAYBE I JUST DID SOMETHING STUPID, BUT...
THAT STUFF...
I HAD A BAD FEELING ABOUT IT.

READ THIS WAY

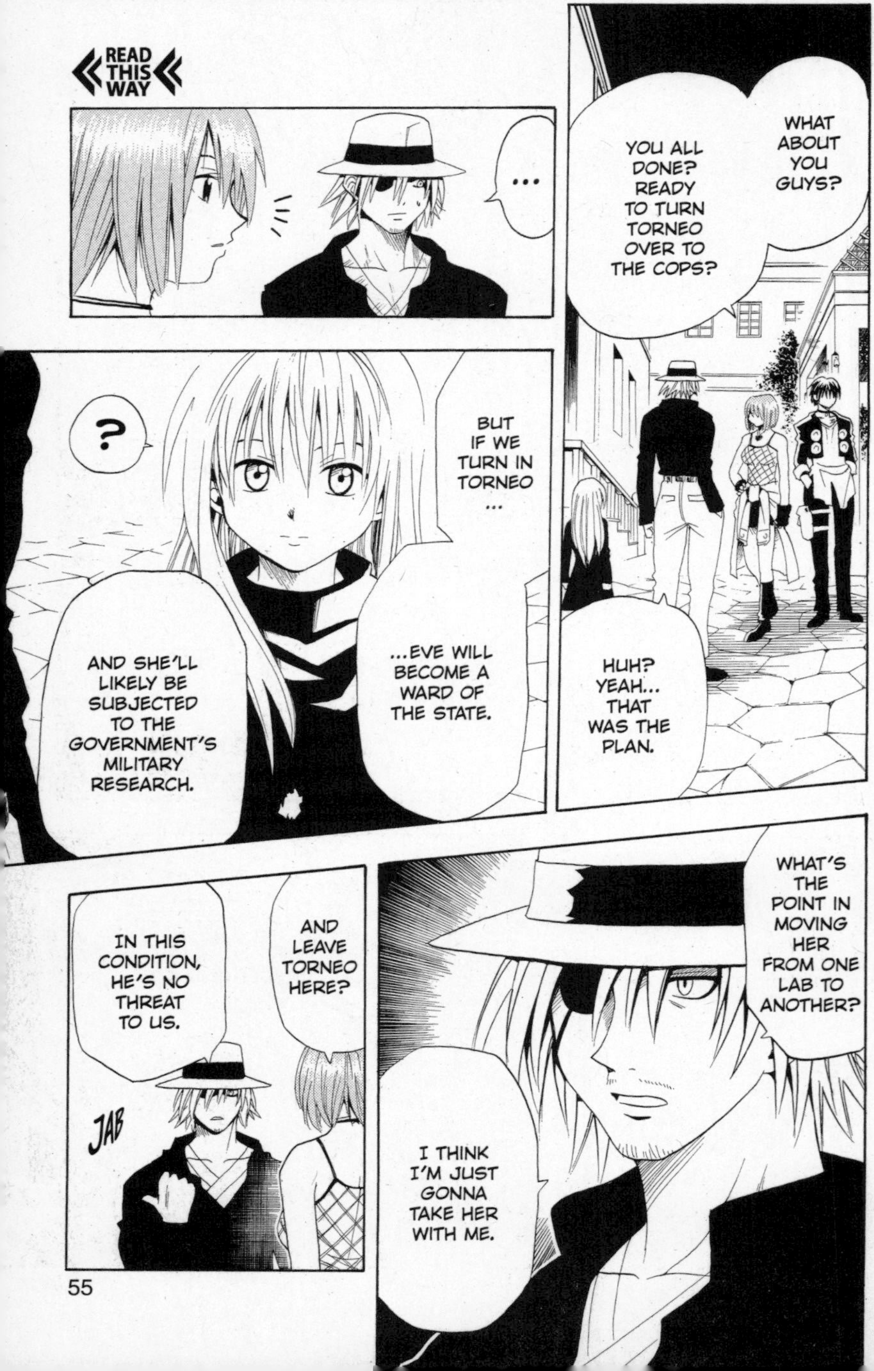
WHAT ABOUT YOU GUYS?
YOU ALL DONE? READY TO TURN TORNEO OVER TO THE COPS?
HUH? YEAH... THAT WAS THE PLAN.
...
BUT IF WE TURN IN TORNEO ...
...EVE WILL BECOME A WARD OF THE STATE.
?
AND SHE'LL LIKELY BE SUBJECTED TO THE GOVERNMENT'S MILITARY RESEARCH.
WHAT'S THE POINT IN MOVING HER FROM ONE LAB TO ANOTHER?
I THINK I'M JUST GONNA TAKE HER WITH ME.
AND LEAVE TORNEO HERE?
IN THIS CONDITION, HE'S NO THREAT TO US.
JAB

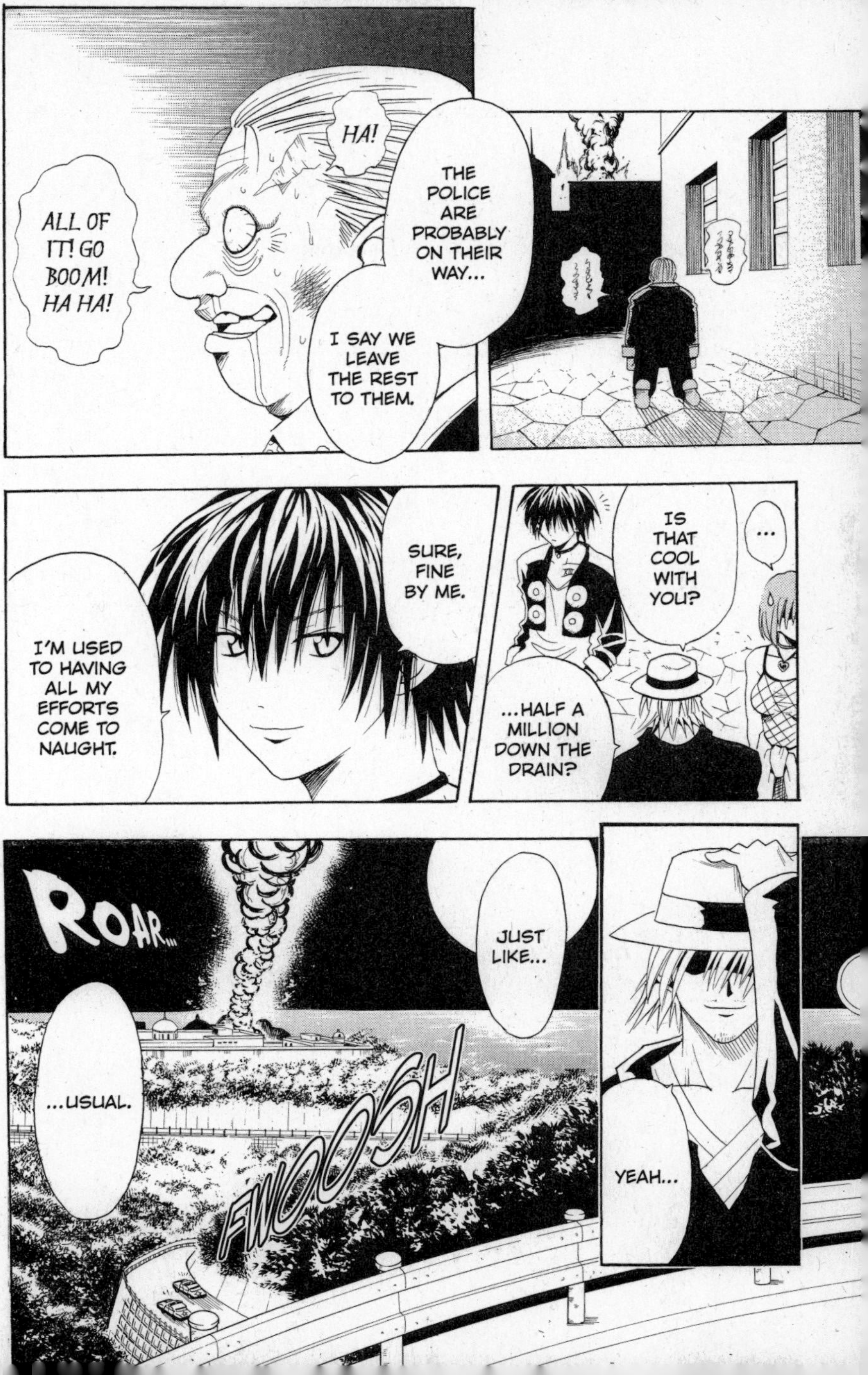
HA!
THE POLICE ARE PROBABLY ON THEIR WAY...
I SAY WE LEAVE THE REST TO THEM.
ALL OF IT! GO BOOM! HA HA!
...
IS THAT COOL WITH YOU?
...HALF A MILLION DOWN THE DRAIN?
SURE, FINE BY ME.
I'M USED TO HAVING ALL MY EFFORTS COME TO NAUGHT.
YEAH...
JUST LIKE...
...USUAL.
ROAR...
FWOOSH

READ THIS WAY

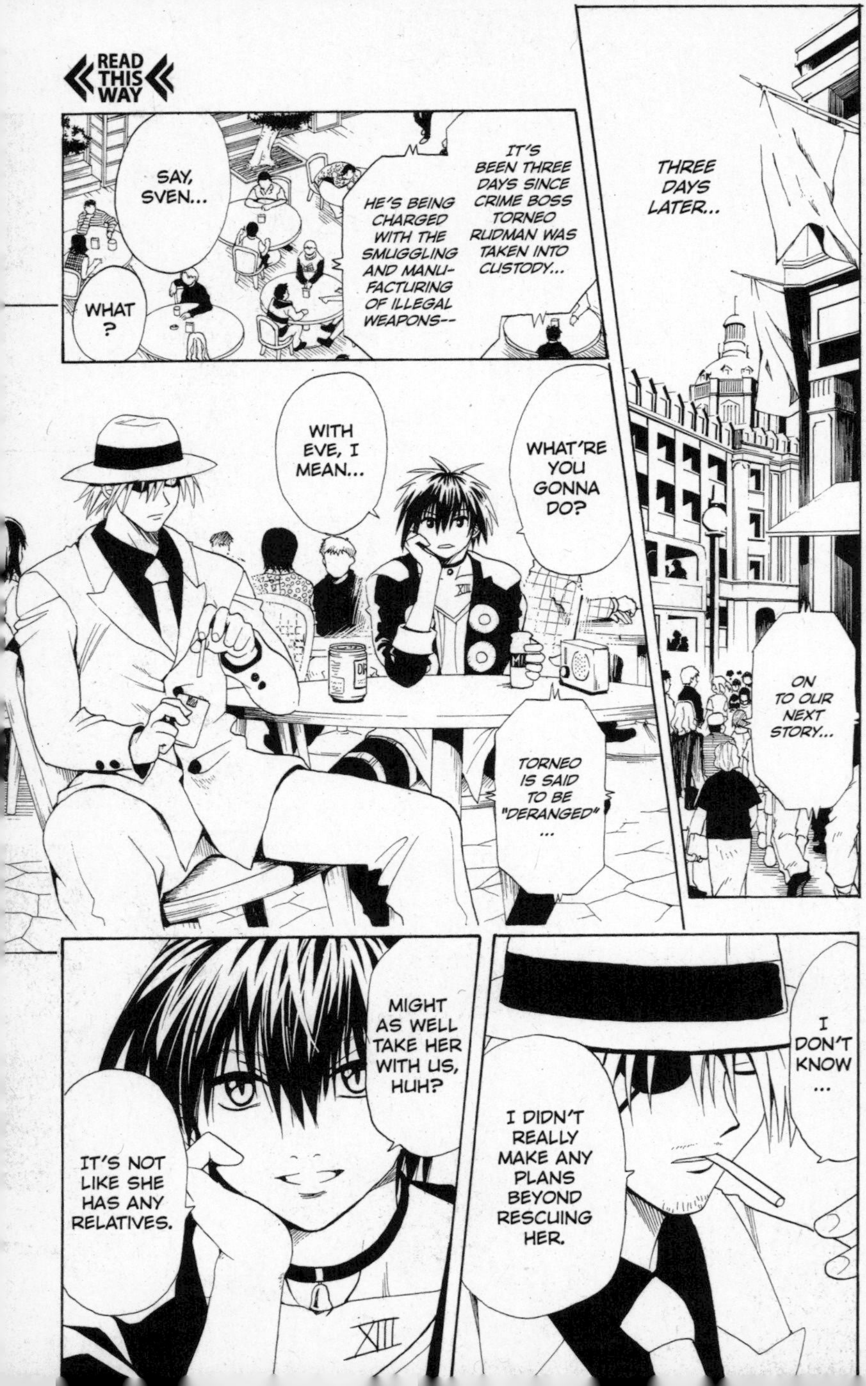
THREE DAYS LATER...
ON TO OUR NEXT STORY...
IT'S BEEN THREE DAYS SINCE CRIME BOSS TORNEO RUDMAN WAS TAKEN INTO CUSTODY...
HE'S BEING CHARGED WITH THE SMUGGLING AND MANU-FACTURING OF ILLEGAL WEAPONS--
SAY, SVEN...
WHAT?
WHAT'RE YOU GONNA DO?
WITH EVE, I MEAN...
TORNEO IS SAID TO BE "DERANGED"...
I DON'T KNOW...
I DIDN'T REALLY MAKE ANY PLANS BEYOND RESCUING HER.
MIGHT AS WELL TAKE HER WITH US, HUH?
IT'S NOT LIKE SHE HAS ANY RELATIVES.

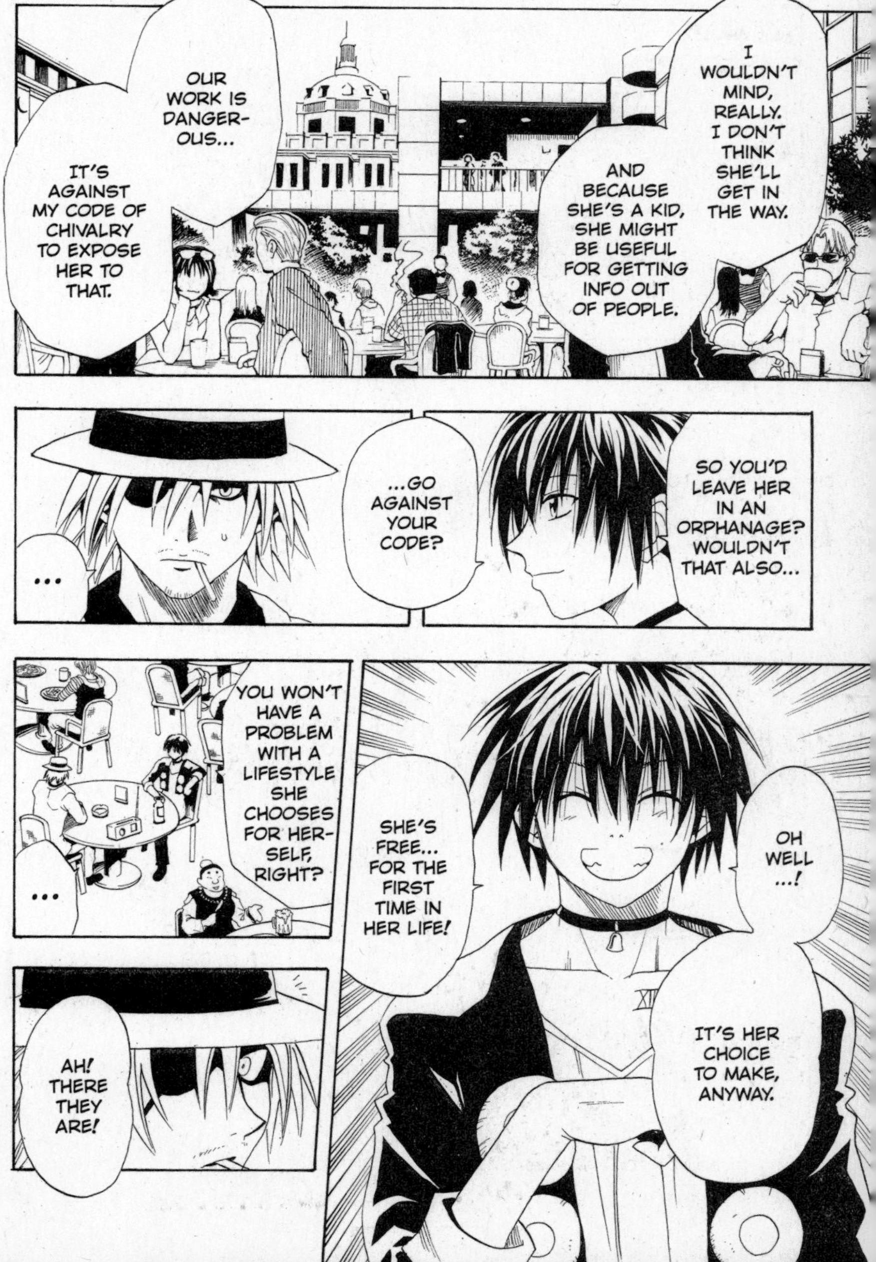
I WOULDN'T MIND, REALLY. I DON'T THINK SHE'LL GET IN THE WAY.
AND BECAUSE SHE'S A KID, SHE MIGHT BE USEFUL FOR GETTING INFO OUT OF PEOPLE.
OUR WORK IS DANGEROUS...
IT'S AGAINST MY CODE OF CHIVALRY TO EXPOSE HER TO THAT.
SO YOU'D LEAVE HER IN AN ORPHANAGE? WOULDN'T THAT ALSO...
...GO AGAINST YOUR CODE?
...
OH WELL...!
SHE'S FREE... FOR THE FIRST TIME IN HER LIFE!
IT'S HER CHOICE TO MAKE, ANYWAY.
YOU WON'T HAVE A PROBLEM WITH A LIFESTYLE SHE CHOOSES FOR HERSELF, RIGHT?
...
AH! THERE THEY ARE!

READ THIS WAY

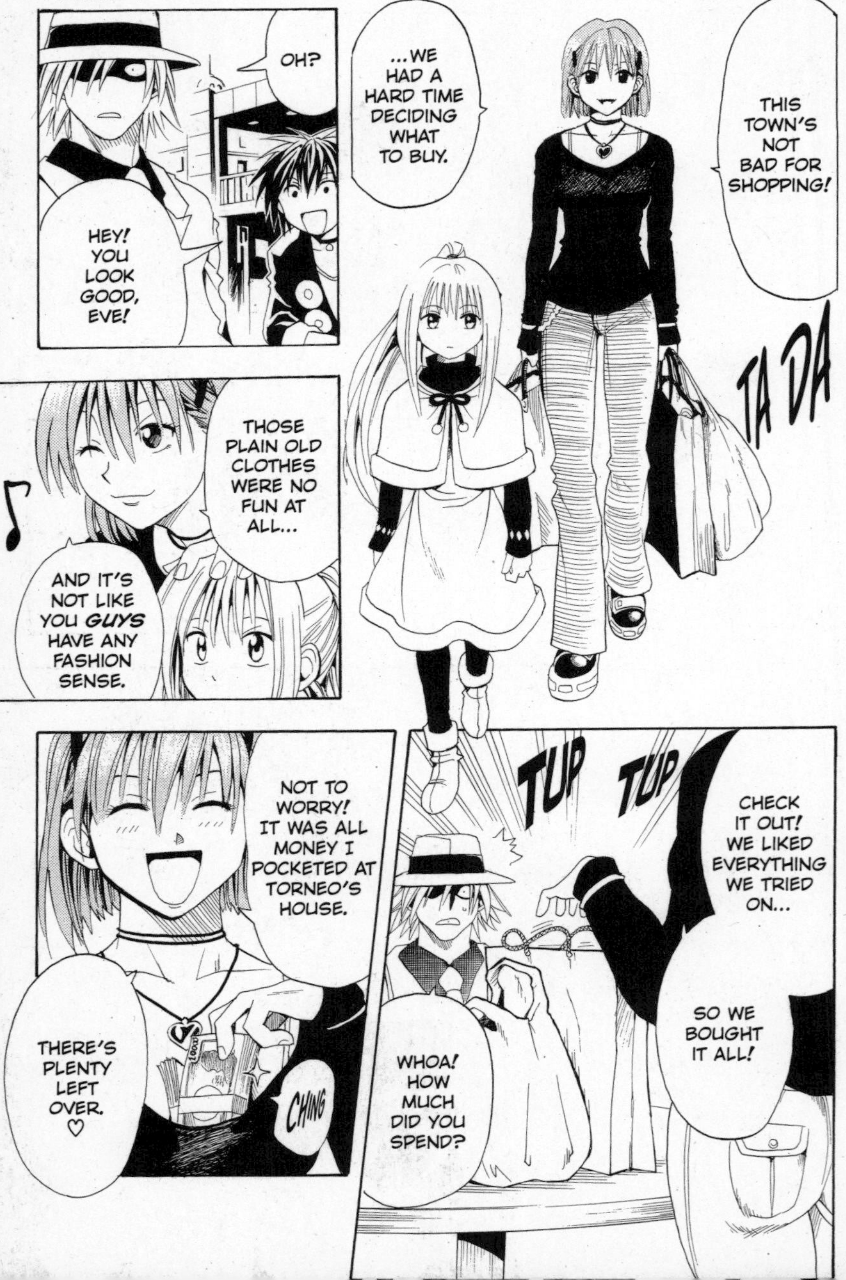
THIS TOWN'S NOT BAD FOR SHOPPING!
...WE HAD A HARD TIME DECIDING WHAT TO BUY.
TA DA
OH?
HEY! YOU LOOK GOOD, EVE!
THOSE PLAIN OLD CLOTHES WERE NO FUN AT ALL...
AND IT'S NOT LIKE YOU *GUYS* HAVE ANY FASHION SENSE.
TUP TUP
CHECK IT OUT! WE LIKED EVERYTHING WE TRIED ON...
SO WE BOUGHT IT ALL!
WHOA! HOW MUCH DID YOU SPEND?
NOT TO WORRY! IT WAS ALL MONEY I POCKETED AT TORNEO'S HOUSE.
CHING
THERE'S PLENTY LEFT OVER. ♡

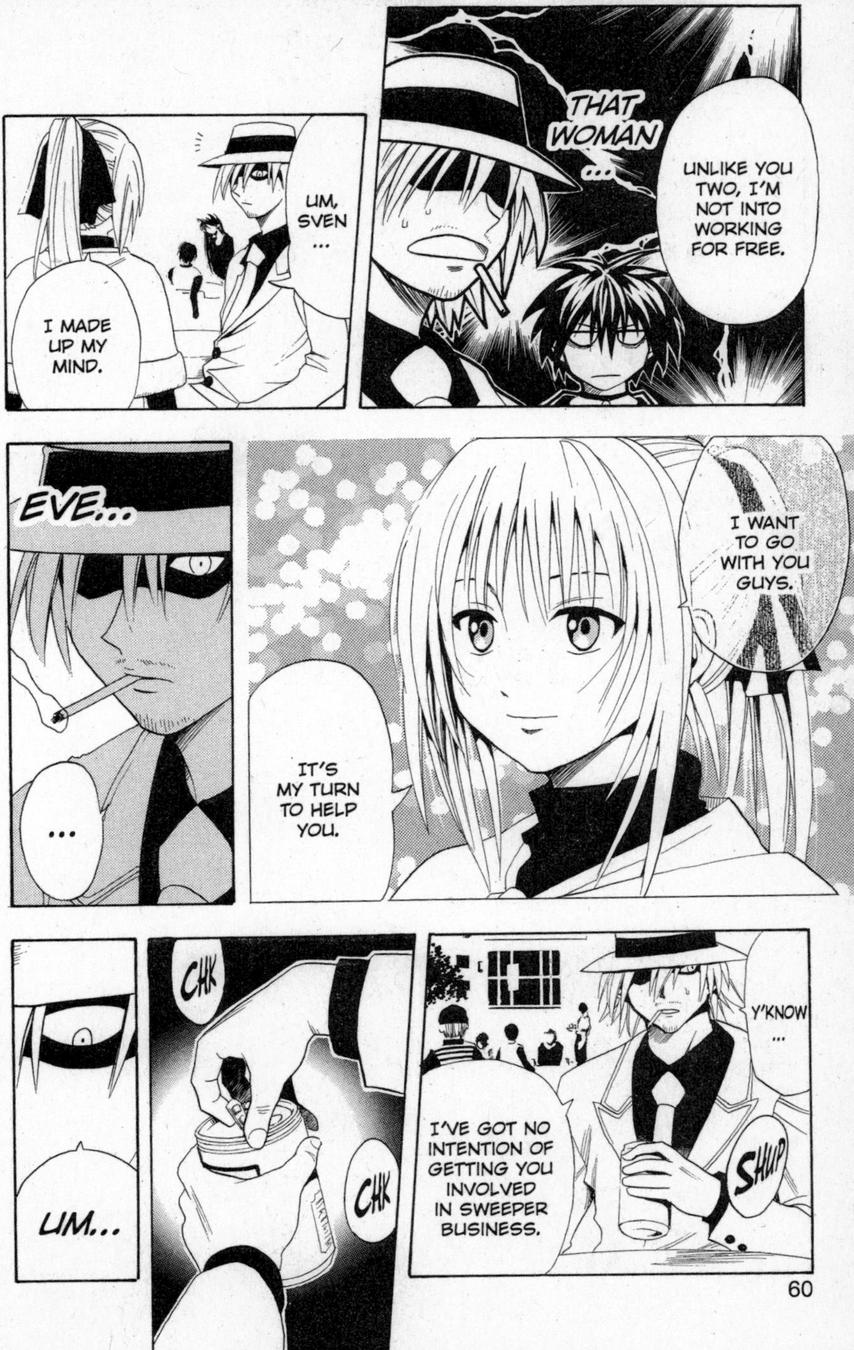

THAT WOMAN...
UNLIKE YOU TWO, I'M NOT INTO WORKING FOR FREE.
UM, SVEN...
I MADE UP MY MIND.
I WANT TO GO WITH YOU GUYS.
IT'S MY TURN TO HELP YOU.
EVE...
...
Y'KNOW...
SHUP
I'VE GOT NO INTENTION OF GETTING YOU INVOLVED IN SWEEPER BUSINESS.
CHK
CHK
UM...

READ THIS WAY

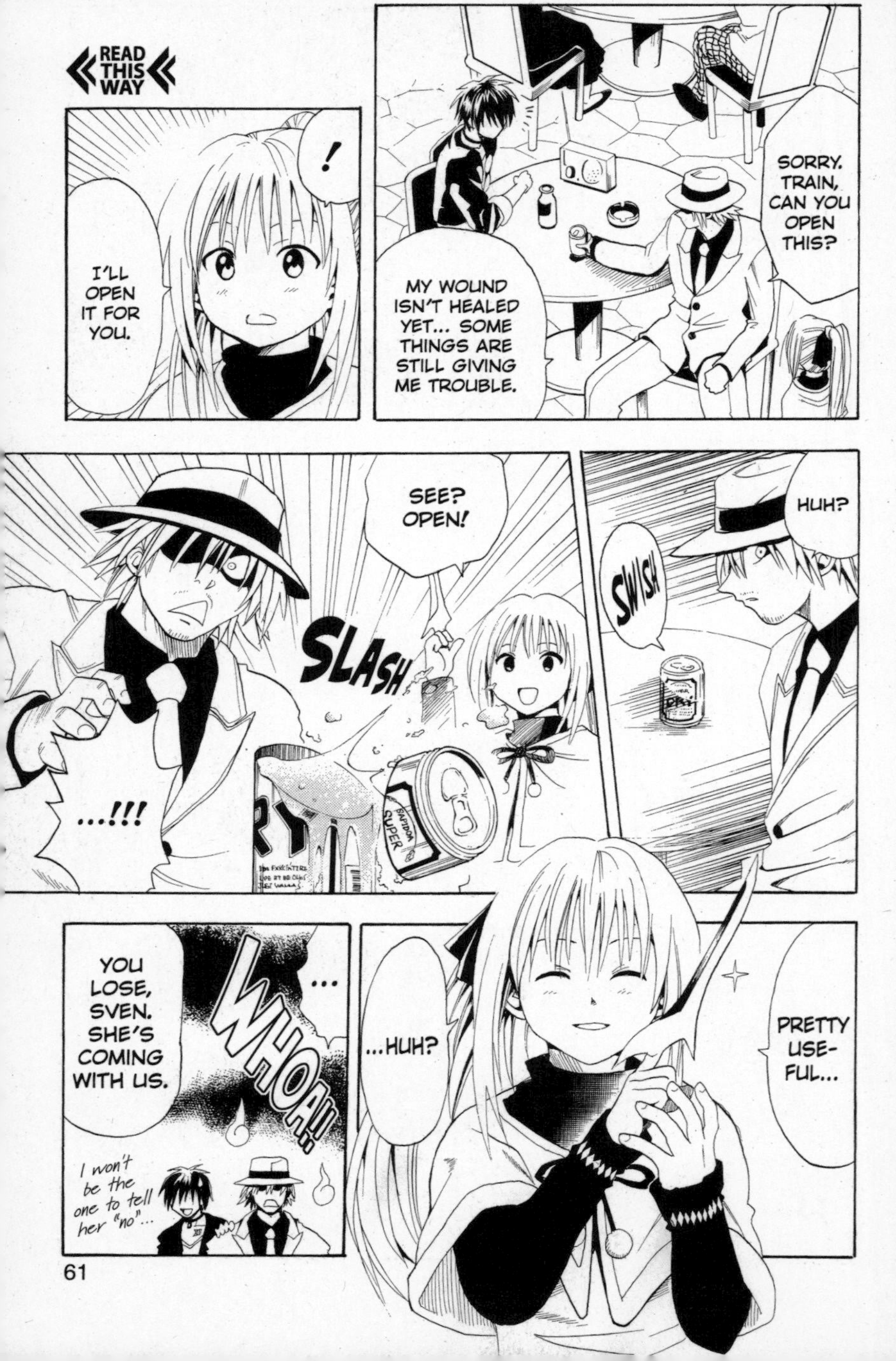

SORRY. TRAIN, CAN YOU OPEN THIS?
MY WOUND ISN'T HEALED YET... SOME THINGS ARE STILL GIVING ME TROUBLE.
!
I'LL OPEN IT FOR YOU.
HUH?
SWISH
SEE? OPEN!
SLASH
...!!!
PRETTY USE-FUL...
...HUH?
...
WHOA!!
YOU LOSE, SVEN. SHE'S COMING WITH US.
I won't be the one to tell her "no"...

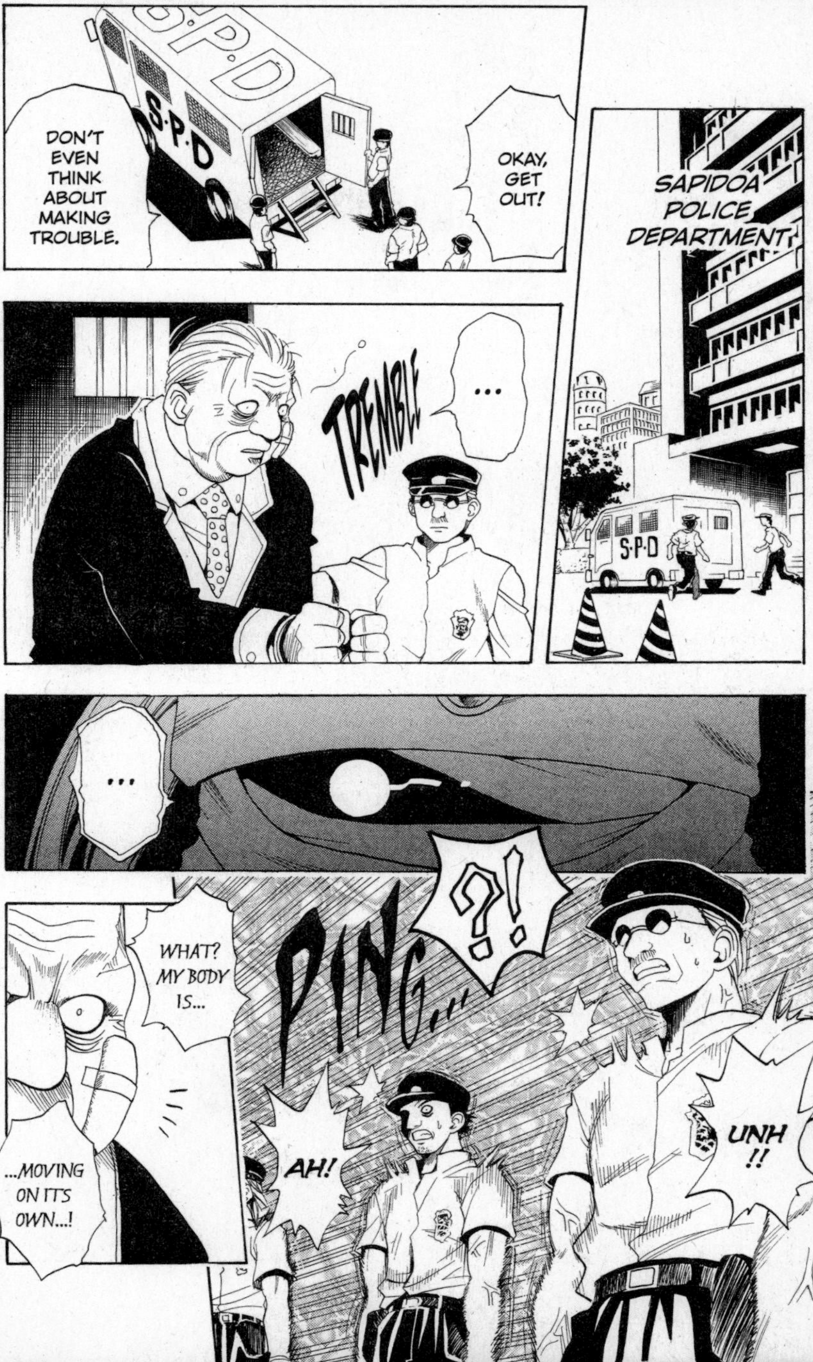
SAPIDOA POLICE DEPARTMENT
OKAY, GET OUT!
DON'T EVEN THINK ABOUT MAKING TROUBLE.
...
TREMBLE
...
?!
PING...
UNH !!
AH!
WHAT? MY BODY IS...
...MOVING ON ITS OWN...!

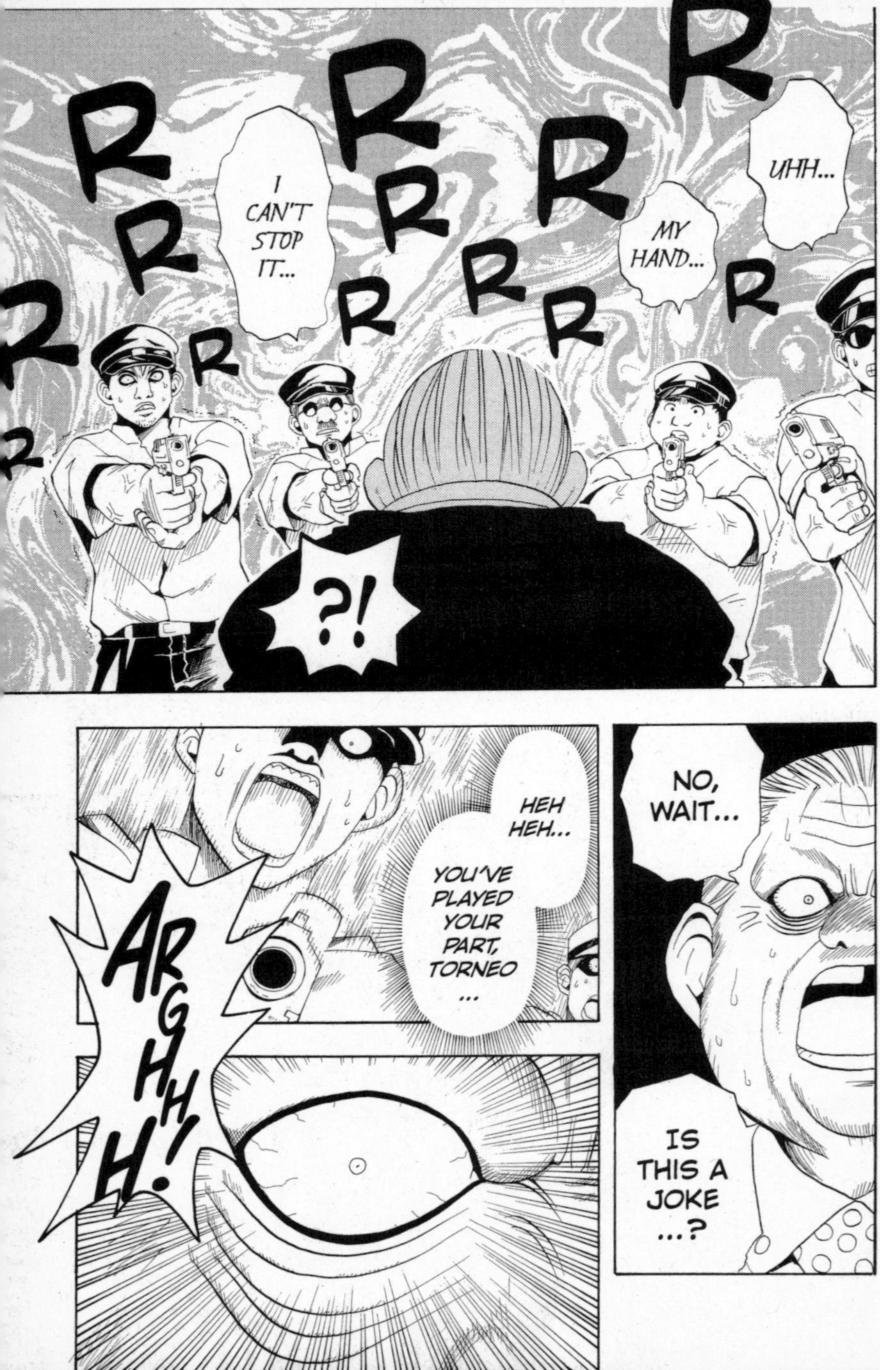
RRRRRRRRRRRRR
UHH...
MY HAND...
I CAN'T STOP IT...
?!
NO, WAIT...
IS THIS A JOKE ...?
HEH HEH...
YOU'VE PLAYED YOUR PART, TORNEO ...
ARGHHH!

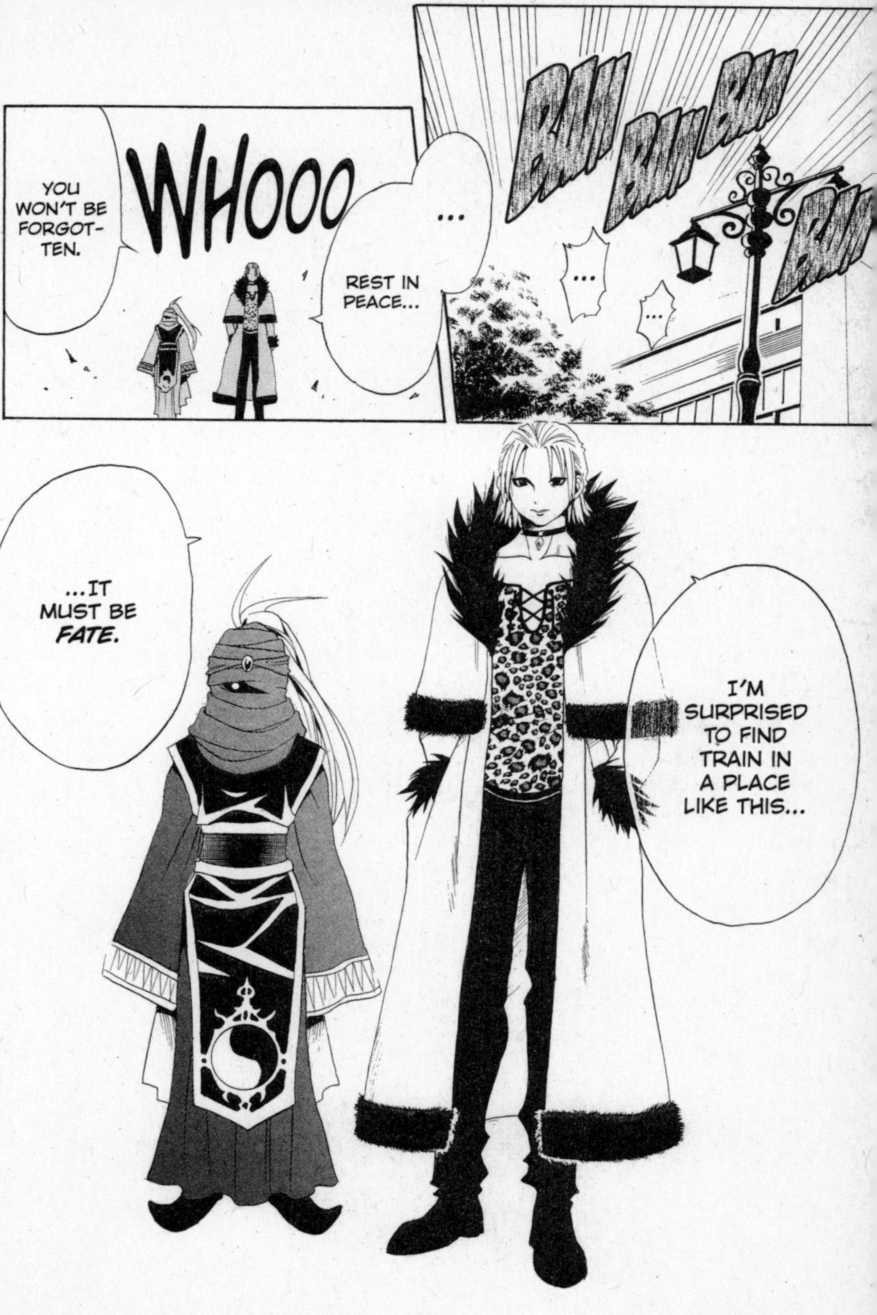
BAM BAM BAM BAM
...
...
... REST IN PEACE...
WHOOO
YOU WON'T BE FORGOT-TEN.
I'M SURPRISED TO FIND TRAIN IN A PLACE LIKE THIS...
...IT MUST BE *FATE*.

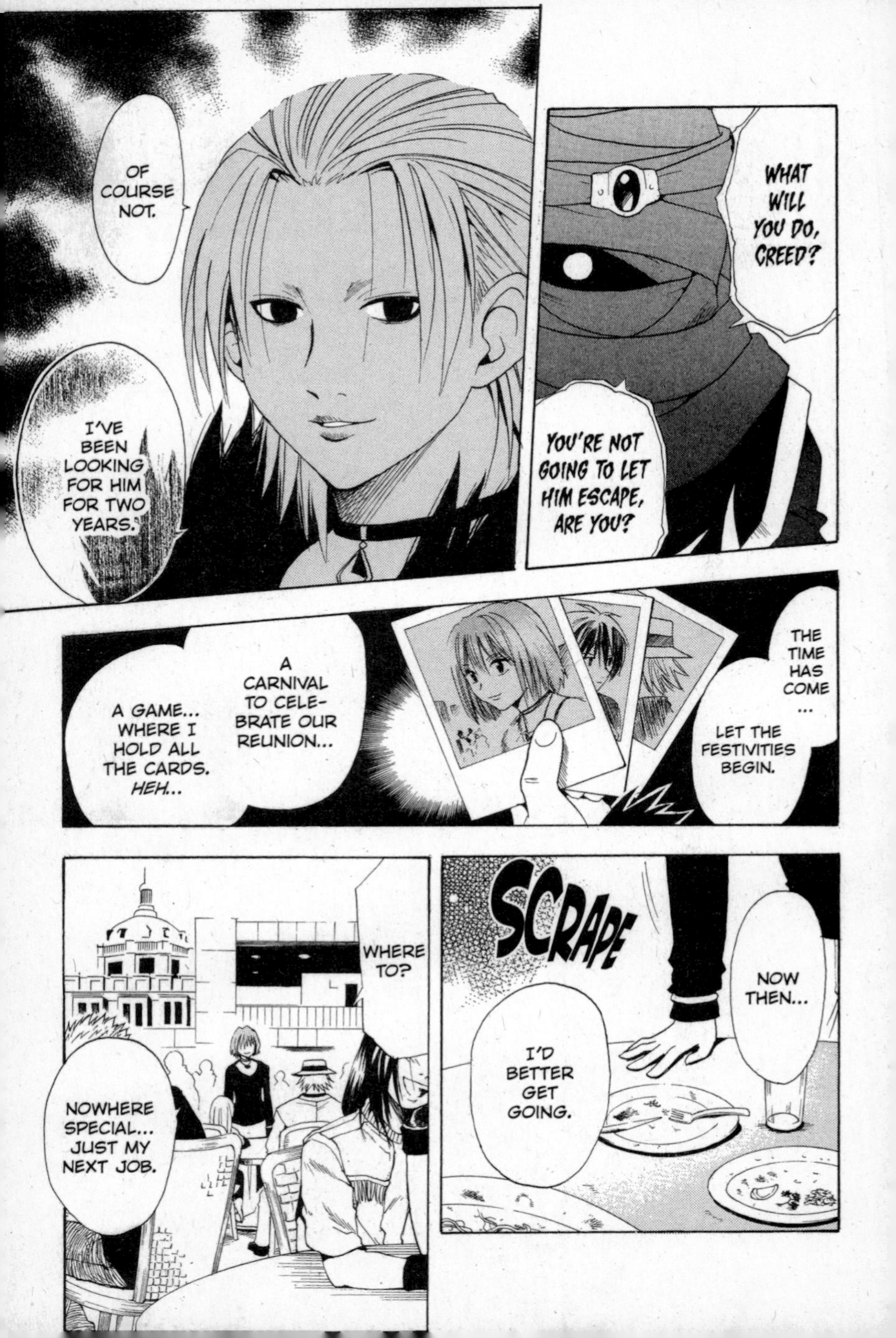
WHAT WILL YOU DO, CREED?
YOU'RE NOT GOING TO LET HIM ESCAPE, ARE YOU?
OF COURSE NOT.
I'VE BEEN LOOKING FOR HIM FOR TWO YEARS.
THE TIME HAS COME...
LET THE FESTIVITIES BEGIN.
A CARNIVAL TO CELE-BRATE OUR REUNION...
A GAME... WHERE I HOLD ALL THE CARDS. *HEH...*
SCRAPE
NOW THEN...
I'D BETTER GET GOING.
WHERE TO?
NOWHERE SPECIAL... JUST MY NEXT JOB.

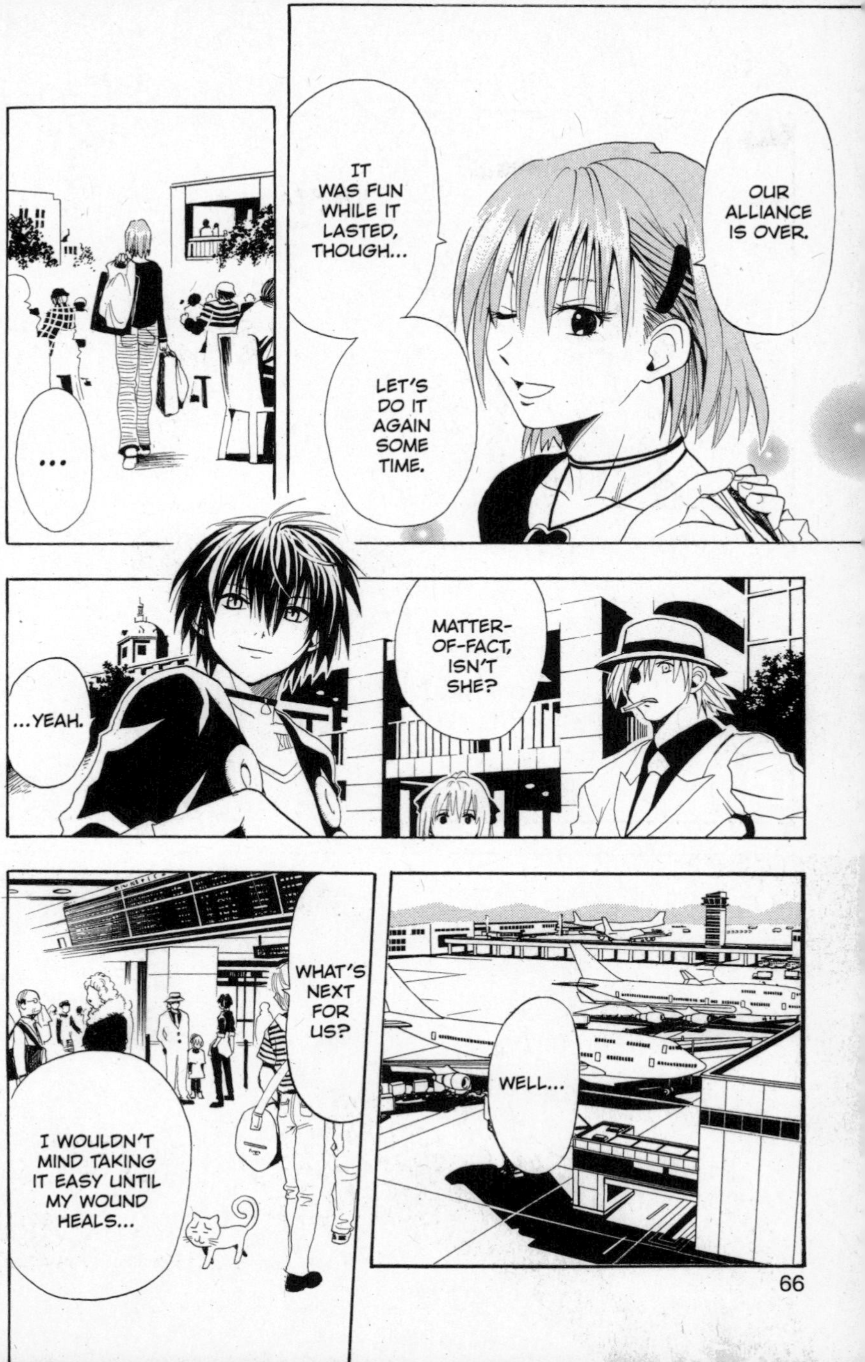
OUR ALLIANCE IS OVER.
IT WAS FUN WHILE IT LASTED, THOUGH...
LET'S DO IT AGAIN SOME TIME.
...
MATTER-OF-FACT, ISN'T SHE?
...YEAH.
WELL...
WHAT'S NEXT FOR US?
I WOULDN'T MIND TAKING IT EASY UNTIL MY WOUND HEALS...

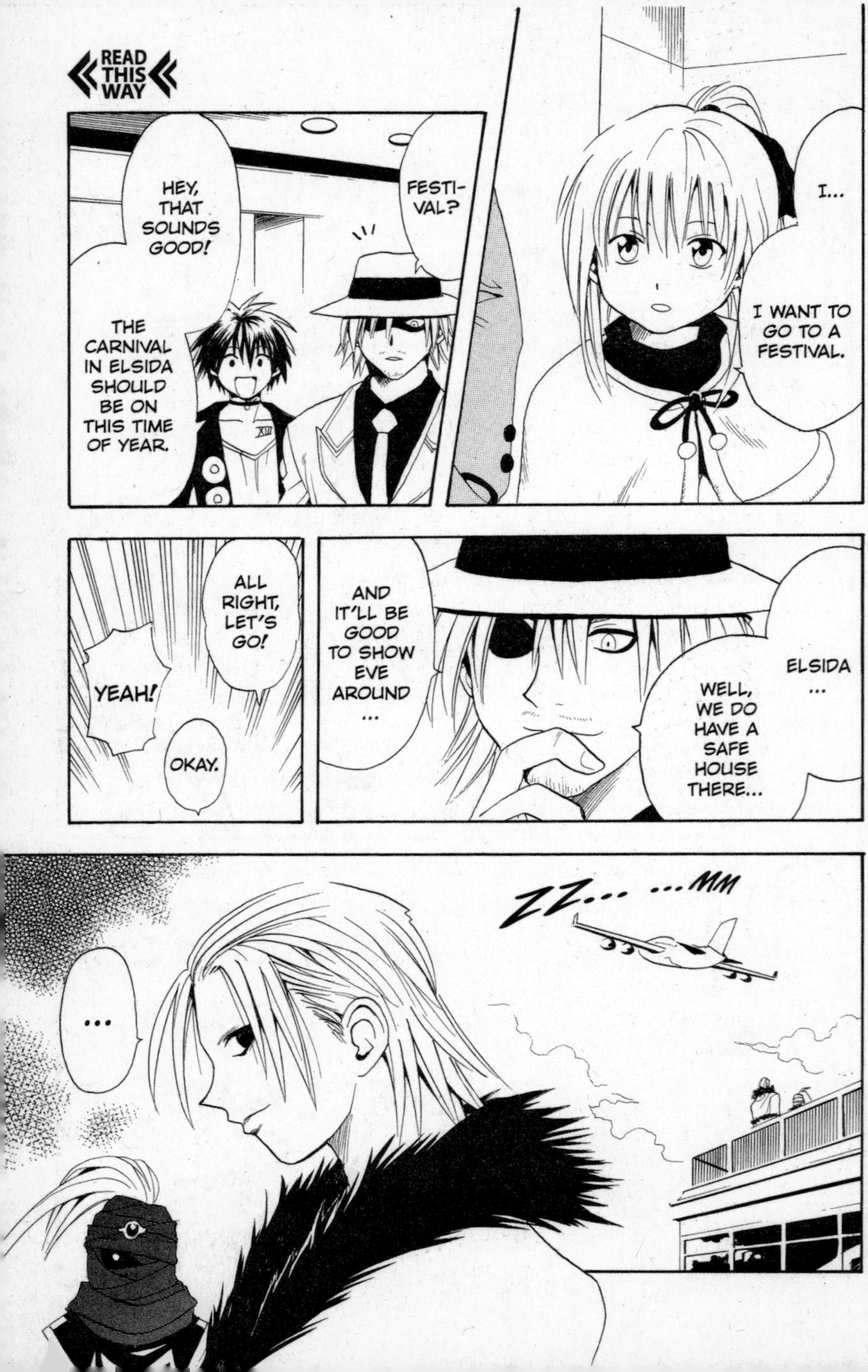
READ THIS WAY
I...
I WANT TO GO TO A FESTIVAL.
FESTI-VAL?
HEY, THAT SOUNDS GOOD!
THE CARNIVAL IN ELSIDA SHOULD BE ON THIS TIME OF YEAR.
ELSIDA...
WELL, WE DO HAVE A SAFE HOUSE THERE...
AND IT'LL BE GOOD TO SHOW EVE AROUND...
ALL RIGHT, LET'S GO!
YEAH!
OKAY.
ZZ... ...MM
...

BLACKCAT **FACTOIDS**

TORNEO'S RESEARCH

TORNEO RUDMAN DEVELOPED EVE THROUGH NANOTECHNOLOGY AND GENETIC ENGINEERING. HIS ULTIMATE GOAL WAS TO REVOLUTIONIZE WARFARE BY CREATING AN ARMY OF WARRIORS WITH POWERS LIKE EVE'S.

EVE WAS THE FIRST STEP IN THIS PLAN AND FROM THE MOMENT SHE WAS BORN, SHE WAS TRAINED AS A WARRIOR. WHEN SHE MATURED, SHE WAS TO BE SENT INTO BATTLE IN ORDER TO GATHER DATA.

TORNEO WAS ALSO AMONG THOSE WHO DONATED FUNDS TO THE MYSTERIOUS GROUP OF REVOLUTIONARIES LED BY CREED DISKENTH. HOWEVER...

OH, YOU...

HEH HEH

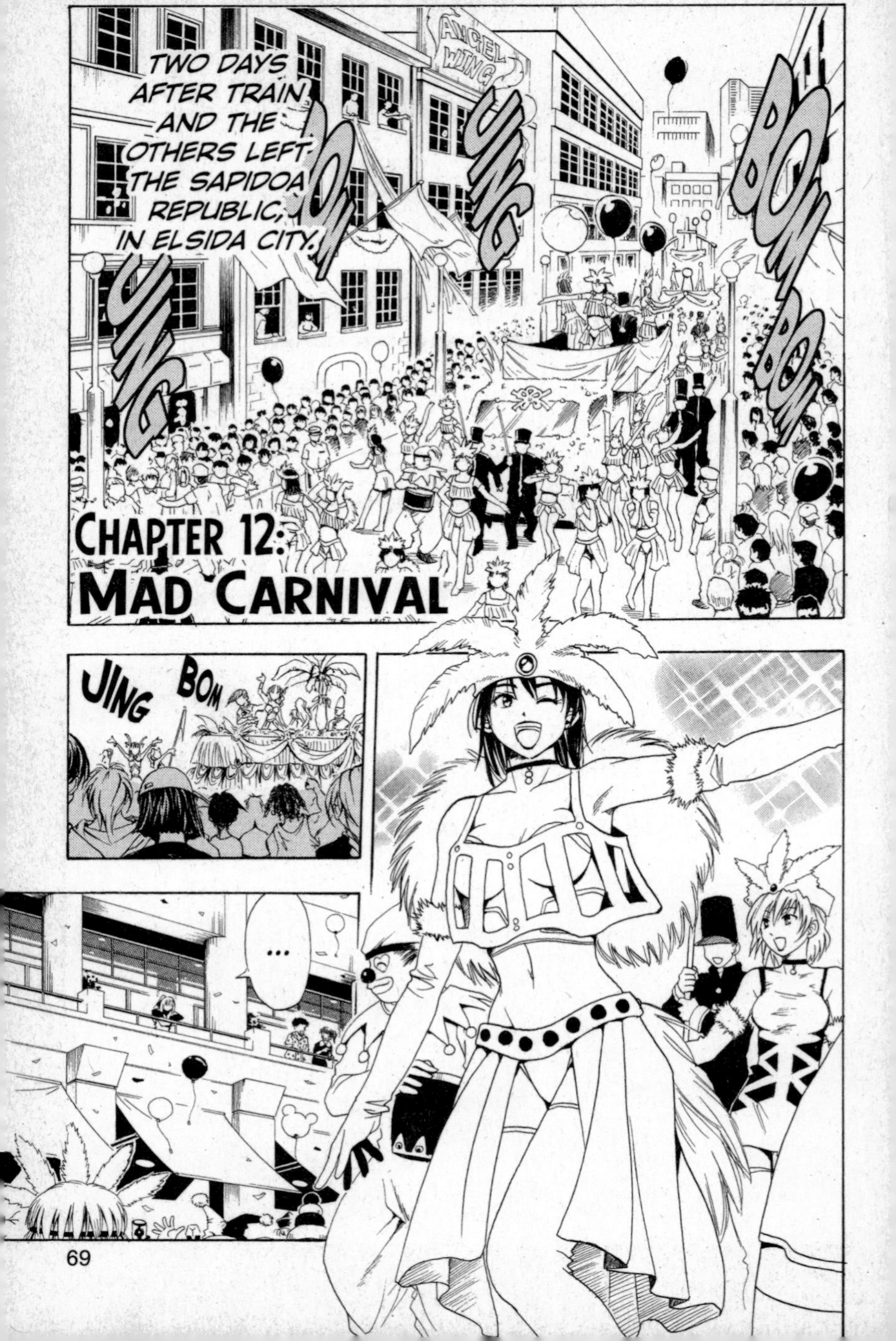
BOM BOM
JING
TWO DAYS AFTER TRAIN AND THE OTHERS LEFT THE SAPIDOA REPUBLIC, IN ELSIDA CITY.
JING
CHAPTER 12: MAD CARNIVAL
JING
BOM
...

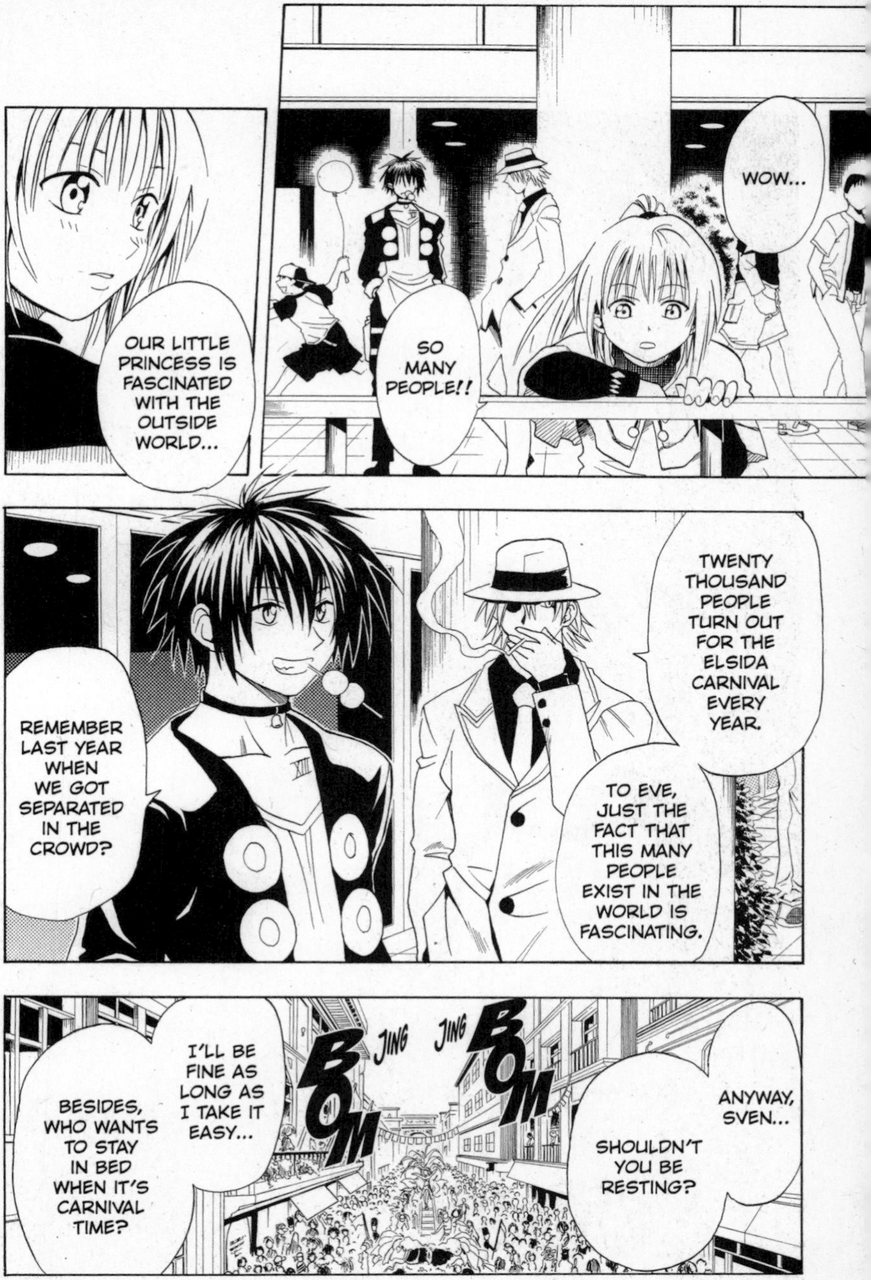
WOW...
SO MANY PEOPLE!!
OUR LITTLE PRINCESS IS FASCINATED WITH THE OUTSIDE WORLD...
TWENTY THOUSAND PEOPLE TURN OUT FOR THE ELSIDA CARNIVAL EVERY YEAR.
TO EVE, JUST THE FACT THAT THIS MANY PEOPLE EXIST IN THE WORLD IS FASCINATING.
REMEMBER LAST YEAR WHEN WE GOT SEPARATED IN THE CROWD?
ANYWAY, SVEN...
SHOULDN'T YOU BE RESTING?
BOOM
JING
JING
BOOM
I'LL BE FINE AS LONG AS I TAKE IT EASY...
BESIDES, WHO WANTS TO STAY IN BED WHEN IT'S CARNIVAL TIME?

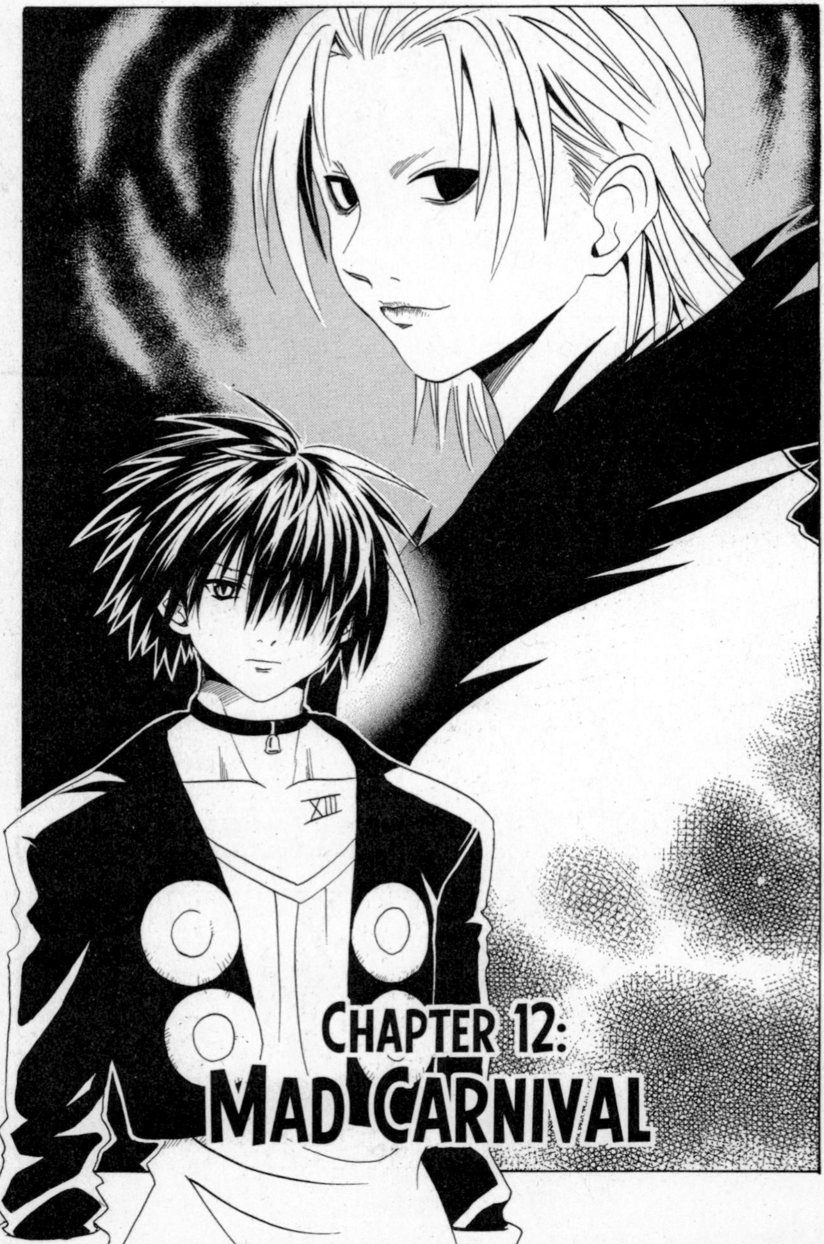

Chapter 12: Mad Carnival

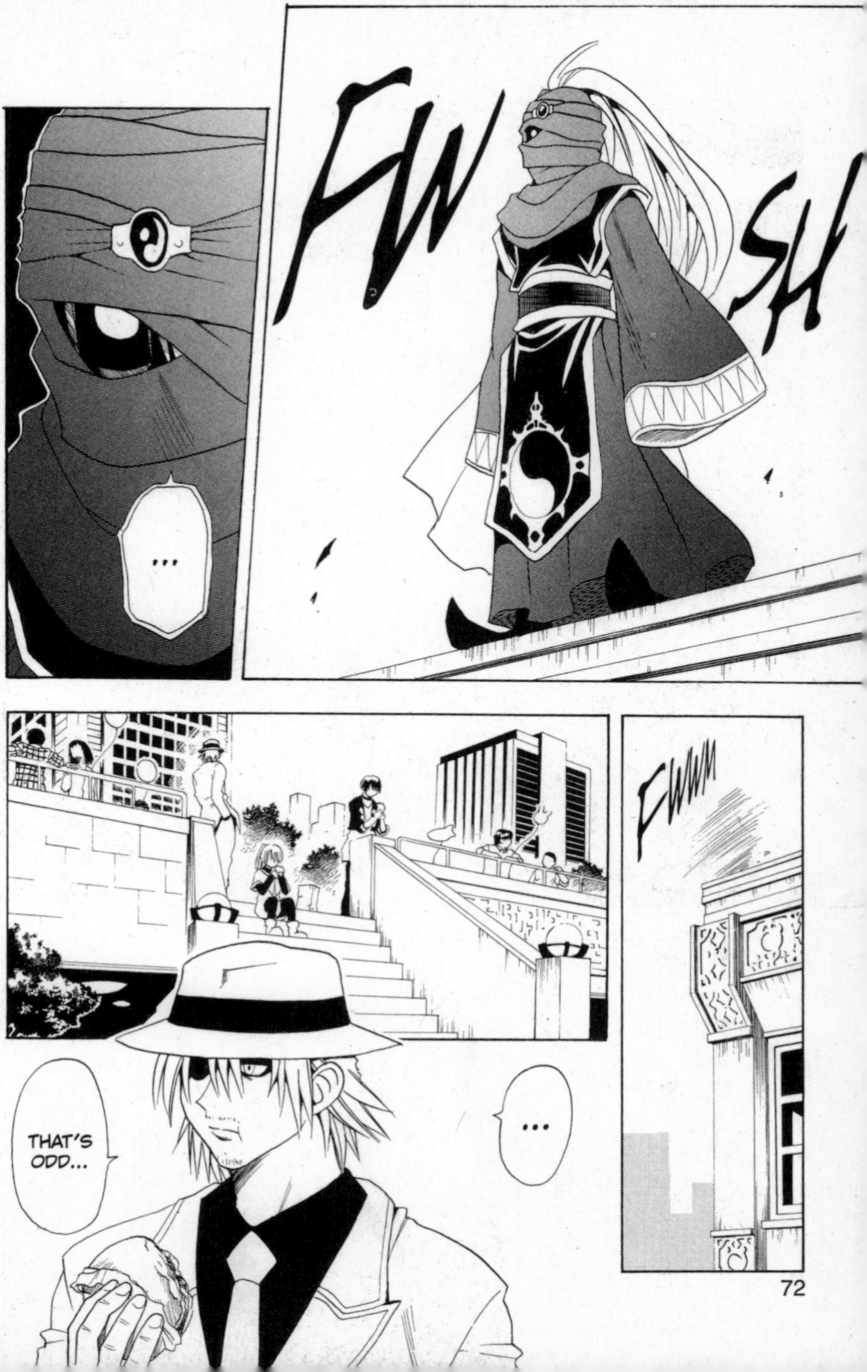
FWSH
...
FWMM
...
THAT'S ODD...

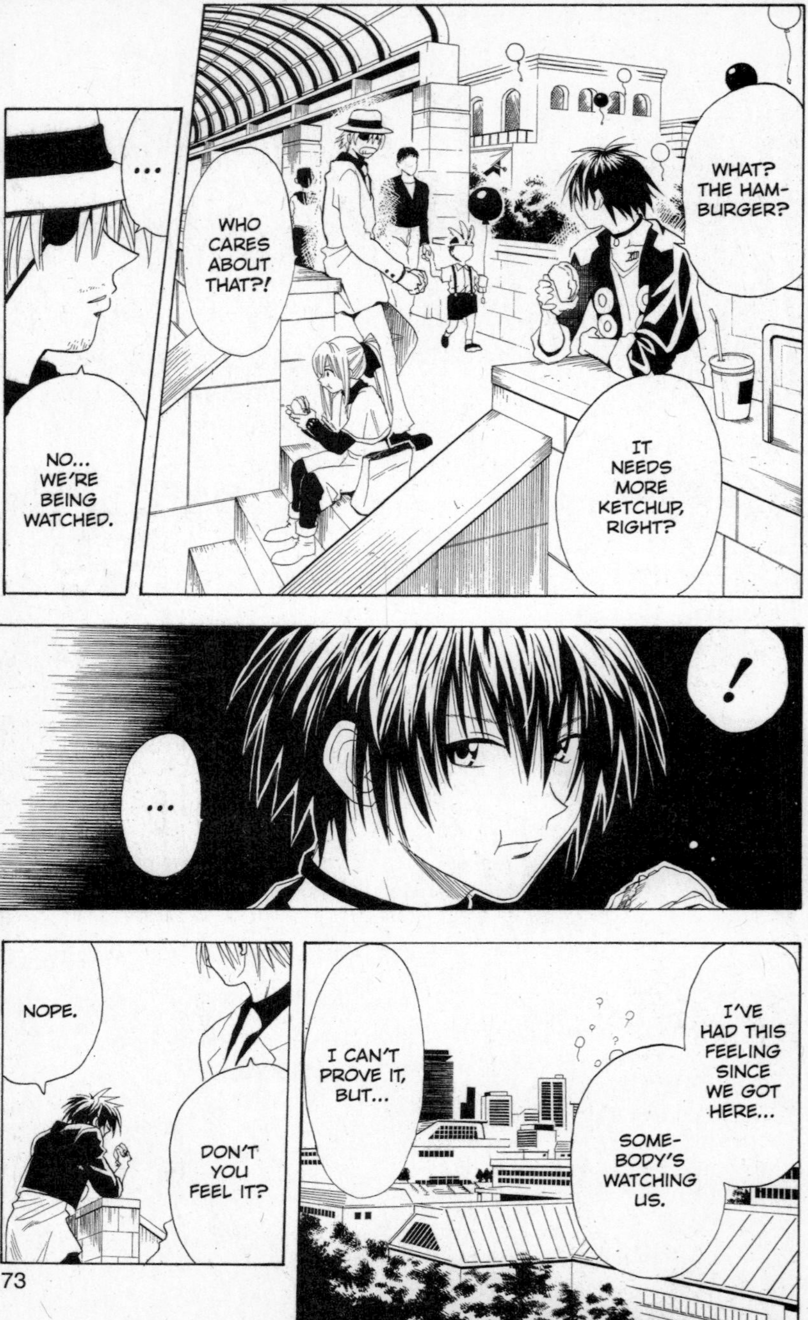
WHAT? THE HAM-BURGER?
IT NEEDS MORE KETCHUP, RIGHT?
WHO CARES ABOUT THAT?!
...
NO... WE'RE BEING WATCHED.
!
...
I'VE HAD THIS FEELING SINCE WE GOT HERE...
SOME-BODY'S WATCHING US.
I CAN'T PROVE IT, BUT...
DON'T YOU FEEL IT?
NOPE.

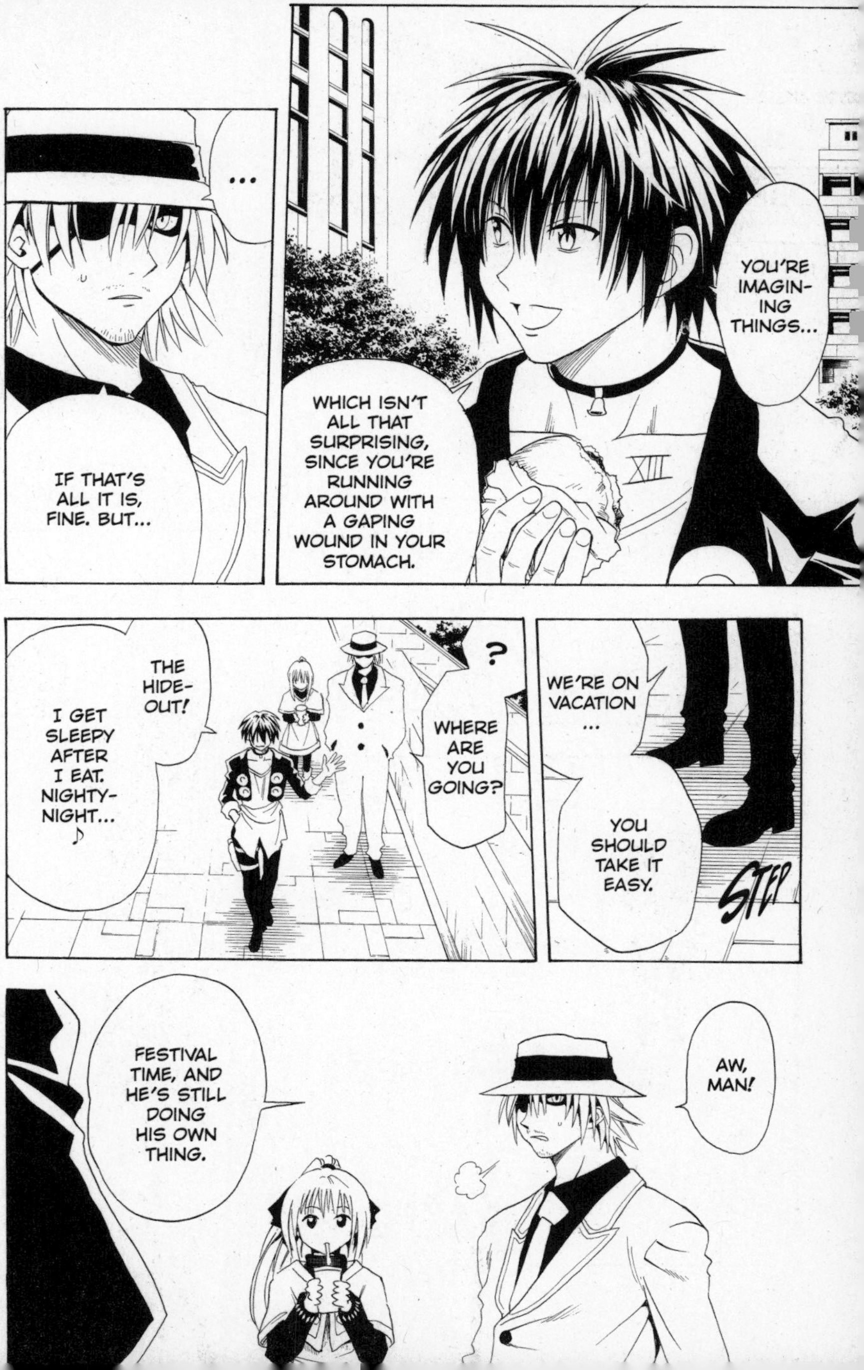
YOU'RE IMAGIN-ING THINGS...
WHICH ISN'T ALL THAT SURPRISING, SINCE YOU'RE RUNNING AROUND WITH A GAPING WOUND IN YOUR STOMACH.
...
IF THAT'S ALL IT IS, FINE. BUT...
WE'RE ON VACATION ...
YOU SHOULD TAKE IT EASY.
STEP
?
WHERE ARE YOU GOING?
THE HIDE-OUT!
I GET SLEEPY AFTER I EAT. NIGHTY-NIGHT... ♪
AW, MAN!
FESTIVAL TIME, AND HE'S STILL DOING HIS OWN THING.

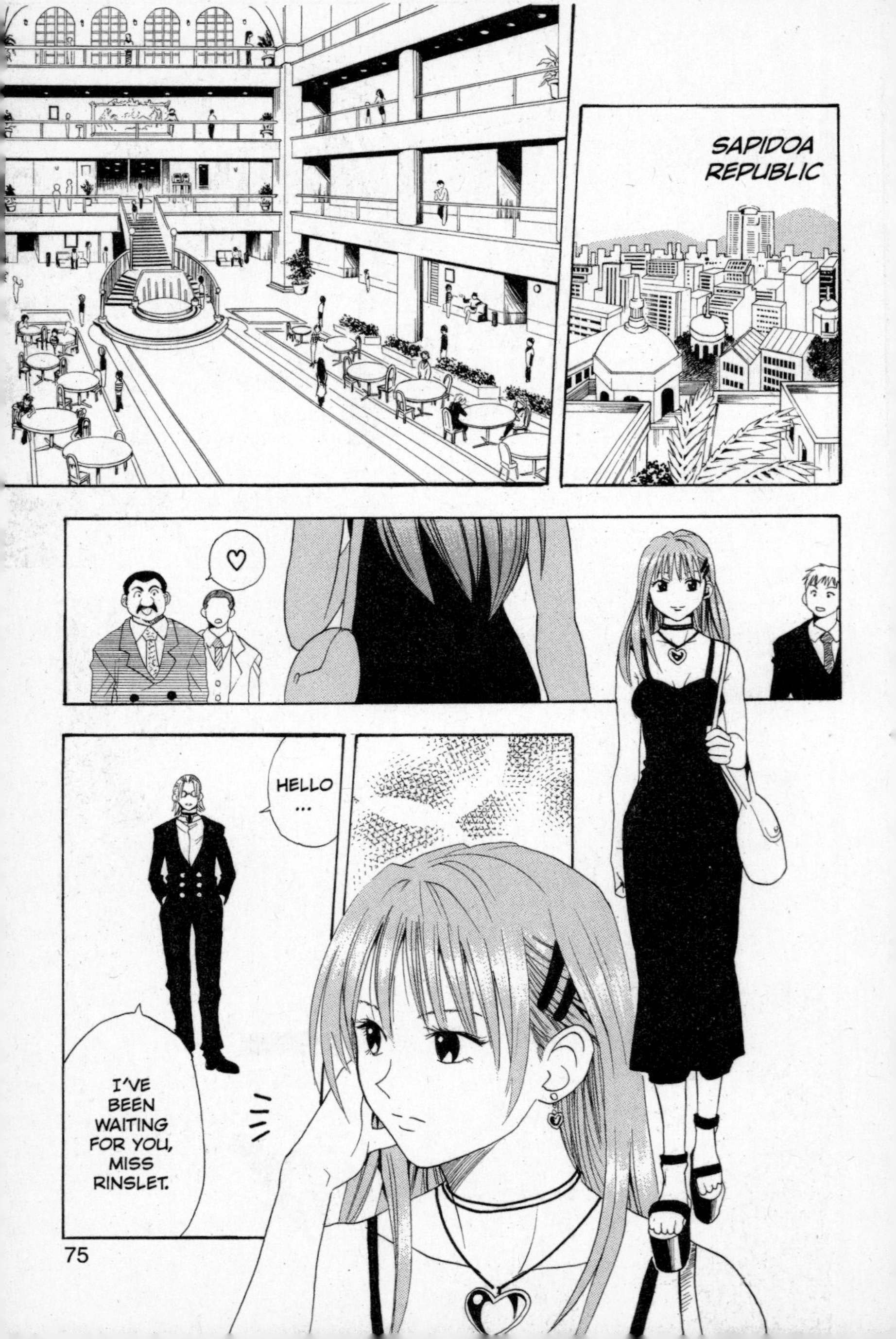
SAPIDOA REPUBLIC
HELLO ...
I'VE BEEN WAITING FOR YOU, MISS RINSLET.

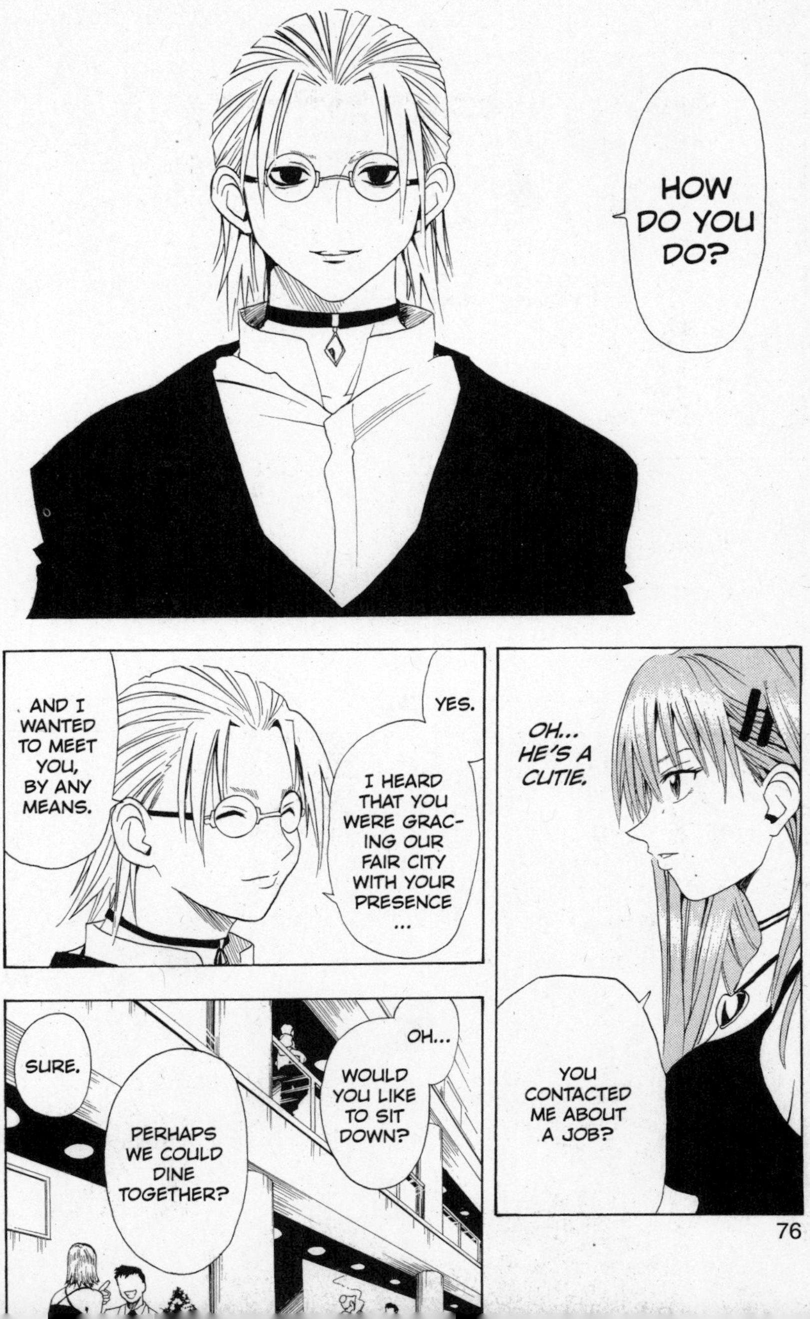
HOW DO YOU DO?
OH... HE'S A CUTIE.
YOU CONTACTED ME ABOUT A JOB?
YES.
I HEARD THAT YOU WERE GRAC-ING OUR FAIR CITY WITH YOUR PRESENCE ...
AND I WANTED TO MEET YOU, BY ANY MEANS.
OH... WOULD YOU LIKE TO SIT DOWN?
PERHAPS WE COULD DINE TOGETHER?
SURE.

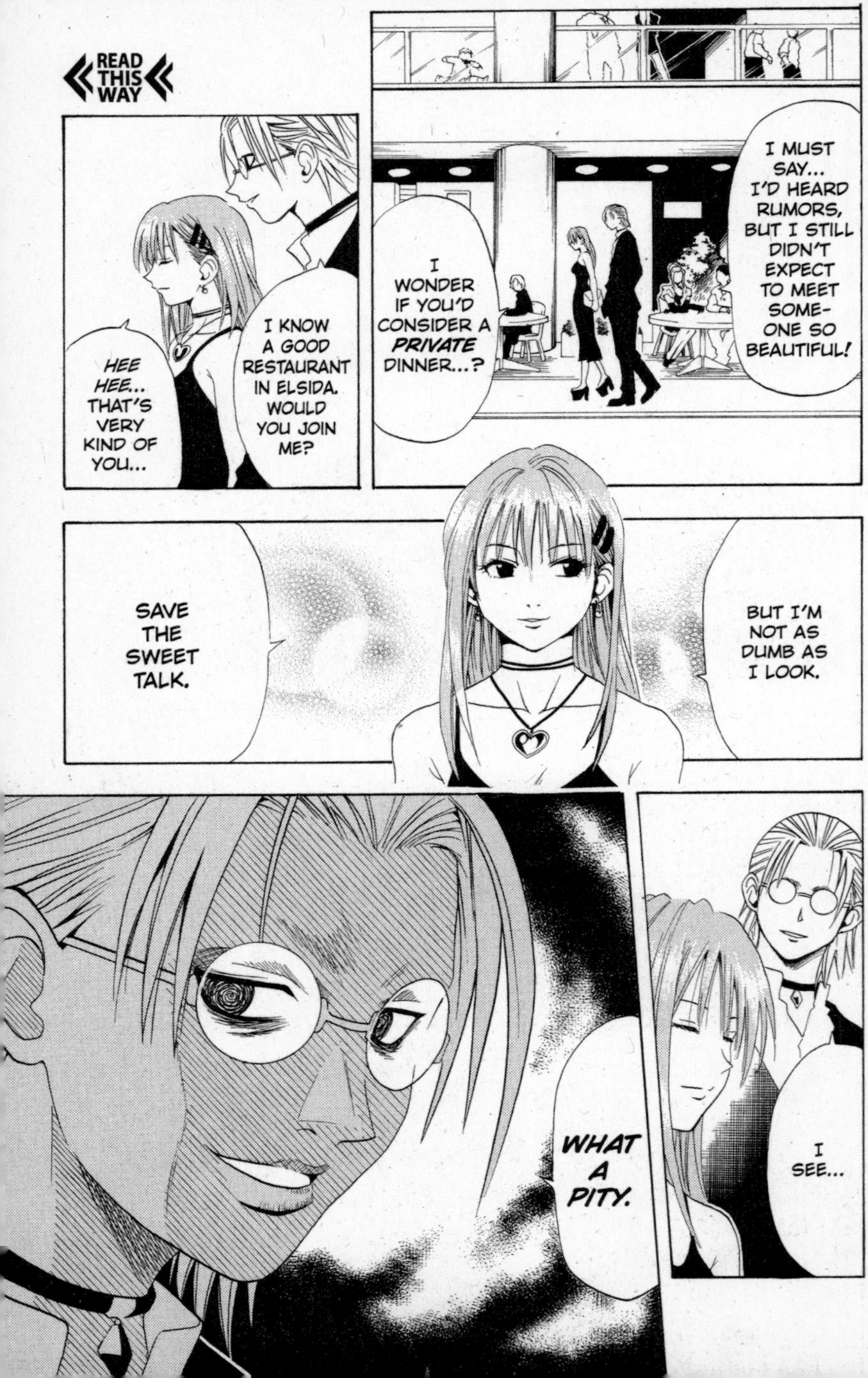
READ THIS WAY
I MUST SAY... I'D HEARD RUMORS, BUT I STILL DIDN'T EXPECT TO MEET SOME-ONE SO BEAUTIFUL!
I WONDER IF YOU'D CONSIDER A *PRIVATE* DINNER...?
I KNOW A GOOD RESTAURANT IN ELSIDA. WOULD YOU JOIN ME?
HEE HEE... THAT'S VERY KIND OF YOU...
BUT I'M NOT AS DUMB AS I LOOK.
SAVE THE SWEET TALK.
I SEE...
WHAT A PITY.

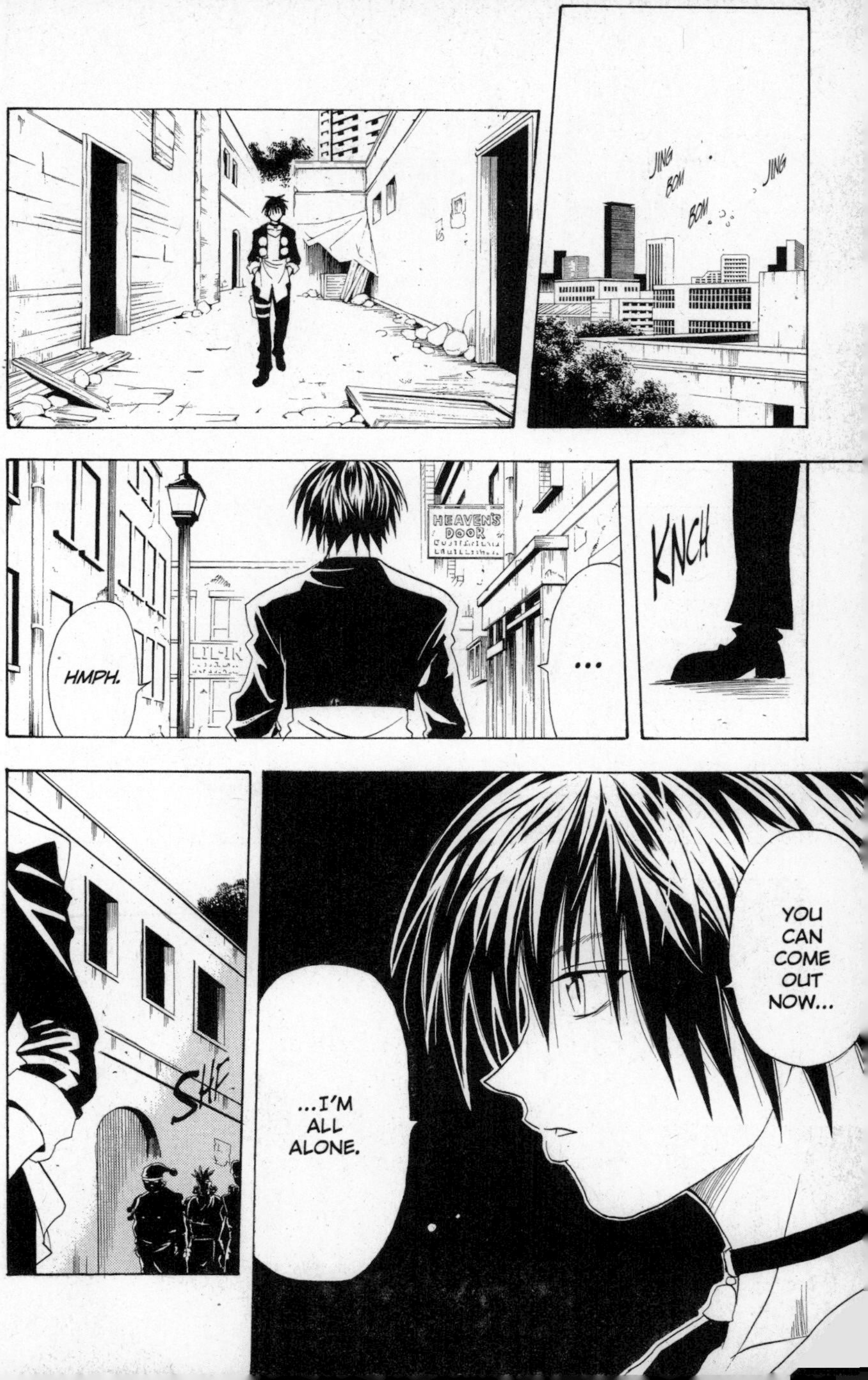
JING
BOM
BOM
JING
KNCH
...
HEAVEN'S DOOR
HMPH.
YOU CAN COME OUT NOW...
...I'M ALL ALONE.
SHF

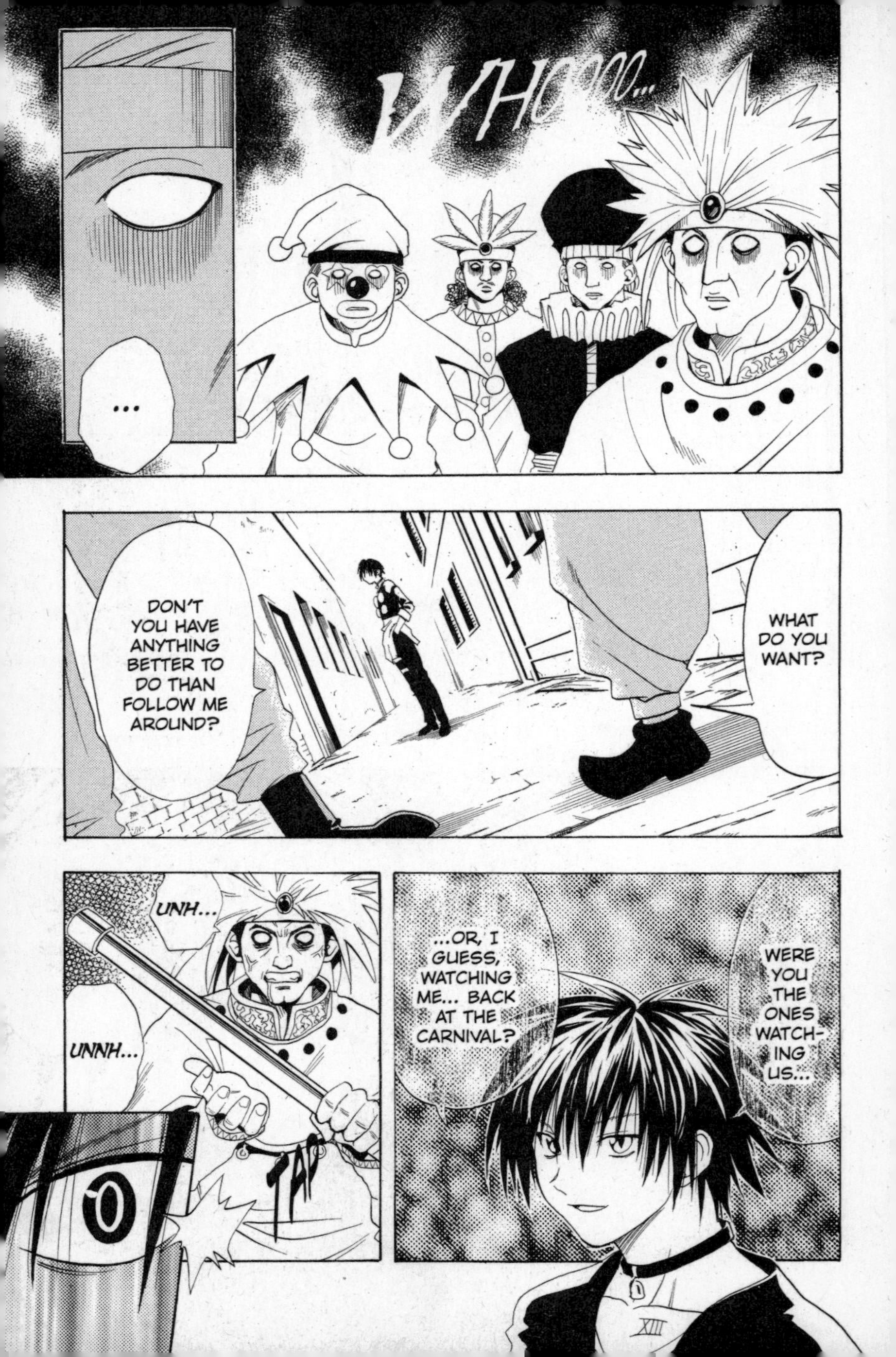
WHOOOO...
...
WHAT DO YOU WANT?
DON'T YOU HAVE ANYTHING BETTER TO DO THAN FOLLOW ME AROUND?
WERE YOU THE ONES WATCHING US...
...OR, I GUESS, WATCHING ME... BACK AT THE CARNIVAL?
UNH...
UNNH...
TAP

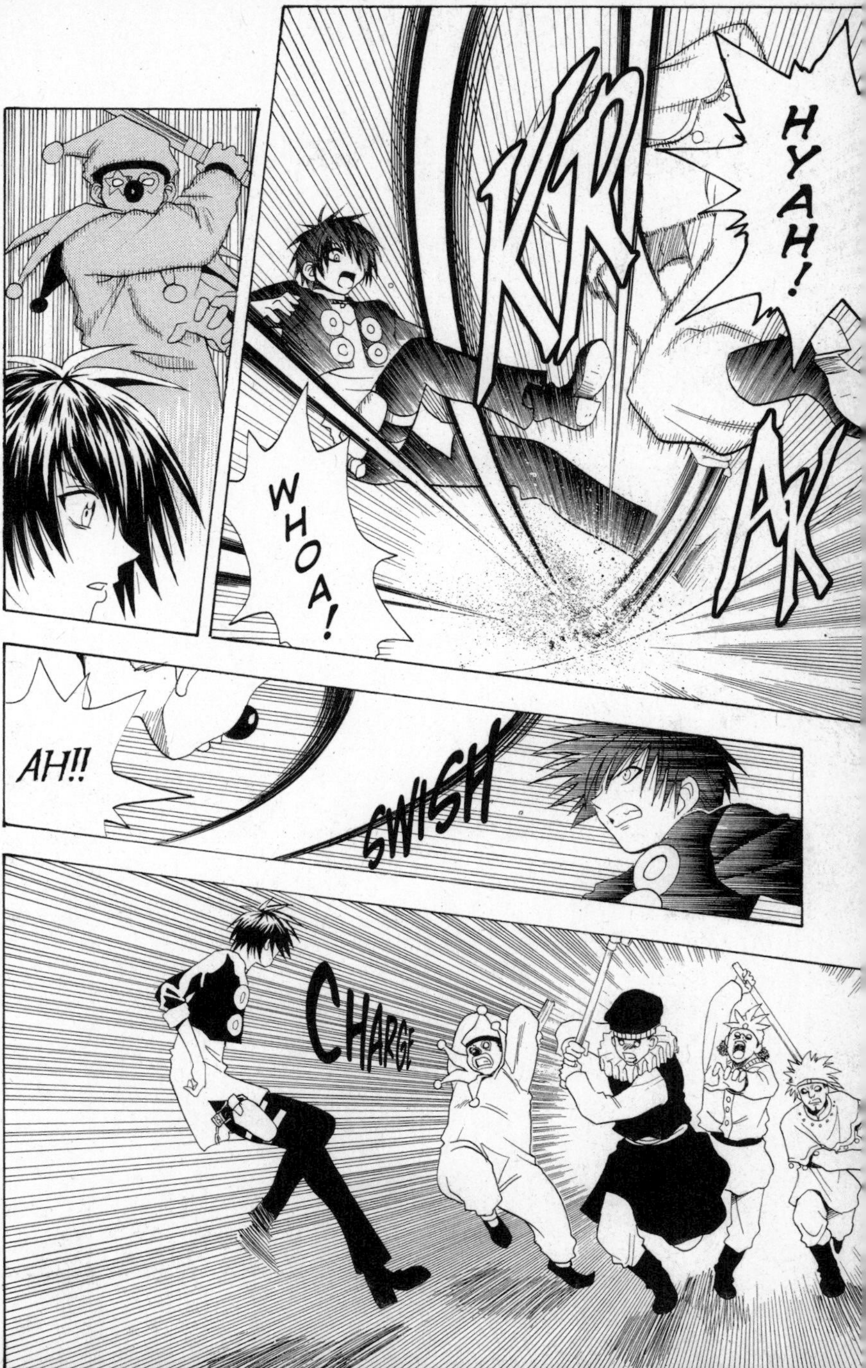
HYAH!
KRR
AK
WHOA!
SWISH
AH!!
CHARGE

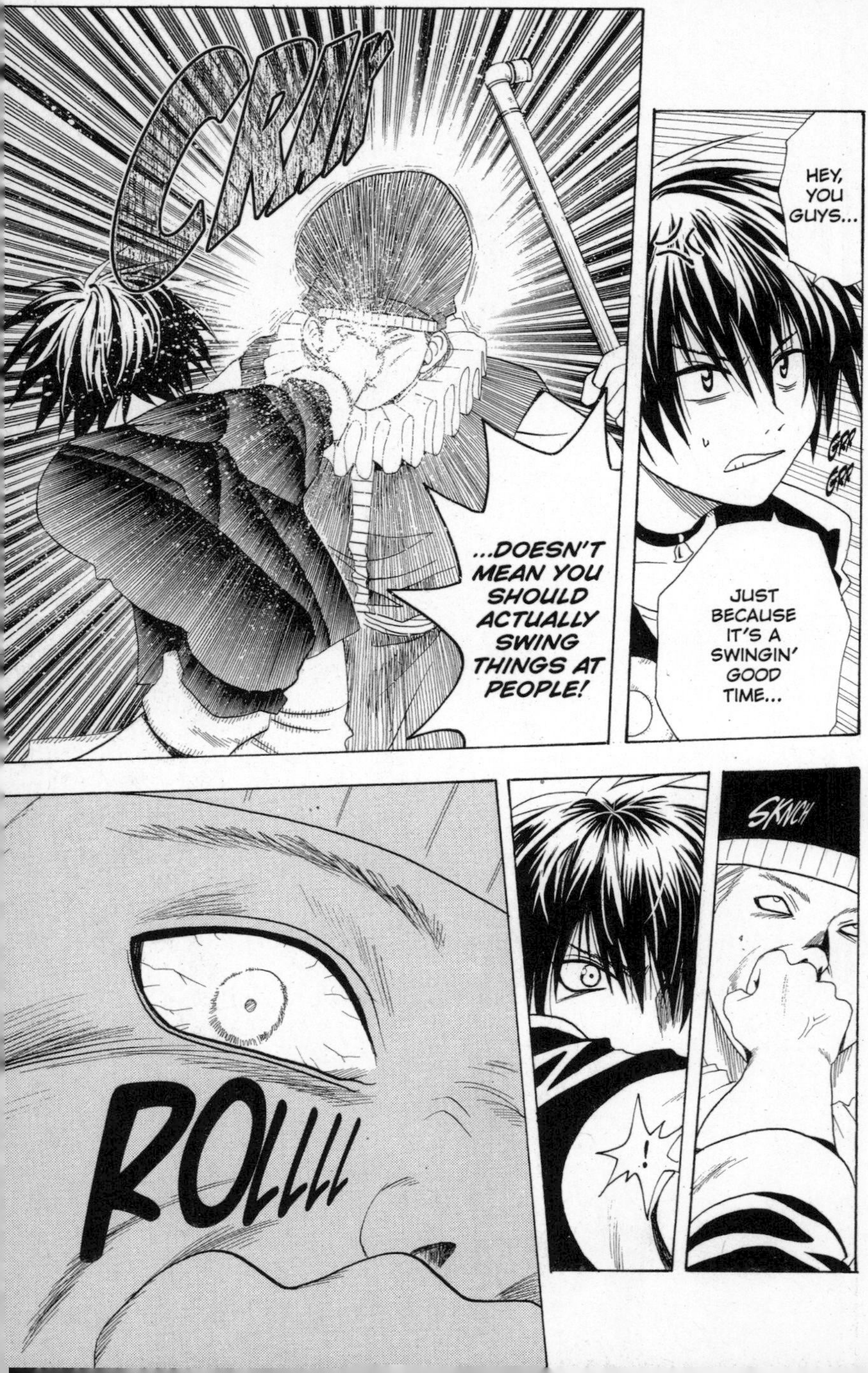
HEY, YOU GUYS...
GRR GRR
JUST BECAUSE IT'S A SWINGIN' GOOD TIME...
CRAK
...DOESN'T MEAN YOU SHOULD ACTUALLY SWING THINGS AT PEOPLE!
SKNCH
!
ROLLL

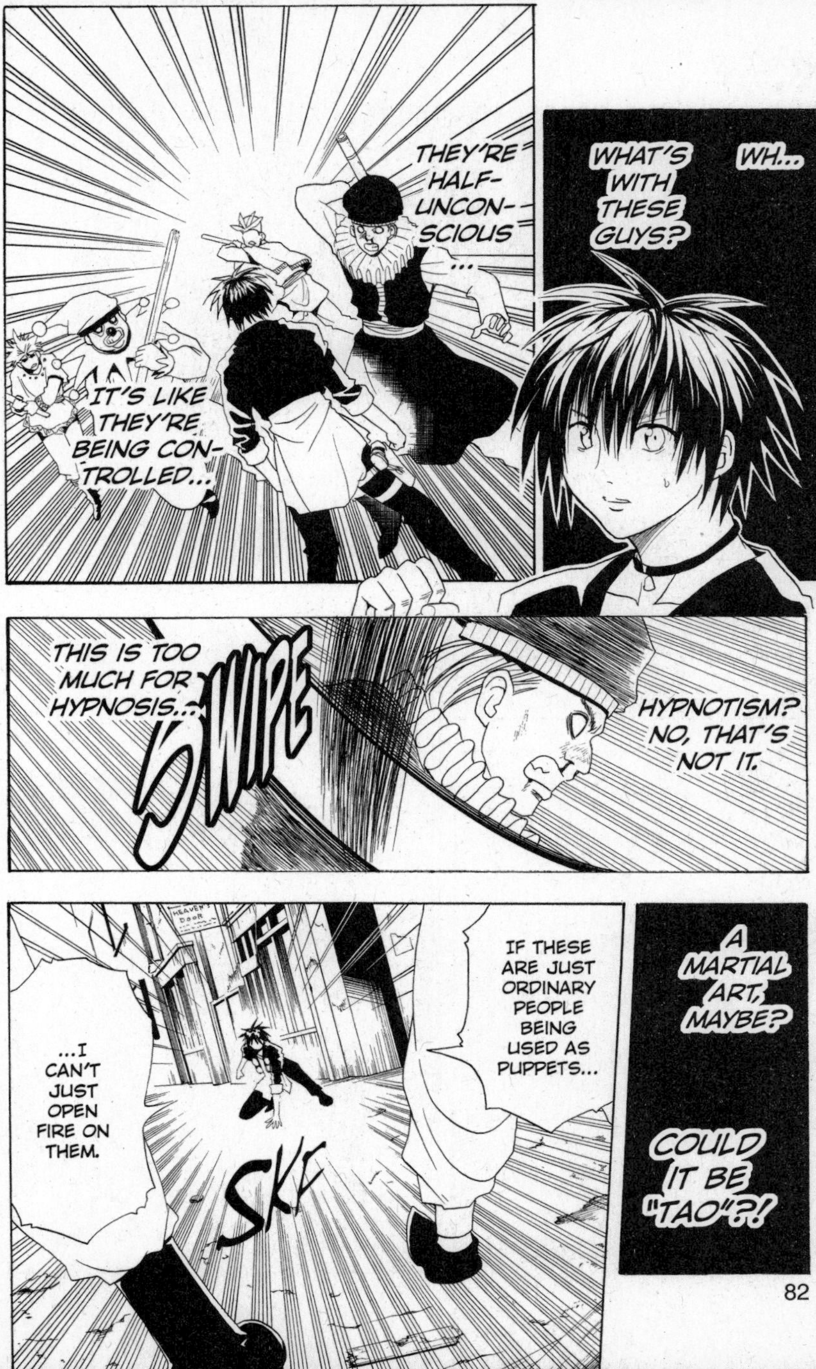
WH...
WHAT'S WITH THESE GUYS?
THEY'RE HALF-UNCONSCIOUS...
IT'S LIKE THEY'RE BEING CONTROLLED...
HYPNOTISM? NO, THAT'S NOT IT.
SWIPE
THIS IS TOO MUCH FOR HYPNOSIS...
A MARTIAL ART, MAYBE?
COULD IT BE "TAO"?!
IF THESE ARE JUST ORDINARY PEOPLE BEING USED AS PUPPETS...
HEAVEN'S DOOR
...I CAN'T JUST OPEN FIRE ON THEM.
SKF

READ THIS WAY

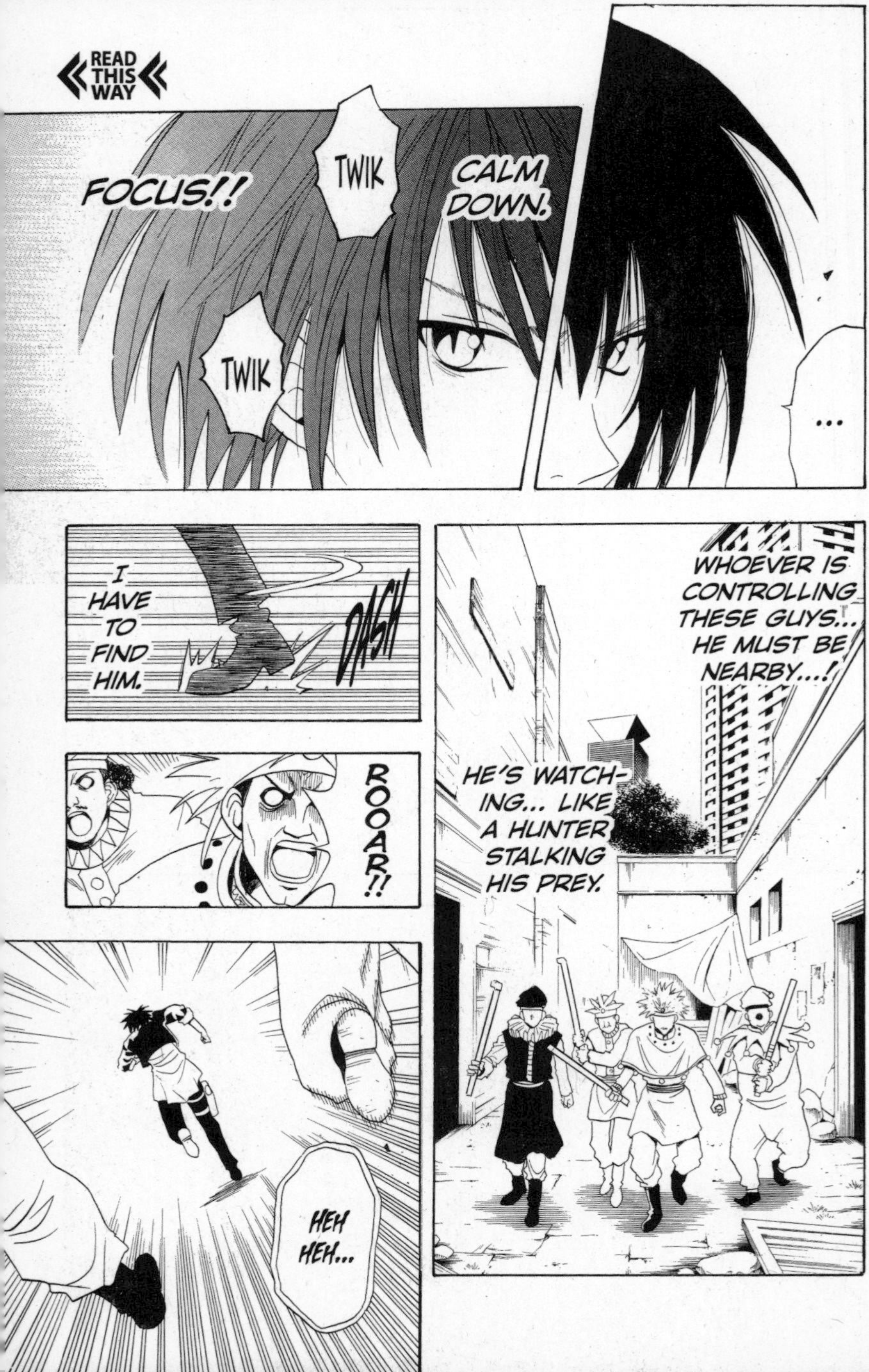

...
CALM DOWN.
TWIK
FOCUS!!
TWIK
WHOEVER IS CONTROLLING THESE GUYS... HE MUST BE NEARBY...!
HE'S WATCHING... LIKE A HUNTER STALKING HIS PREY.
I HAVE TO FIND HIM.
DASH
ROOOAR!!
HEH HEH...

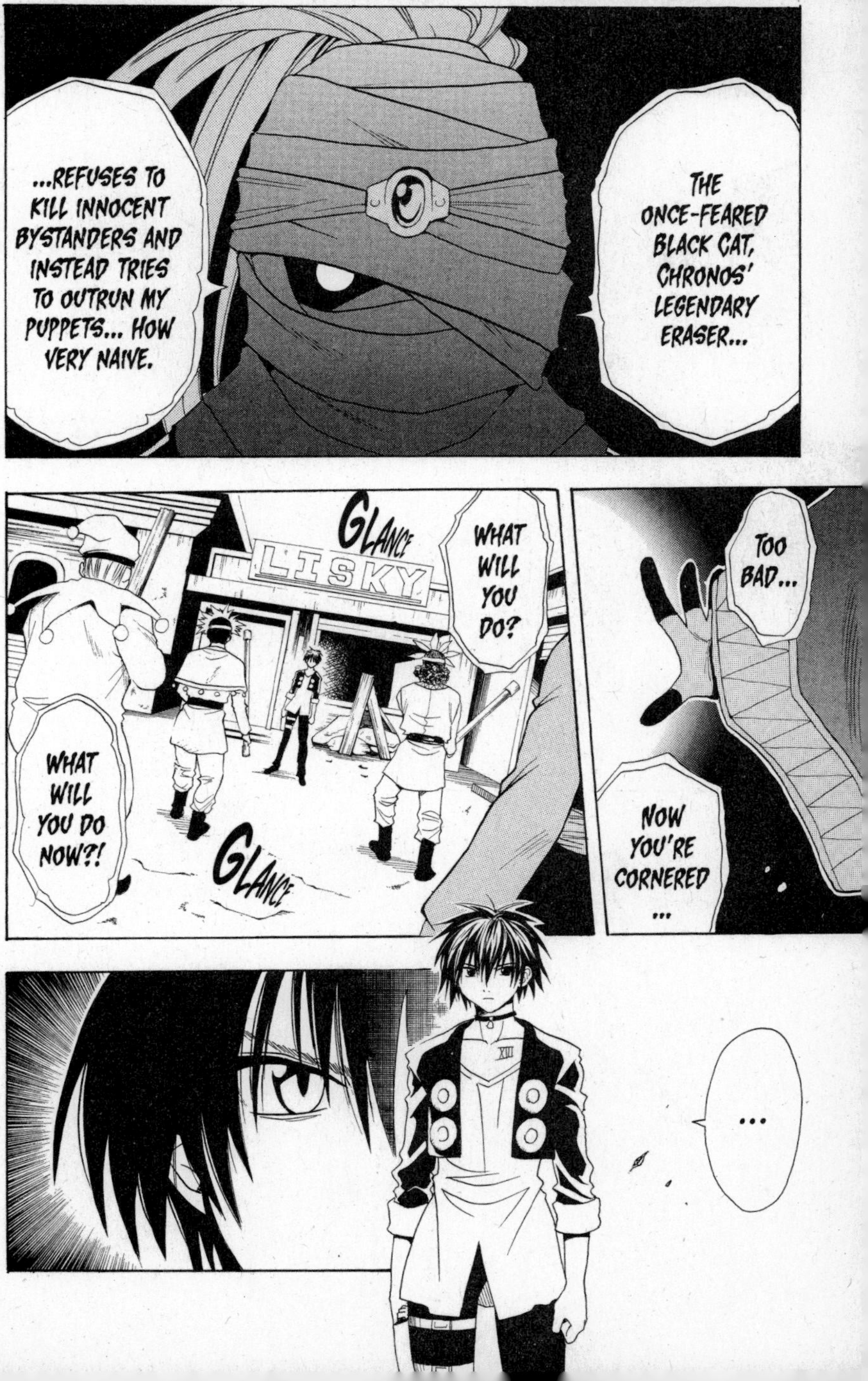
THE ONCE-FEARED BLACK CAT, CHRONOS' LEGENDARY ERASER...
...REFUSES TO KILL INNOCENT BYSTANDERS AND INSTEAD TRIES TO OUTRUN MY PUPPETS... HOW VERY NAIVE.
TOO BAD...
NOW YOU'RE CORNERED ...
WHAT WILL YOU DO?
GLANCE
LISKY
WHAT WILL YOU DO NOW?!
GLANCE
...

READ THIS WAY

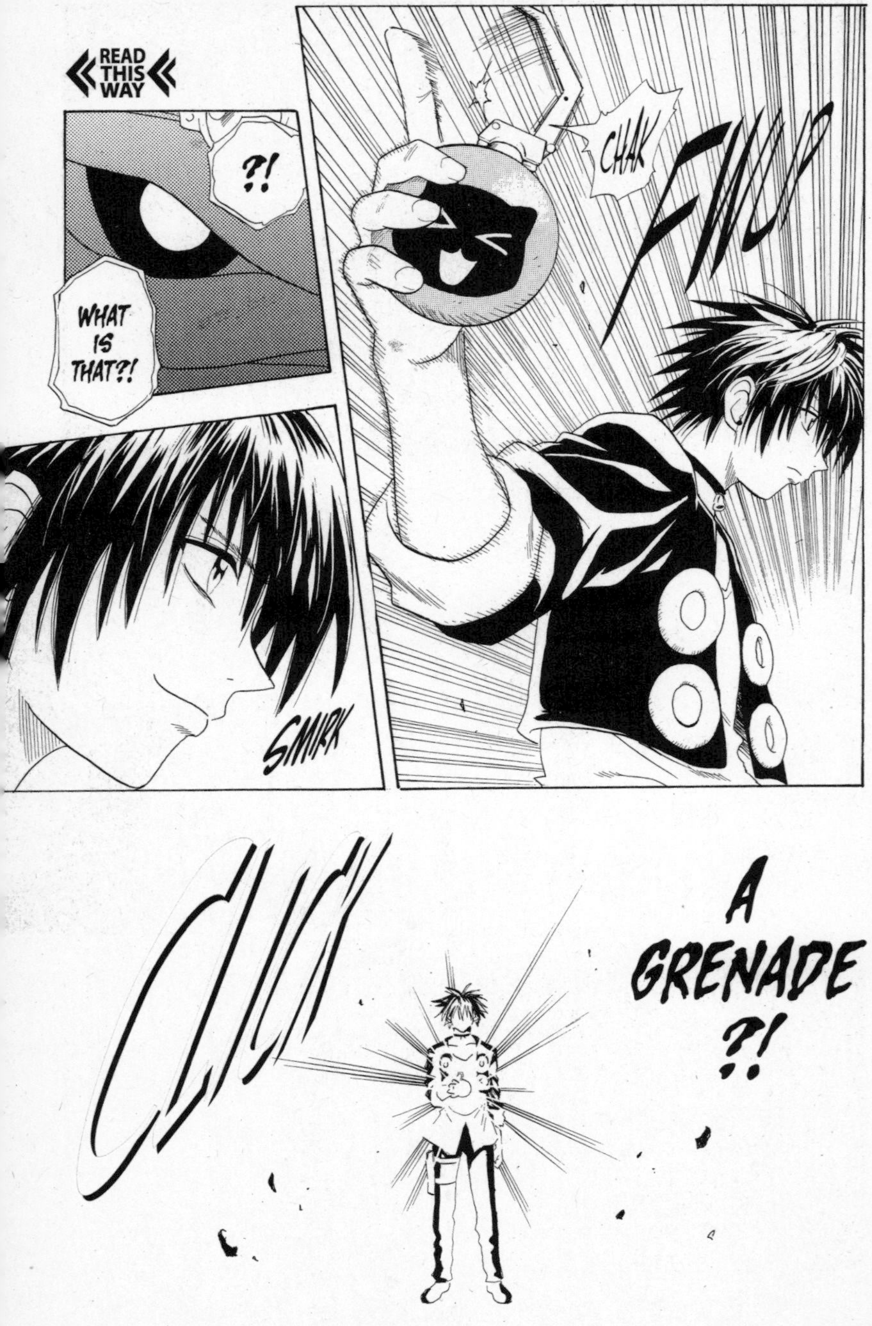
CHAK
FWUP
?!
WHAT IS THAT?!
SMIRK
A GRENADE ?!

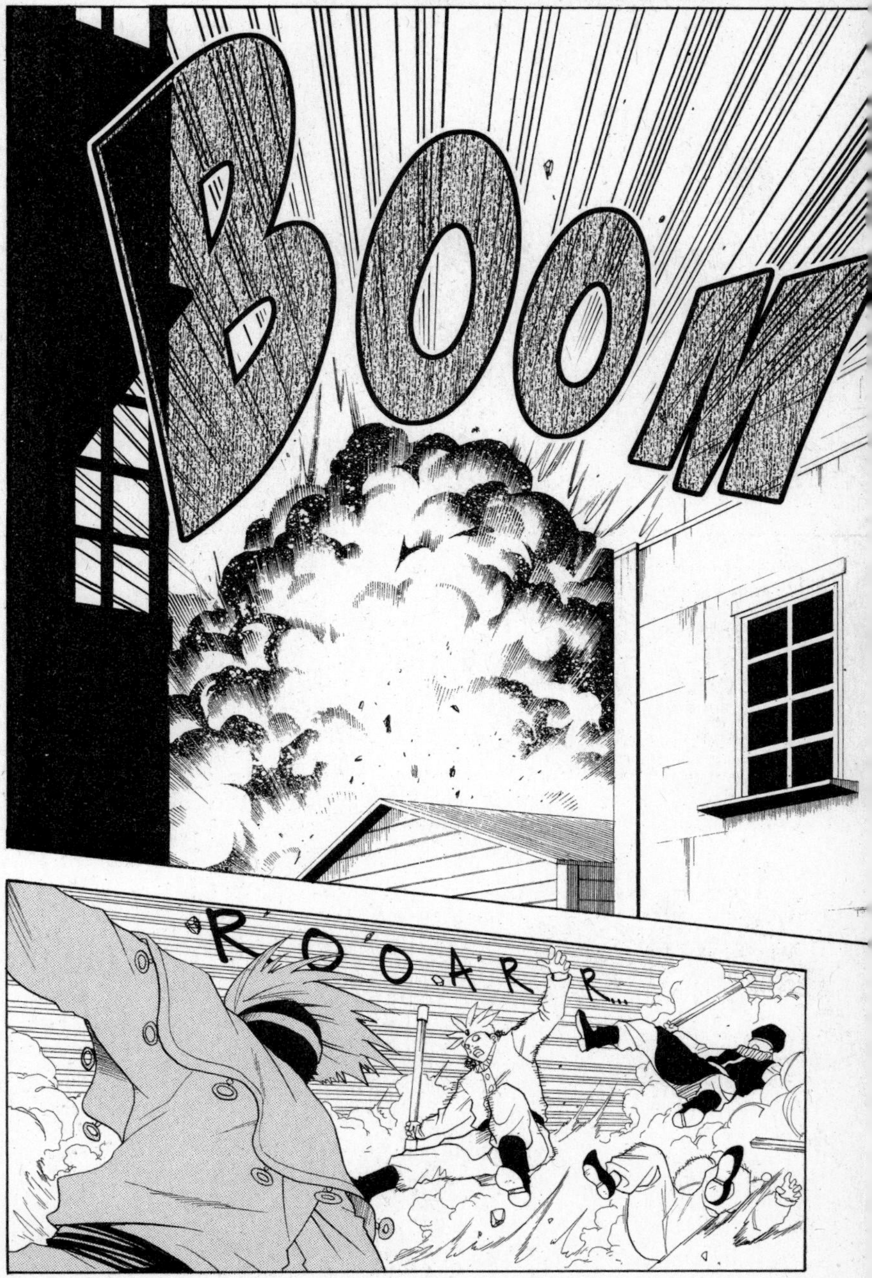
BOOM
ROOARR...

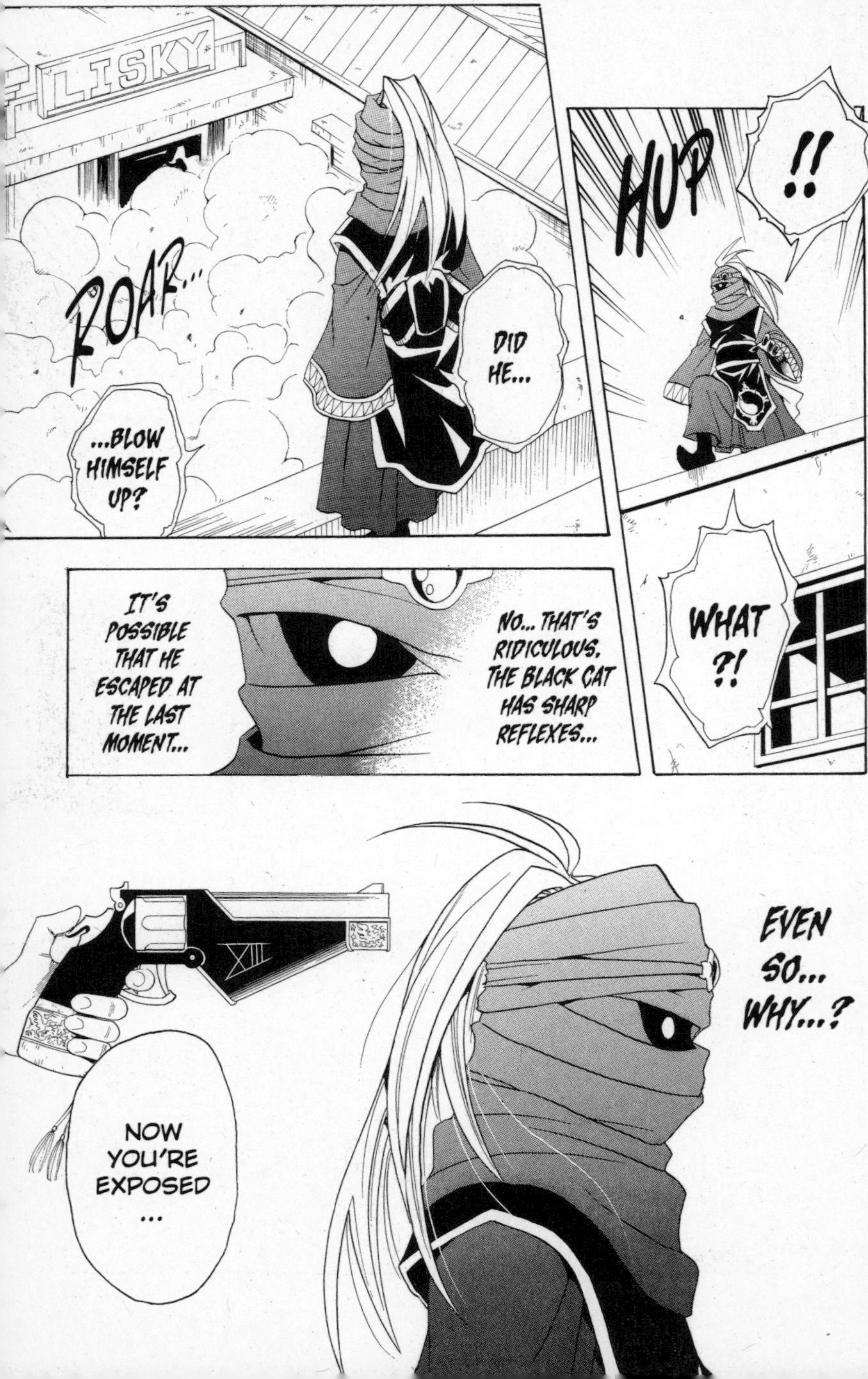
HUP
!!
LISKY
ROAR...
DID HE...
...BLOW HIMSELF UP?
WHAT ?!
NO... THAT'S RIDICULOUS. THE BLACK CAT HAS SHARP REFLEXES...
IT'S POSSIBLE THAT HE ESCAPED AT THE LAST MOMENT...
EVEN SO... WHY...?
XIII
NOW YOU'RE EXPOSED ...

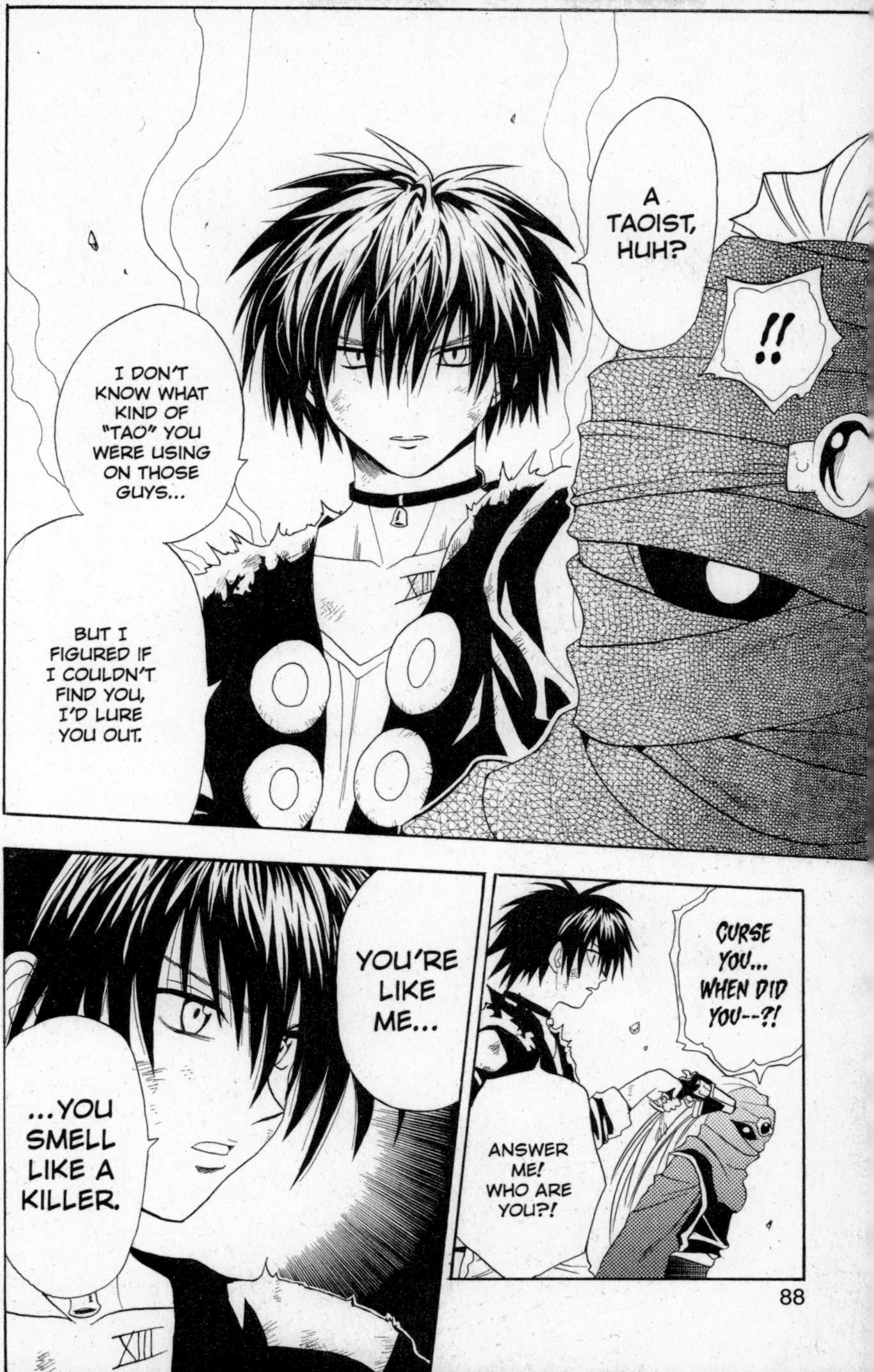
A TAOIST, HUH?
!!
I DON'T KNOW WHAT KIND OF "TAO" YOU WERE USING ON THOSE GUYS...
BUT I FIGURED IF I COULDN'T FIND YOU, I'D LURE YOU OUT.
CURSE YOU... WHEN DID YOU--?!
ANSWER ME! WHO ARE YOU?!
YOU'RE LIKE ME...
...YOU SMELL LIKE A KILLER.

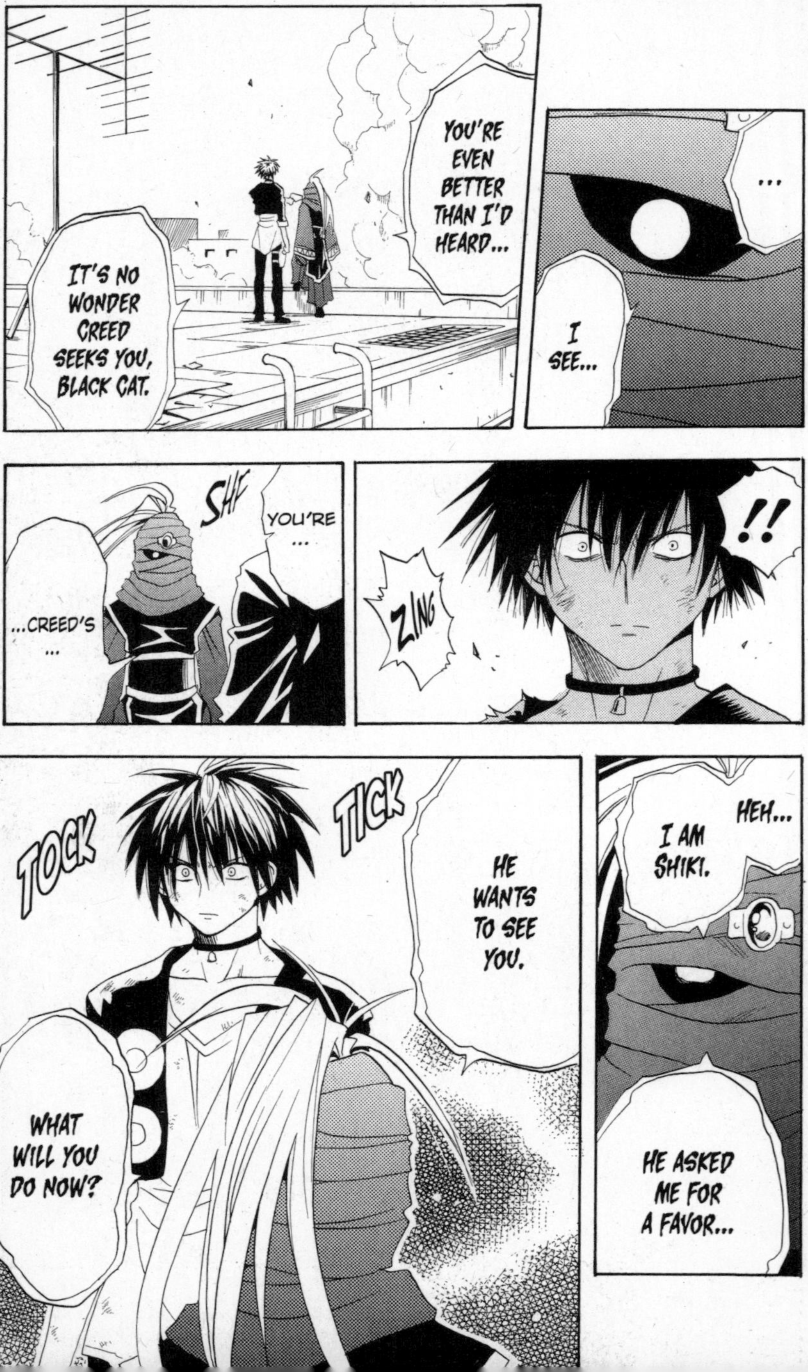
...
I SEE...
YOU'RE EVEN BETTER THAN I'D HEARD...
IT'S NO WONDER CREED SEEKS YOU, BLACK CAT.
!!
ZING
SHF
YOU'RE ...
...CREED'S ...
HEH... I AM SHIKI.
HE ASKED ME FOR A FAVOR...
HE WANTS TO SEE YOU.
TICK
TOCK
WHAT WILL YOU DO NOW?

BLACK CAT

profile

RINSLET WALKER

DATA	
BIRTHDAY:	AUGUST 1
AGE:	21 YEARS OLD
BLOOD TYPE:	B
HEIGHT:	167 CM
WEIGHT:	48 KG
OCCUPATION:	THIEF-FOR-HIRE
HOBBIES:	DISGUISES, SHOPPING, TAROT CARD READING
LIKES:	MONEY, JEWELRY, HANDSOME MEN, CUTE GIRLS, ETC.
DISLIKES:	GHOSTS, NARCISSISTS, ETC.
HANDEDNESS:	RIGHT-HANDED
COMMENTS:	HER ACTIONS ARE ALWAYS IN LINE WITH HER BELIEFS. SHE IS VERY INDEPENDENT AND WON'T DO ANYTHING SHE DOESN'T WANT TO. SENSING A COMMONALITY BETWEEN HERSELF AND TRAIN, SHE'S HARBORED AN INTEREST IN HIM SINCE SAPIDOA.

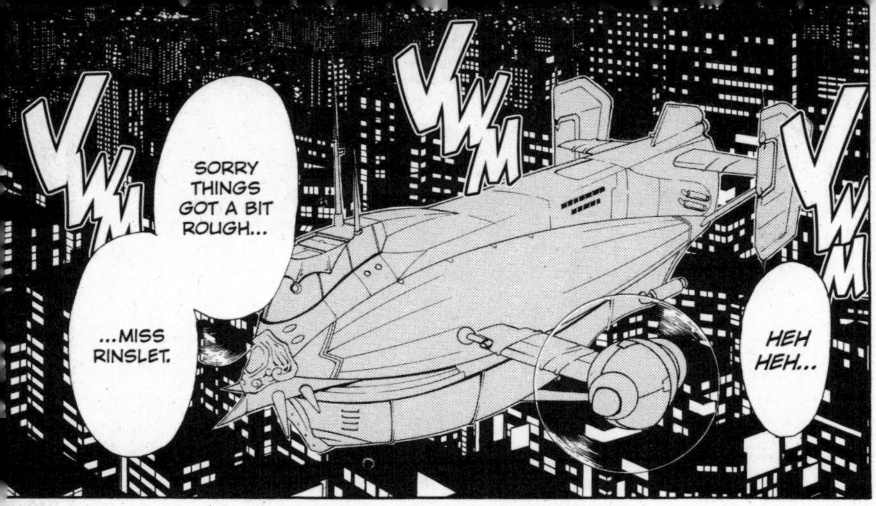
VWM
VWM
VWM
HEH HEH...
SORRY THINGS GOT A BIT ROUGH...
...MISS RINSLET.

Chapter 13: Black Coat

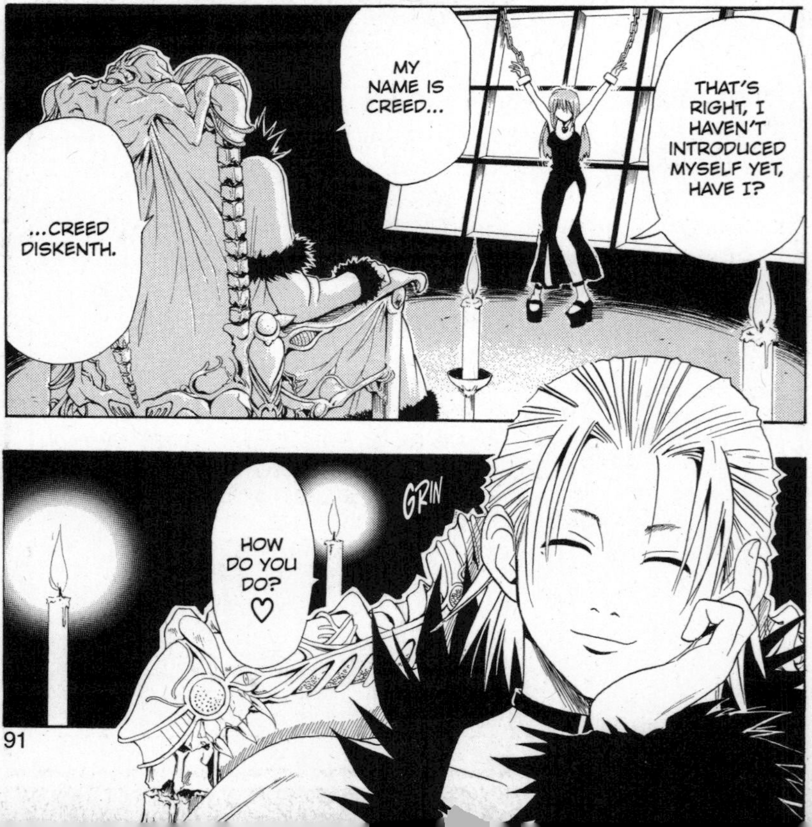
THAT'S RIGHT, I HAVEN'T INTRODUCED MYSELF YET, HAVE I?
MY NAME IS CREED...
...CREED DISKENTH.
GRIN
HOW DO YOU DO? ♡

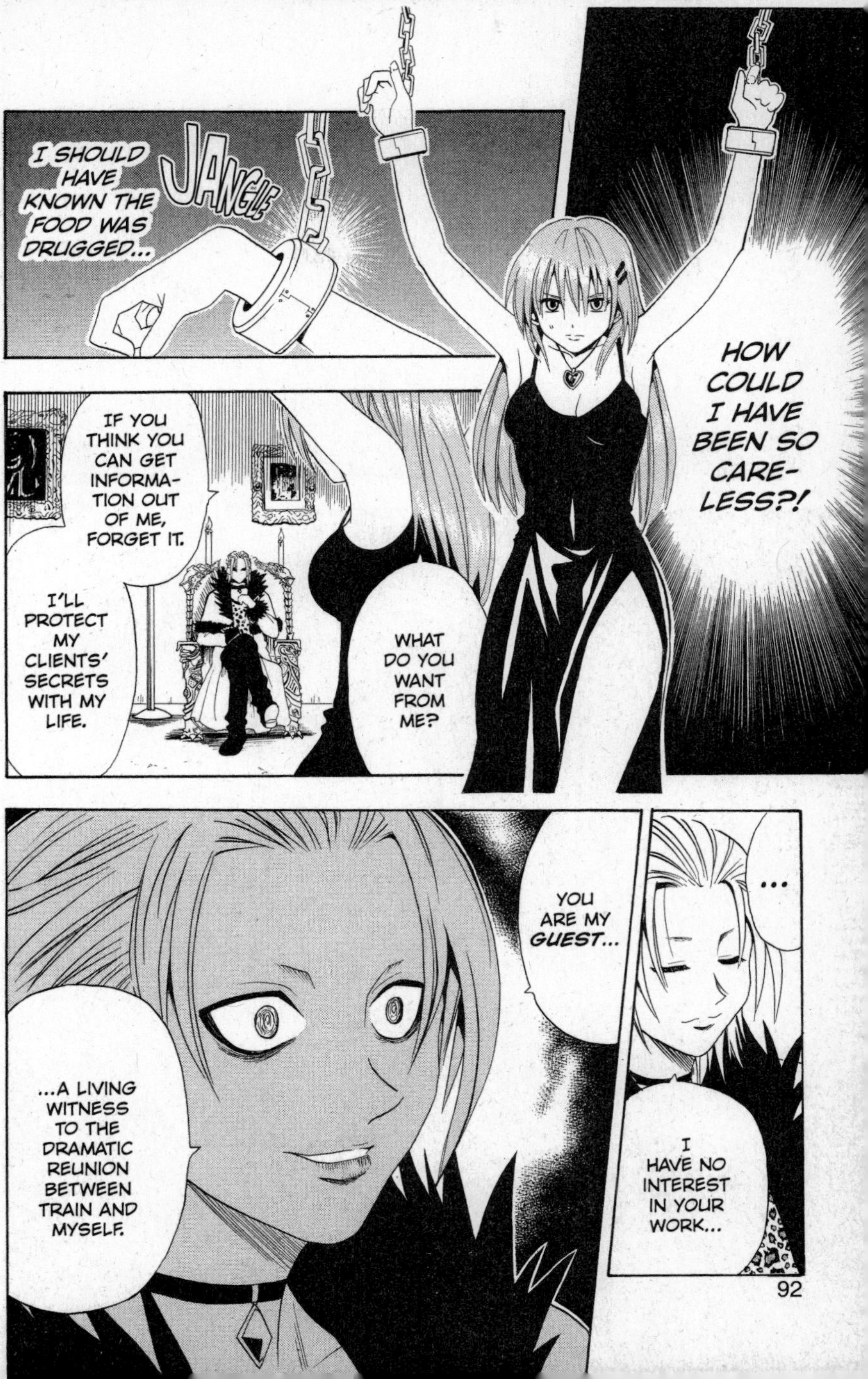
HOW COULD I HAVE BEEN SO CARELESS?!
I SHOULD HAVE KNOWN THE FOOD WAS DRUGGED...
JANGLE
WHAT DO YOU WANT FROM ME?
IF YOU THINK YOU CAN GET INFORMATION OUT OF ME, FORGET IT.
I'LL PROTECT MY CLIENTS' SECRETS WITH MY LIFE.
...
I HAVE NO INTEREST IN YOUR WORK...
YOU ARE MY *GUEST*...
...A LIVING WITNESS TO THE DRAMATIC REUNION BETWEEN TRAIN AND MYSELF.

READ THIS WAY

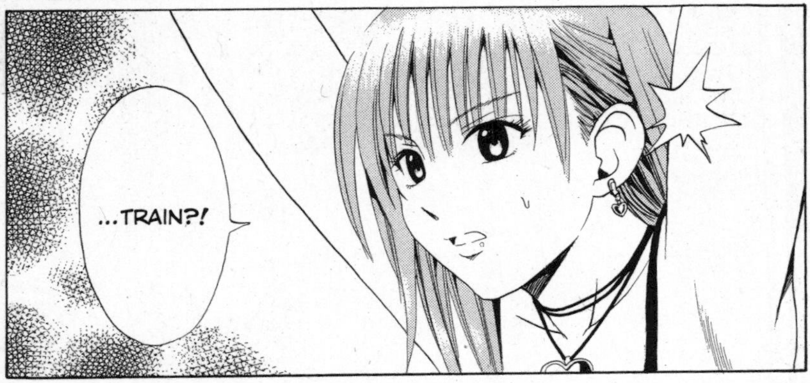
...TRAIN?!

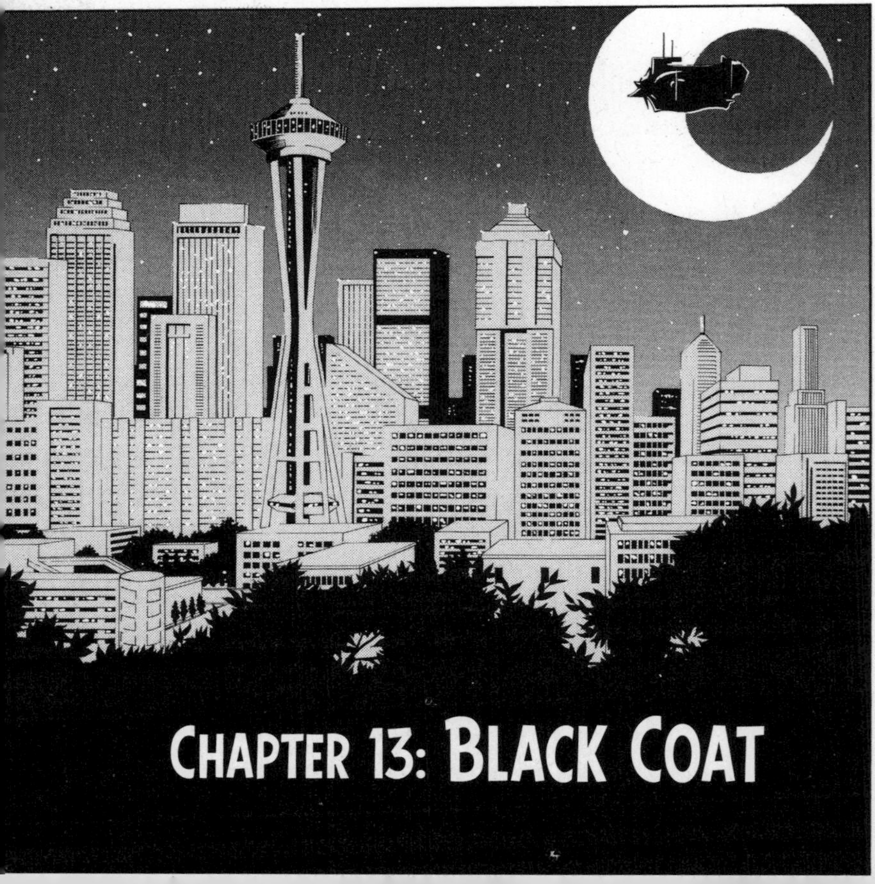

CHAPTER 13: BLACK COAT

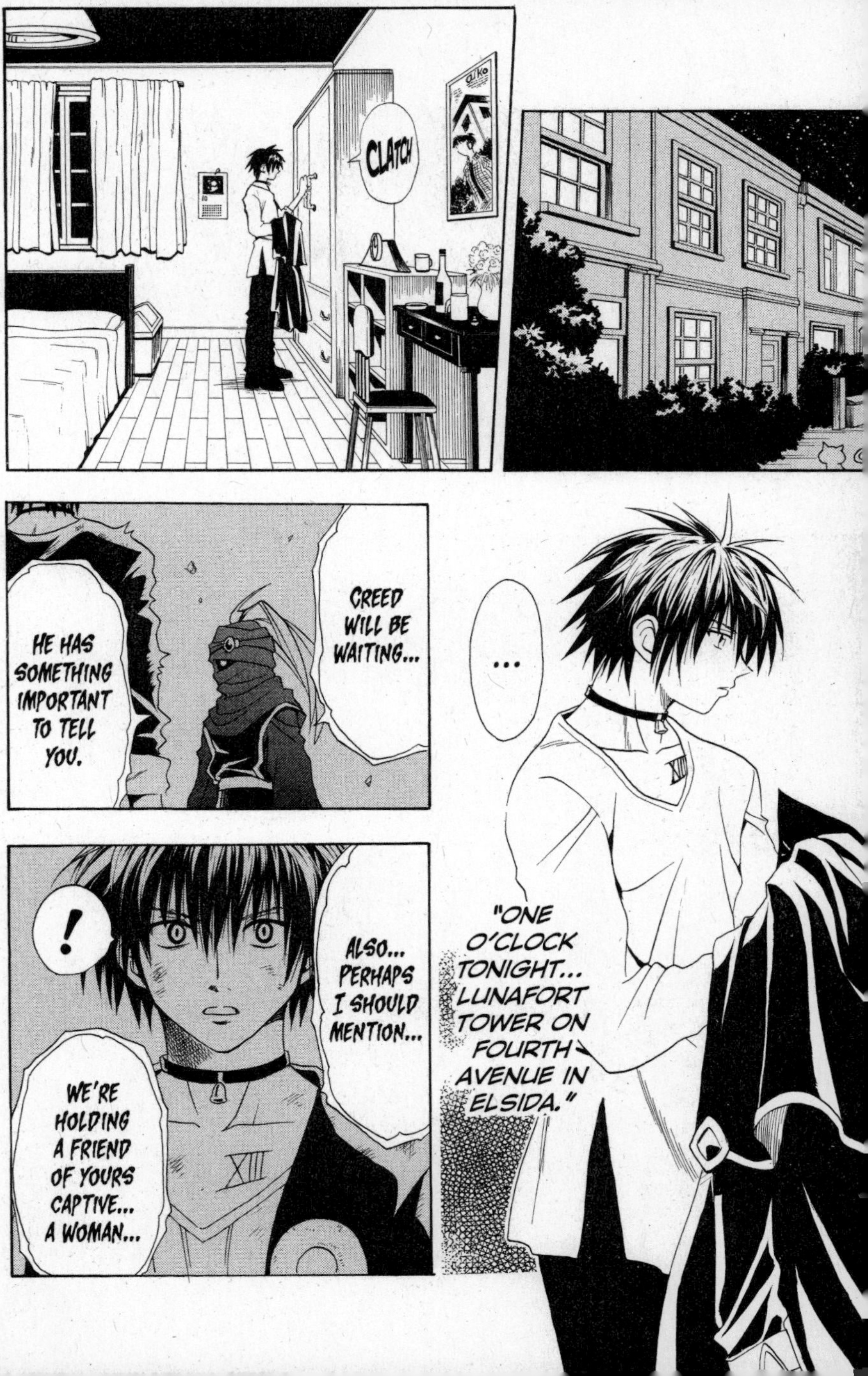
CLATCH
...
"ONE O'CLOCK TONIGHT... LUNAFORT TOWER ON FOURTH AVENUE IN ELSIDA."
CREED WILL BE WAITING...
HE HAS SOMETHING IMPORTANT TO TELL YOU.
ALSO... PERHAPS I SHOULD MENTION...
!
WE'RE HOLDING A FRIEND OF YOURS CAPTIVE... A WOMAN...

READ THIS WAY

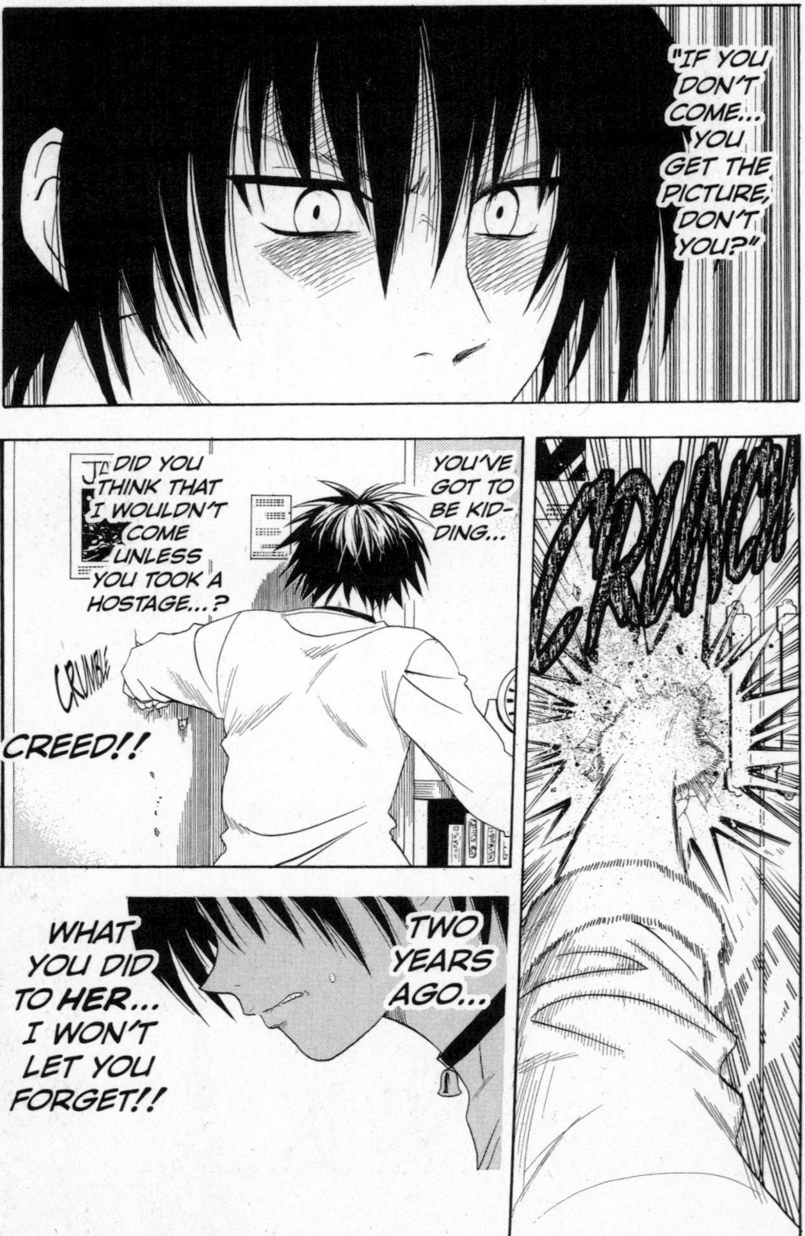
"IF YOU DON'T COME... YOU GET THE PICTURE, DON'T YOU?"
CRUNCH
YOU'VE GOT TO BE KID-DING...
DID YOU THINK THAT I WOULDN'T COME UNLESS YOU TOOK A HOSTAGE...?
CRUMBLE
CREED!!
TWO YEARS AGO...
WHAT YOU DID TO HER... I WON'T LET YOU FORGET!!

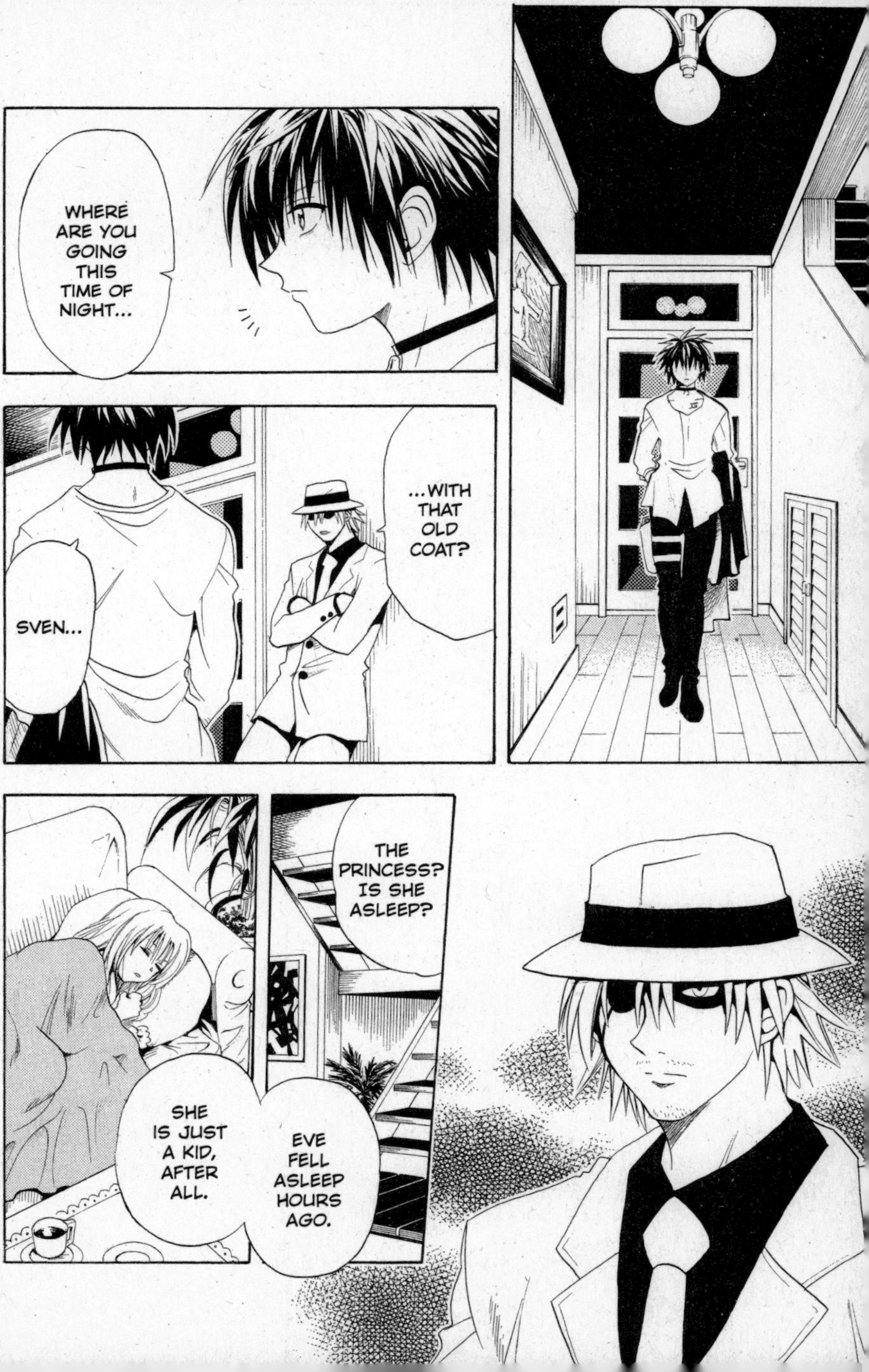
WHERE ARE YOU GOING THIS TIME OF NIGHT...
...WITH THAT OLD COAT?
SVEN...
THE PRINCESS? IS SHE ASLEEP?
EVE FELL ASLEEP HOURS AGO.
SHE IS JUST A KID, AFTER ALL.

READ THIS WAY

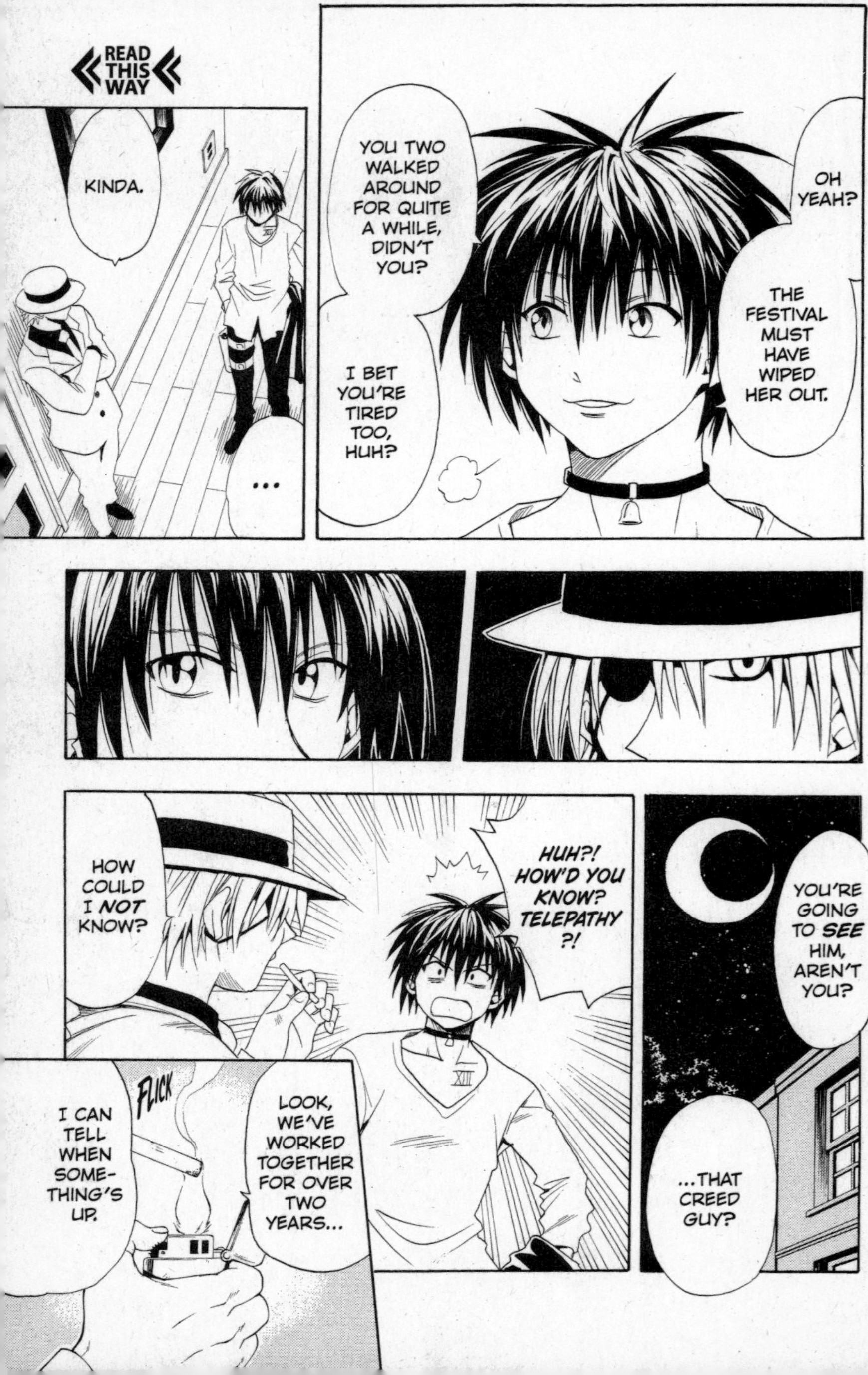
OH YEAH?
THE FESTIVAL MUST HAVE WIPED HER OUT.
YOU TWO WALKED AROUND FOR QUITE A WHILE, DIDN'T YOU?
I BET YOU'RE TIRED TOO, HUH?
KINDA.
...
YOU'RE GOING TO *SEE* HIM, AREN'T YOU?
...THAT CREED GUY?
HUH?! HOW'D YOU KNOW? TELEPATHY?!
HOW COULD I *NOT* KNOW?
LOOK, WE'VE WORKED TOGETHER FOR OVER TWO YEARS...
FLICK
I CAN TELL WHEN SOME-THING'S UP.

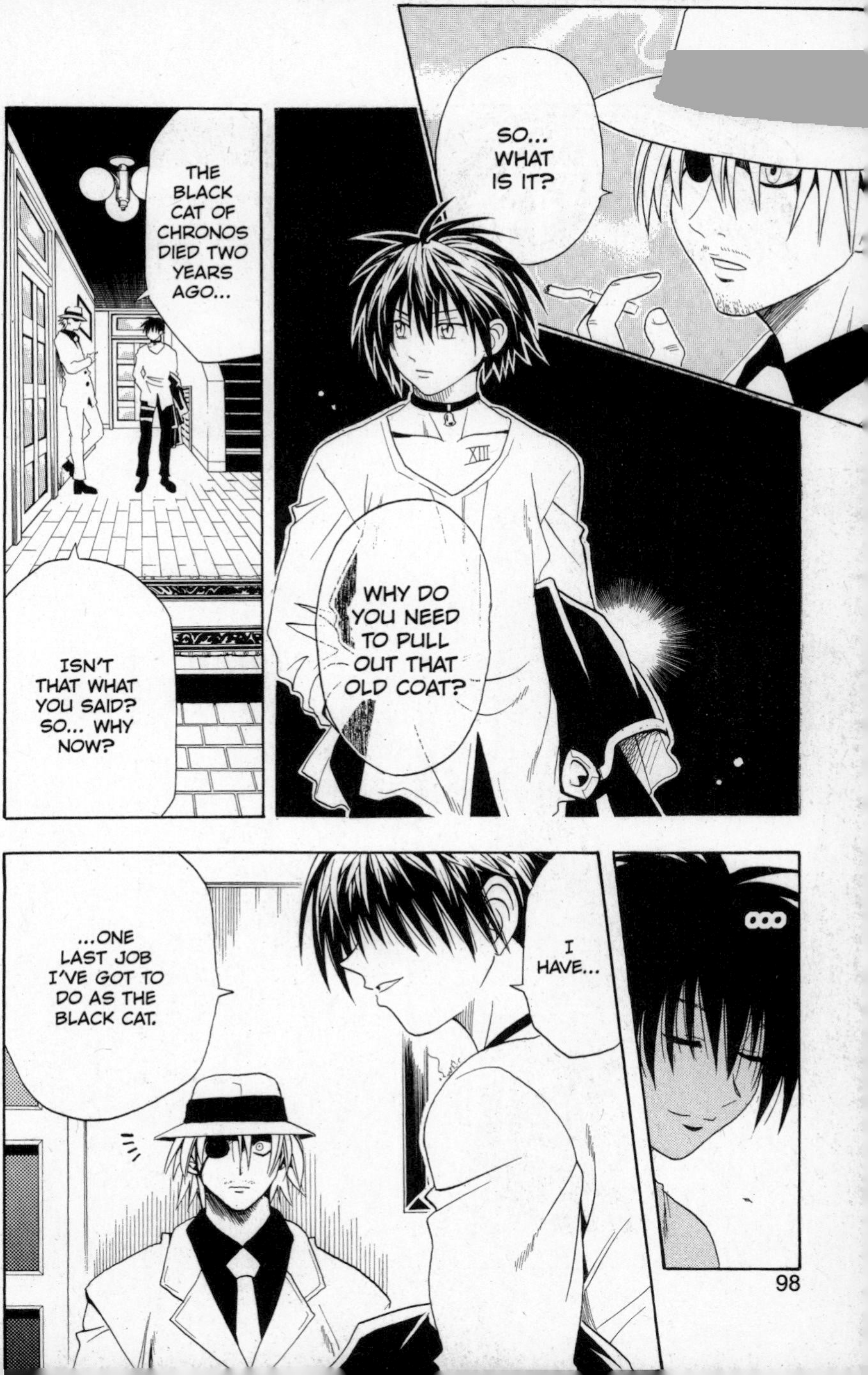
SO... WHAT IS IT?
WHY DO YOU NEED TO PULL OUT THAT OLD COAT?
THE BLACK CAT OF CHRONOS DIED TWO YEARS AGO...
ISN'T THAT WHAT YOU SAID? SO... WHY NOW?
I HAVE...
...ONE LAST JOB I'VE GOT TO DO AS THE BLACK CAT.

READ THIS WAY

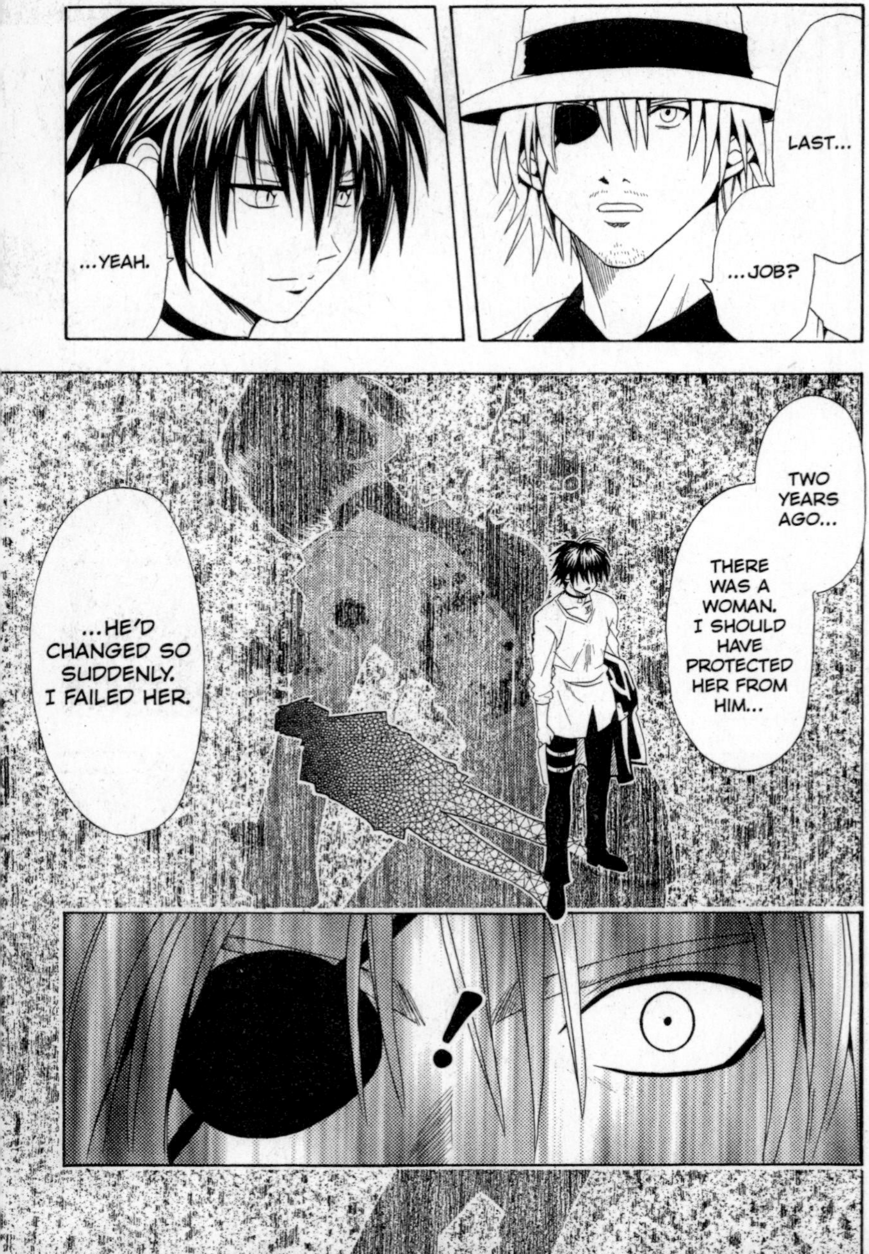
LAST...
...JOB?
...YEAH.
TWO YEARS AGO...
THERE WAS A WOMAN. I SHOULD HAVE PROTECTED HER FROM HIM...
...HE'D CHANGED SO SUDDENLY. I FAILED HER.
!

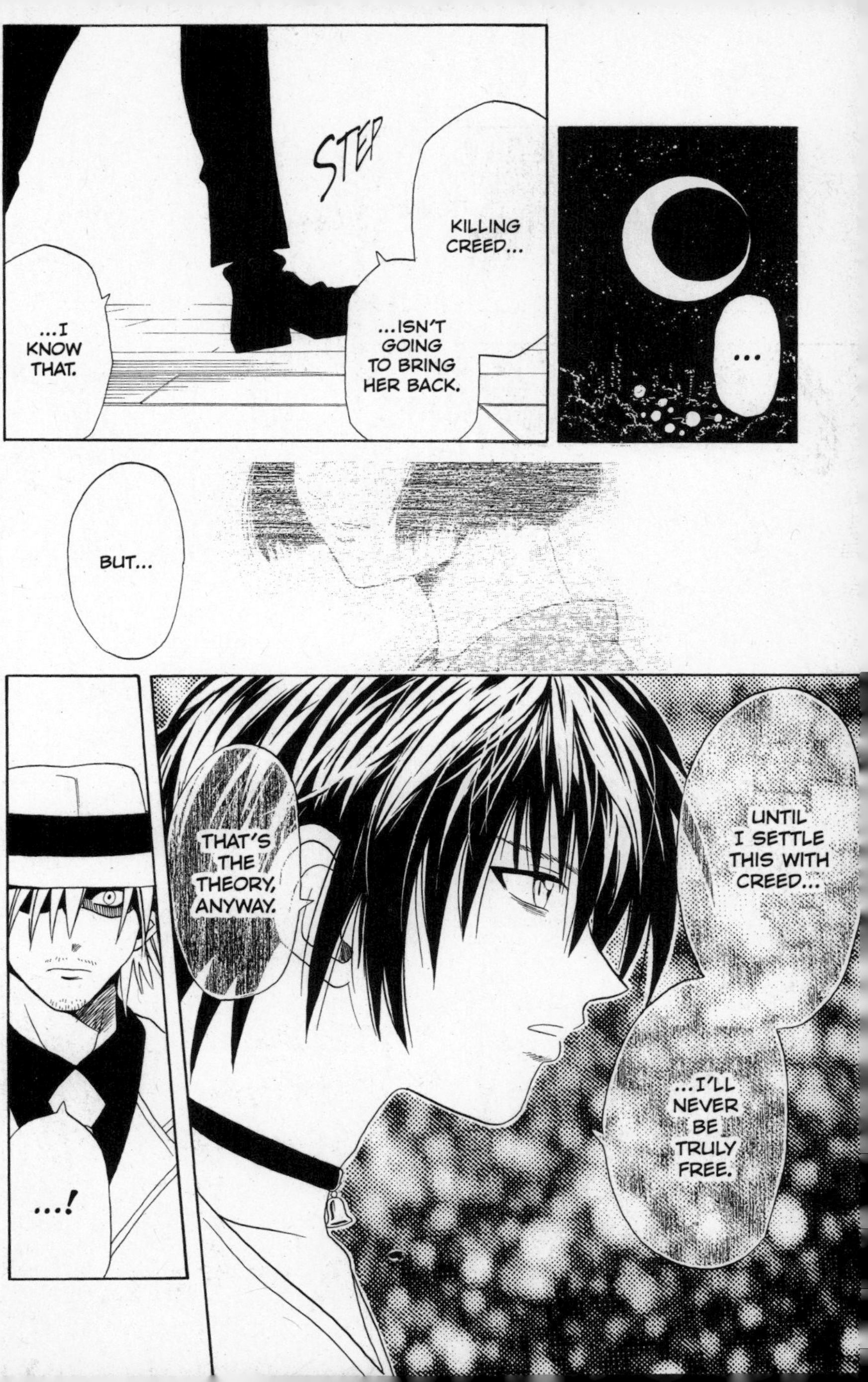
...
STEP
KILLING CREED...
...ISN'T GOING TO BRING HER BACK.
...I KNOW THAT.
BUT...
UNTIL I SETTLE THIS WITH CREED...
...I'LL NEVER BE TRULY FREE.
THAT'S THE THEORY, ANYWAY.
...!

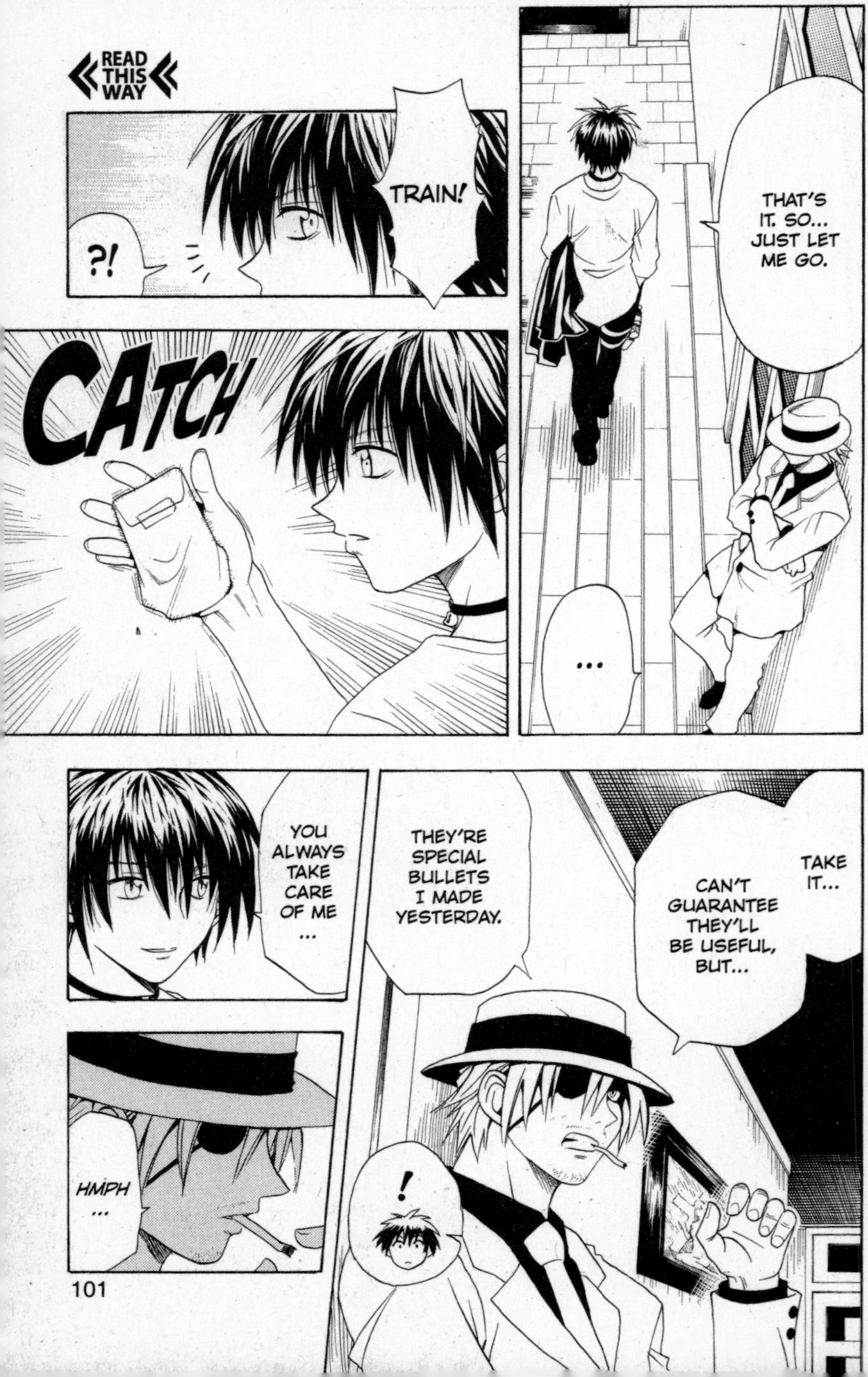
READ THIS WAY
THAT'S IT. SO... JUST LET ME GO.
...
TRAIN!
?!
CATCH
TAKE IT...
CAN'T GUARANTEE THEY'LL BE USEFUL, BUT...
THEY'RE SPECIAL BULLETS I MADE YESTERDAY.
!
YOU ALWAYS TAKE CARE OF ME ...
HMPH ...

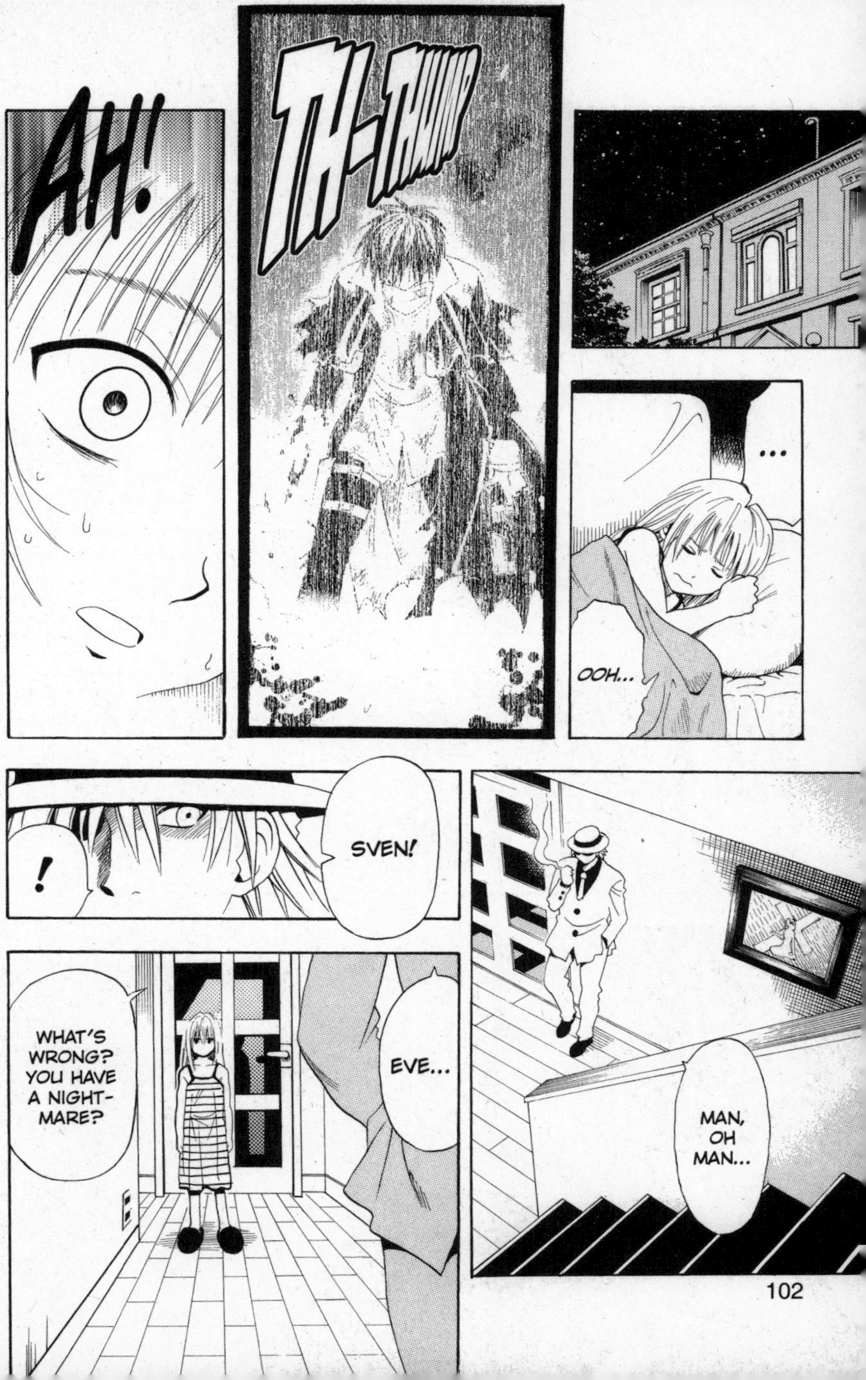
...
OOH...
TH-THUMP
AH!
MAN, OH MAN...
!
SVEN!
EVE...
WHAT'S WRONG? YOU HAVE A NIGHT-MARE?

READ THIS WAY

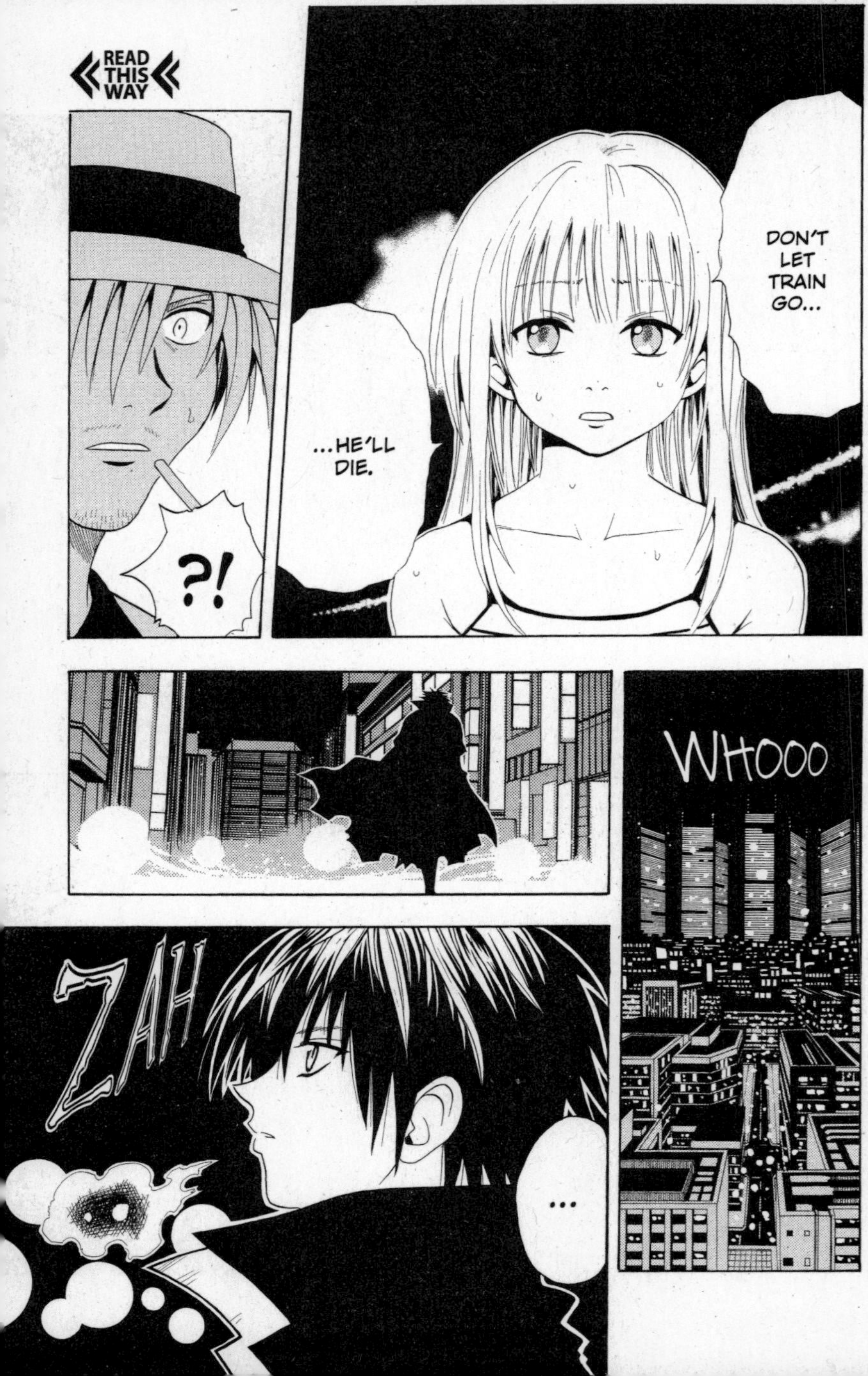
DON'T LET TRAIN GO...
...HE'LL DIE.
?!
WHOOO
ZAH
...

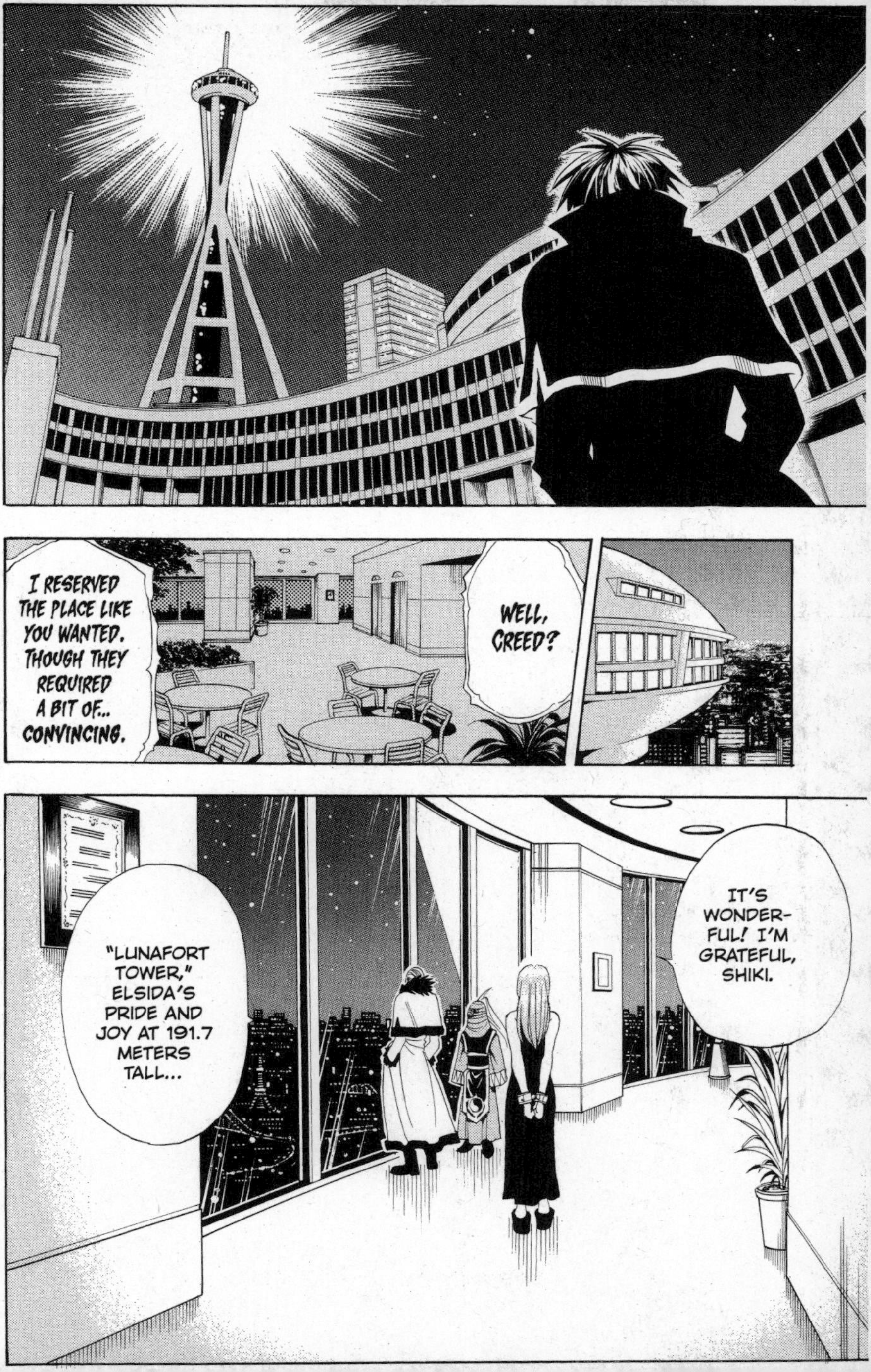

WELL, CREED?
I RESERVED THE PLACE LIKE YOU WANTED. THOUGH THEY REQUIRED A BIT OF... CONVINCING.
IT'S WONDER-FUL! I'M GRATEFUL, SHIKI.
"LUNAFORT TOWER," ELSIDA'S PRIDE AND JOY AT 191.7 METERS TALL...

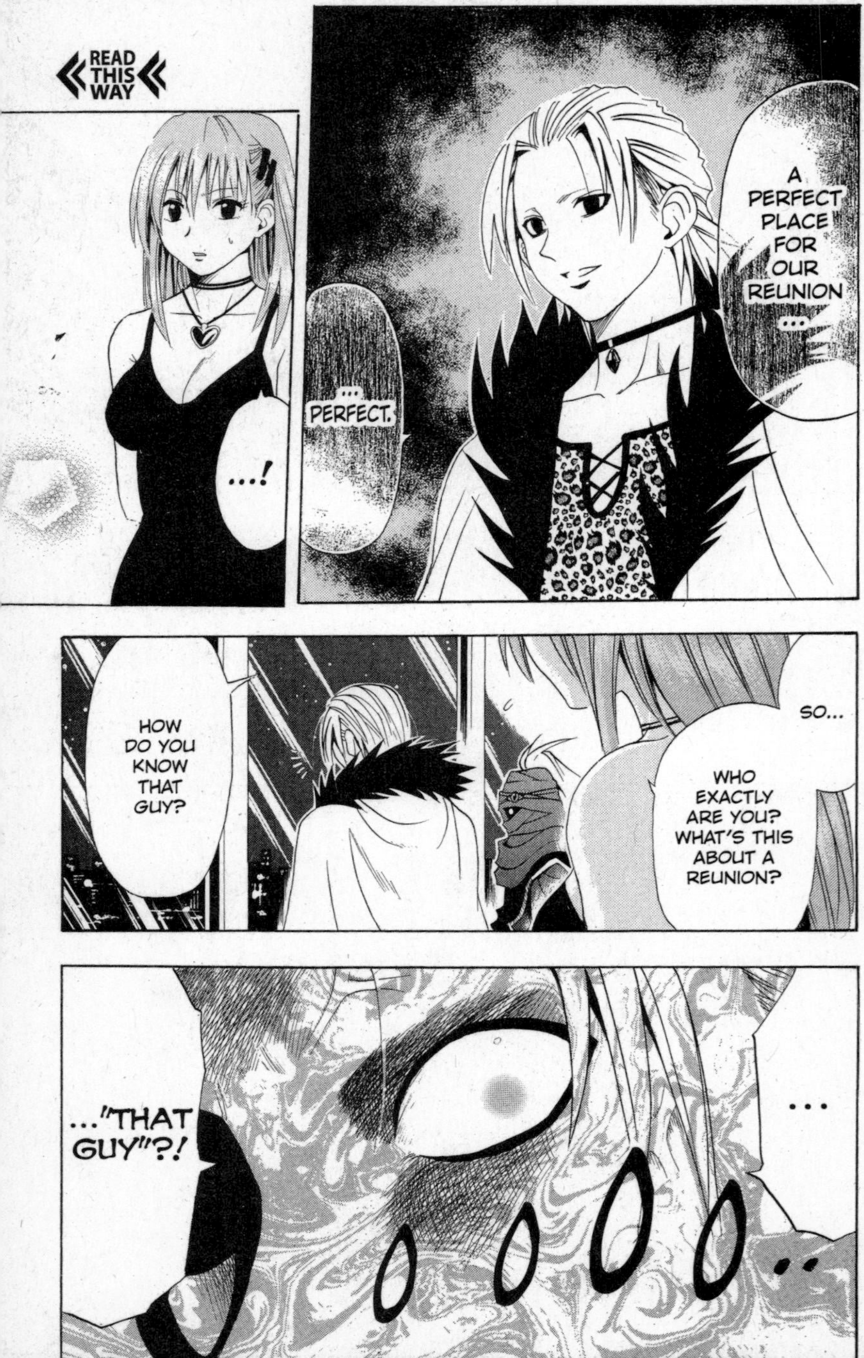
READ THIS WAY
A PERFECT PLACE FOR OUR REUNION ...
... PERFECT.
...!
SO...
WHO EXACTLY ARE YOU? WHAT'S THIS ABOUT A REUNION?
HOW DO YOU KNOW THAT GUY?
...
..."THAT GUY"?!

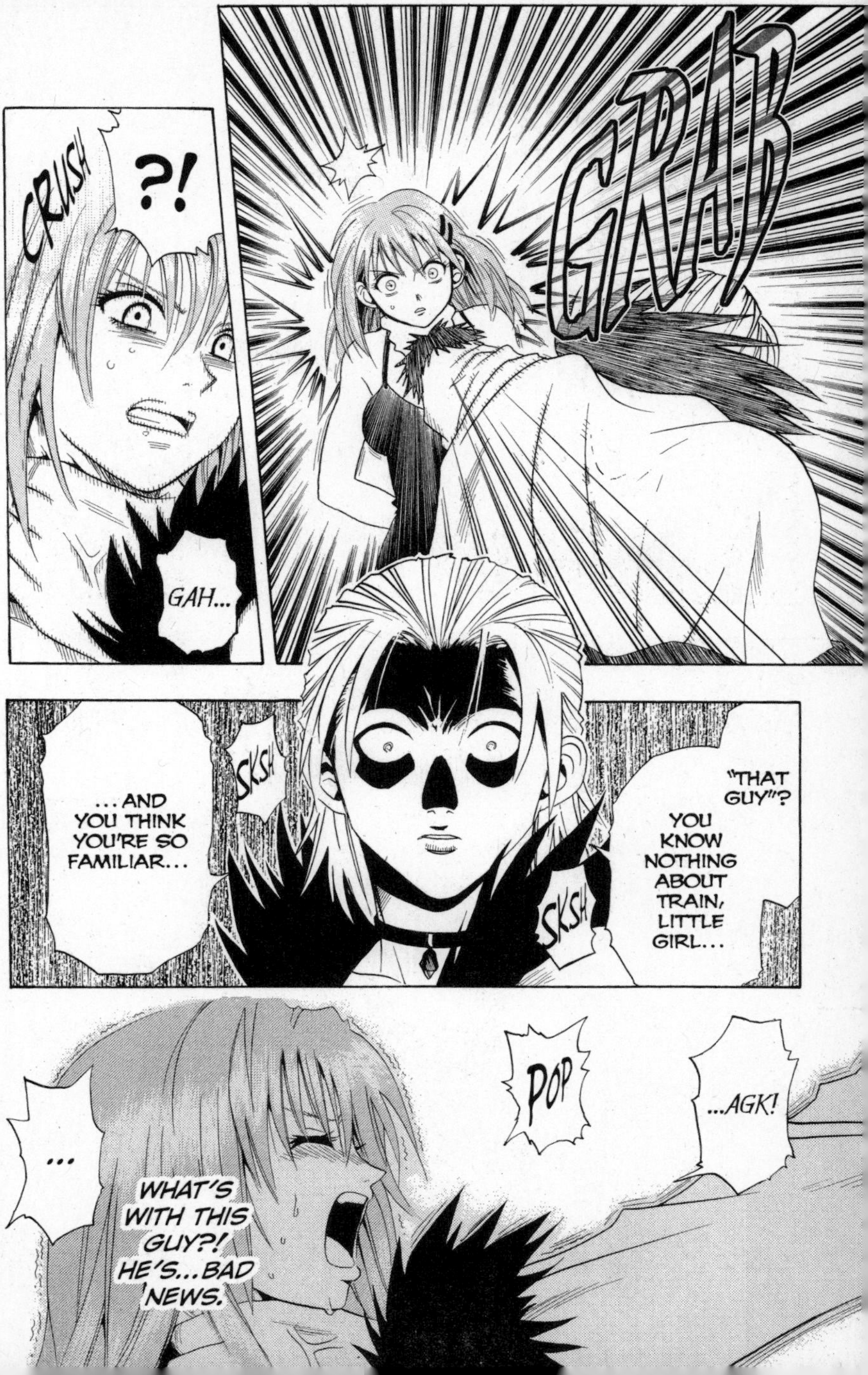
GRAB
CRUSH
?!
GAH...
"THAT GUY"? YOU KNOW NOTHING ABOUT TRAIN, LITTLE GIRL...
SKSH
SKSH
...AND YOU THINK YOU'RE SO FAMILIAR...
...AGK!
POP
...
WHAT'S WITH THIS GUY?! HE'S...BAD NEWS.

READ THIS WAY

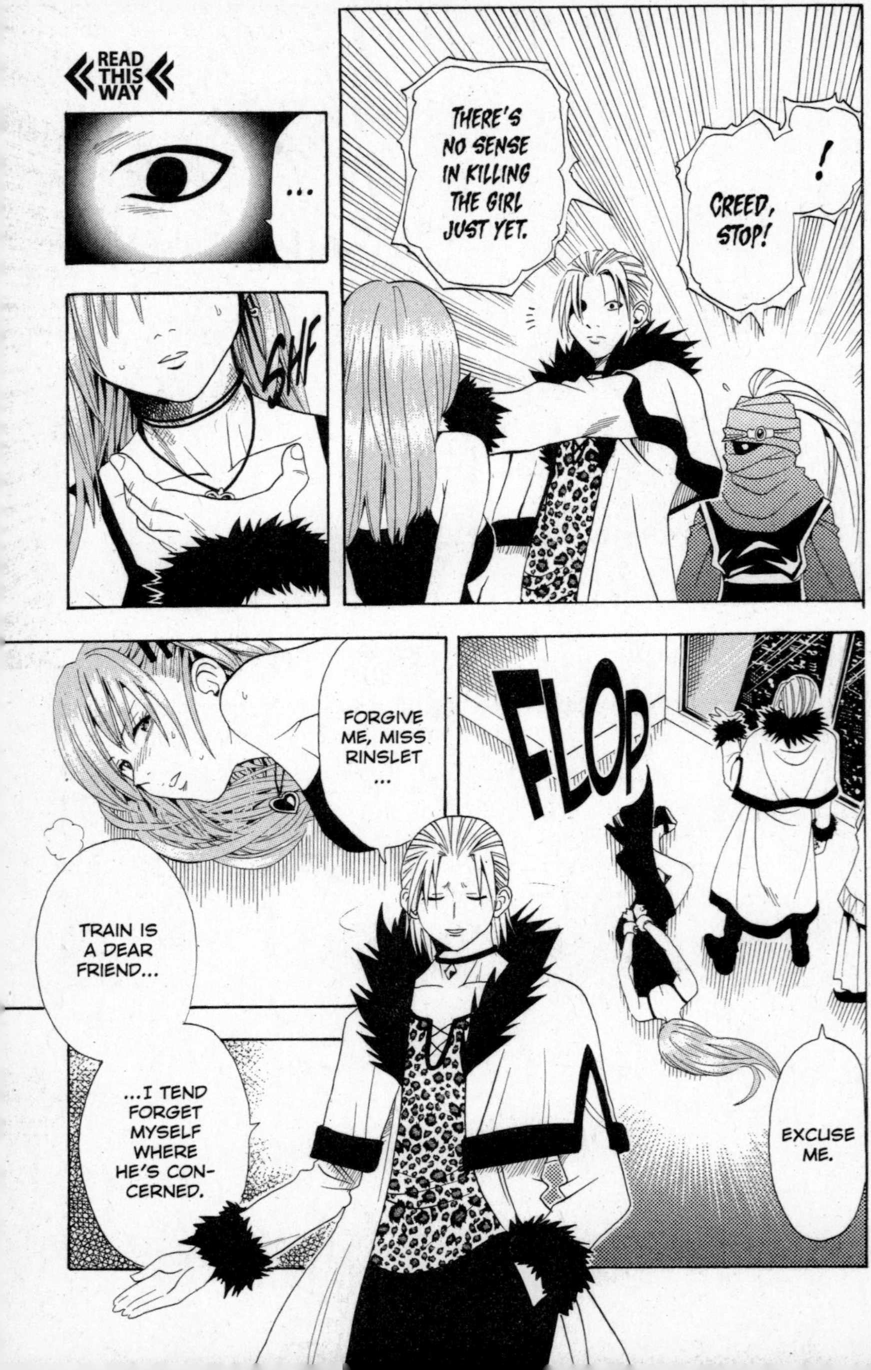
!
CREED, STOP!
THERE'S NO SENSE IN KILLING THE GIRL JUST YET.
...
SHF
FLOP
EXCUSE ME.
FORGIVE ME, MISS RINSLET ...
TRAIN IS A DEAR FRIEND...
...I TEND FORGET MYSELF WHERE HE'S CONCERNED.

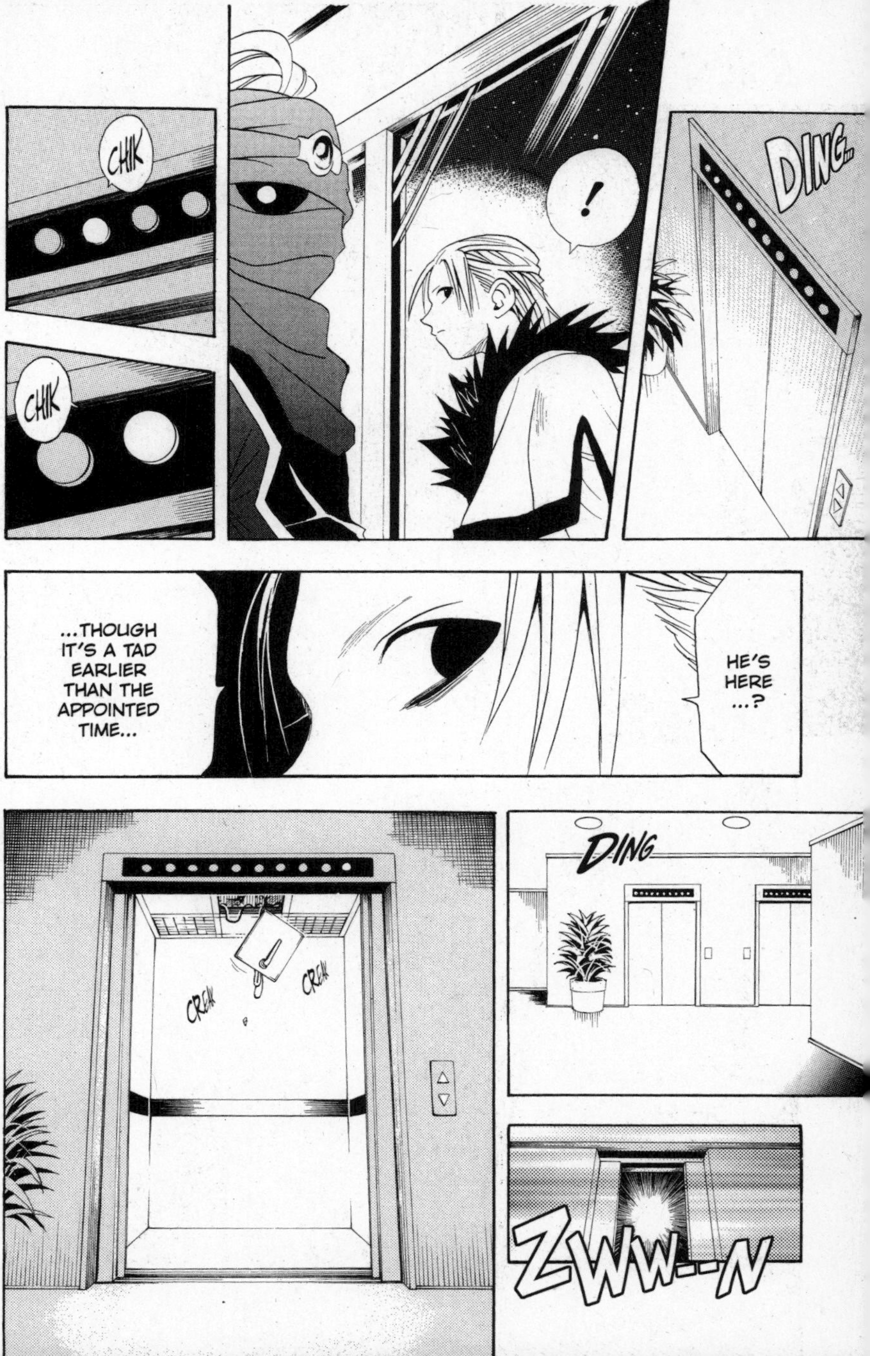
DING..
!
CHIK
CHIK
HE'S HERE ...?
...THOUGH IT'S A TAD EARLIER THAN THE APPOINTED TIME...
DING
ZWW--N
CREAK
CREAK

READ THIS WAY

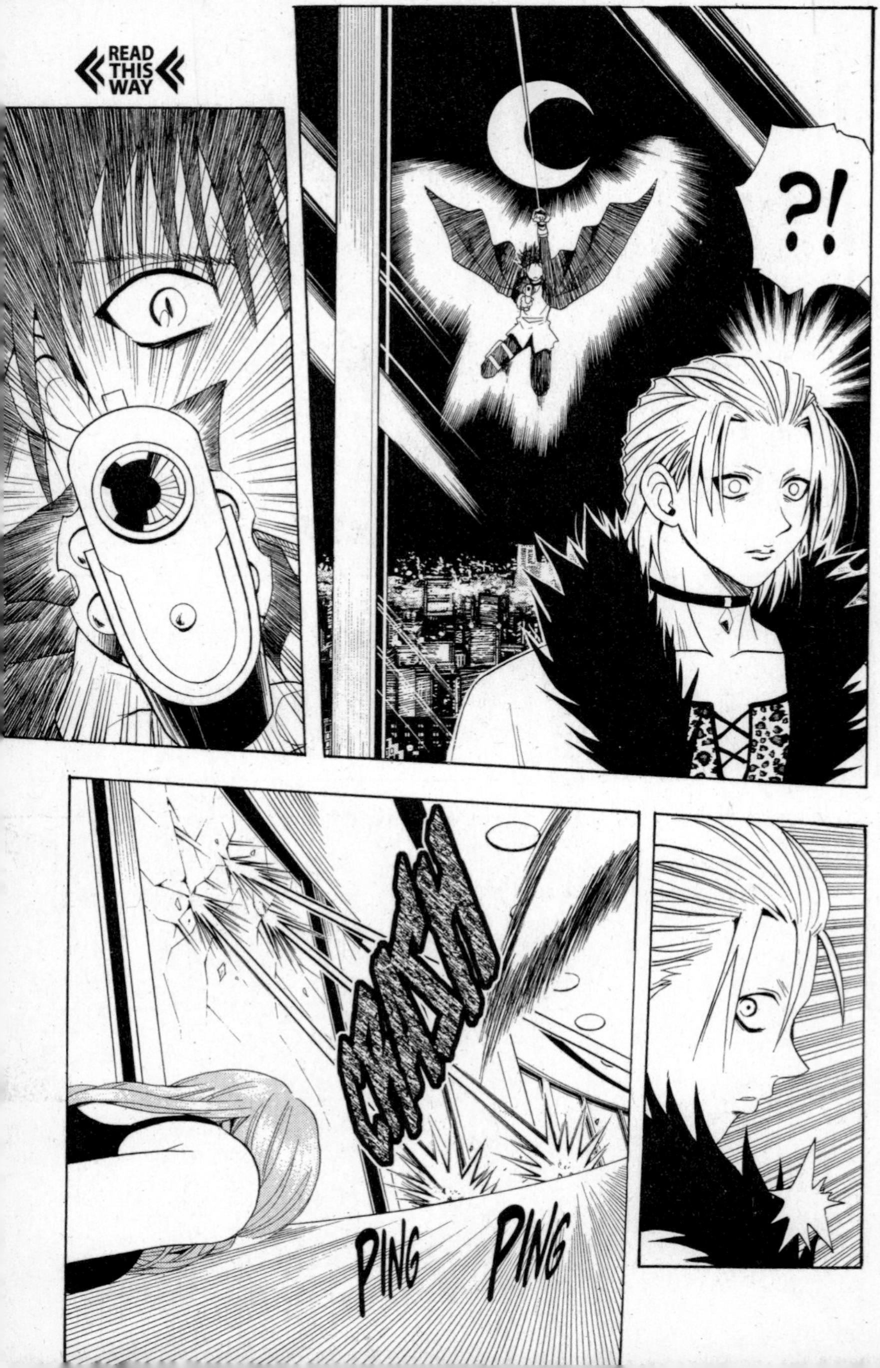
?!
PING
PING

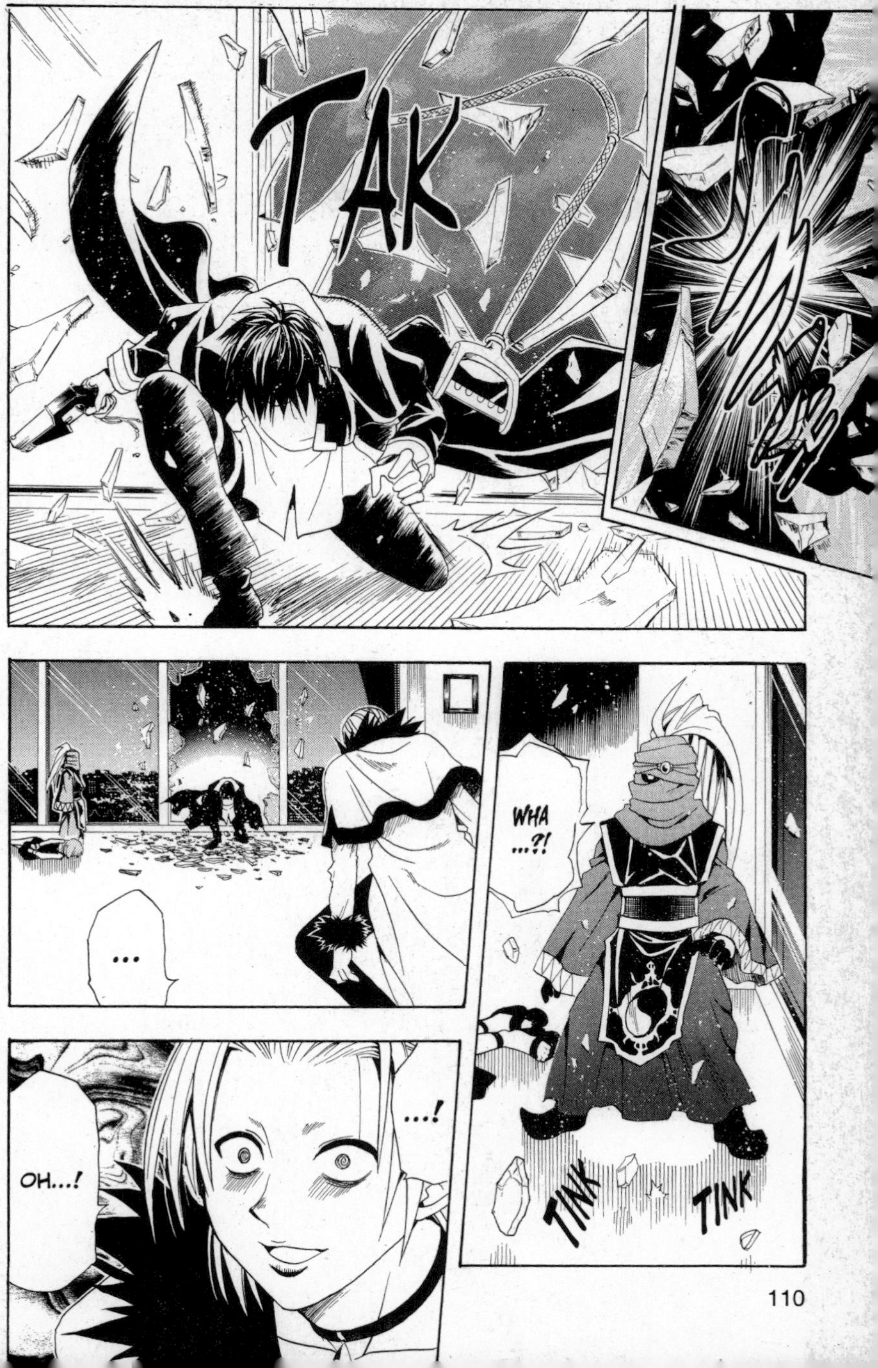
TAK
WHA ...?!
TINK
TINK
...
...!
OH...!

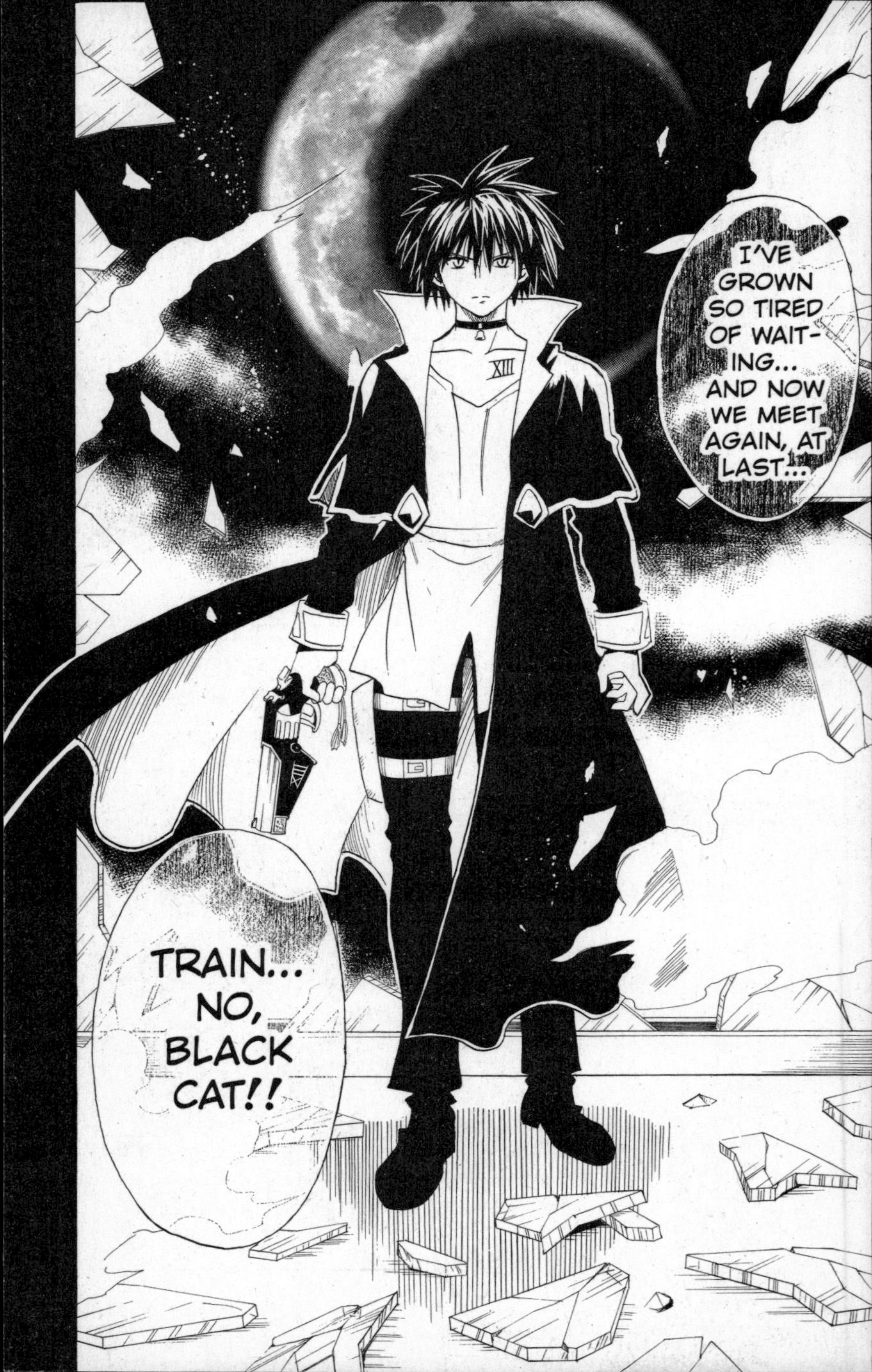
I'VE GROWN SO TIRED OF WAIT- ING... AND NOW WE MEET AGAIN, AT LAST...
TRAIN... NO, BLACK CAT!!

BLACK CAT

profile

EVE

DATA	
BIRTHDAY:	?
AGE:	? (FOR NOW, I'M MAKING HER 11 YEARS OLD)
BLOOD TYPE:	AB
HEIGHT:	133 CM
WEIGHT:	30 KG
HOBBIES:	READING, OBSERVING, WATCHING SVEN IN PARTICULAR
RECENT FAVORITE BOOKS:	"MASTER AND APPRENTICE" (ELSIDA PUBLISHING); "HEART-POUNDING SURVIVAL" (MARRON BOOKSTORE)
DISLIKES:	WINDOWLESS ROOMS, SCARY PEOPLE
FAVORITE FOOD:	ICE CREAM
COMMENTS:	SHE HAS A PRETTY HIGH IQ AND NEVER FORGETS A BOOK ONCE SHE'S READ IT. BECAUSE SHE POSSESSES HEALING NANOMACHINES, HER WOUNDS HEAL AT AN ACCELERATED RATE. (EVE WILL GROW, INCIDENTALLY. OTHER THAN THE FACT THAT SHE HAS AN ORGAN INSIDE HER BODY THAT GENERATES NANOMACHINES, SHE IS NO DIFFERENT FROM AN ORDINARY HUMAN GIRL.)

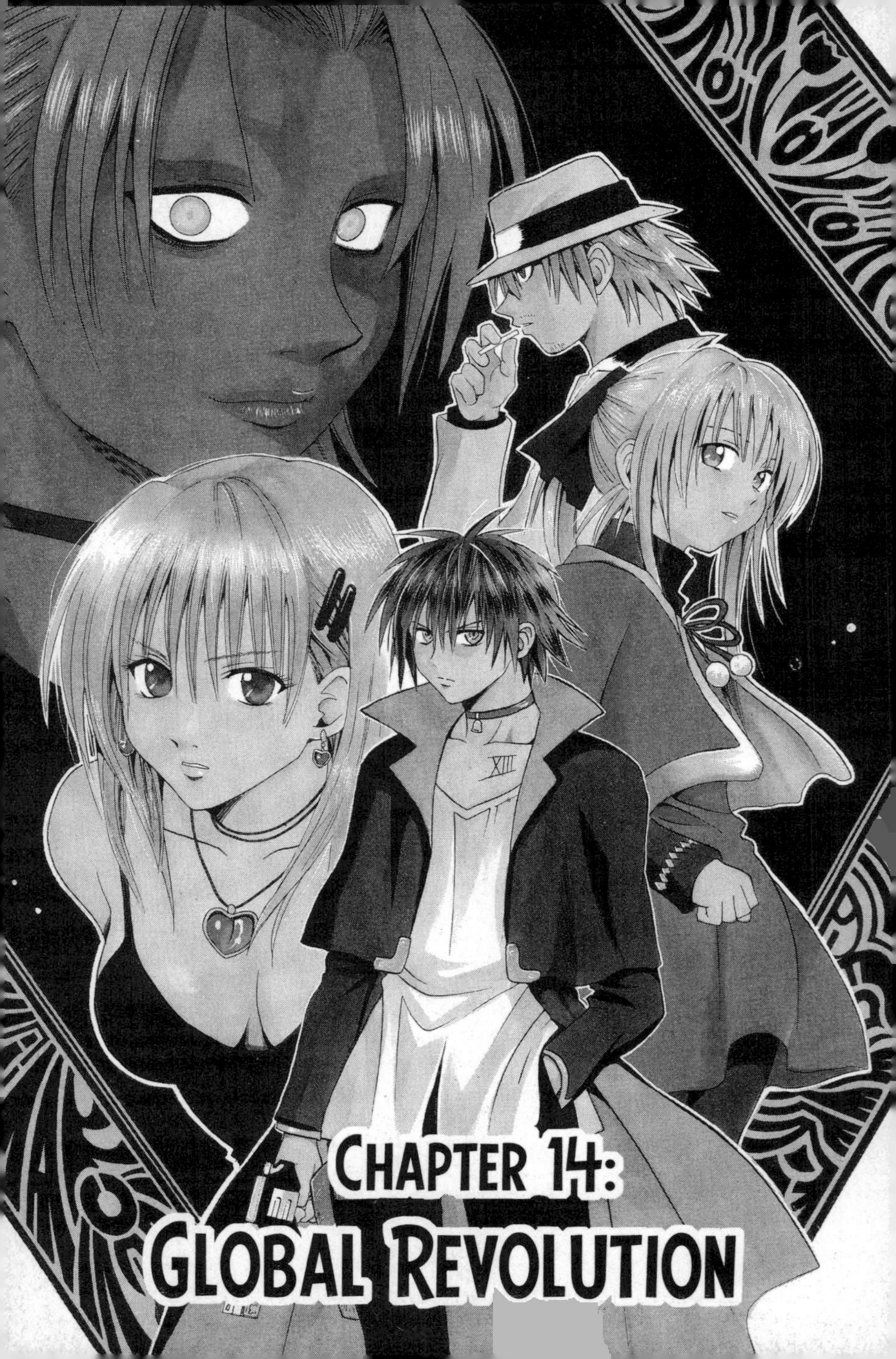
Chapter 14:
Global Revolution

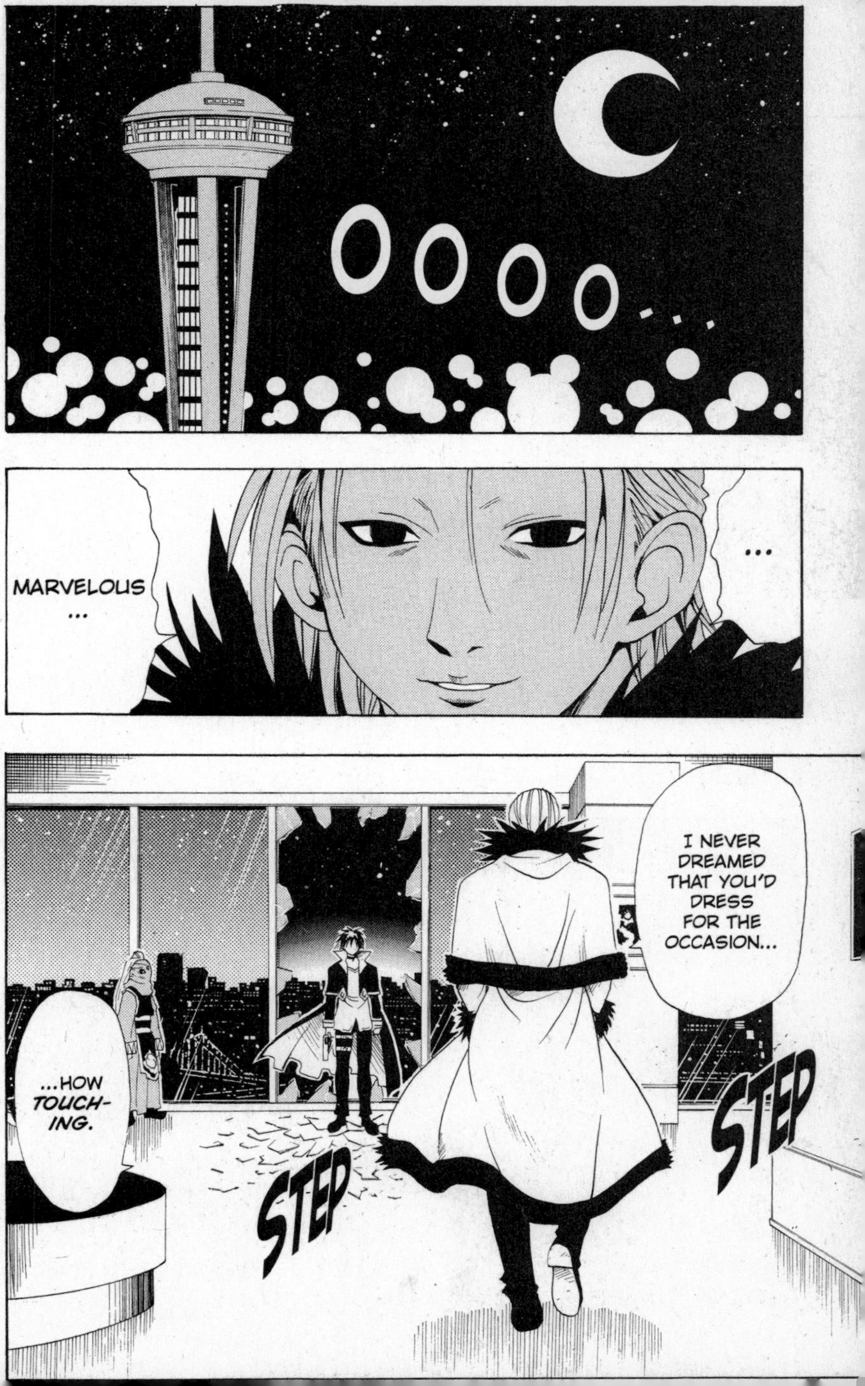
OOOO...
...
MARVELOUS ...
I NEVER DREAMED THAT YOU'D DRESS FOR THE OCCASION...
STEP
...HOW TOUCHING.
STEP

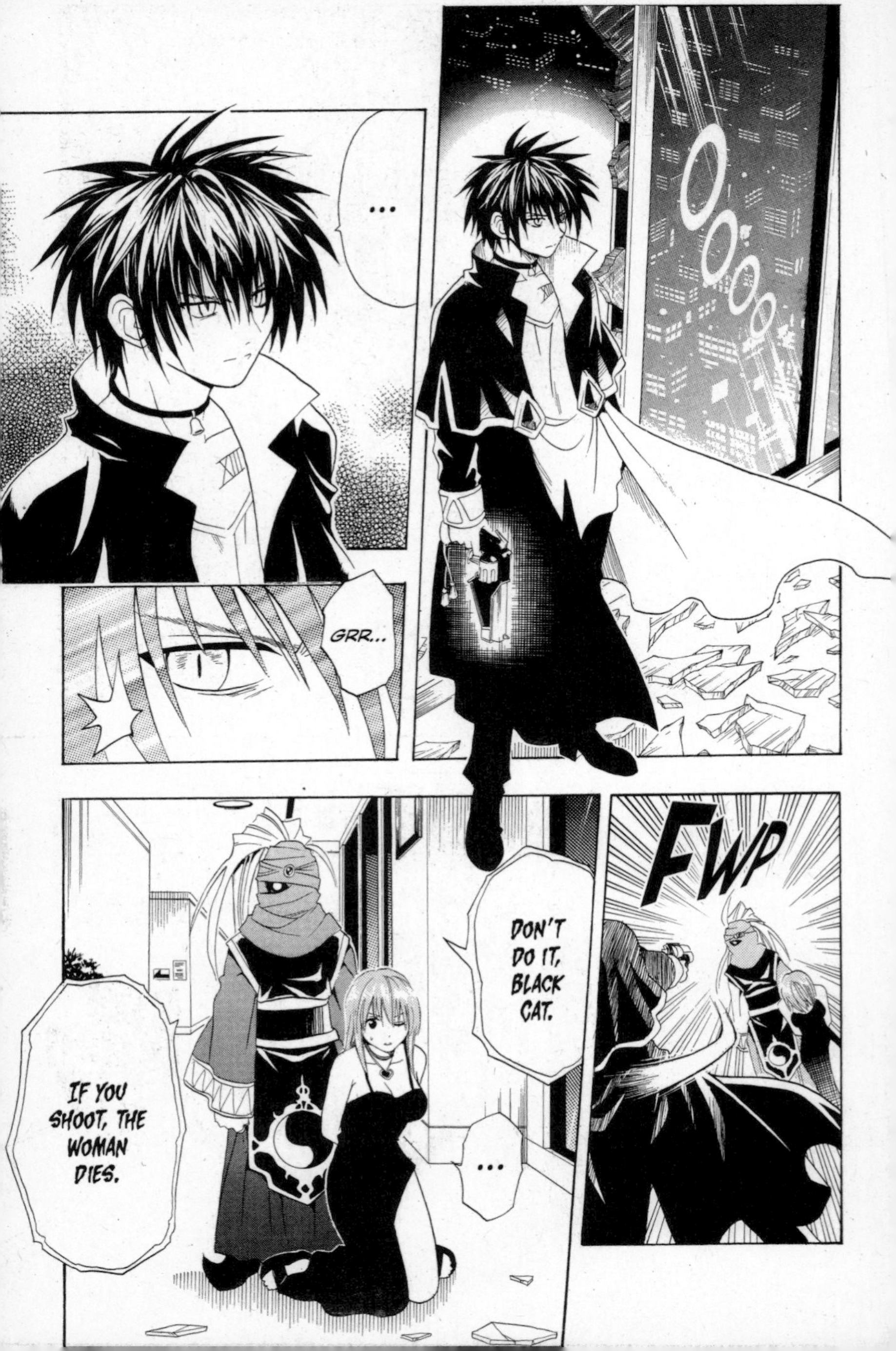
...
GRR...
FWP
DON'T DO IT, BLACK CAT.
IF YOU SHOOT, THE WOMAN DIES.
...

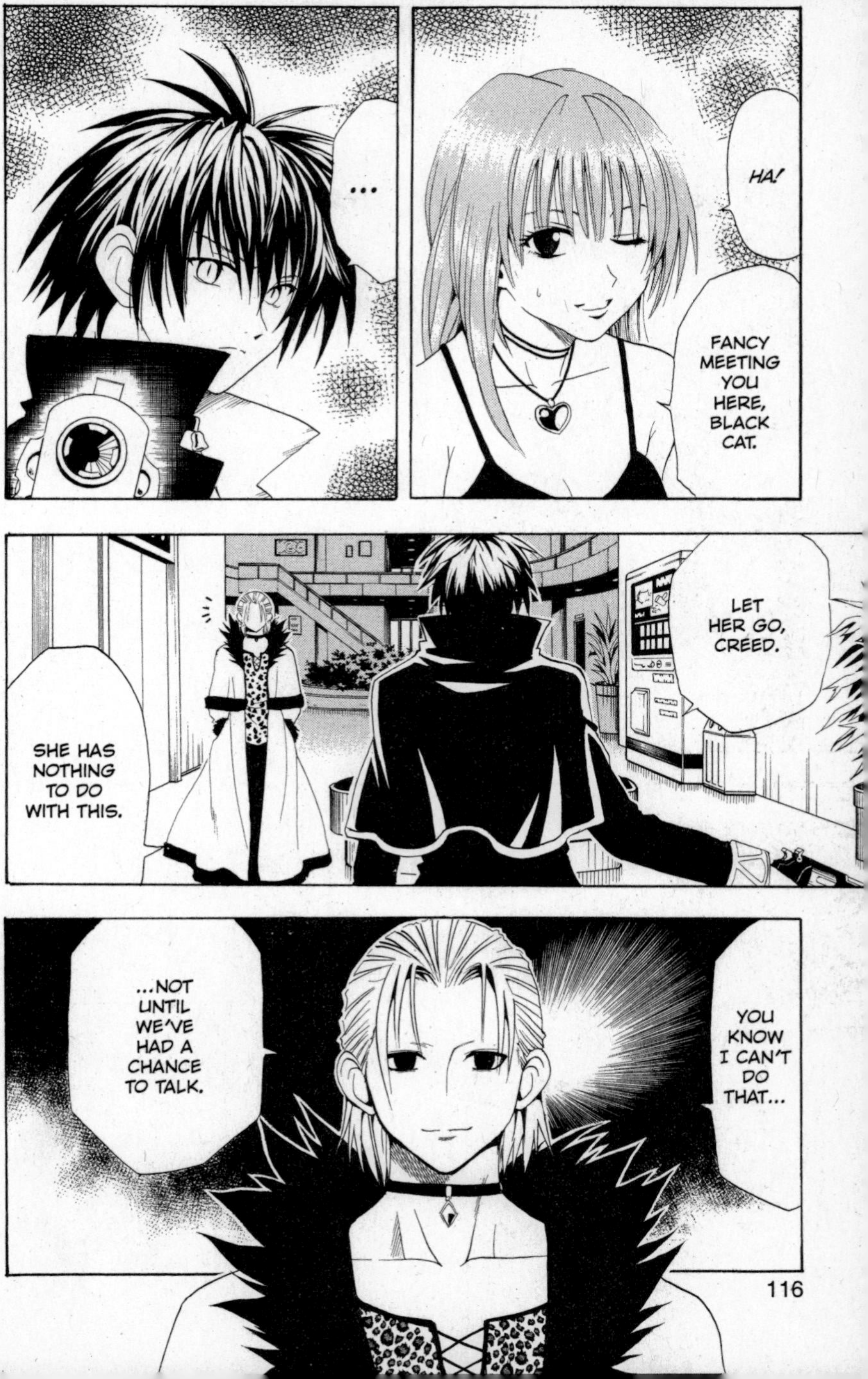
HA!
FANCY MEETING YOU HERE, BLACK CAT.
...
LET HER GO, CREED.
SHE HAS NOTHING TO DO WITH THIS.
YOU KNOW I CAN'T DO THAT...
...NOT UNTIL WE'VE HAD A CHANCE TO TALK.

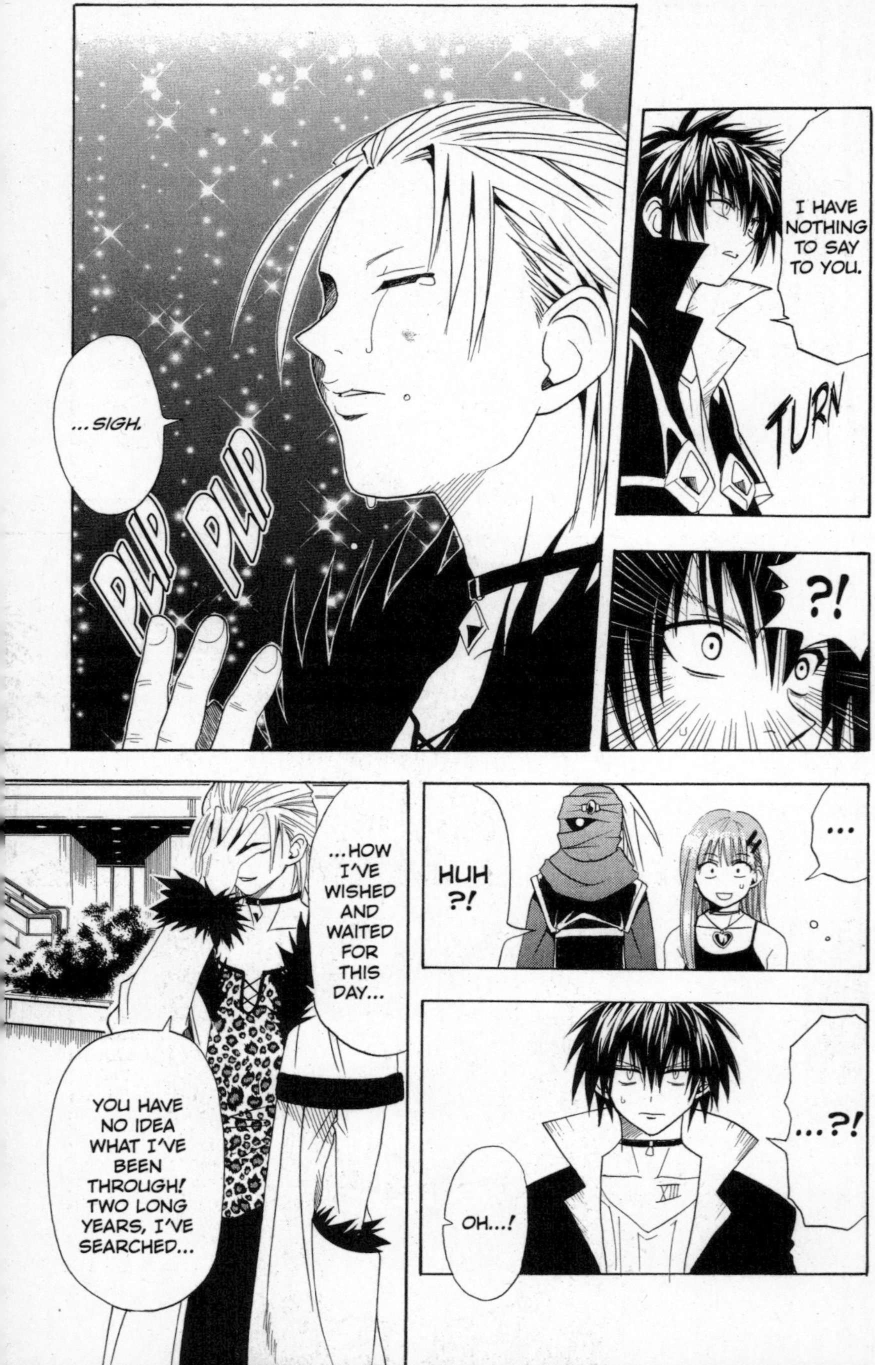

I HAVE NOTHING TO SAY TO YOU.
TURN
?!
...SIGH.
PLIP PLIP
...
HUH ?!
...?!
OH...!
...HOW I'VE WISHED AND WAITED FOR THIS DAY...
YOU HAVE NO IDEA WHAT I'VE BEEN THROUGH! TWO LONG YEARS, I'VE SEARCHED...

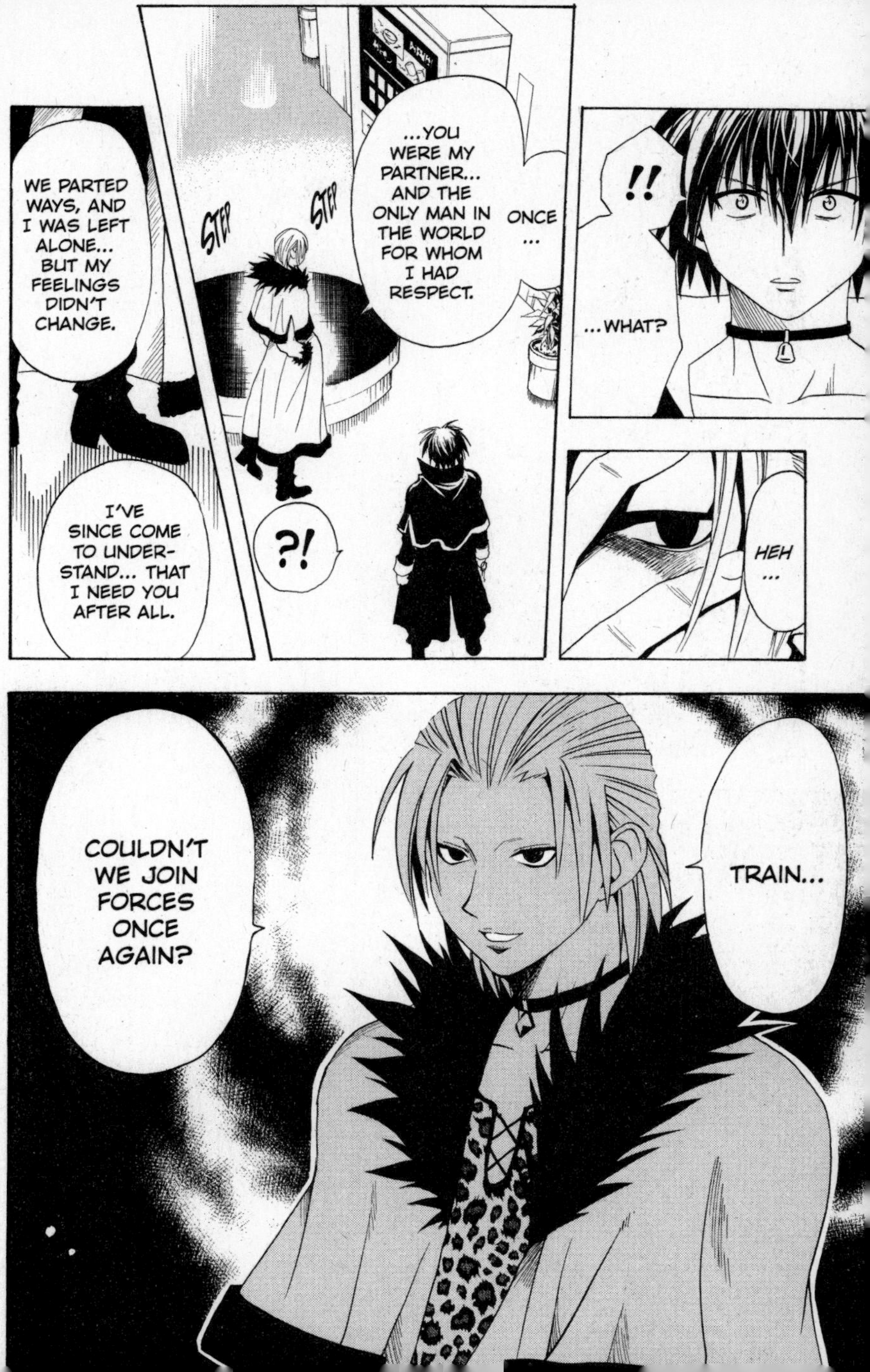
!!
...WHAT?
HEH ...
ONCE ...
...YOU WERE MY PARTNER... AND THE ONLY MAN IN THE WORLD FOR WHOM I HAD RESPECT.
STEP
STEP
?!
WE PARTED WAYS, AND I WAS LEFT ALONE... BUT MY FEELINGS DIDN'T CHANGE.
I'VE SINCE COME TO UNDER-STAND... THAT I NEED YOU AFTER ALL.
TRAIN...
COULDN'T WE JOIN FORCES ONCE AGAIN?

READ THIS WAY

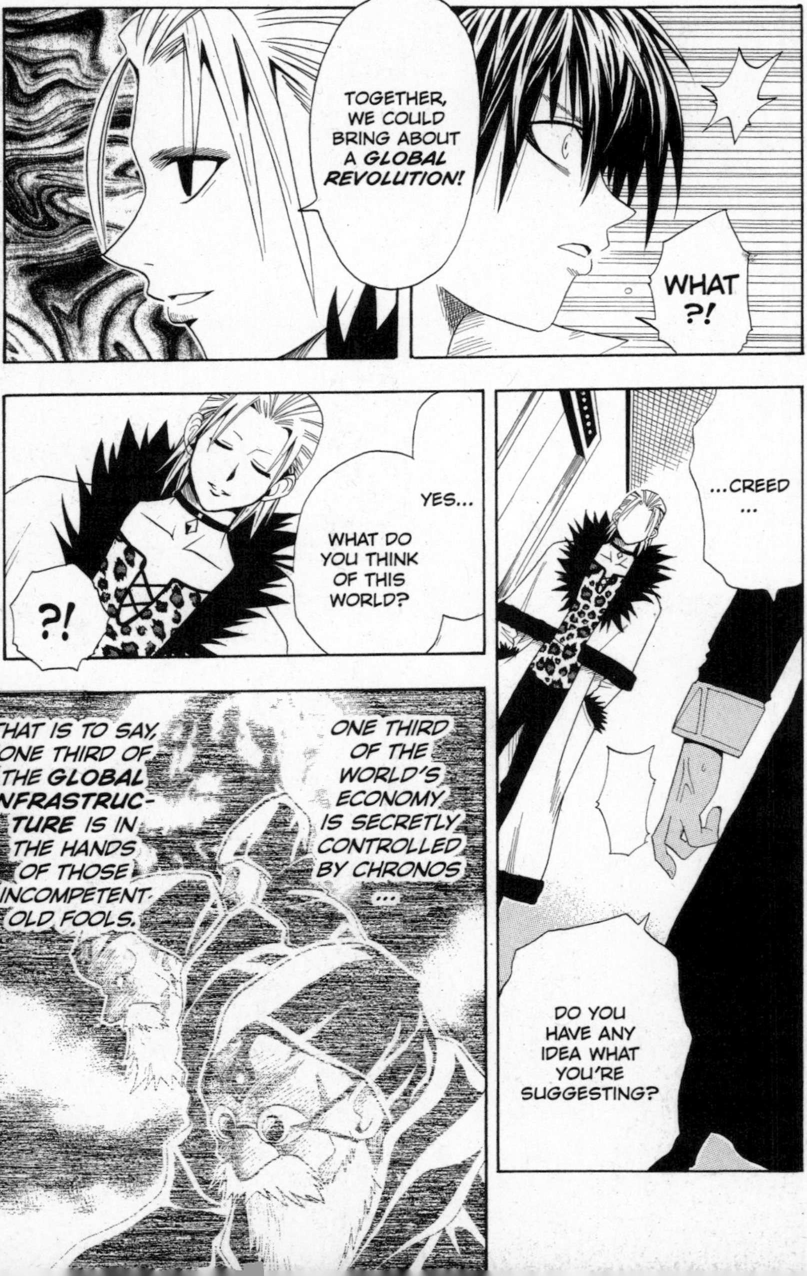

TOGETHER, WE COULD BRING ABOUT A ***GLOBAL REVOLUTION!***
WHAT ?!
...CREED ...
DO YOU HAVE ANY IDEA WHAT YOU'RE SUGGESTING?
YES...
WHAT DO YOU THINK OF THIS WORLD?
?!
ONE THIRD OF THE WORLD'S ECONOMY IS SECRETLY CONTROLLED BY CHRONOS ...
*THAT IS TO SAY, ONE THIRD OF THE **GLOBAL INFRASTRUCTURE** IS IN THE HANDS OF THOSE INCOMPETENT OLD FOOLS.*

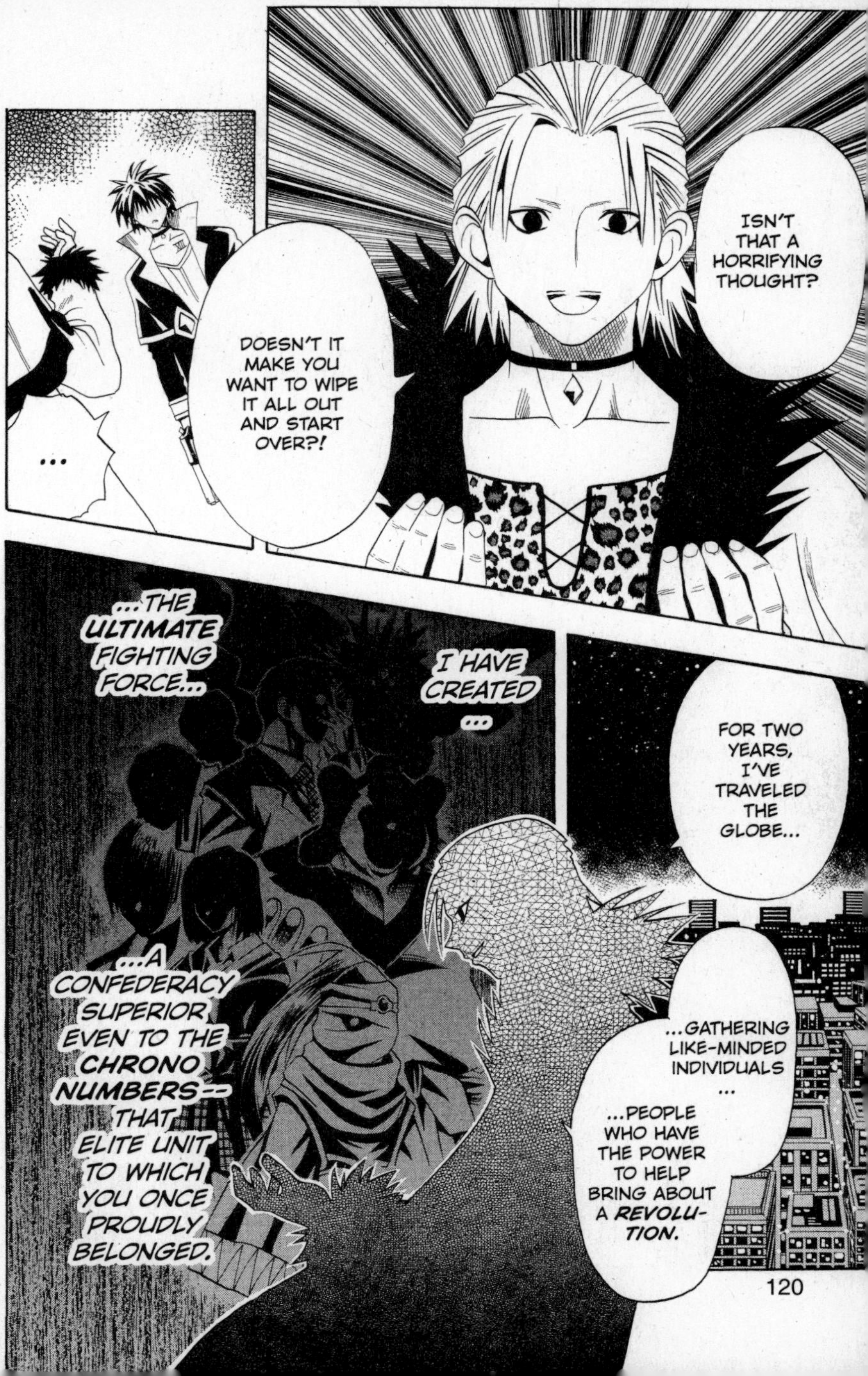
ISN'T THAT A HORRIFYING THOUGHT?
DOESN'T IT MAKE YOU WANT TO WIPE IT ALL OUT AND START OVER?!
...
FOR TWO YEARS, I'VE TRAVELED THE GLOBE...
...GATHERING LIKE-MINDED INDIVIDUALS...
...PEOPLE WHO HAVE THE POWER TO HELP BRING ABOUT A REVOLUTION.
I HAVE CREATED...
...THE ULTIMATE FIGHTING FORCE...
...A CONFEDERACY SUPERIOR EVEN TO THE CHRONO NUMBERS-- THAT ELITE UNIT TO WHICH YOU ONCE PROUDLY BELONGED.

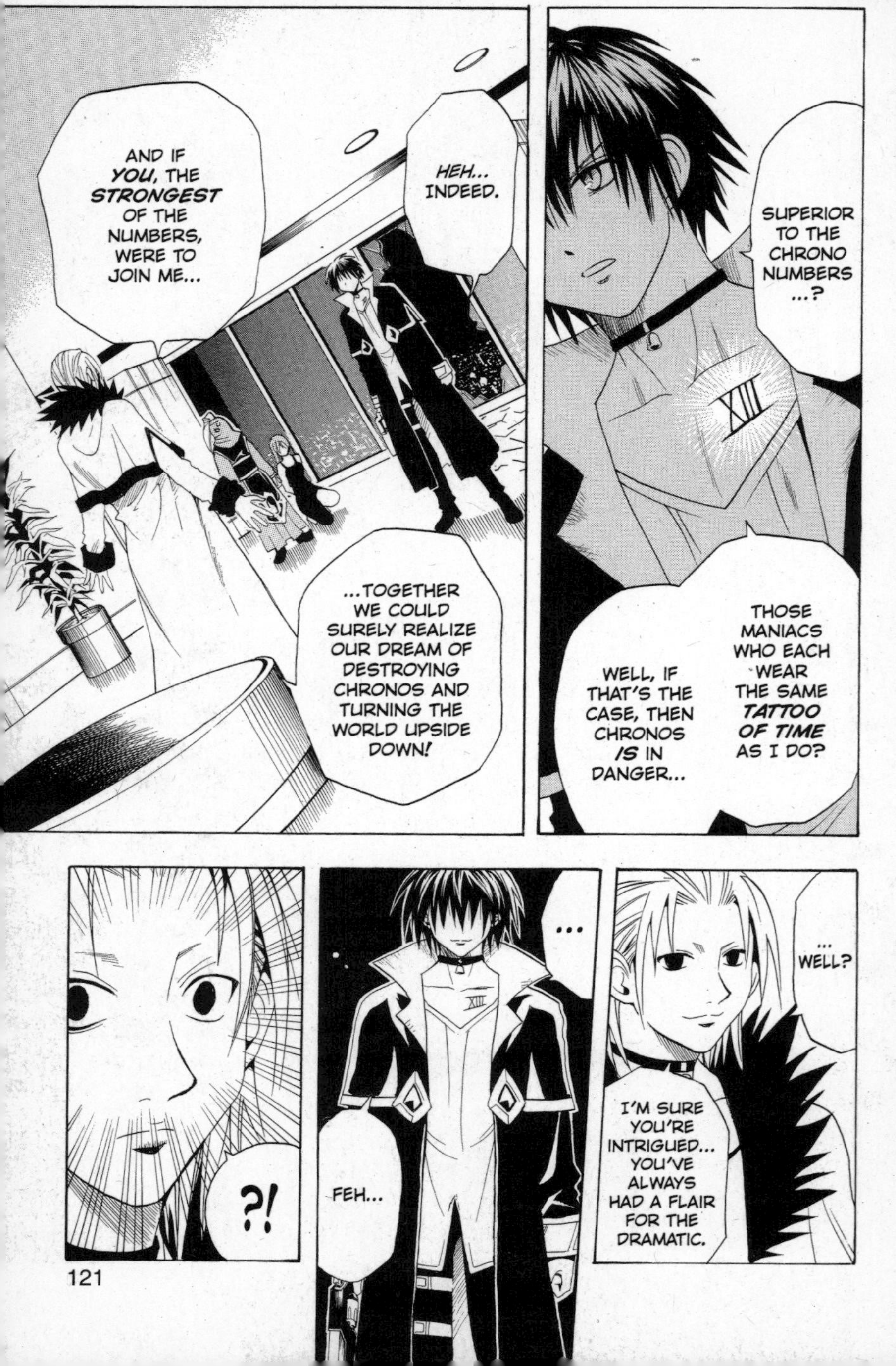
SUPERIOR TO THE CHRONO NUMBERS ...?
THOSE MANIACS WHO EACH WEAR THE SAME *TATTOO OF TIME* AS I DO?
WELL, IF THAT'S THE CASE, THEN CHRONOS *IS* IN DANGER...
HEH... INDEED.
AND IF *YOU*, THE *STRONGEST* OF THE NUMBERS, WERE TO JOIN ME...
...TOGETHER WE COULD SURELY REALIZE OUR DREAM OF DESTROYING CHRONOS AND TURNING THE WORLD UPSIDE DOWN!
... WELL?
I'M SURE YOU'RE INTRIGUED... YOU'VE ALWAYS HAD A FLAIR FOR THE DRAMATIC.
...
FEH...
?!

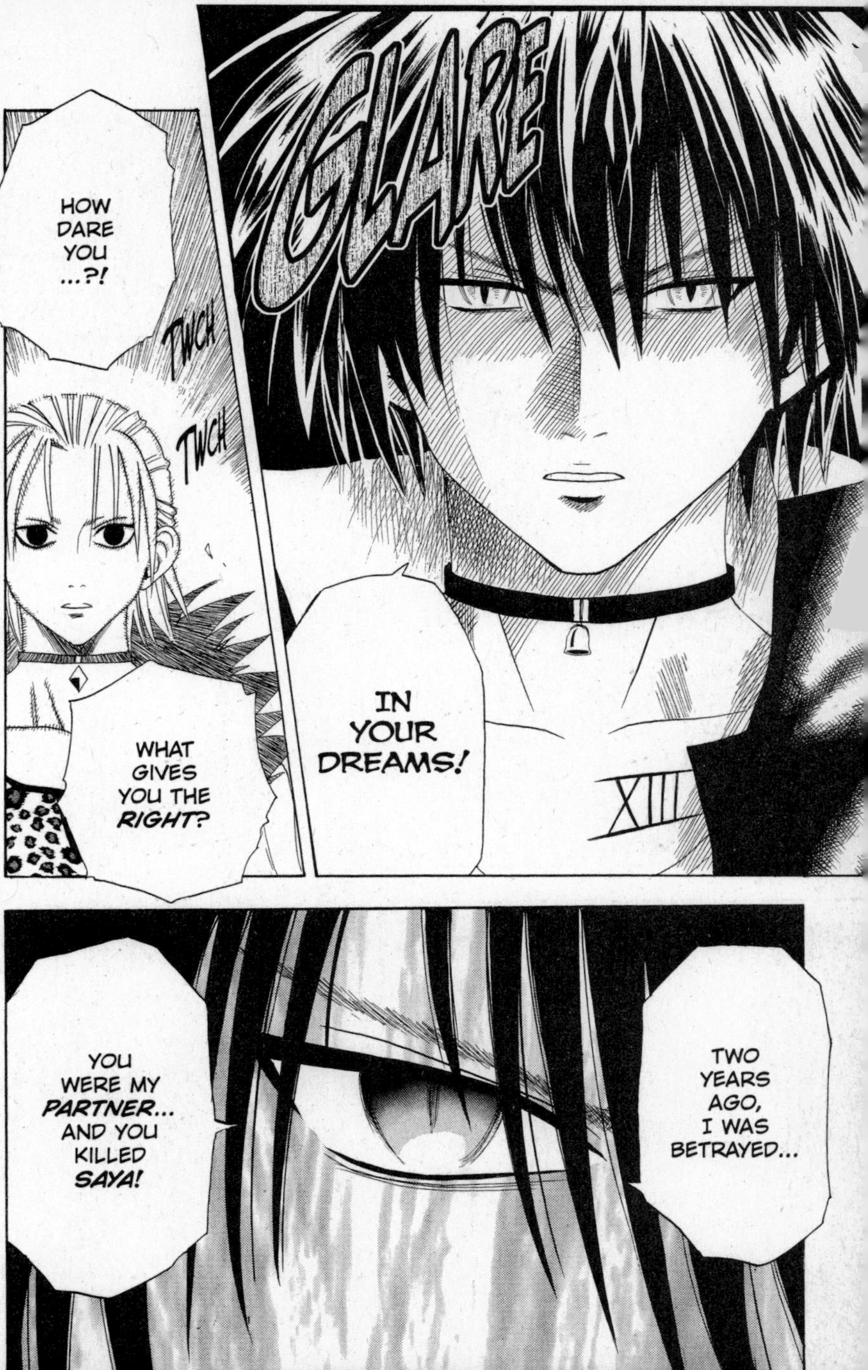
GLARE
IN YOUR DREAMS!
HOW DARE YOU ...?!
TWCH
TWCH
WHAT GIVES YOU THE *RIGHT*?
TWO YEARS AGO, I WAS BETRAYED...
YOU WERE MY *PARTNER*... AND YOU KILLED *SAYA*!

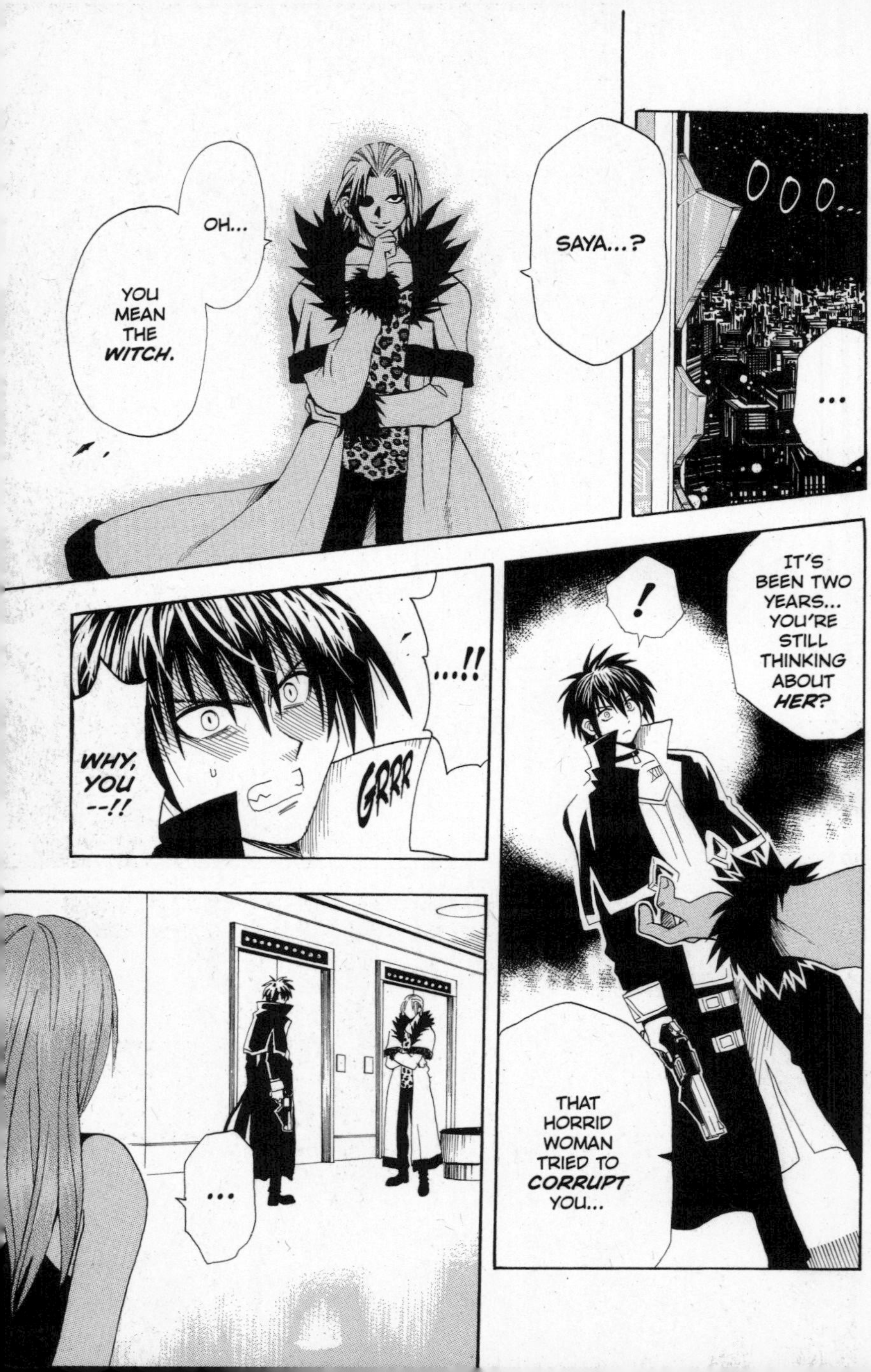

OOO...
SAYA...?
...
OH...
YOU MEAN THE *WITCH.*
IT'S BEEN TWO YEARS... YOU'RE STILL THINKING ABOUT *HER?*
!
THAT HORRID WOMAN TRIED TO *CORRUPT* YOU...
...!!
GRRR
WHY, YOU --!!
...

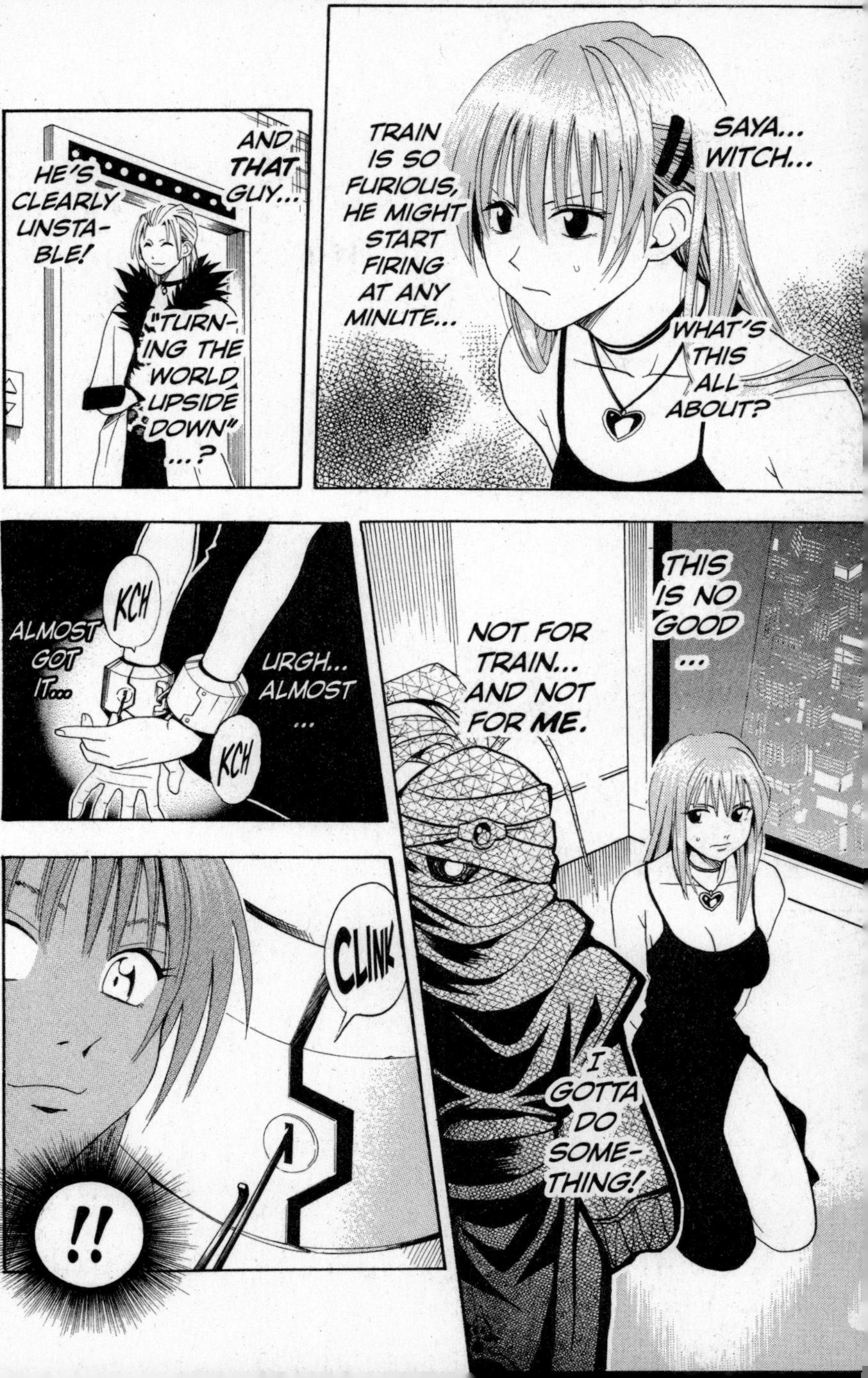
SAYA... WITCH...
TRAIN IS SO FURIOUS, HE MIGHT START FIRING AT ANY MINUTE...
WHAT'S THIS ALL ABOUT?
AND THAT GUY...
HE'S CLEARLY UNSTABLE!
"TURNING THE WORLD UPSIDE DOWN"...?
THIS IS NO GOOD...
NOT FOR TRAIN... AND NOT FOR ME.
I GOTTA DO SOMETHING!
KCH
URGH... ALMOST...
ALMOST GOT IT...
KCH
CLINK
!!

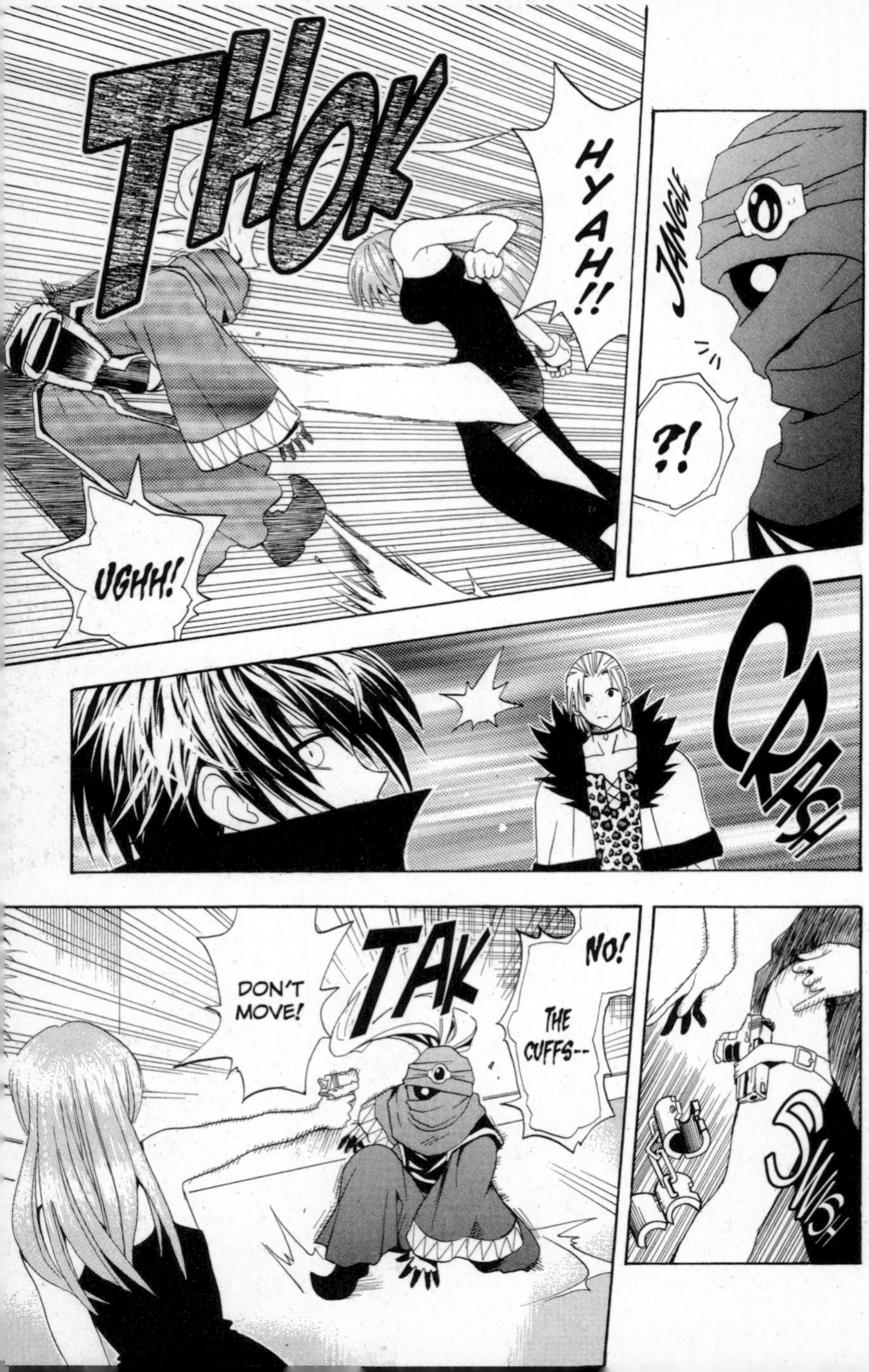
JANGLE
?!
THOK
HYAH!!
UGHH!
CRASH
DON'T MOVE!
TAK
NO!
THE CUFFS--

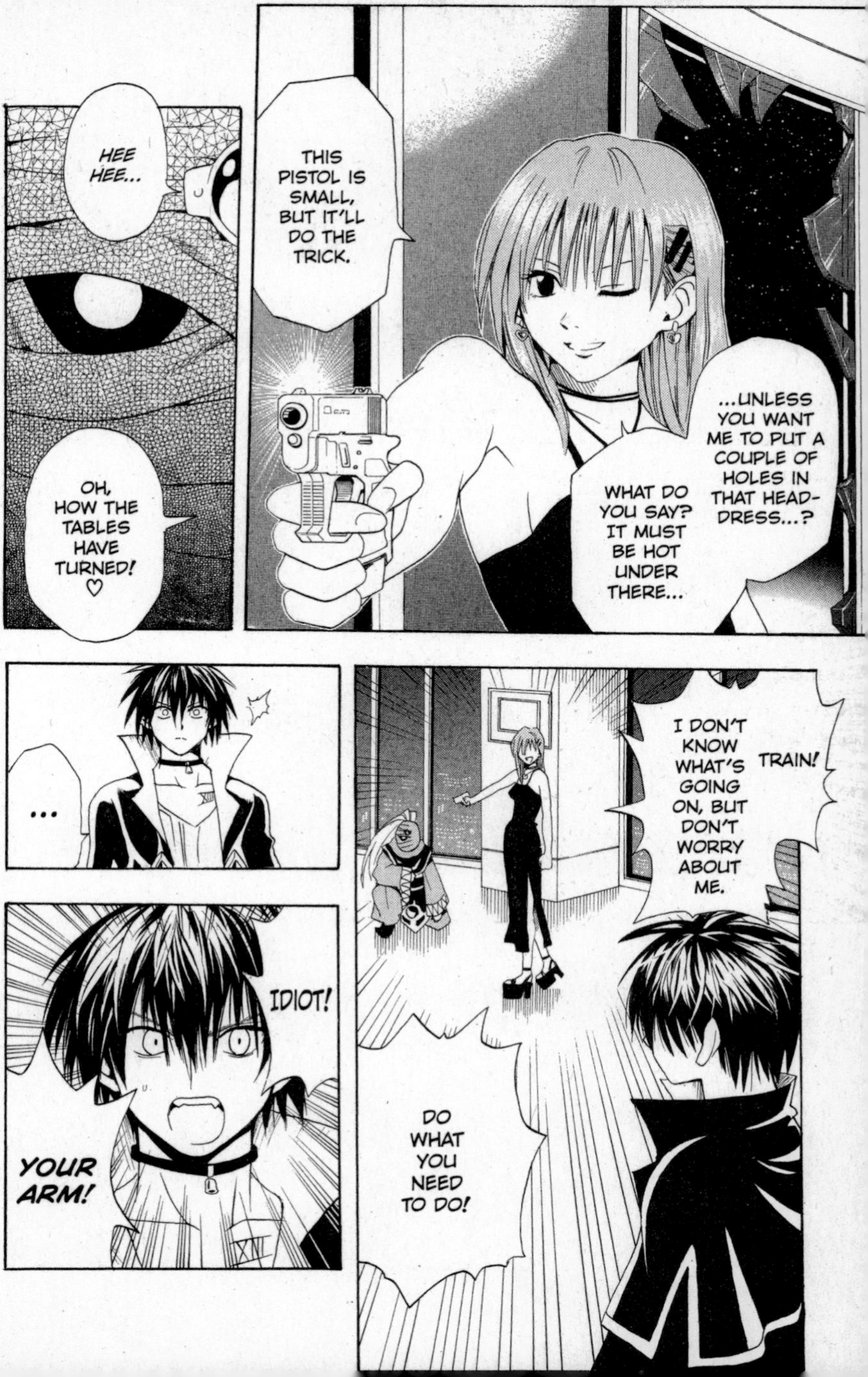
THIS PISTOL IS SMALL, BUT IT'LL DO THE TRICK.
WHAT DO YOU SAY? IT MUST BE HOT UNDER THERE...
...UNLESS YOU WANT ME TO PUT A COUPLE OF HOLES IN THAT HEAD-DRESS...?
HEE HEE...
OH, HOW THE TABLES HAVE TURNED! ♡
TRAIN!
I DON'T KNOW WHAT'S GOING ON, BUT DON'T WORRY ABOUT ME.
DO WHAT YOU NEED TO DO!
...
IDIOT!
YOUR ARM!

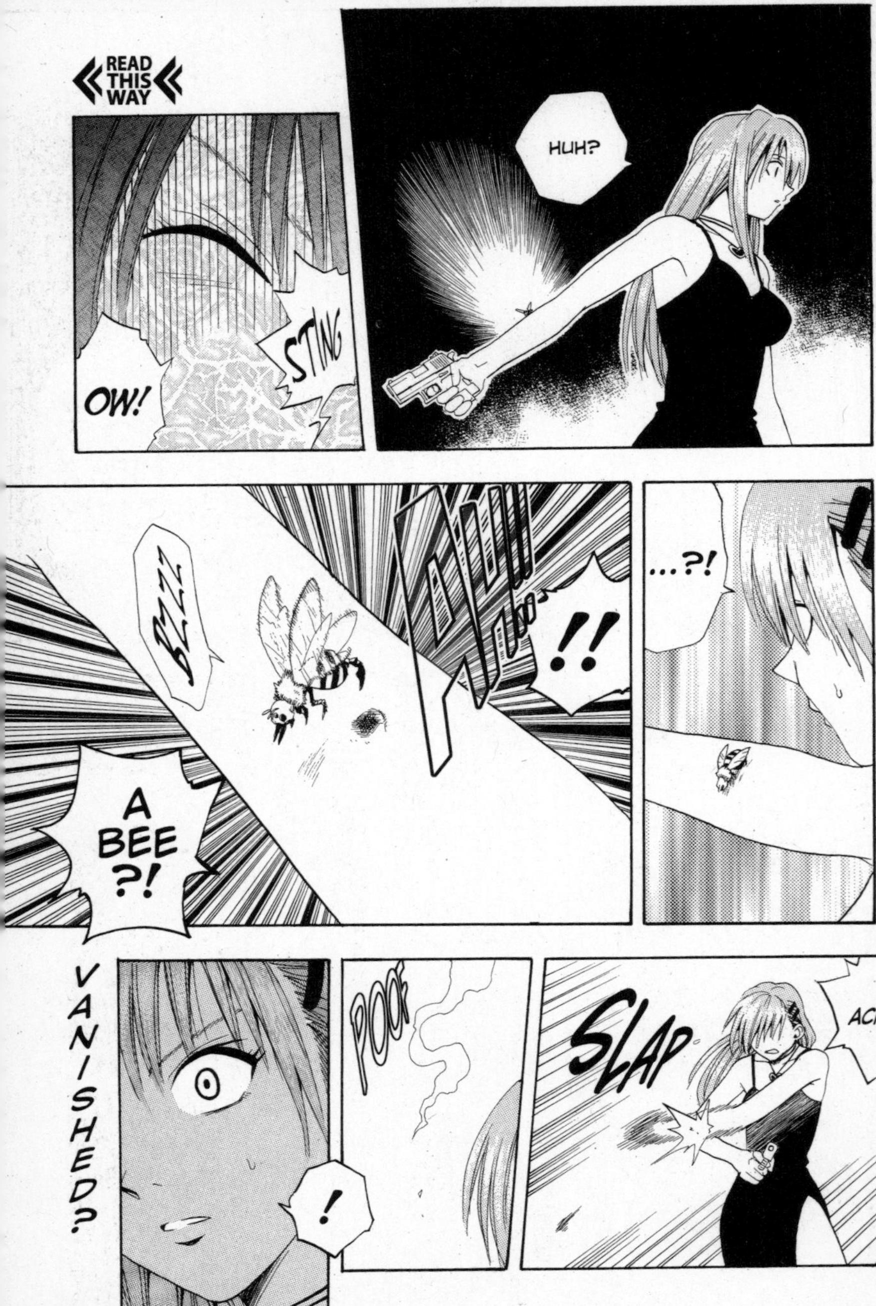
READ THIS WAY
HUH?
STING
OW!
...?!
!!
BZZZ
A BEE?!
ACK!!
SLAP
POOF
!
VANISHED?

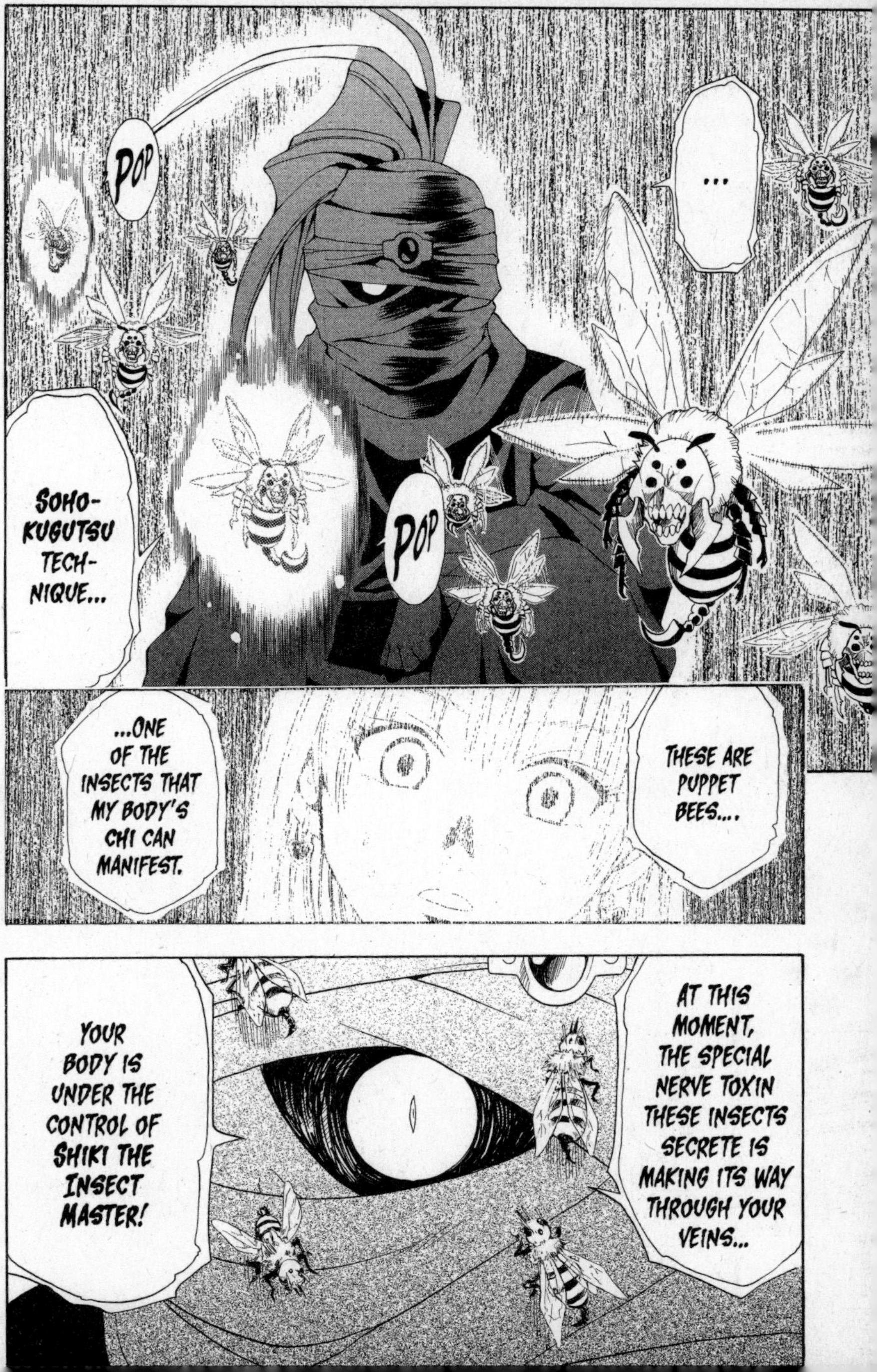
...
POP
POP
SOHO-KUGUTSU TECHNIQUE...
THESE ARE PUPPET BEES....
...ONE OF THE INSECTS THAT MY BODY'S CHI CAN MANIFEST.
AT THIS MOMENT, THE SPECIAL NERVE TOXIN THESE INSECTS SECRETE IS MAKING ITS WAY THROUGH YOUR VEINS...
YOUR BODY IS UNDER THE CONTROL OF SHIKI THE INSECT MASTER!

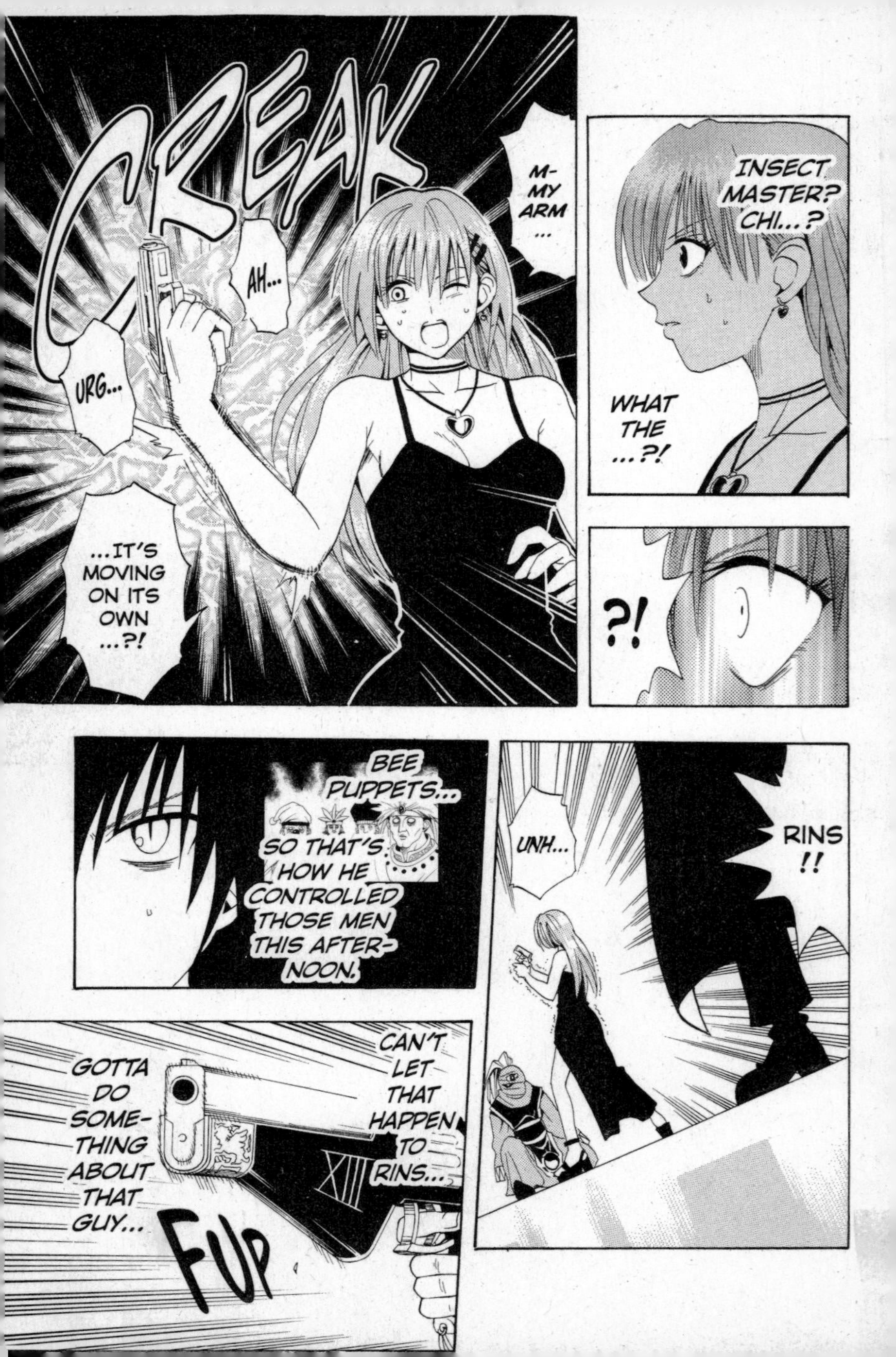
INSECT MASTER? CHI...?
WHAT THE ...?!
?!
M-MY ARM ...
CREAK
AH...
URG...
...IT'S MOVING ON ITS OWN ...?!
RINS !!
UNH...
BEE PUPPETS... SO THAT'S HOW HE CONTROLLED THOSE MEN THIS AFTER-NOON.
CAN'T LET THAT HAPPEN TO RINS...
GOTTA DO SOME-THING ABOUT THAT GUY...
FUP

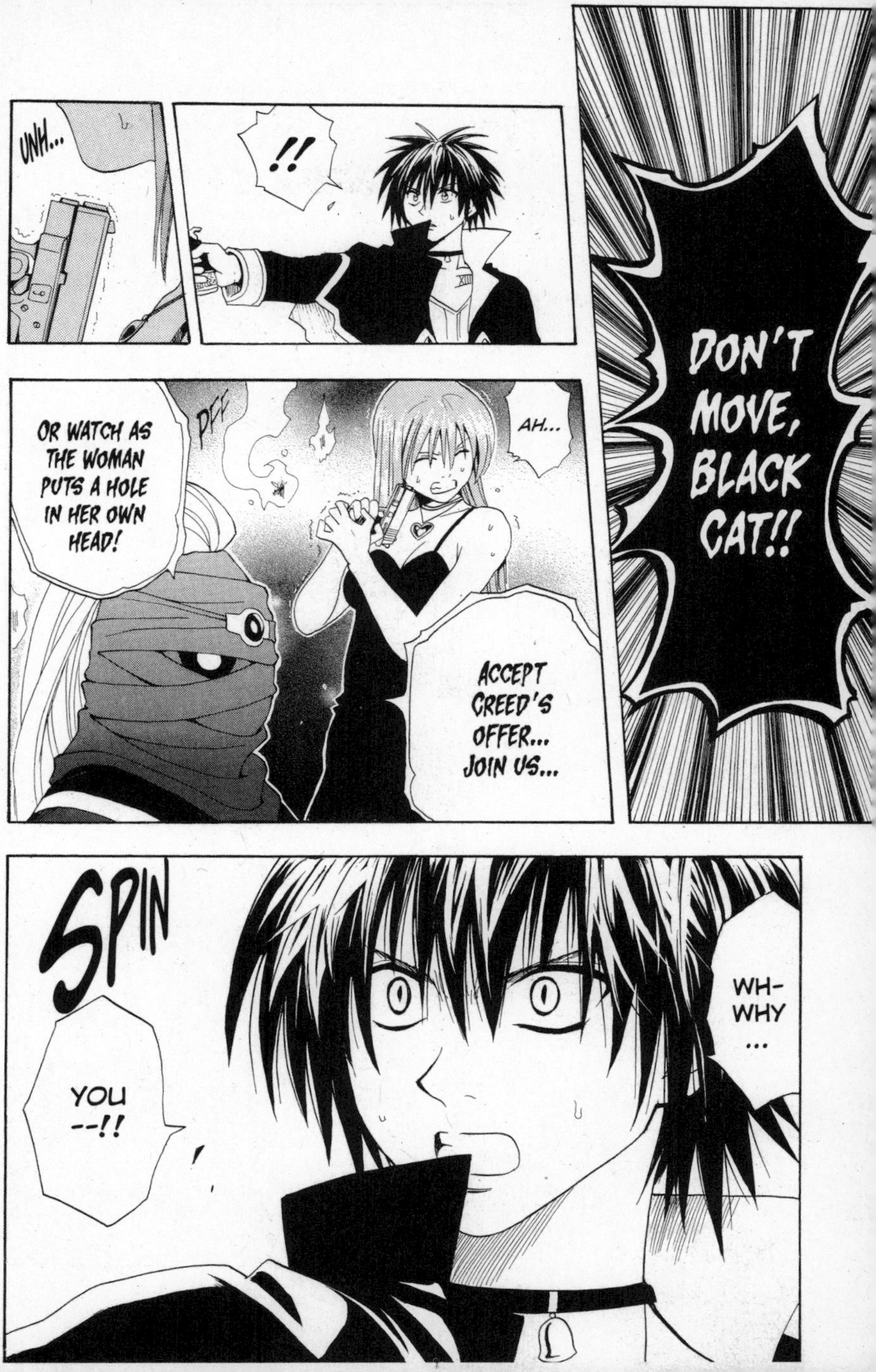
DON'T MOVE, BLACK CAT!!
!!
UNH...
AH...
ACCEPT CREED'S OFFER... JOIN US...
PFF
OR WATCH AS THE WOMAN PUTS A HOLE IN HER OWN HEAD!
WH- WHY ...
SPIN
YOU --!!

READ THIS WAY

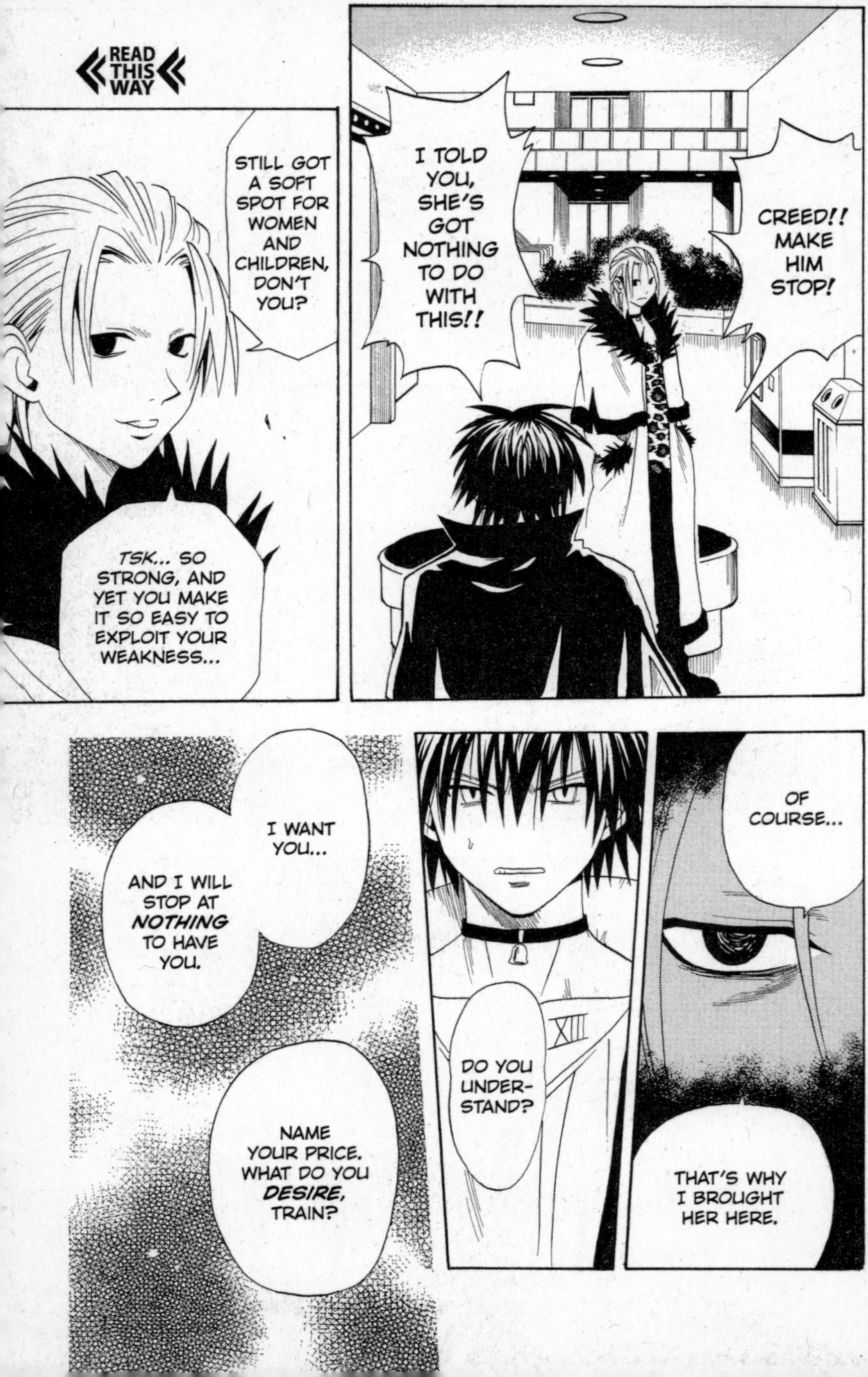
CREED!! MAKE HIM STOP!
I TOLD YOU, SHE'S GOT NOTHING TO DO WITH THIS!!
STILL GOT A SOFT SPOT FOR WOMEN AND CHILDREN, DON'T YOU?
TSK... SO STRONG, AND YET YOU MAKE IT SO EASY TO EXPLOIT YOUR WEAKNESS...
OF COURSE...
THAT'S WHY I BROUGHT HER HERE.
DO YOU UNDER-STAND?
I WANT YOU...
AND I WILL STOP AT NOTHING TO HAVE YOU.
NAME YOUR PRICE. WHAT DO YOU DESIRE, TRAIN?

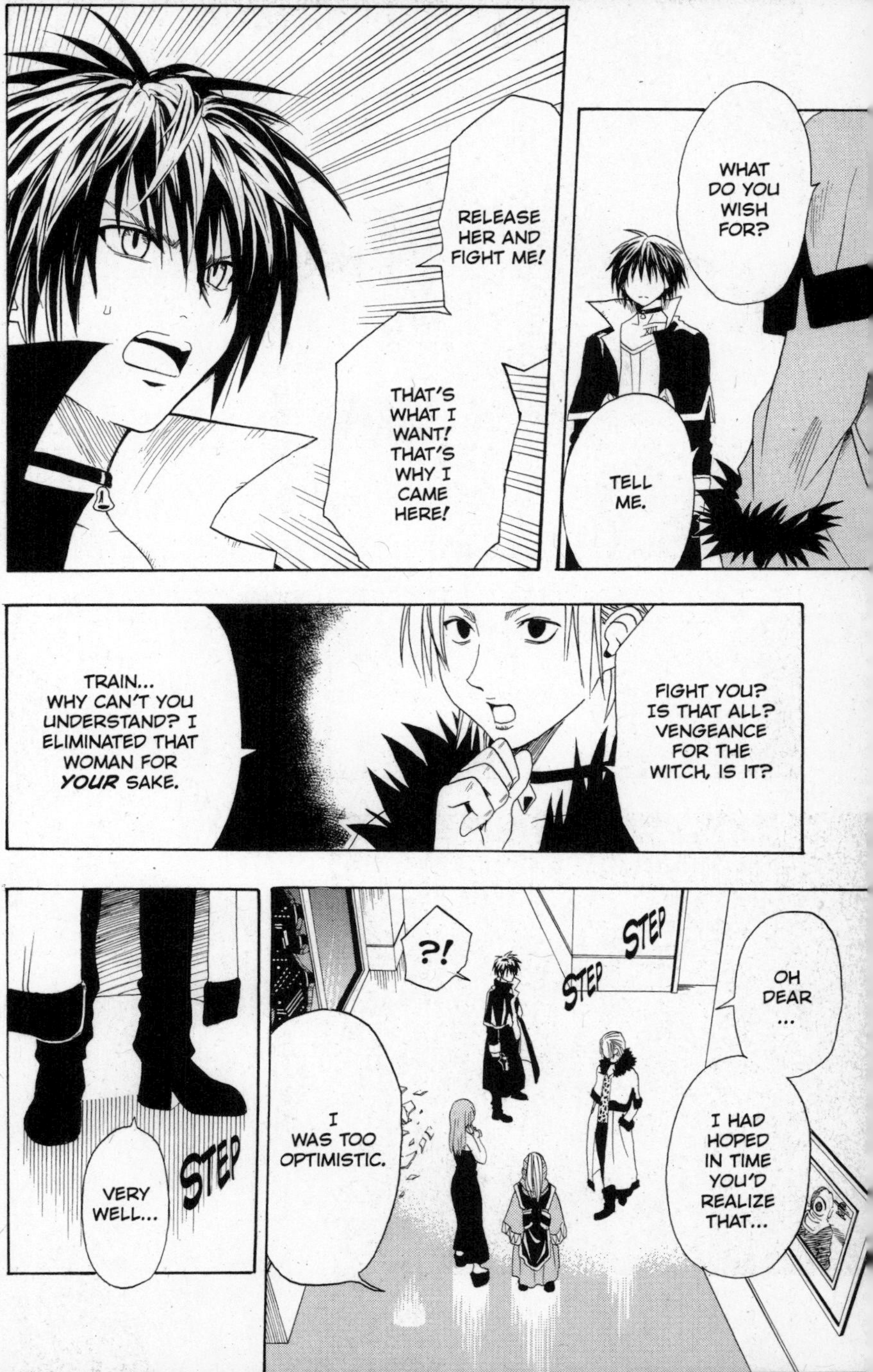
WHAT DO YOU WISH FOR?
TELL ME.
RELEASE HER AND FIGHT ME!
THAT'S WHAT I WANT! THAT'S WHY I CAME HERE!
FIGHT YOU? IS THAT ALL? VENGEANCE FOR THE WITCH, IS IT?
TRAIN... WHY CAN'T YOU UNDERSTAND? I ELIMINATED THAT WOMAN FOR *YOUR* SAKE.
OH DEAR ...
I HAD HOPED IN TIME YOU'D REALIZE THAT...
STEP
STEP
?!
I WAS TOO OPTIMISTIC.
STEP
VERY WELL...

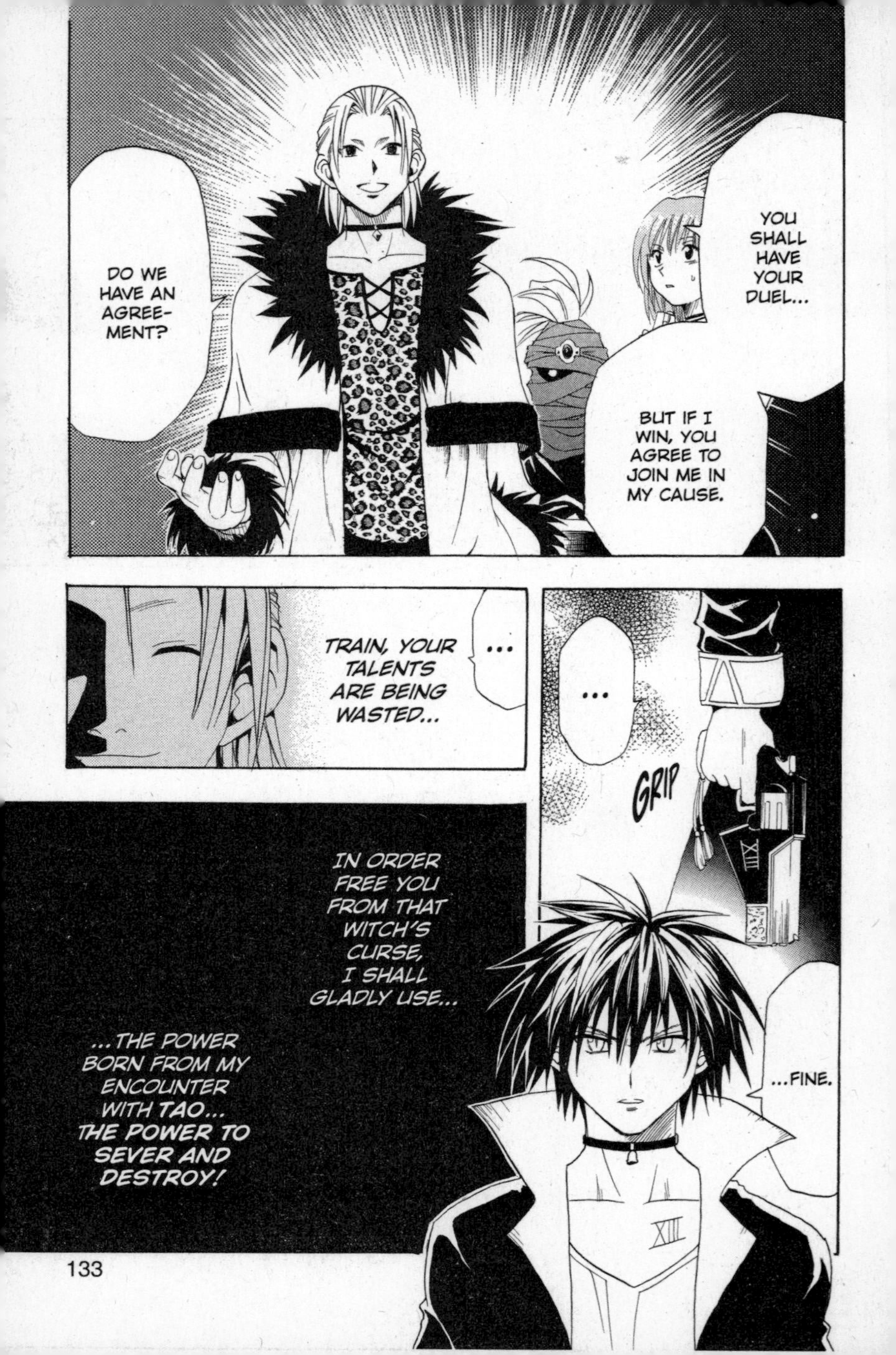
YOU SHALL HAVE YOUR DUEL...
BUT IF I WIN, YOU AGREE TO JOIN ME IN MY CAUSE.
DO WE HAVE AN AGREEMENT?
...
GRIP
...FINE.
...
TRAIN, YOUR TALENTS ARE BEING WASTED...
IN ORDER FREE YOU FROM THAT WITCH'S CURSE, I SHALL GLADLY USE...
...THE POWER BORN FROM MY ENCOUNTER WITH TAO... THE POWER TO SEVER AND DESTROY!

◎ ON A WHIM, I'M INCLUDING SOME PICTURES I DREW FOR THE NEW YEAR'S CARDS THAT I SENT TO MY ASSISTANTS AND FRIENDS THIS YEAR (2001).

NEW YEAR'S CARD PICS I

RINSLET WALKER

EVE ①

KYOKO KIRISAKI ①

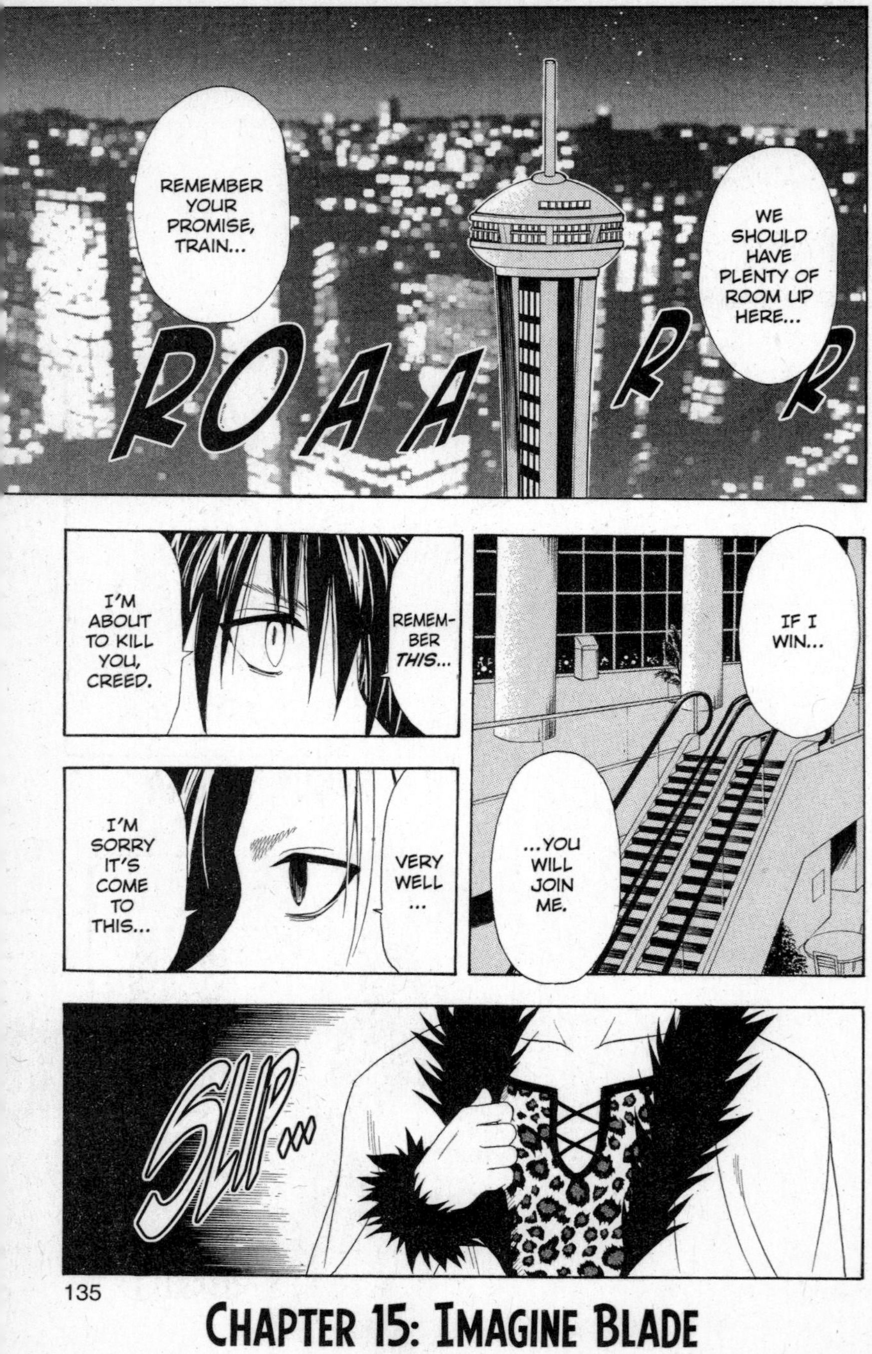
WE SHOULD HAVE PLENTY OF ROOM UP HERE...
REMEMBER YOUR PROMISE, TRAIN...
ROAARR
IF I WIN...
...YOU WILL JOIN ME.
REMEMBER THIS...
I'M ABOUT TO KILL YOU, CREED.
VERY WELL...
I'M SORRY IT'S COME TO THIS...
SLIP...

Chapter 15: Imagine Blade

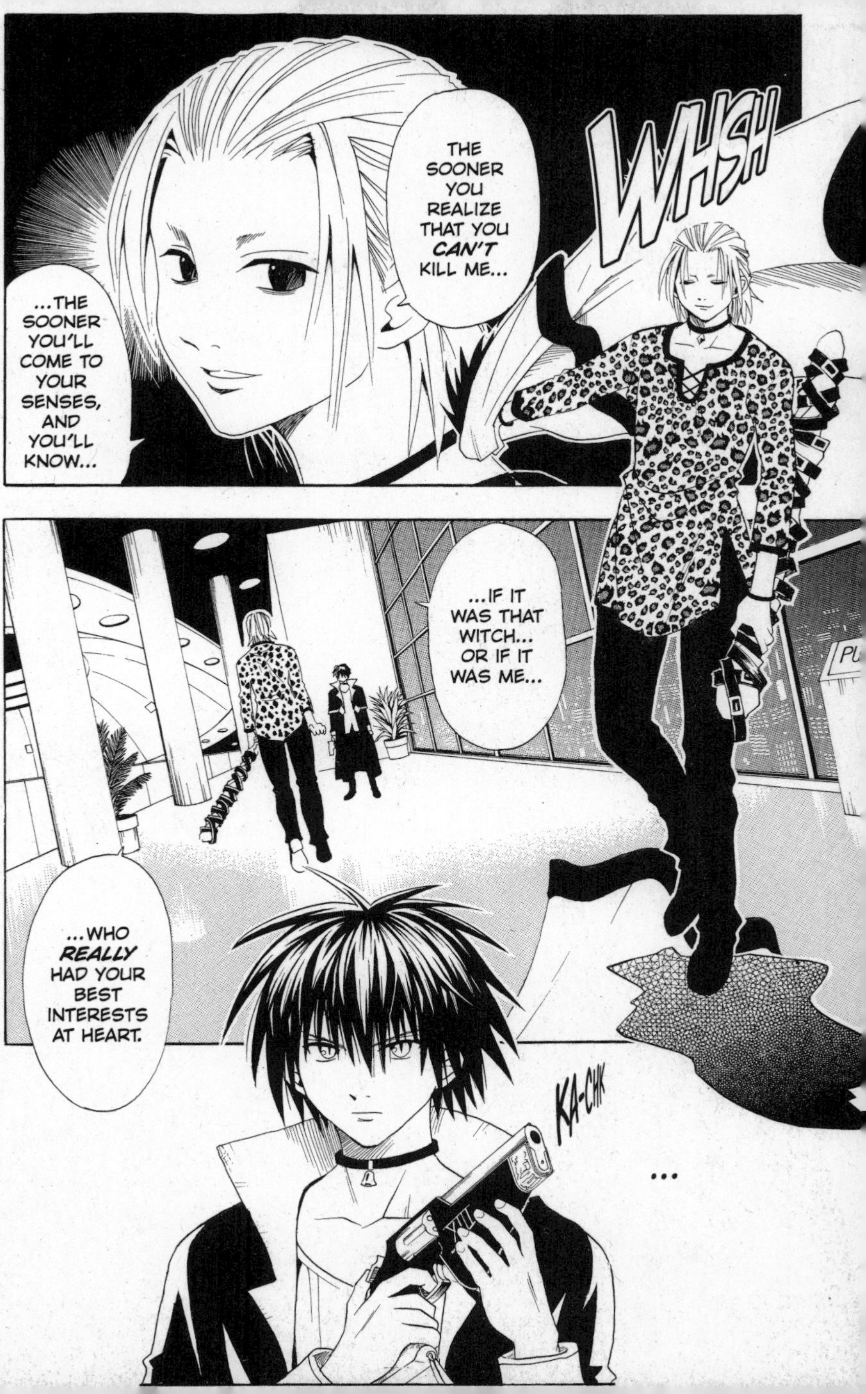
WHSH
THE SOONER YOU REALIZE THAT YOU CAN'T KILL ME...
...THE SOONER YOU'LL COME TO YOUR SENSES, AND YOU'LL KNOW...
...IF IT WAS THAT WITCH... OR IF IT WAS ME...
...WHO REALLY HAD YOUR BEST INTERESTS AT HEART.
KA-CHK
...

Chapter 15: Imagine Blade

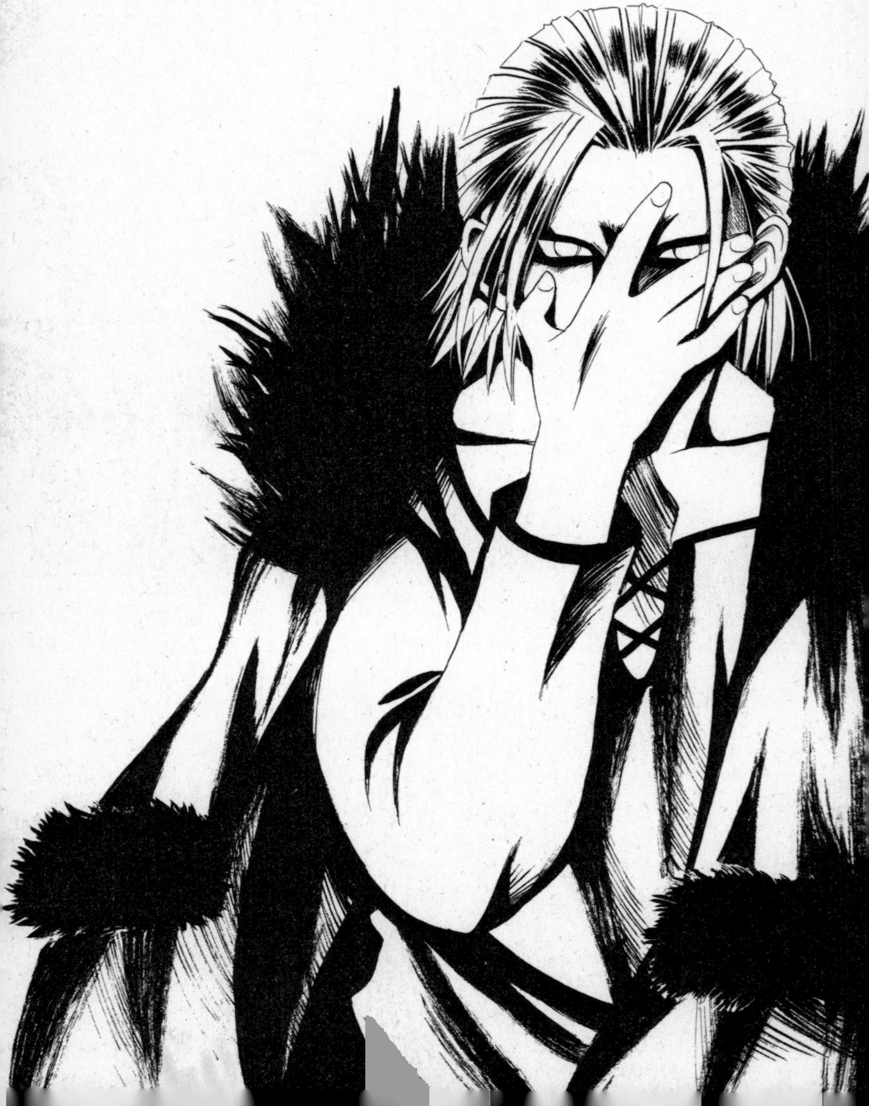

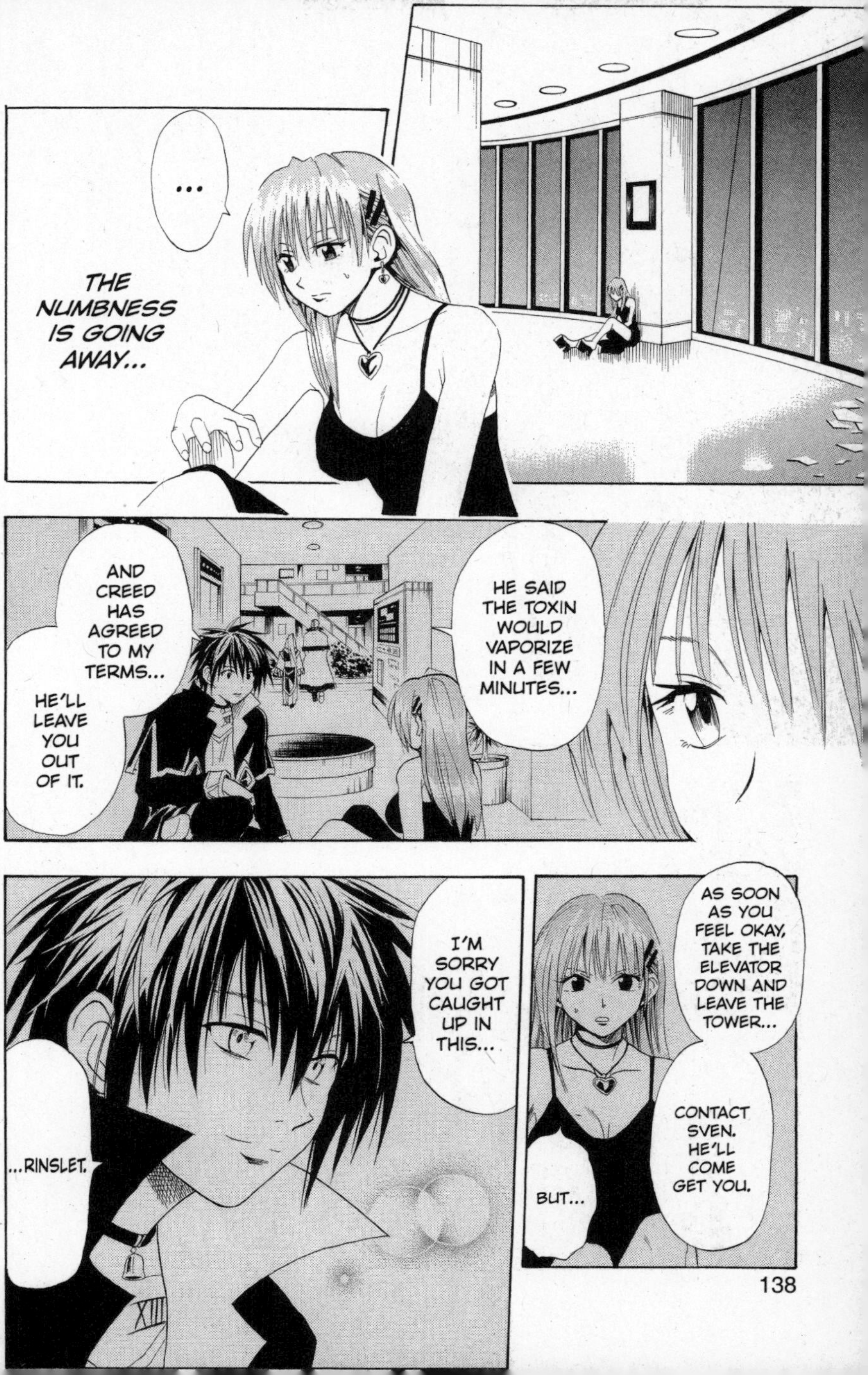
...
THE NUMBNESS IS GOING AWAY...
HE SAID THE TOXIN WOULD VAPORIZE IN A FEW MINUTES...
AND CREED HAS AGREED TO MY TERMS...
HE'LL LEAVE YOU OUT OF IT.
AS SOON AS YOU FEEL OKAY, TAKE THE ELEVATOR DOWN AND LEAVE THE TOWER...
CONTACT SVEN. HE'LL COME GET YOU.
BUT...
I'M SORRY YOU GOT CAUGHT UP IN THIS...
...RINSLET.

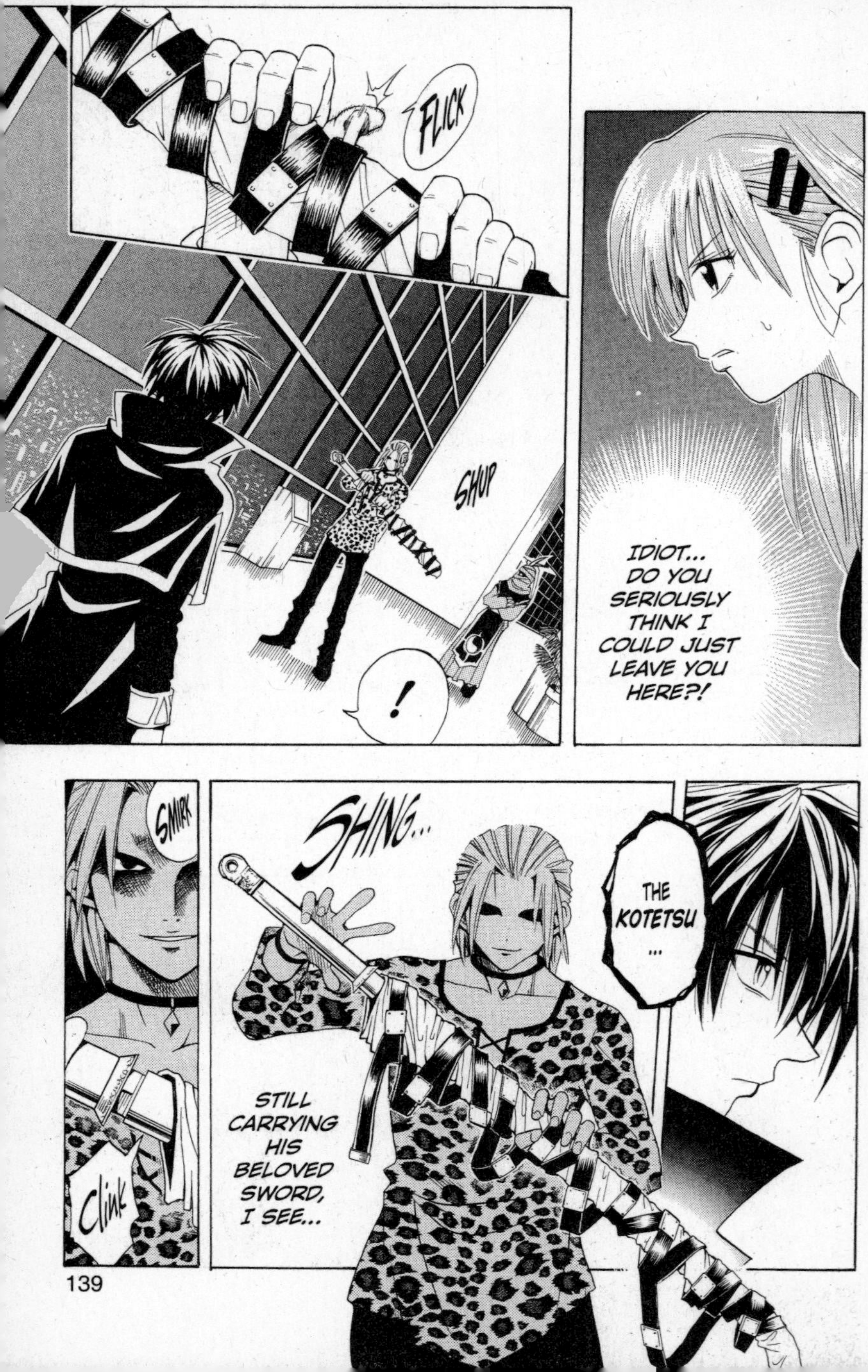
IDIOT... DO YOU SERIOUSLY THINK I COULD JUST LEAVE YOU HERE?!
FLICK
SHUP
!
THE KOTETSU ...
SHING...
STILL CARRYING HIS BELOVED SWORD, I SEE...
SMIRK
Clink

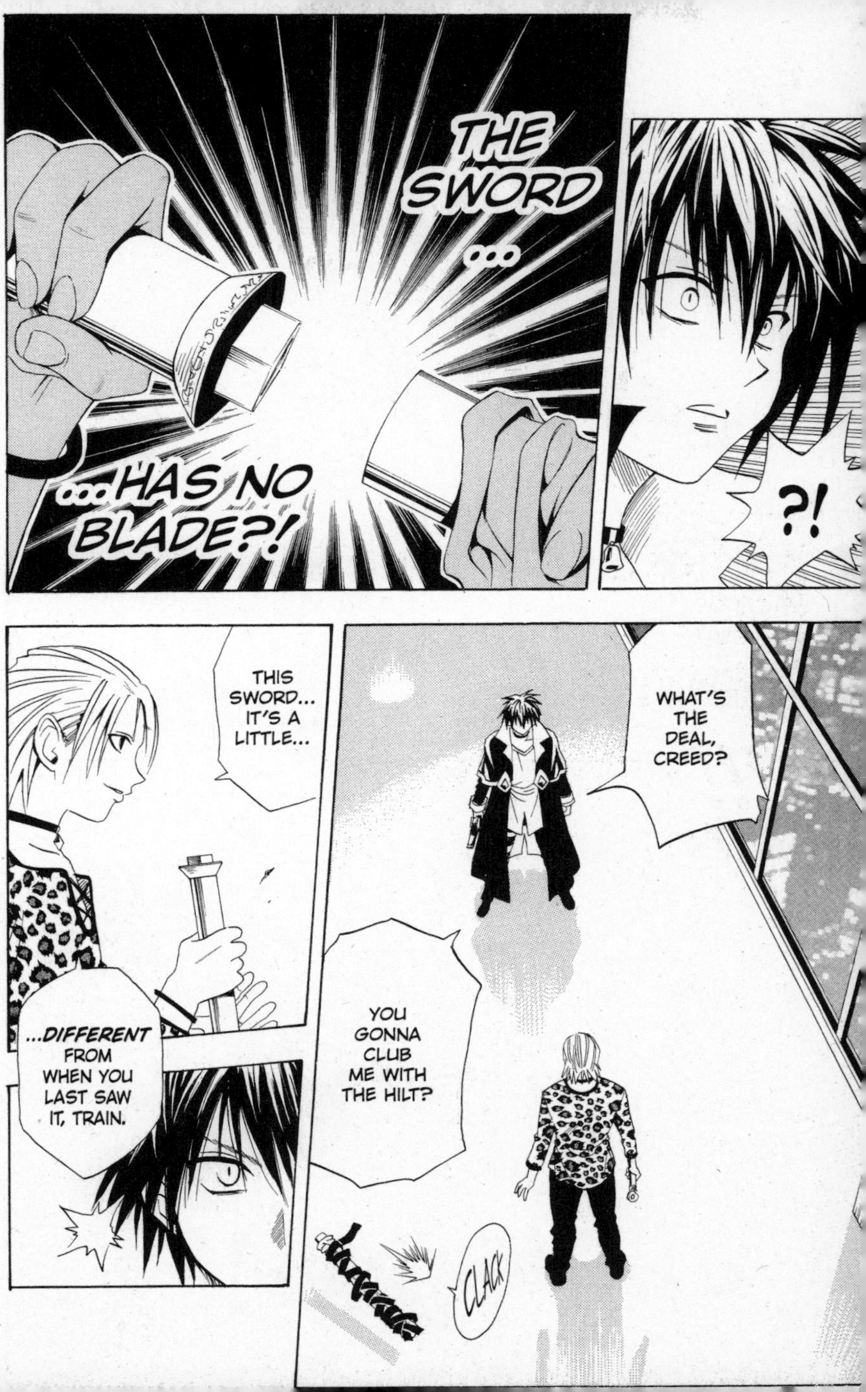
?!
THE SWORD ...
...HAS NO BLADE?!
WHAT'S THE DEAL, CREED?
YOU GONNA CLUB ME WITH THE HILT?
CLACK
THIS SWORD... IT'S A LITTLE...
...*DIFFERENT* FROM WHEN YOU LAST SAW IT, TRAIN.

READ THIS WAY

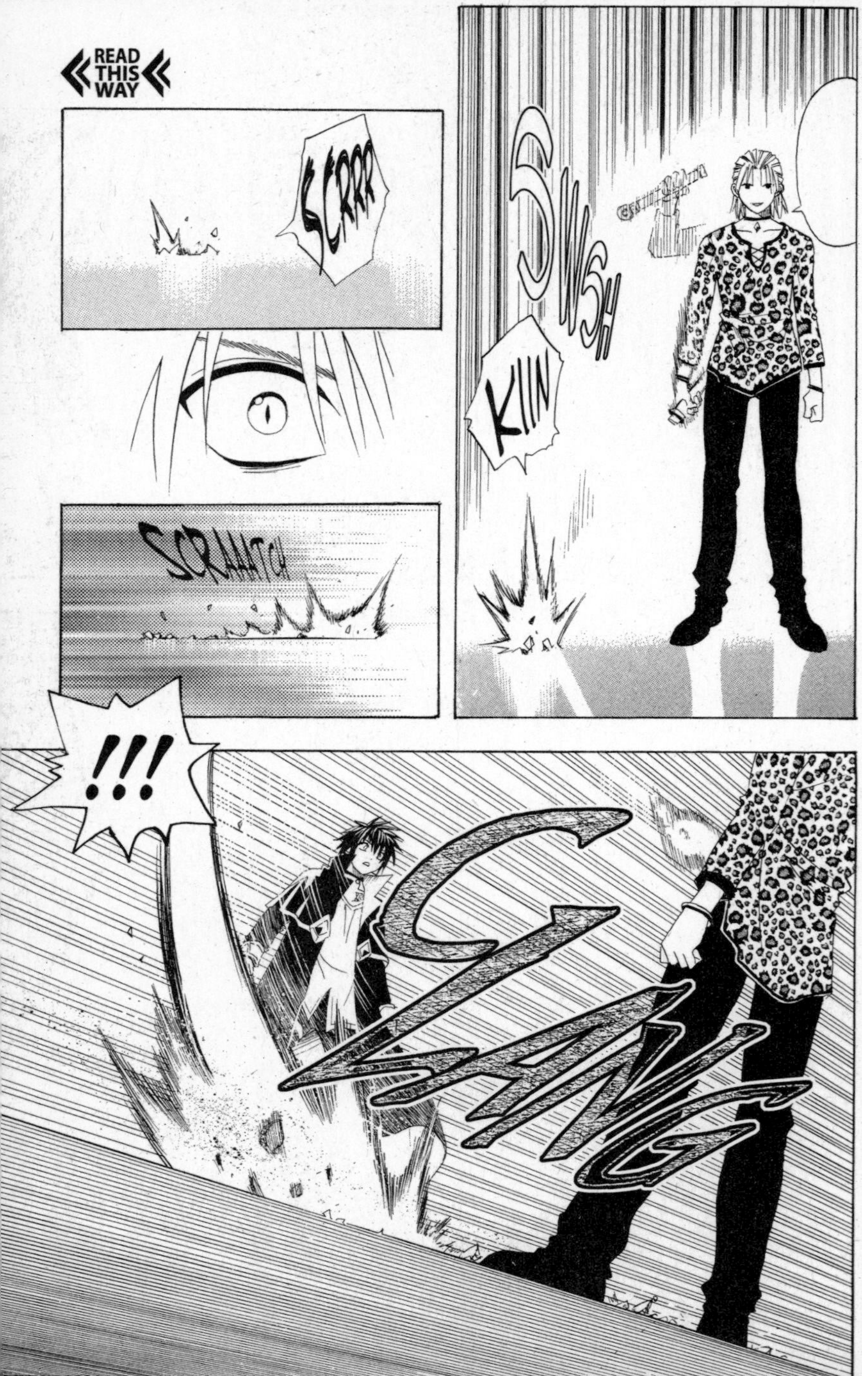
SWISH
KIIN
SCRRR
SCRAATCH
!!!
CLANG

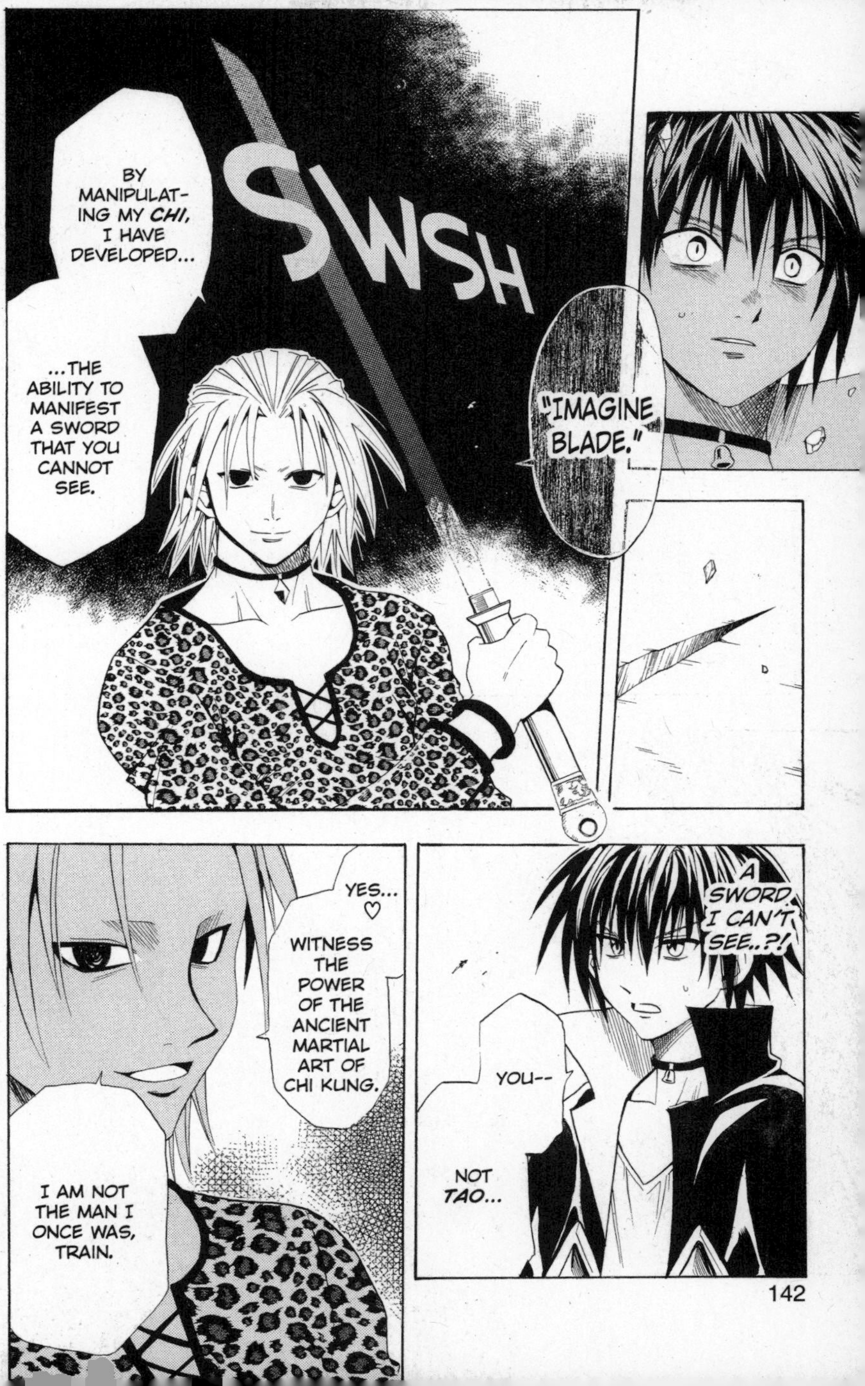
BY MANIPULATING MY *CHI*, I HAVE DEVELOPED...
...THE ABILITY TO MANIFEST A SWORD THAT YOU CANNOT SEE.
SWSH
"IMAGINE BLADE."
A SWORD I CAN'T SEE..?!
YOU--
NOT *TAO*...
YES... ♡
WITNESS THE POWER OF THE ANCIENT MARTIAL ART OF CHI KUNG.
I AM NOT THE MAN I ONCE WAS, TRAIN.

READ THIS WAY

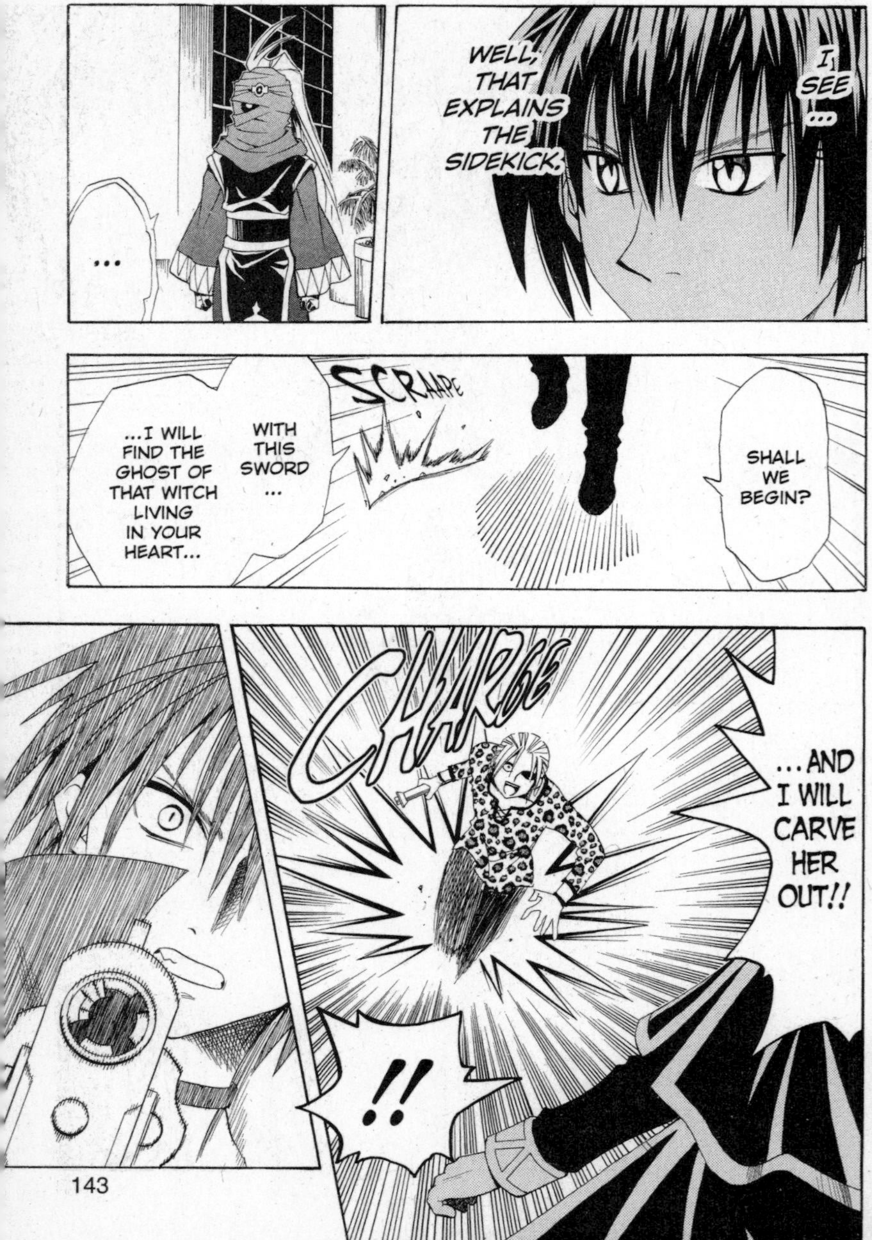
I SEE ...
WELL, THAT EXPLAINS THE SIDEKICK.
...
SHALL WE BEGIN?
SCRAAPE
WITH THIS SWORD ...
...I WILL FIND THE GHOST OF THAT WITCH LIVING IN YOUR HEART...
...AND I WILL CARVE HER OUT!!
CHARGE
!!

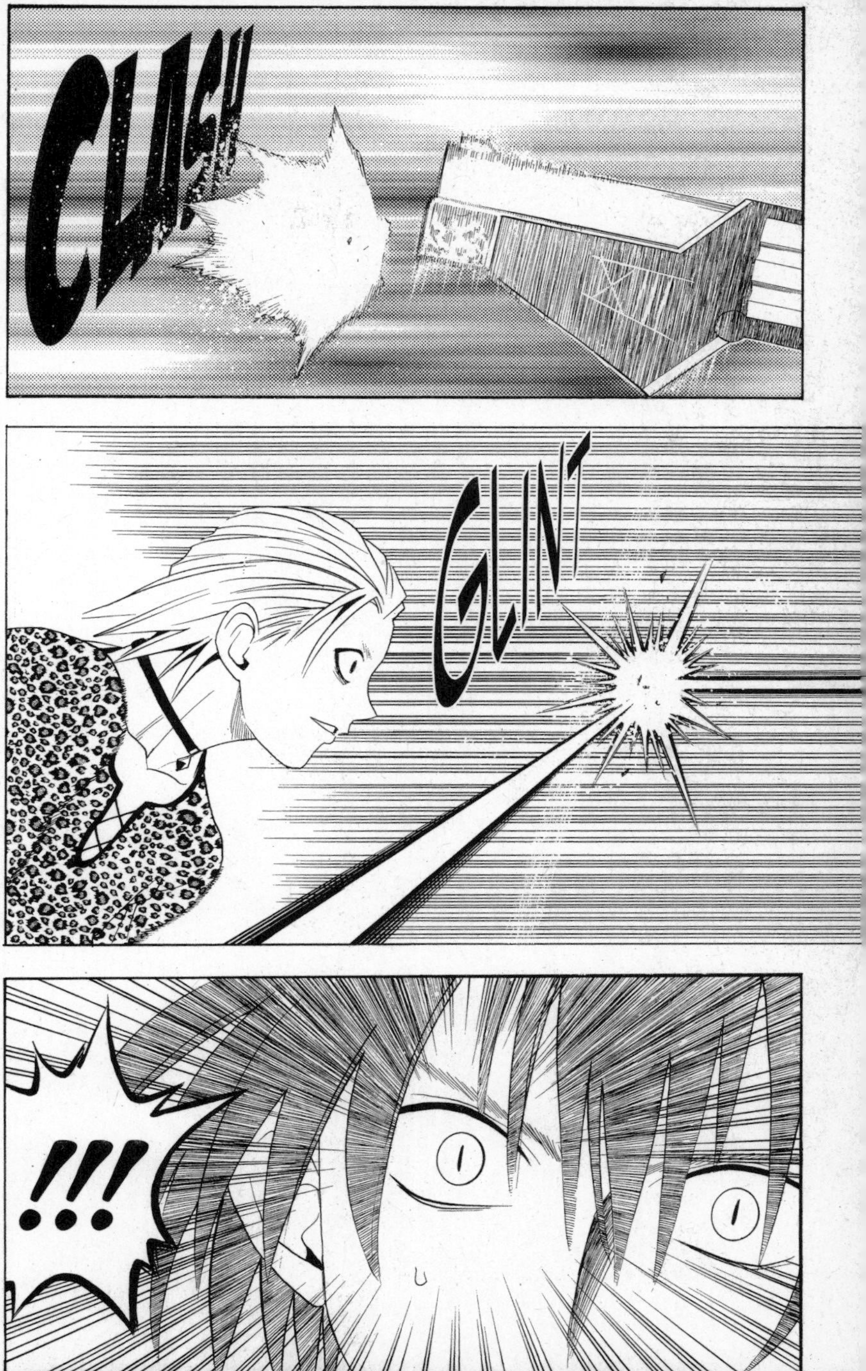
CLASH
GLINT
!!!

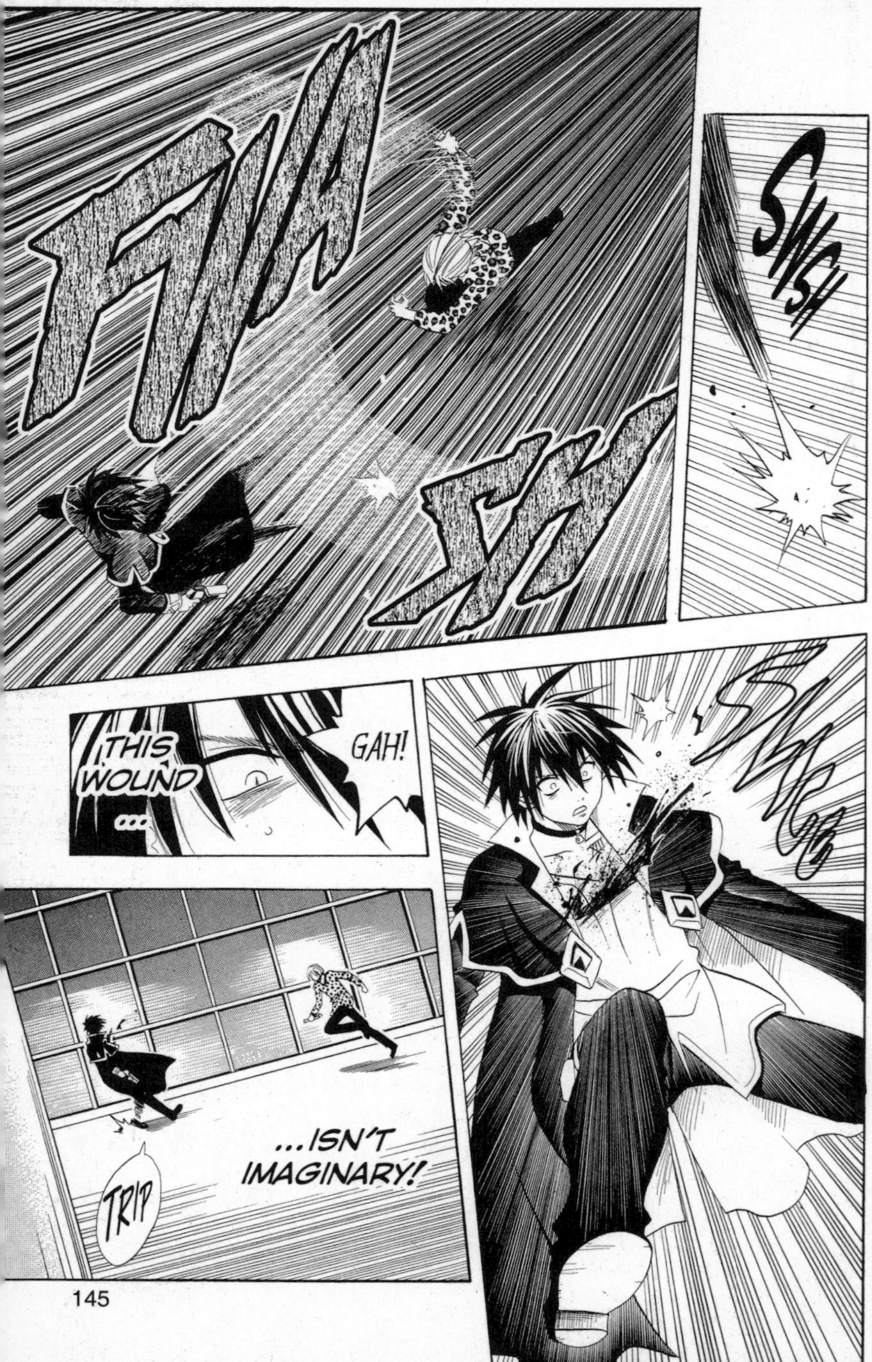
SWISH
GAH!
THIS WOUND ...
...ISN'T IMAGINARY!
TRIP

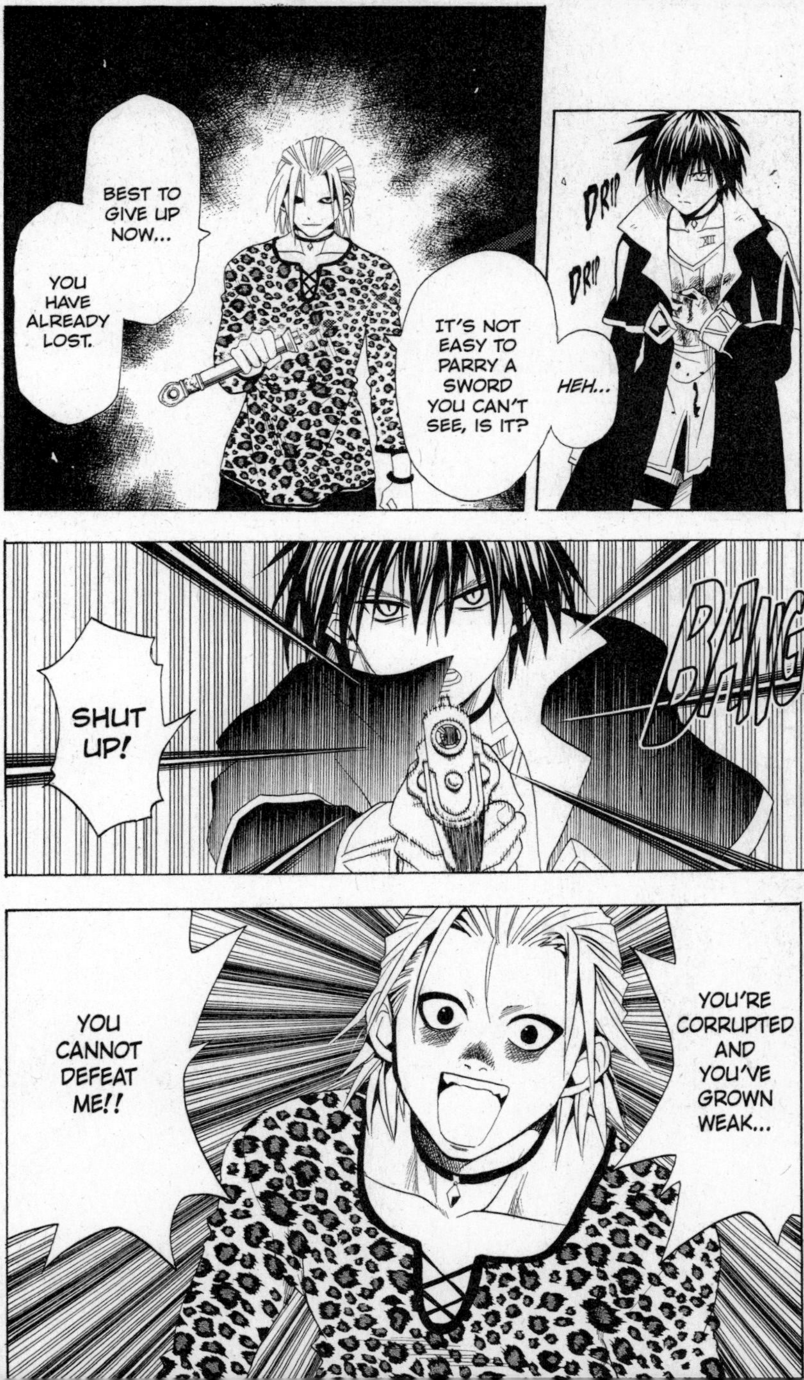
DRIP
DRIP
HEH...
IT'S NOT EASY TO PARRY A SWORD YOU CAN'T SEE, IS IT?
BEST TO GIVE UP NOW...
YOU HAVE ALREADY LOST.
BANG
SHUT UP!
YOU'RE CORRUPTED AND YOU'VE GROWN WEAK...
YOU CANNOT DEFEAT ME!!

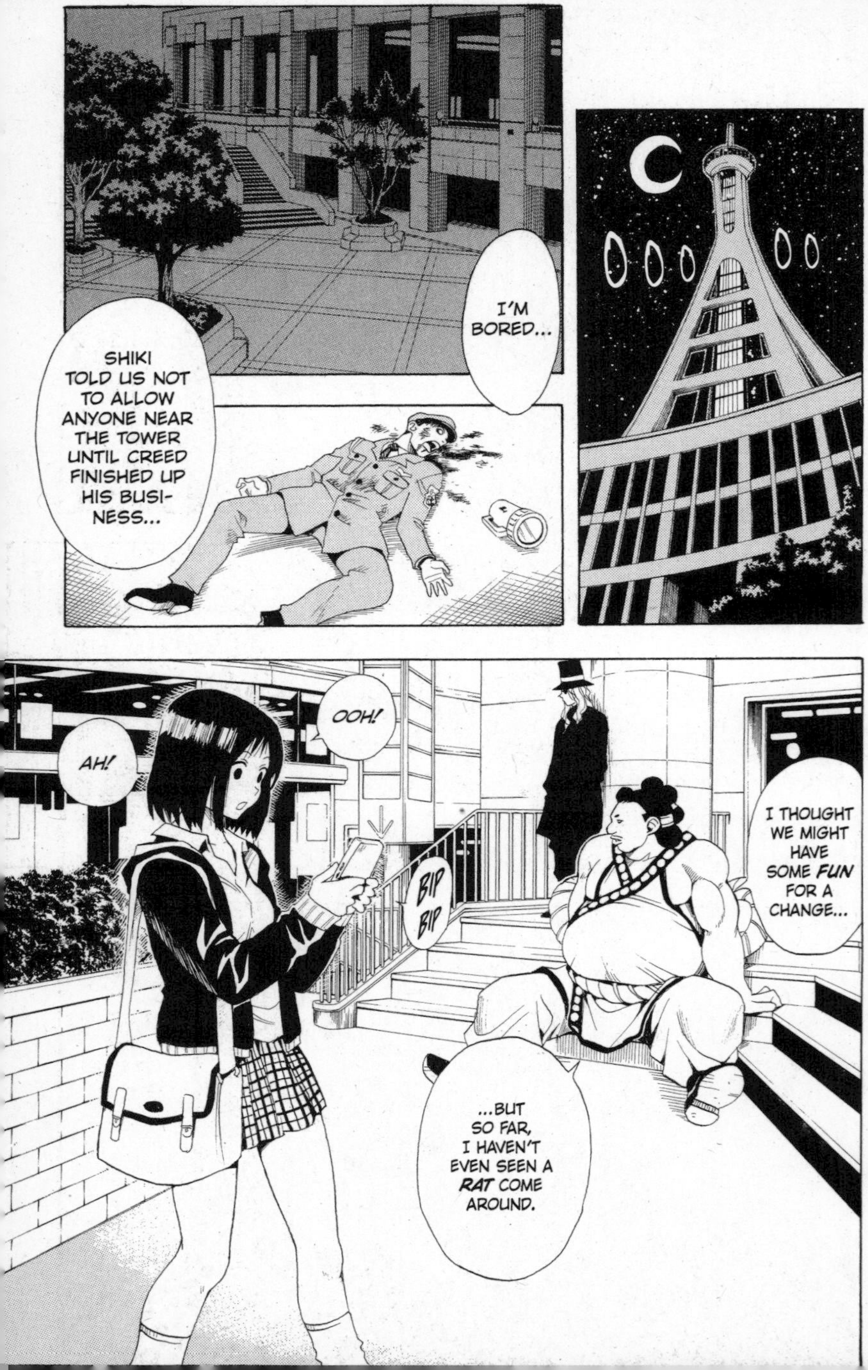
I'M BORED...
SHIKI TOLD US NOT TO ALLOW ANYONE NEAR THE TOWER UNTIL CREED FINISHED UP HIS BUSINESS...
I THOUGHT WE MIGHT HAVE SOME FUN FOR A CHANGE...
...BUT SO FAR, I HAVEN'T EVEN SEEN A RAT COME AROUND.
OOH!
BIP BIP
AH!

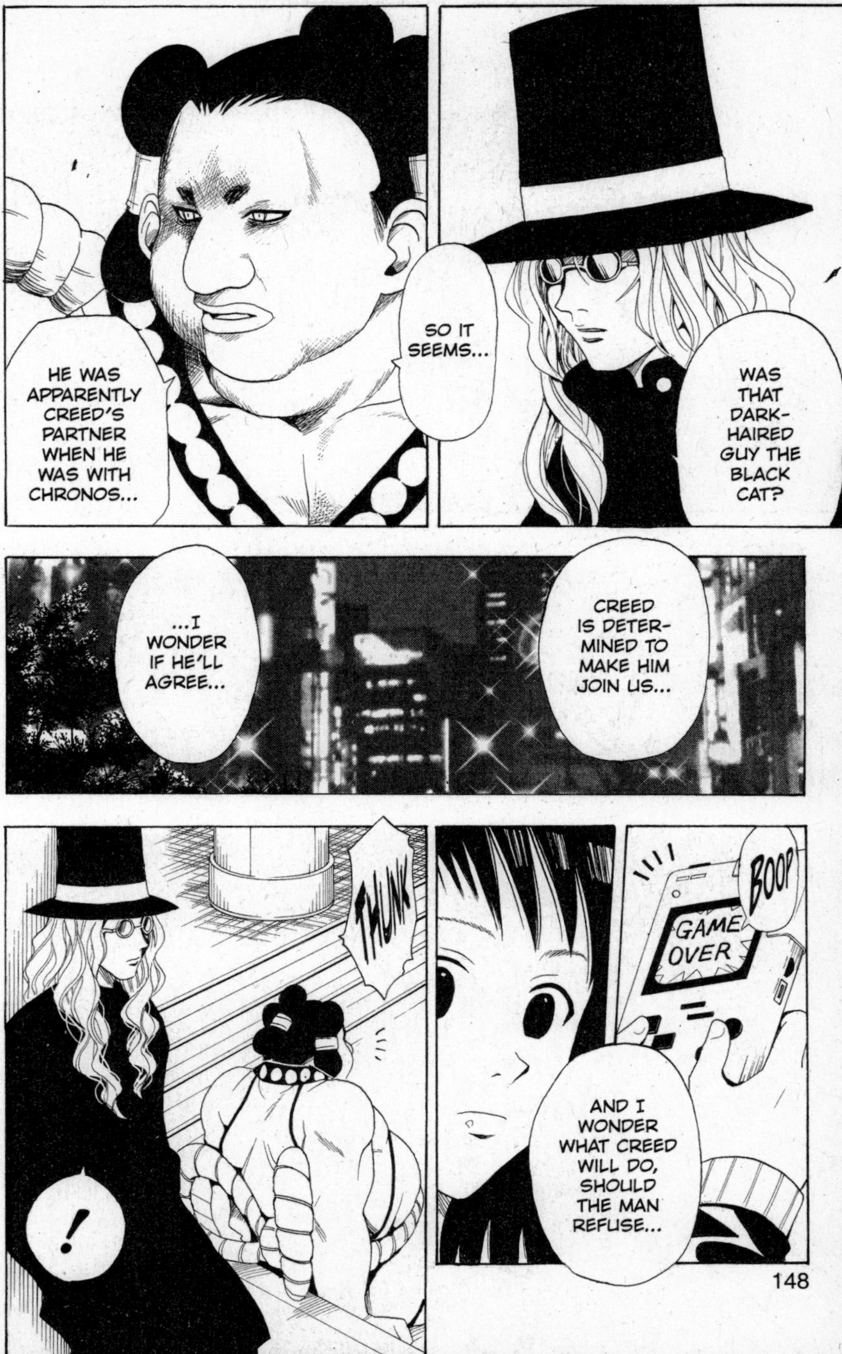
WAS THAT DARK-HAIRED GUY THE BLACK CAT?
SO IT SEEMS...
HE WAS APPARENTLY CREED'S PARTNER WHEN HE WAS WITH CHRONOS...
CREED IS DETERMINED TO MAKE HIM JOIN US...
...I WONDER IF HE'LL AGREE...
BOOP
GAME OVER
AND I WONDER WHAT CREED WILL DO, SHOULD THE MAN REFUSE...
THUNK
!

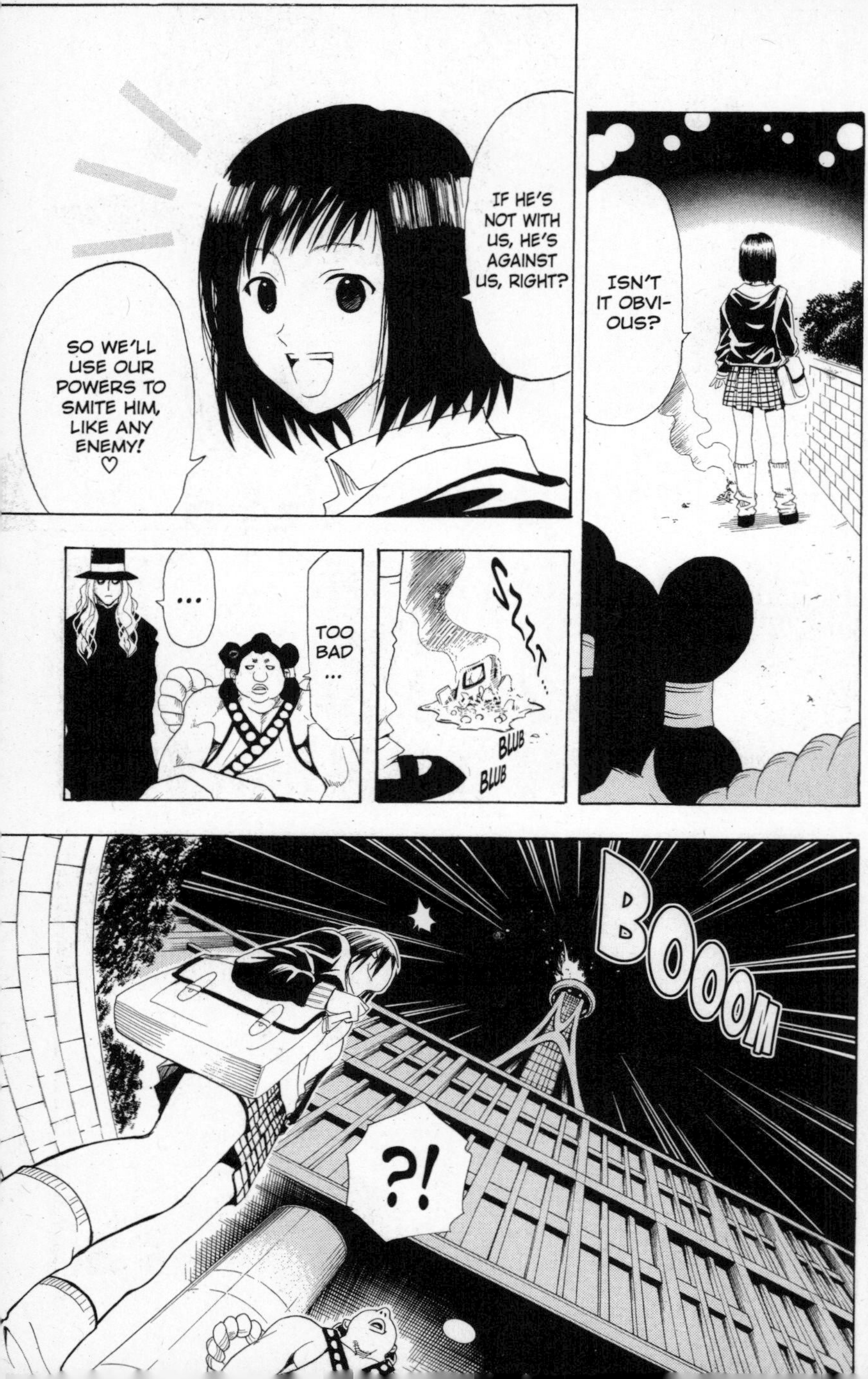
ISN'T IT OBVI-OUS?
IF HE'S NOT WITH US, HE'S AGAINST US, RIGHT?
SO WE'LL USE OUR POWERS TO SMITE HIM, LIKE ANY ENEMY! ♡
SZZZT...
BLUB
BLUB
TOO BAD...
...
BOOOOM
?!

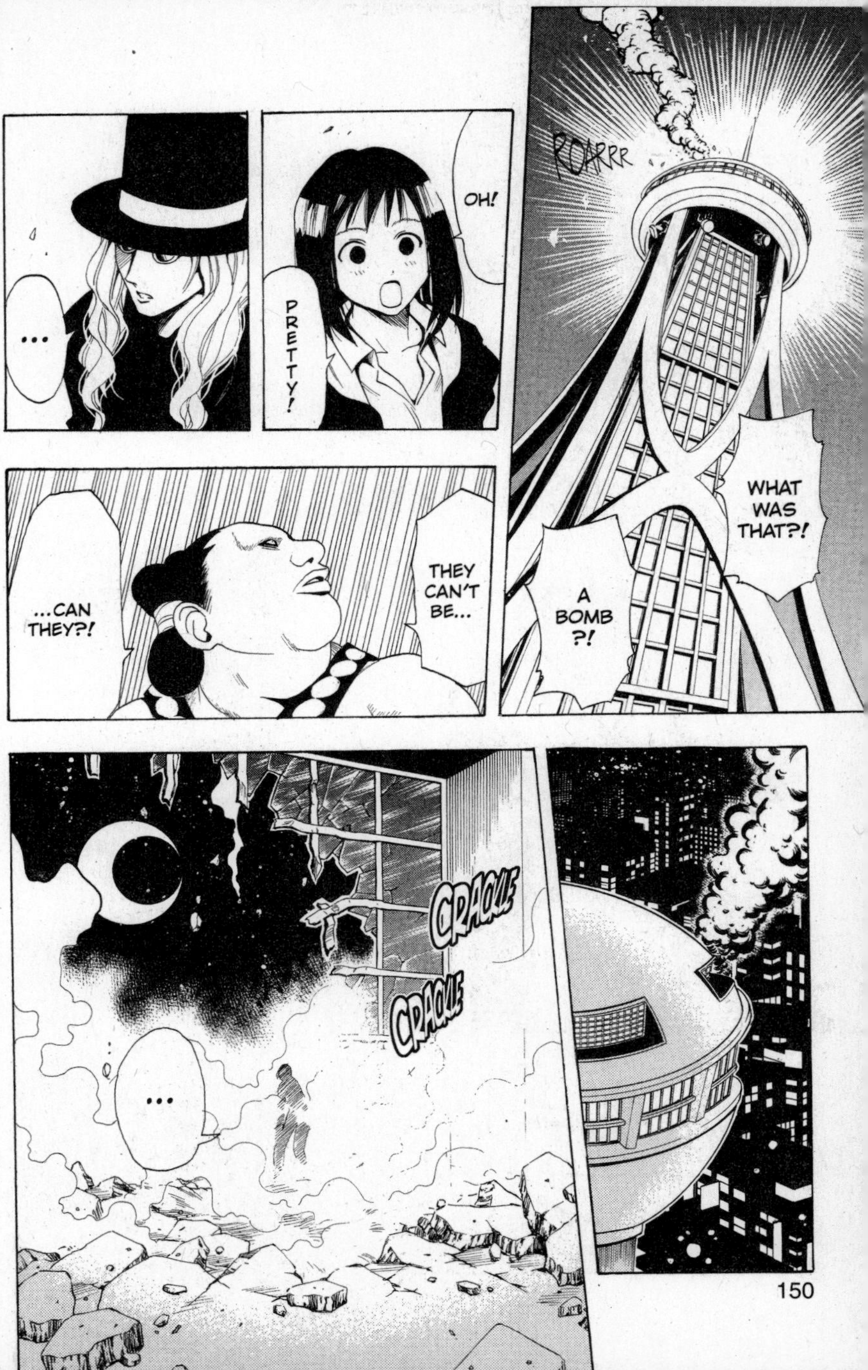
ROARRR
WHAT WAS THAT?!
A BOMB ?!
OH!
PRETTY!
...
THEY CAN'T BE...
...CAN THEY?!
CRACKLE
CRACKLE
...

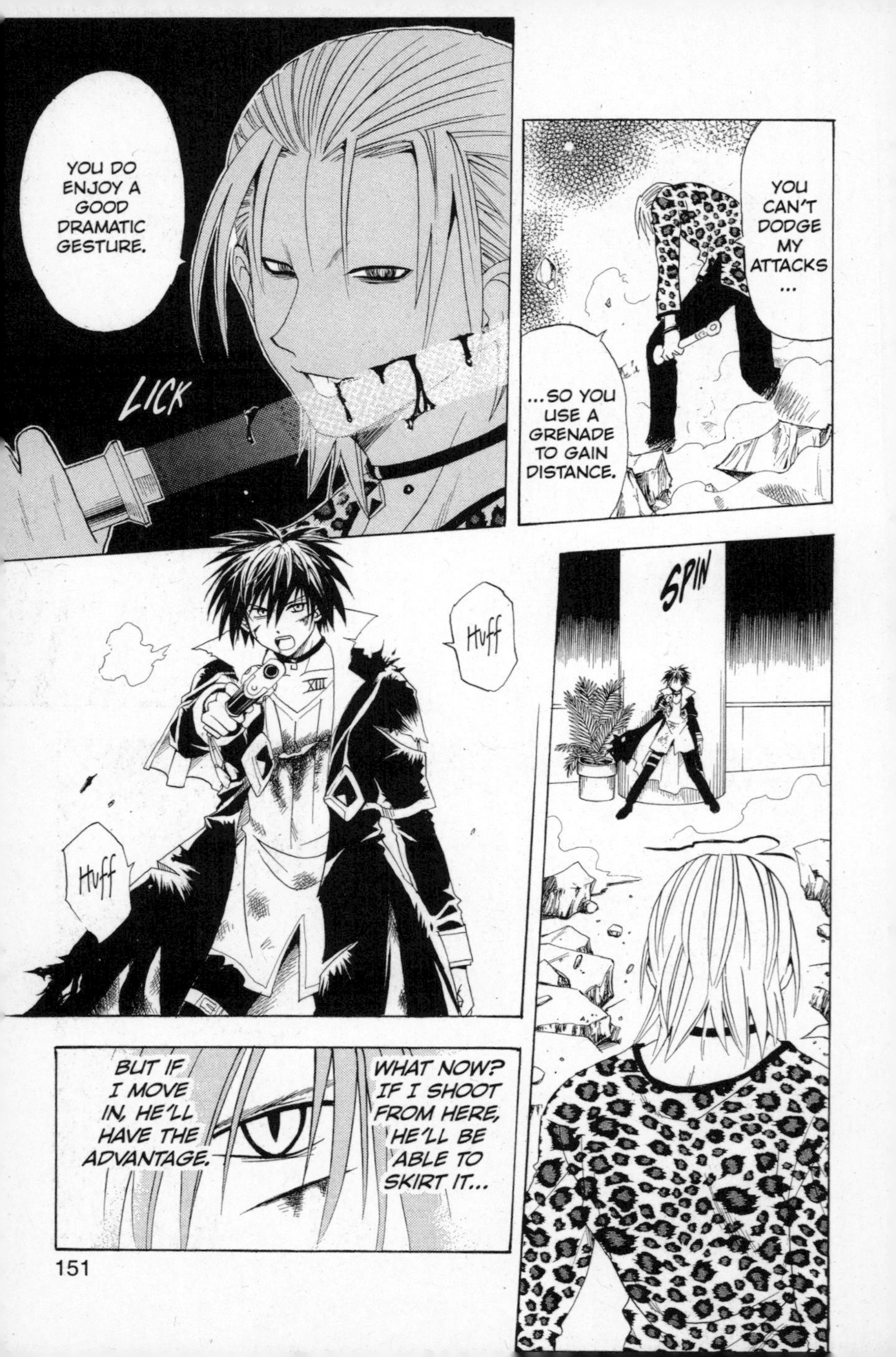
YOU CAN'T DODGE MY ATTACKS ...
...SO YOU USE A GRENADE TO GAIN DISTANCE.
YOU DO ENJOY A GOOD DRAMATIC GESTURE.
LICK
SPIN
Huff
Huff
WHAT NOW? IF I SHOOT FROM HERE, HE'LL BE ABLE TO SKIRT IT...
BUT IF I MOVE IN, HE'LL HAVE THE ADVANTAGE.

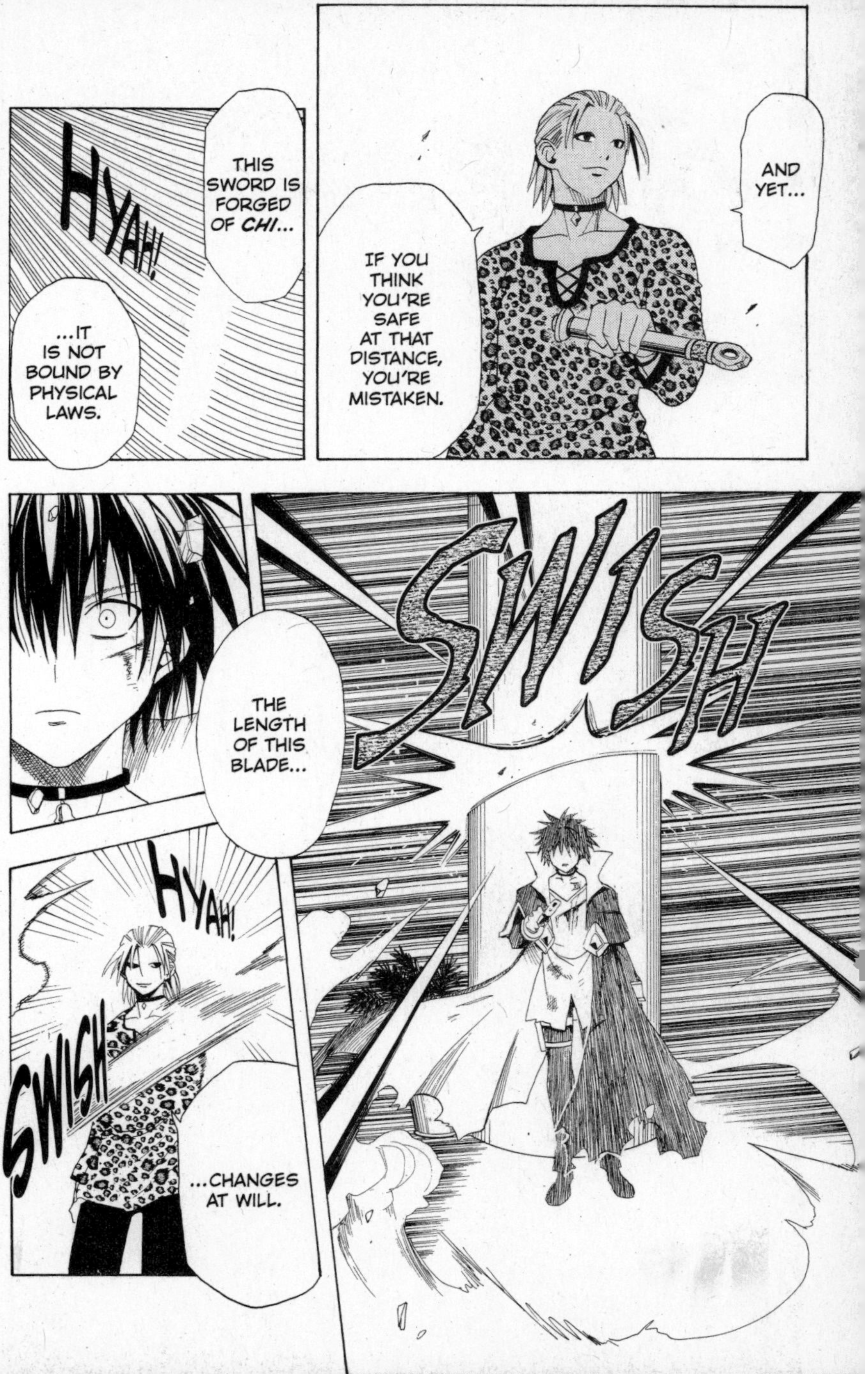
AND YET...
IF YOU THINK YOU'RE SAFE AT THAT DISTANCE, YOU'RE MISTAKEN.
HYAH!
THIS SWORD IS FORGED OF *CHI*...
...IT IS NOT BOUND BY PHYSICAL LAWS.
SWISH
THE LENGTH OF THIS BLADE...
HYAH!
SWISH
...CHANGES AT WILL.

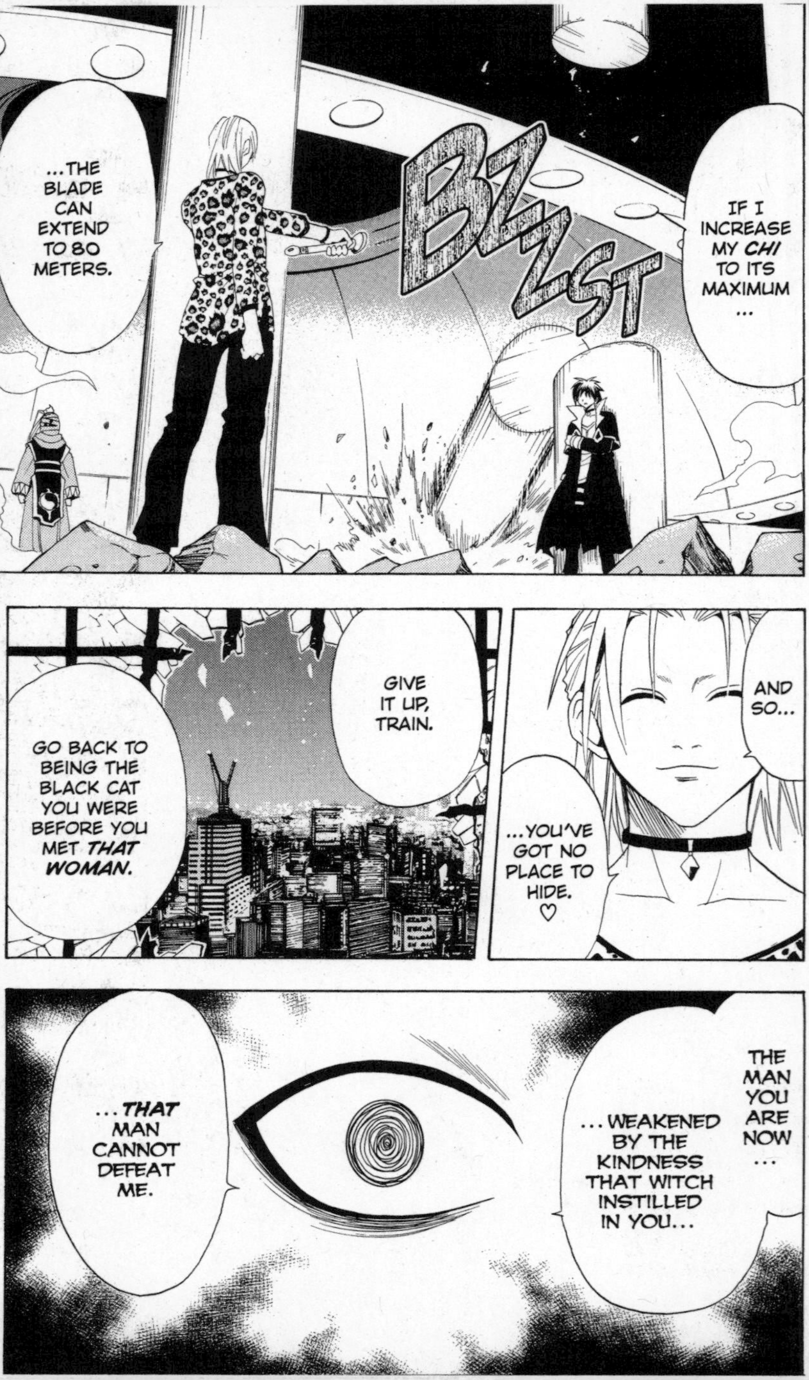
IF I INCREASE MY *CHI* TO ITS MAXIMUM ...
BZZST
...THE BLADE CAN EXTEND TO 80 METERS.
AND SO...
...YOU'VE GOT NO PLACE TO HIDE. ♡
GIVE IT UP, TRAIN.
GO BACK TO BEING THE BLACK CAT YOU WERE BEFORE YOU MET *THAT WOMAN*.
THE MAN YOU ARE NOW ...
...WEAKENED BY THE KINDNESS THAT WITCH INSTILLED IN YOU...
...*THAT* MAN CANNOT DEFEAT ME.

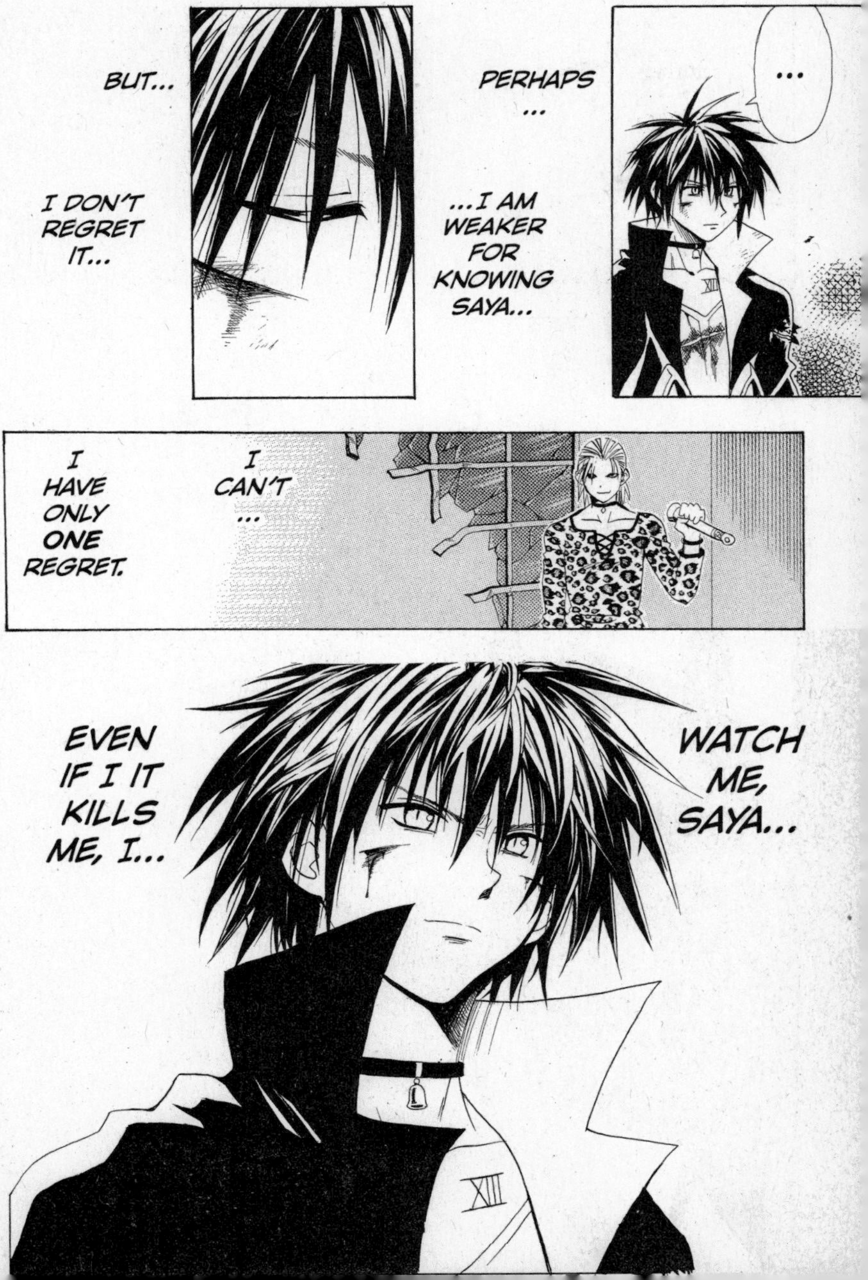
...
PERHAPS ...
...I AM WEAKER FOR KNOWING SAYA...
BUT...
I DON'T REGRET IT...
I CAN'T ...
I HAVE ONLY ONE REGRET.
WATCH ME, SAYA...
EVEN IF I IT KILLS ME, I...

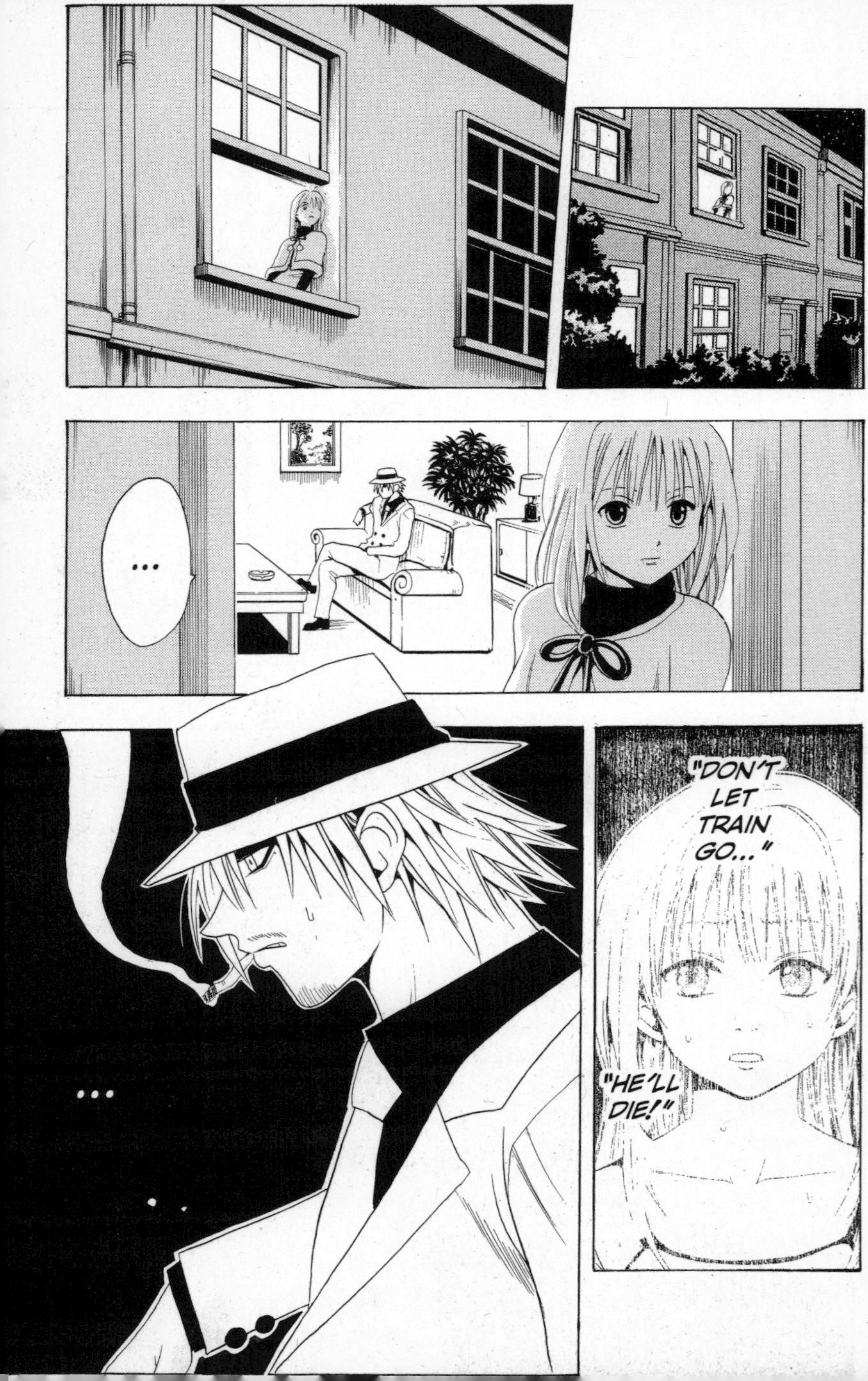
...
"DON'T LET TRAIN GO..."
"HE'LL DIE!"
...
. . .

NEW YEAR'S CARD PICS II

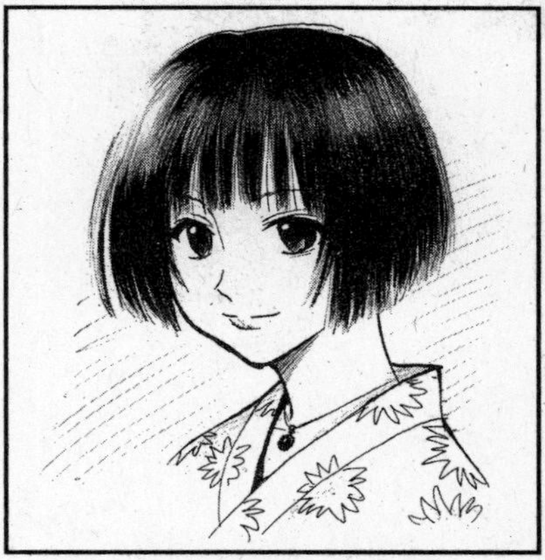

SAYA MINATSUKI

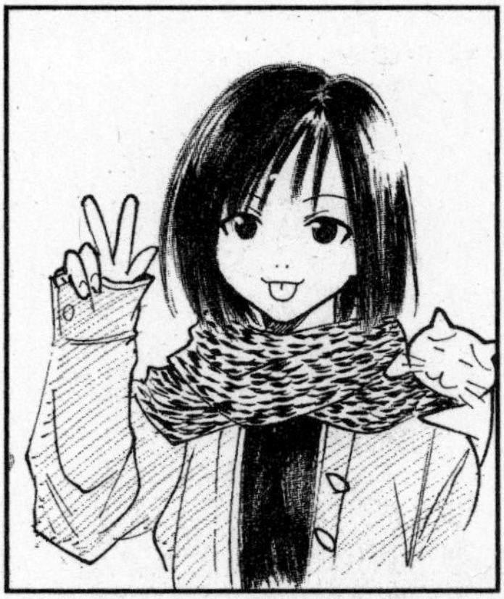

KYOKO KIRISAKI ②

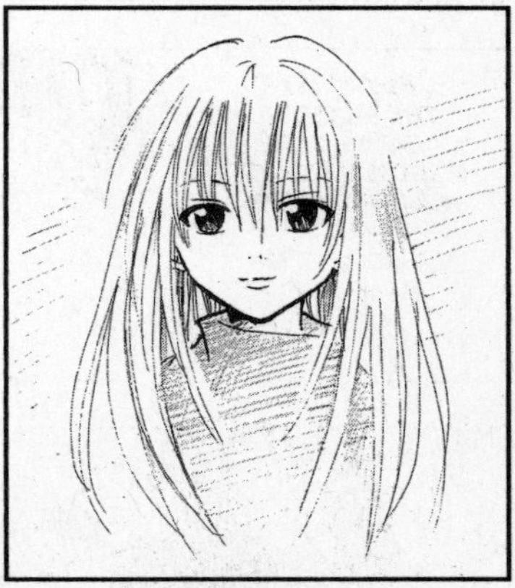

EVE ②

◎ WOMEN ONLY (HA!). OH WELL, THE RECIPIENTS WERE MOSTLY MEN... PRIVATE DRAWINGS LIKE THESE ARE FUN BECAUSE I CAN DO ANYTHING I WANT. IF I HAVE ROOM IN FUTURE VOLUMES, I'LL INCLUDE A FEW MORE.

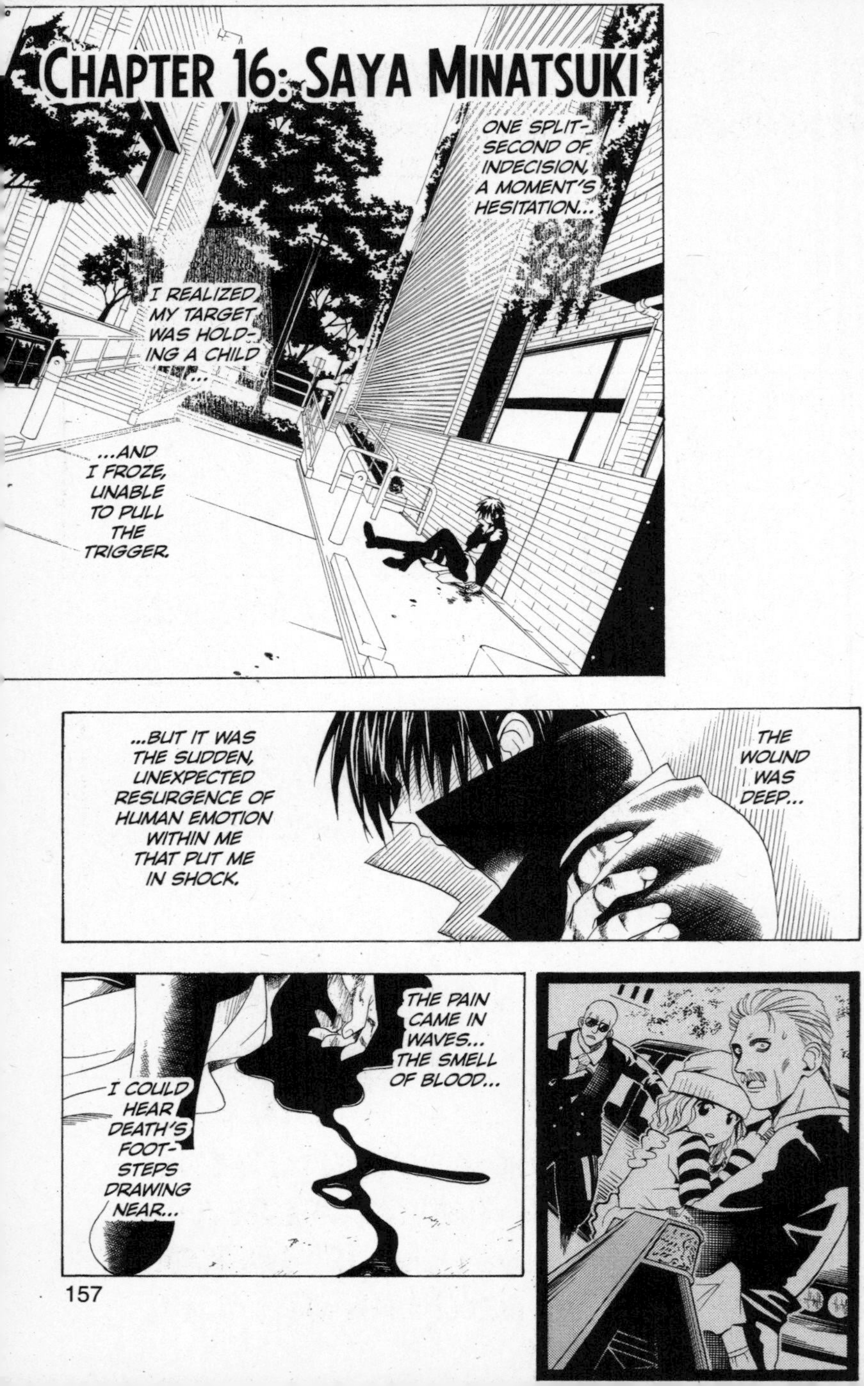
CHAPTER 16: SAYA MINATSUKI
ONE SPLIT-SECOND OF INDECISION, A MOMENT'S HESITATION...
I REALIZED MY TARGET WAS HOLDING A CHILD...
...AND I FROZE, UNABLE TO PULL THE TRIGGER.
THE WOUND WAS DEEP...
...BUT IT WAS THE SUDDEN, UNEXPECTED RESURGENCE OF HUMAN EMOTION WITHIN ME THAT PUT ME IN SHOCK.
THE PAIN CAME IN WAVES... THE SMELL OF BLOOD...
I COULD HEAR DEATH'S FOOTSTEPS DRAWING NEAR...

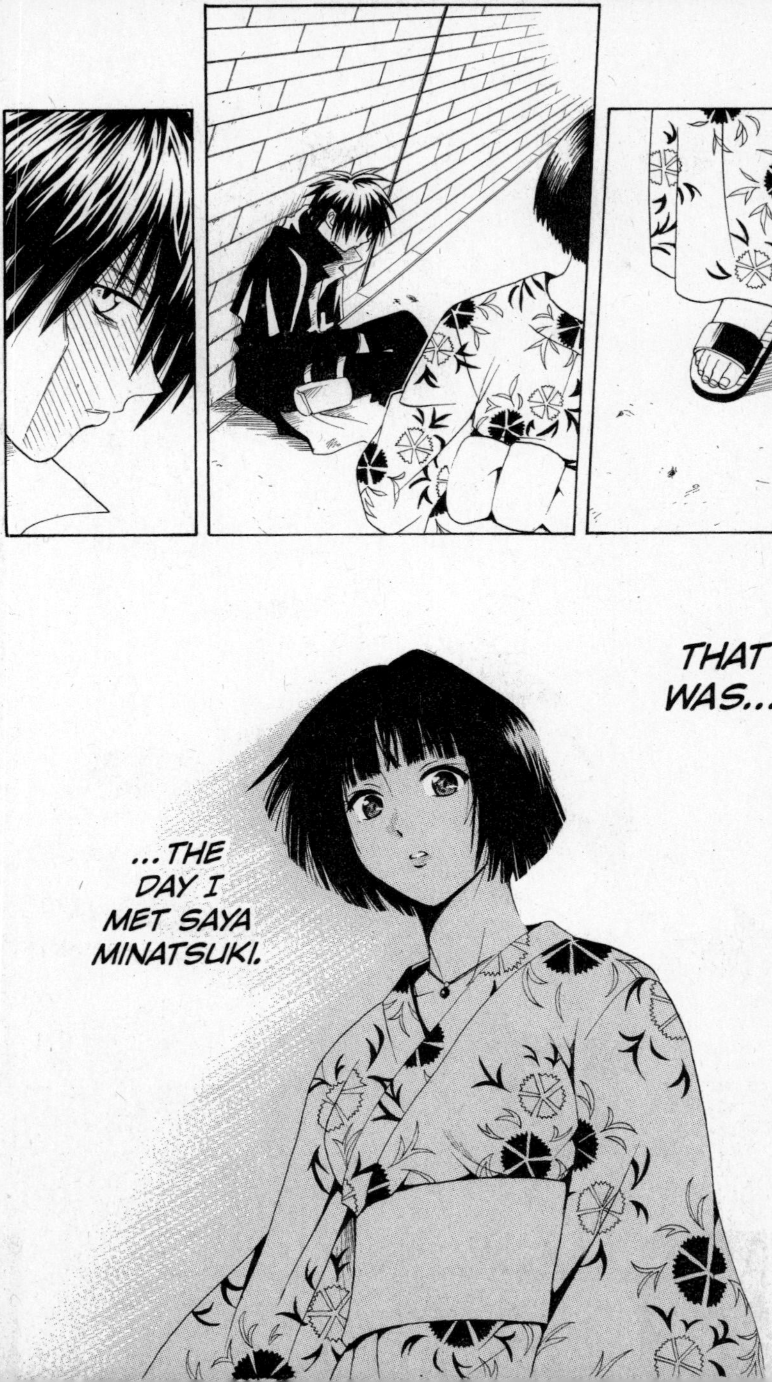
THAT WAS...
...THE DAY I MET SAYA MINATSUKI.

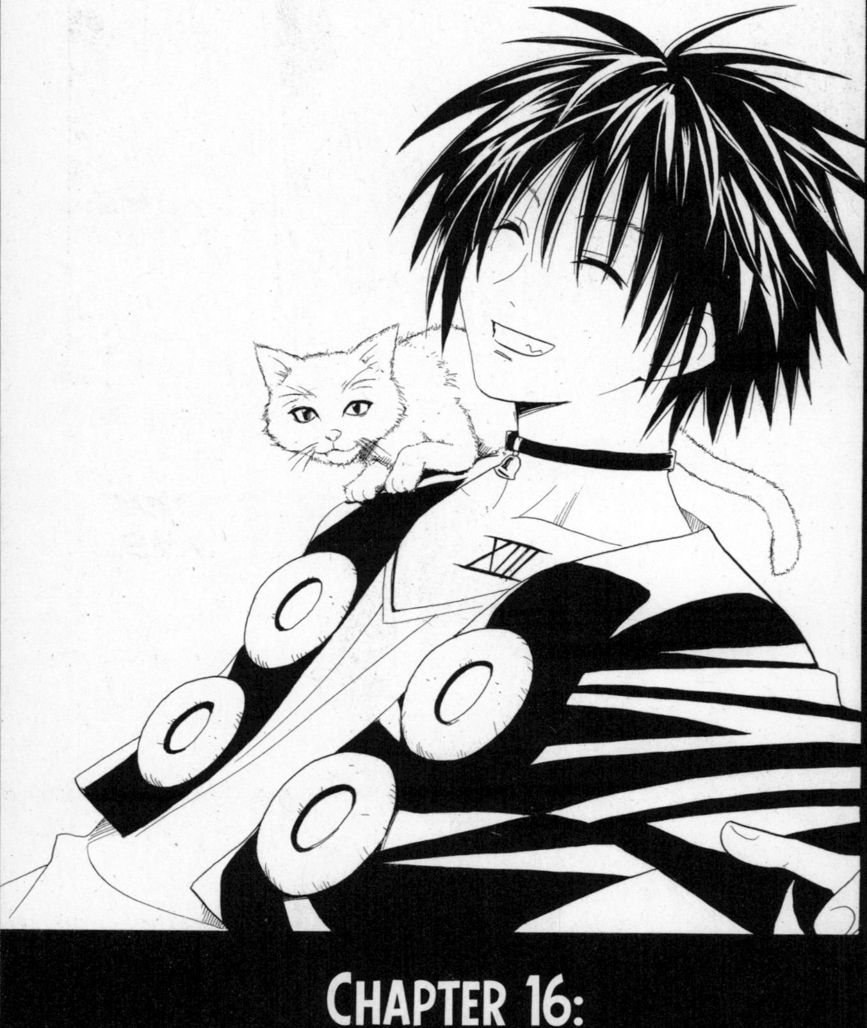
XIII

CHAPTER 16:

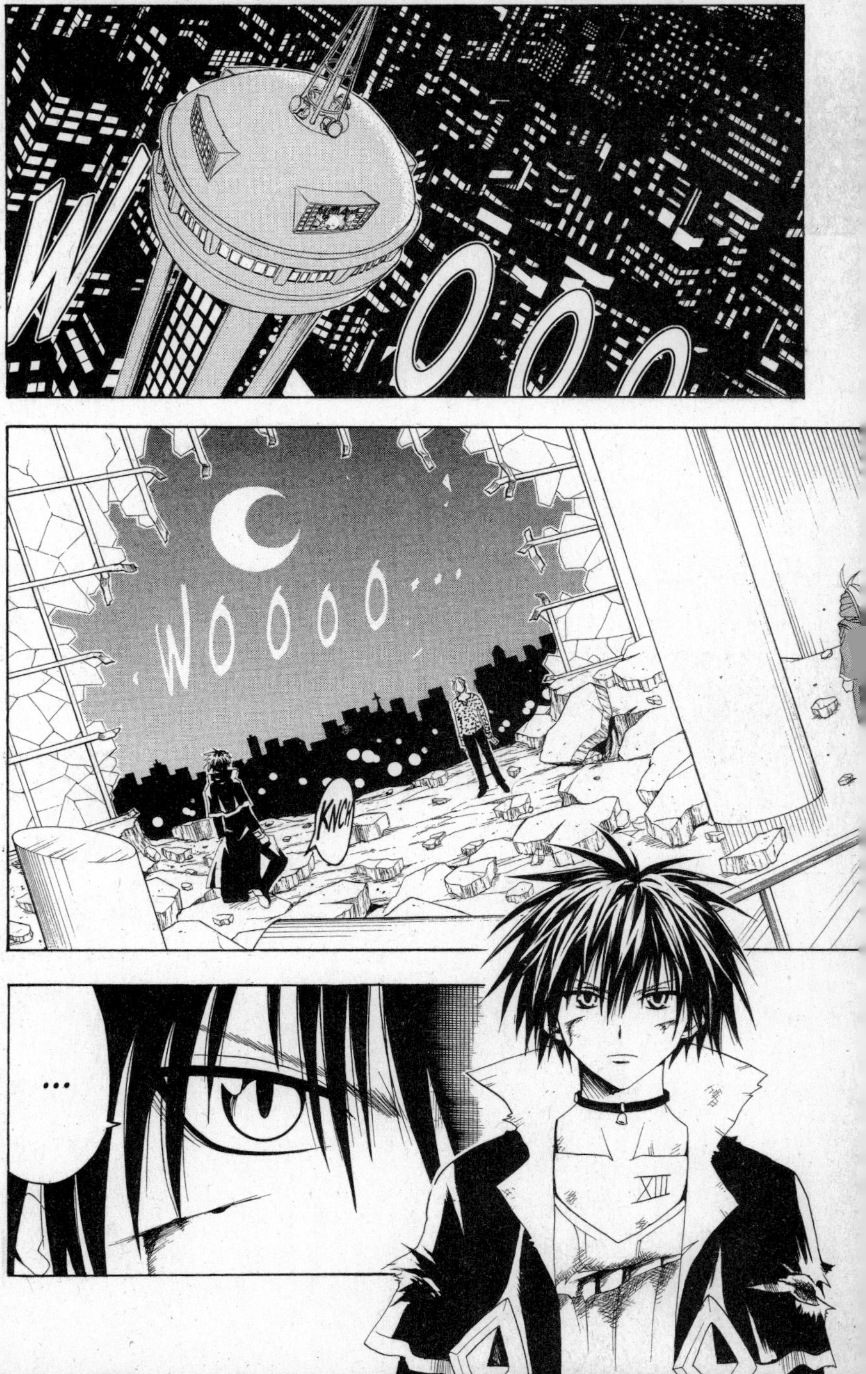

WOOOO
WOOOO...
KNCH
...

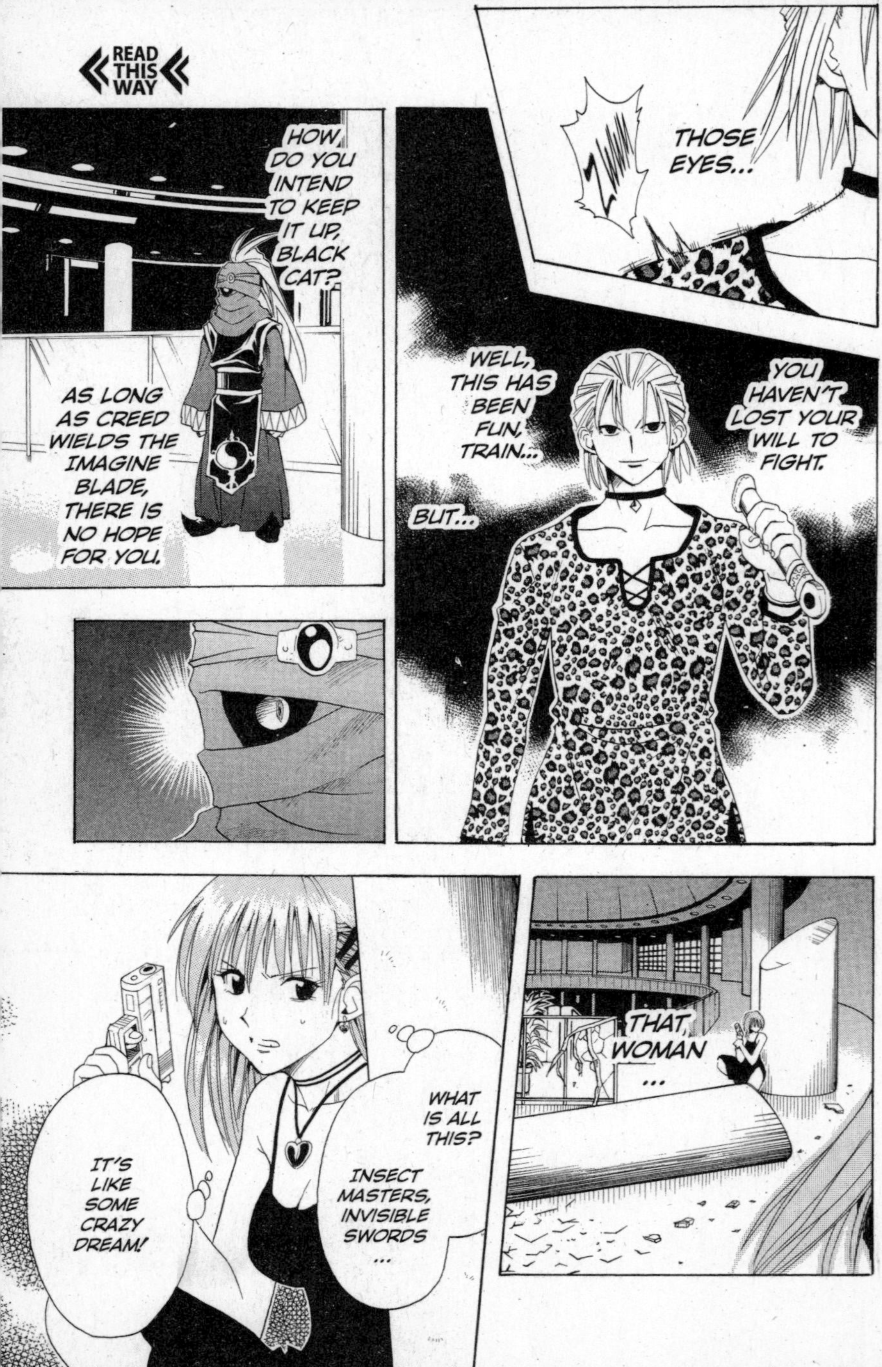
READ THIS WAY
THOSE EYES...
YOU HAVEN'T LOST YOUR WILL TO FIGHT.
WELL, THIS HAS BEEN FUN, TRAIN...
BUT...
HOW DO YOU INTEND TO KEEP IT UP, BLACK CAT?
AS LONG AS CREED WIELDS THE IMAGINE BLADE, THERE IS NO HOPE FOR YOU.
THAT WOMAN ...
WHAT IS ALL THIS?
INSECT MASTERS, INVISIBLE SWORDS ...
IT'S LIKE SOME CRAZY DREAM!

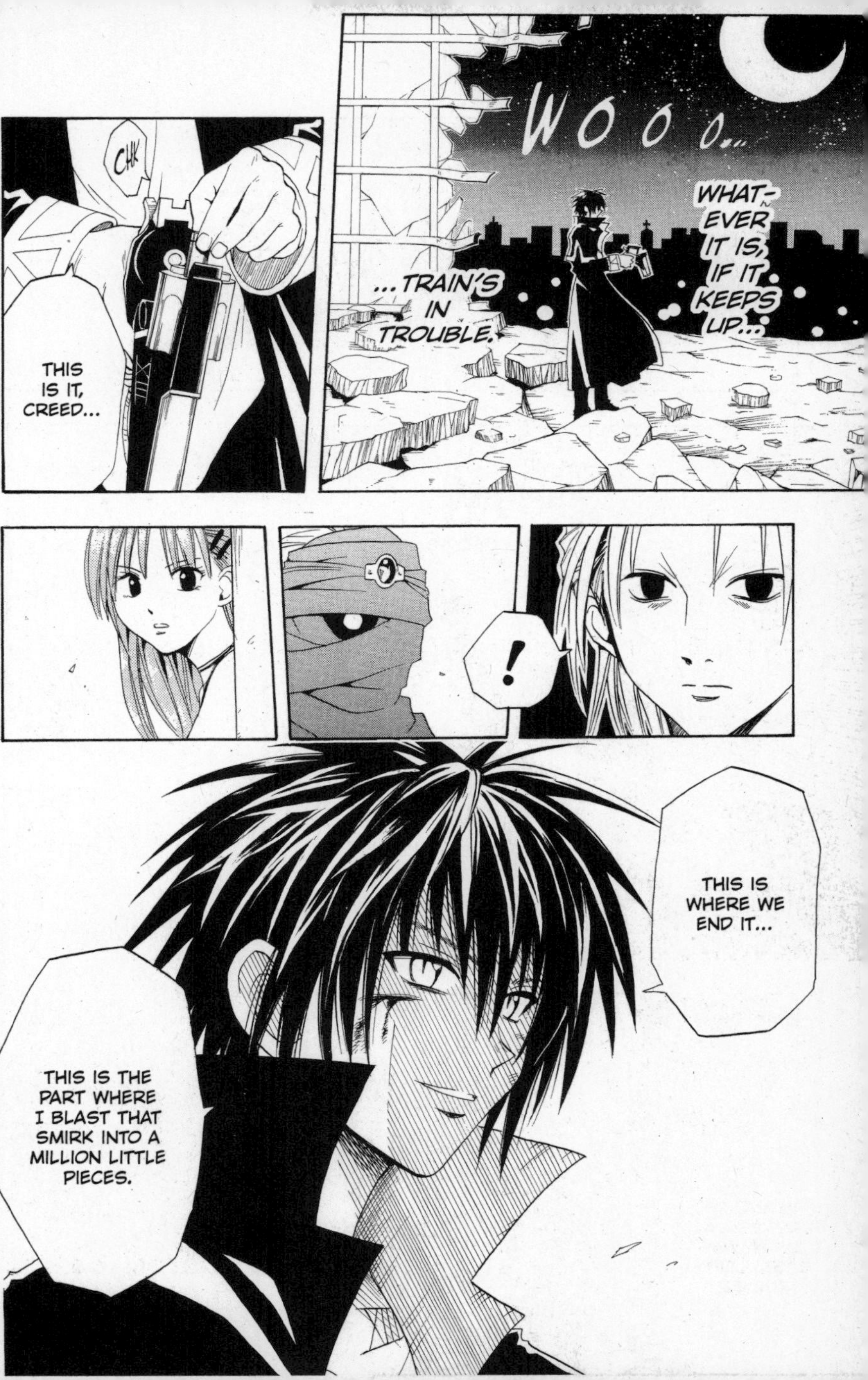
WOOO...
WHAT-EVER IT IS, IF IT KEEPS UP...
...TRAIN'S IN TROUBLE.
CHK
THIS IS IT, CREED...
!
THIS IS WHERE WE END IT...
THIS IS THE PART WHERE I BLAST THAT SMIRK INTO A MILLION LITTLE PIECES.

READ THIS WAY

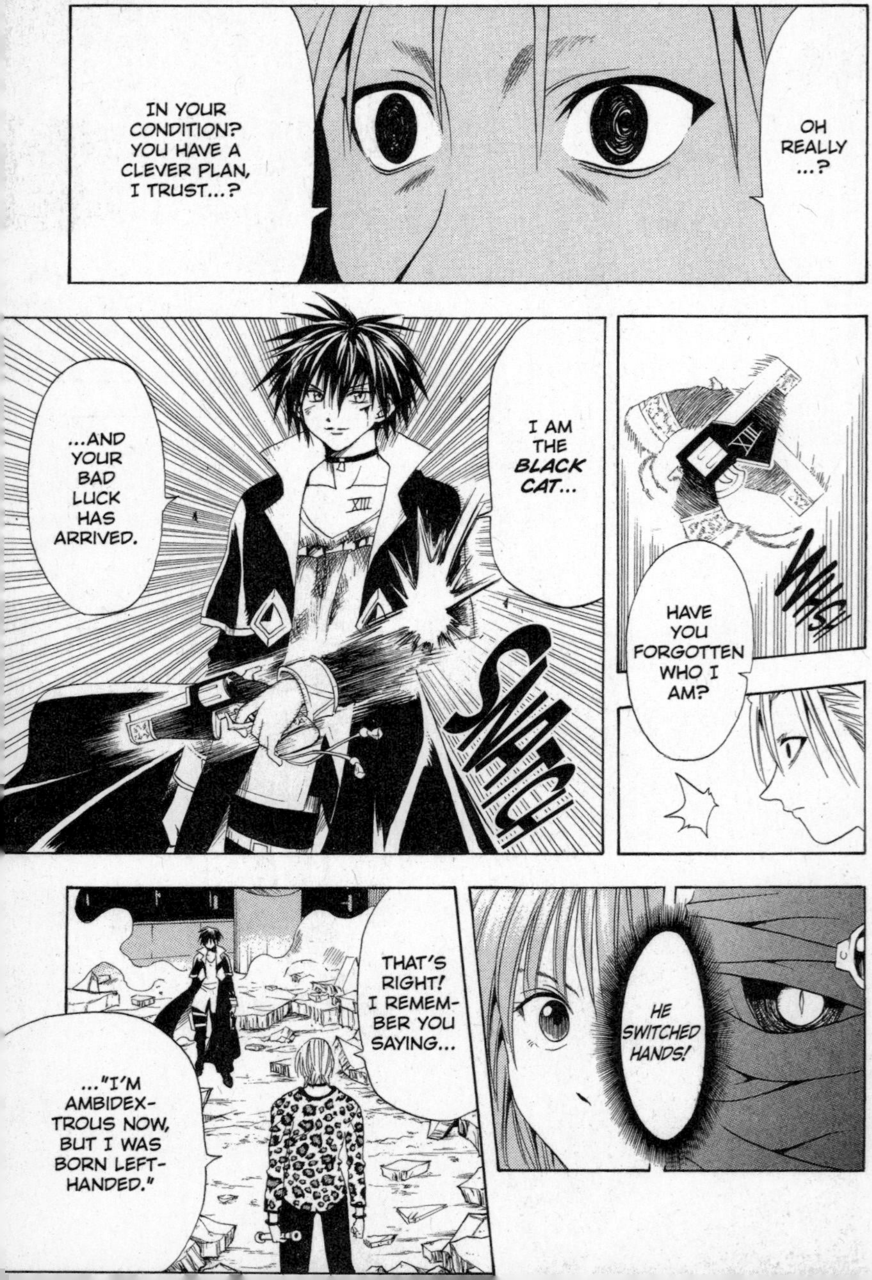
OH REALLY ...?
IN YOUR CONDITION? YOU HAVE A CLEVER PLAN, I TRUST...?
HAVE YOU FORGOTTEN WHO I AM?
I AM THE *BLACK CAT*...
SNATCH
...AND YOUR BAD LUCK HAS ARRIVED.
HE SWITCHED HANDS!
THAT'S RIGHT! I REMEMBER YOU SAYING...
..."I'M AMBIDEXTROUS NOW, BUT I WAS BORN LEFT-HANDED."

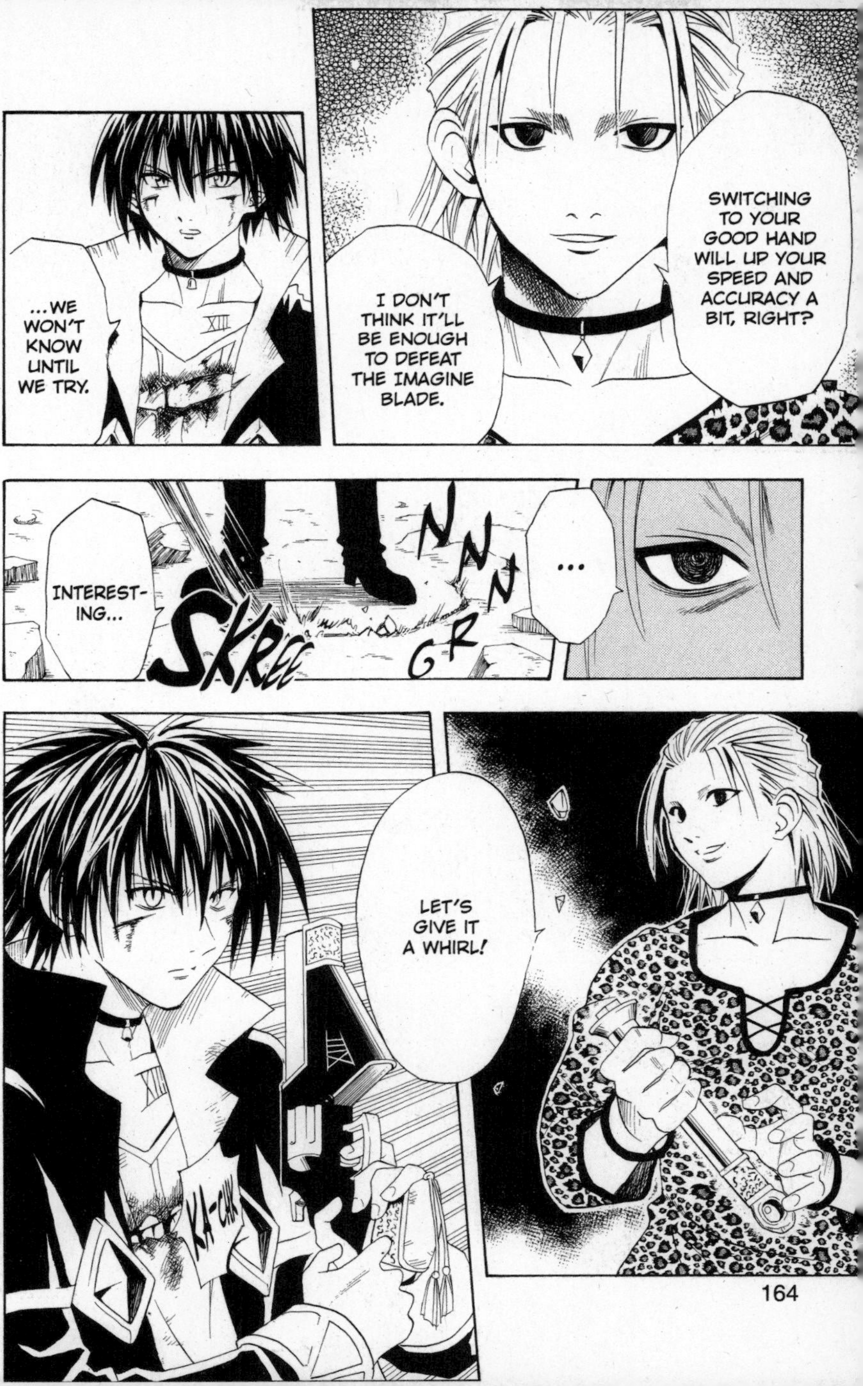
SWITCHING TO YOUR GOOD HAND WILL UP YOUR SPEED AND ACCURACY A BIT, RIGHT?
I DON'T THINK IT'LL BE ENOUGH TO DEFEAT THE IMAGINE BLADE.
...WE WON'T KNOW UNTIL WE TRY.
...
NNNNGRR
SKREE
INTEREST-ING...
LET'S GIVE IT A WHIRL!
KA-CHK

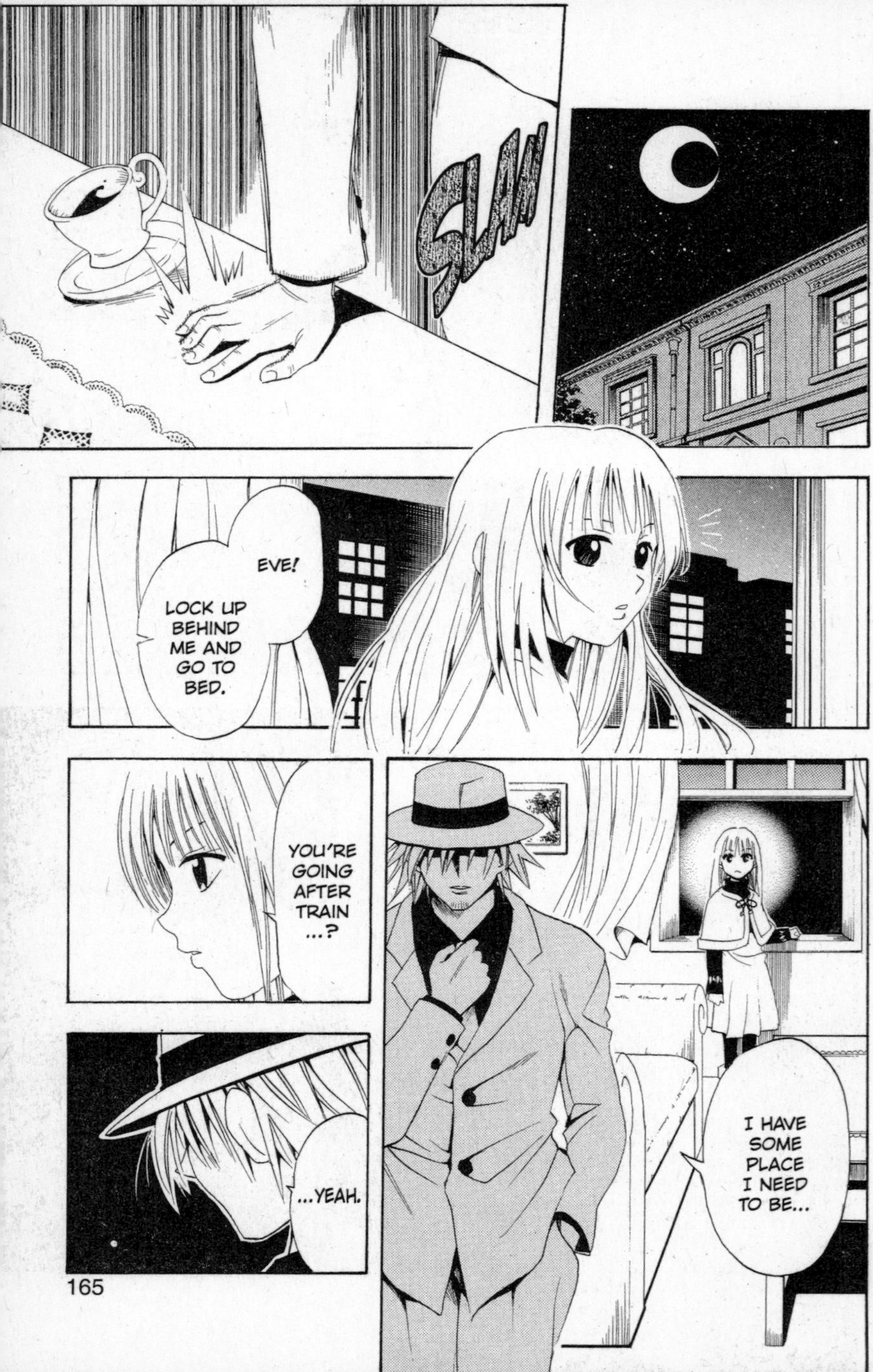
SLAM
EVE!
LOCK UP BEHIND ME AND GO TO BED.
I HAVE SOME PLACE I NEED TO BE...
YOU'RE GOING AFTER TRAIN ...?
...YEAH.

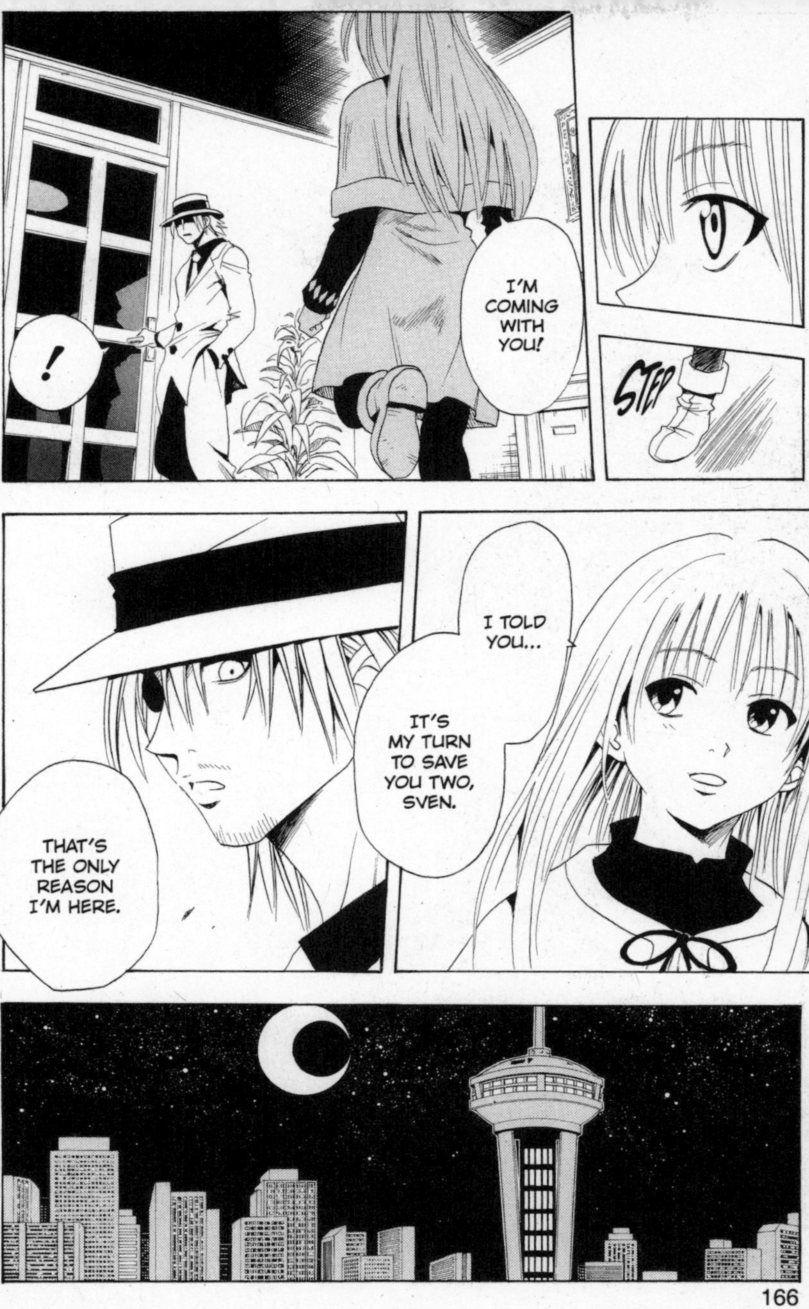
STEP
I'M COMING WITH YOU!
!
I TOLD YOU...
IT'S MY TURN TO SAVE YOU TWO, SVEN.
THAT'S THE ONLY REASON I'M HERE.

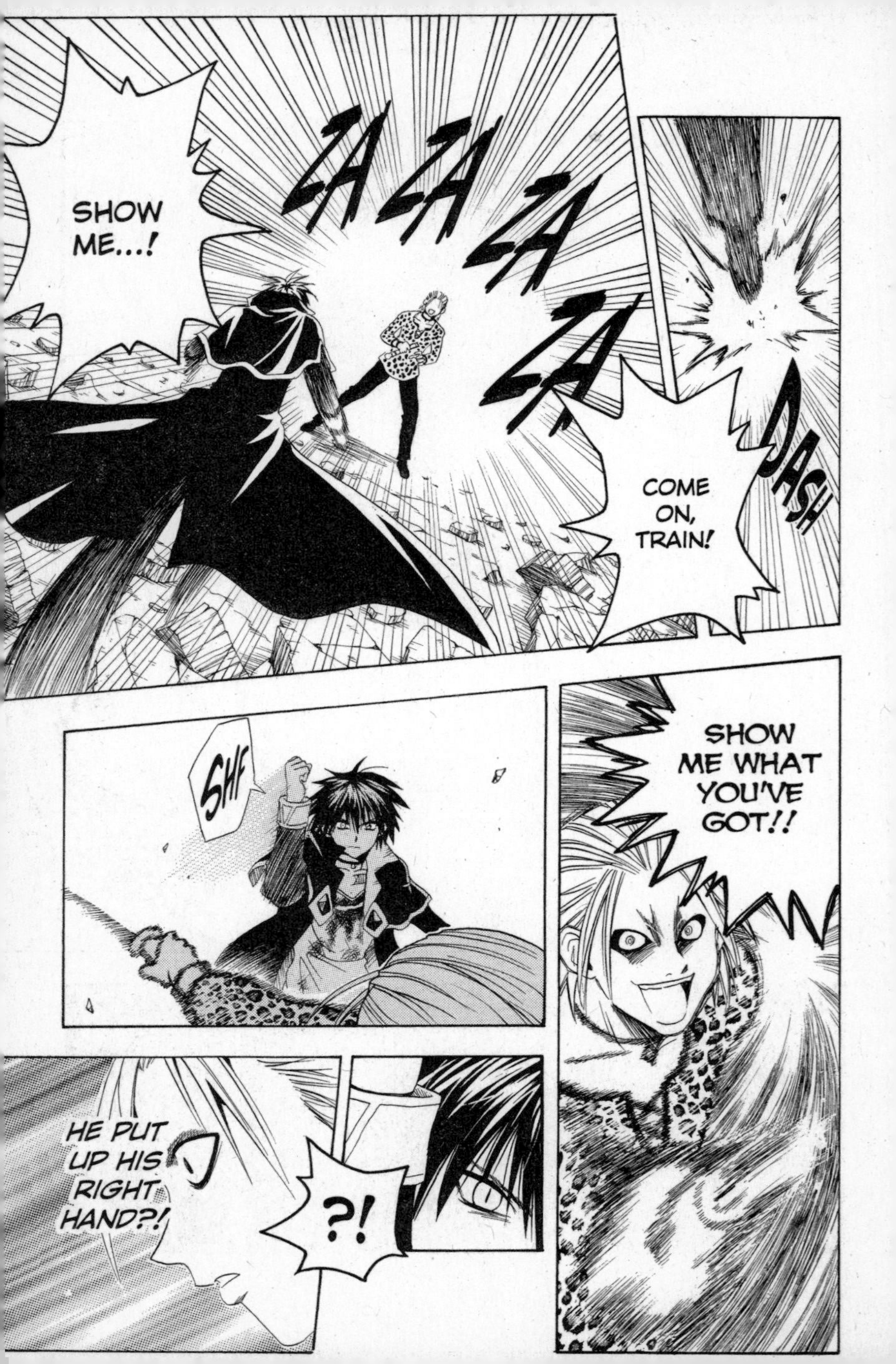
DASH
COME ON, TRAIN!
ZA ZA ZA ZA ZA ZA
SHOW ME...!
SHOW ME WHAT YOU'VE GOT!!
SHF
?!
HE PUT UP HIS RIGHT HAND?!

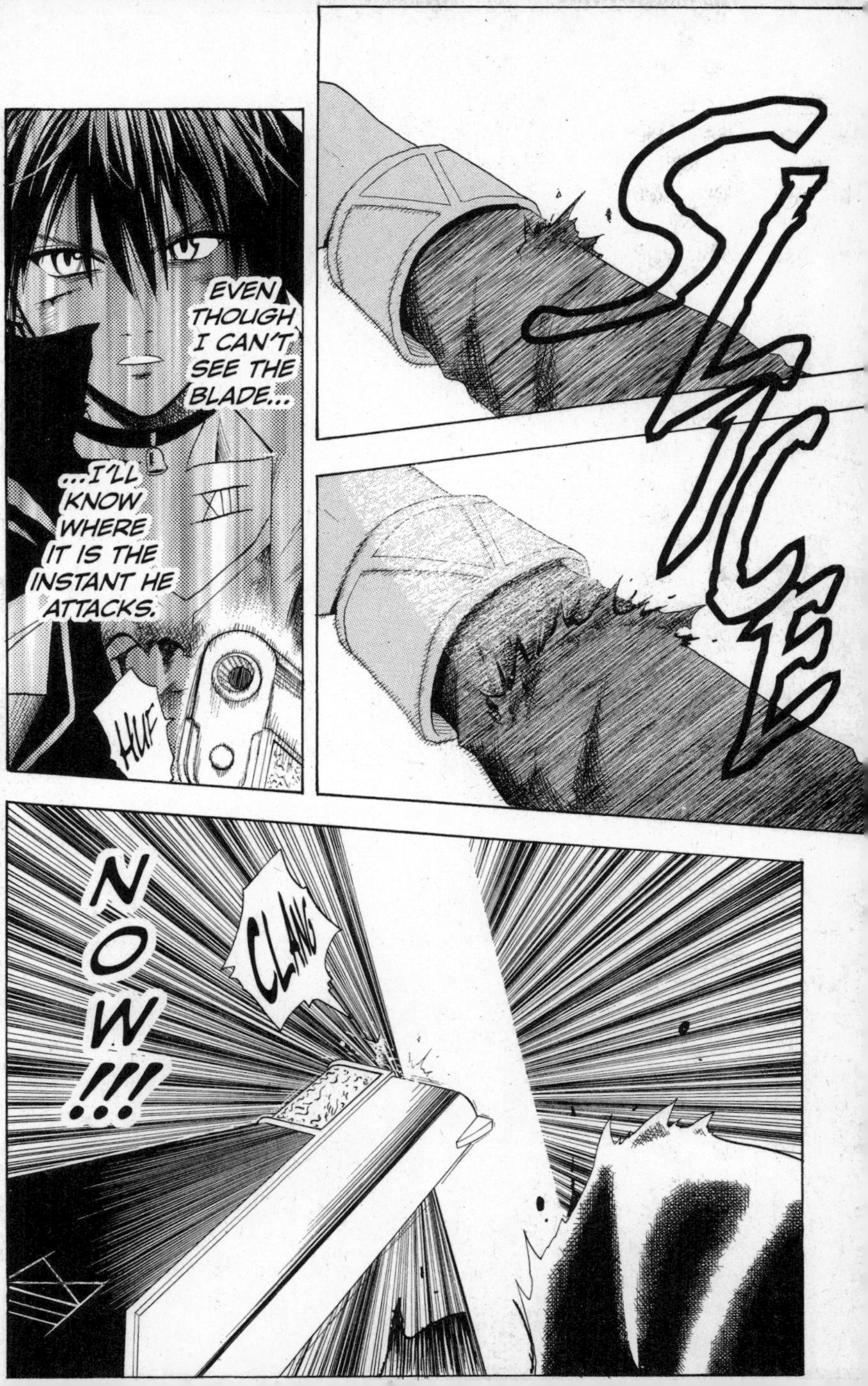
EVEN THOUGH I CAN'T SEE THE BLADE...
...I'LL KNOW WHERE IT IS THE INSTANT HE ATTACKS.
HUF
CLANG
NOW!!!

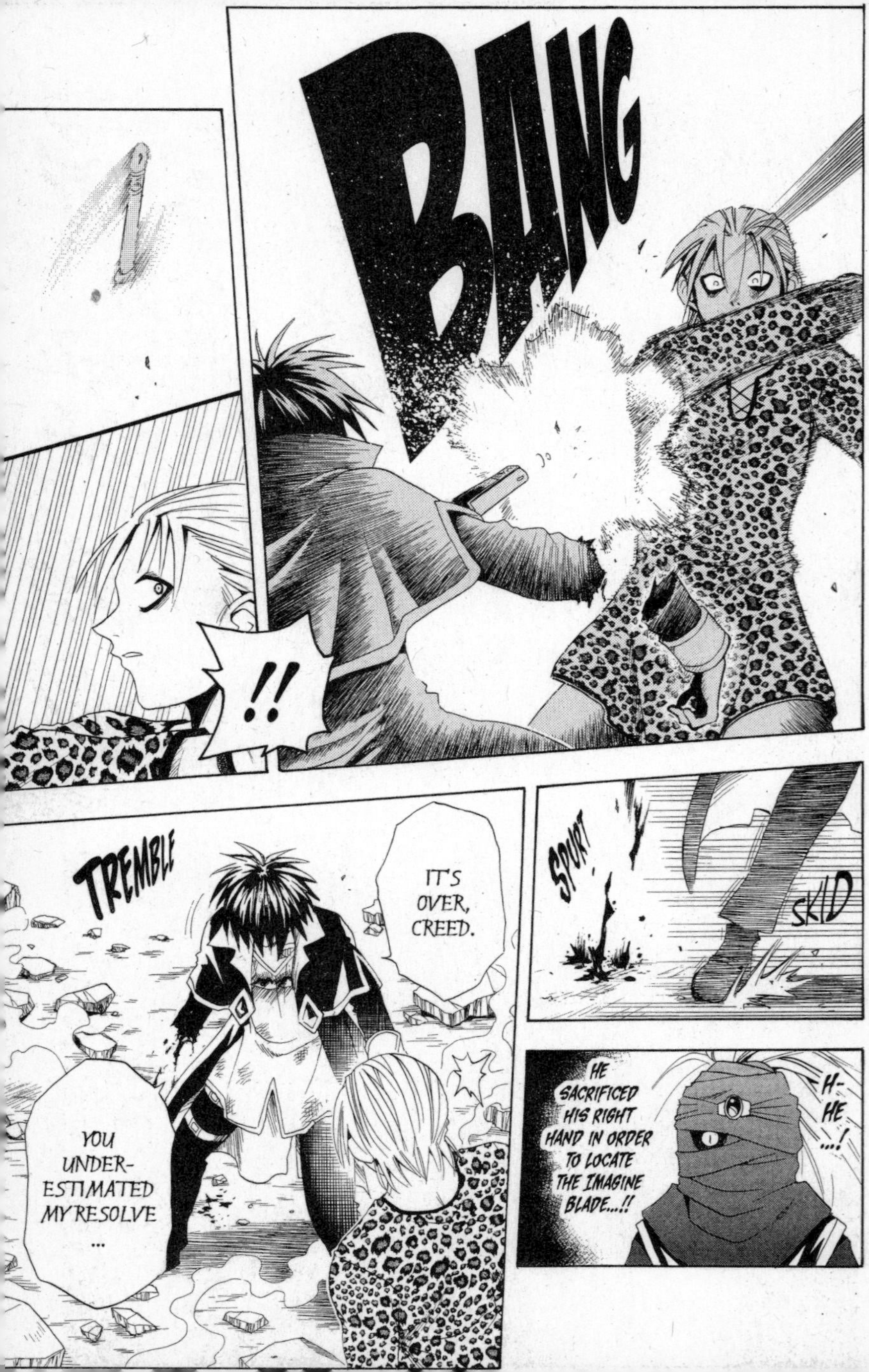
BANG
!!
SPURT
SKID
H-HE...!
HE SACRIFICED HIS RIGHT HAND IN ORDER TO LOCATE THE IMAGINE BLADE...!!
TREMBLE
IT'S OVER, CREED.
YOU UNDER-ESTIMATED MY RESOLVE ...

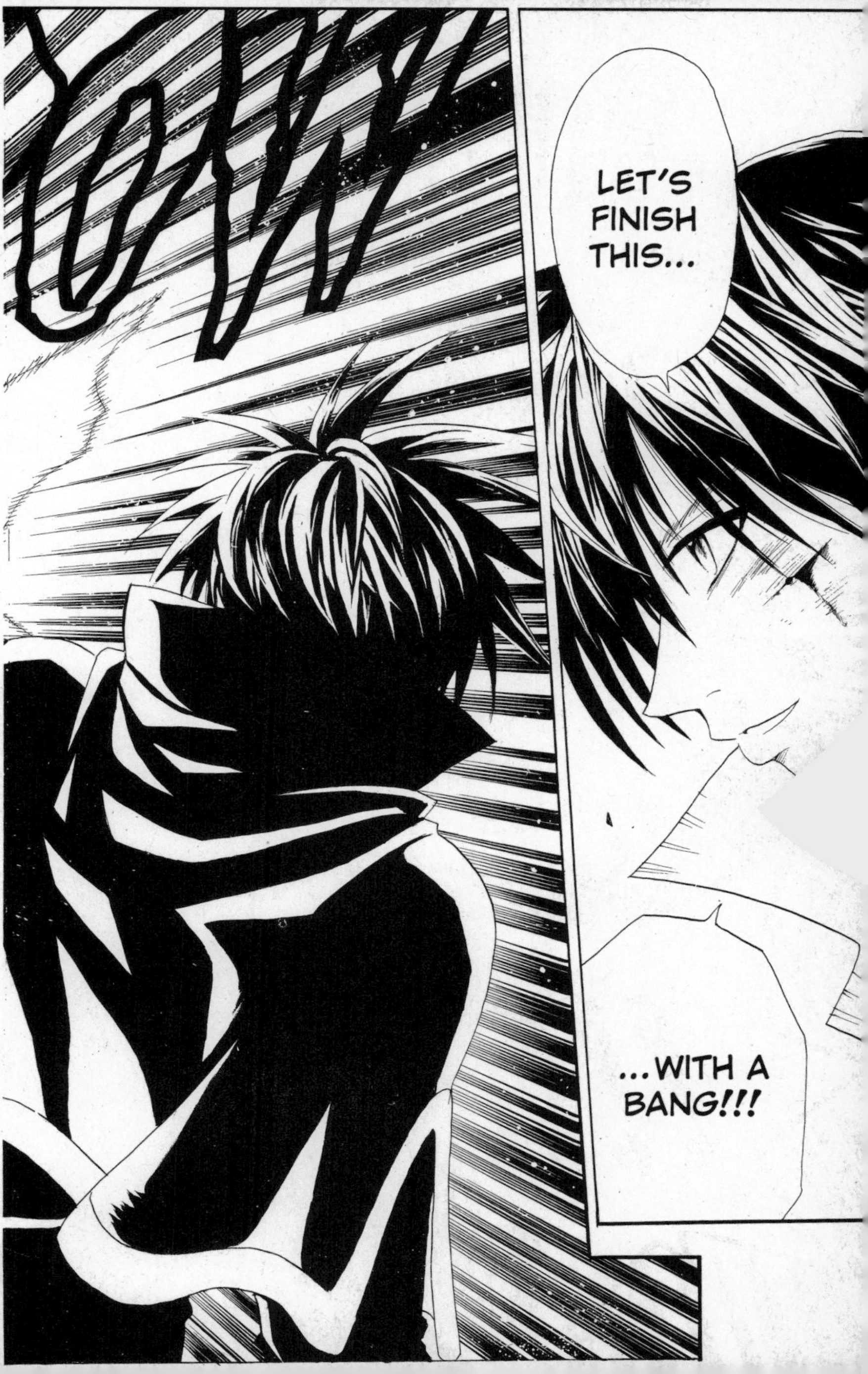
LET'S FINISH THIS...
...WITH A BANG!!!

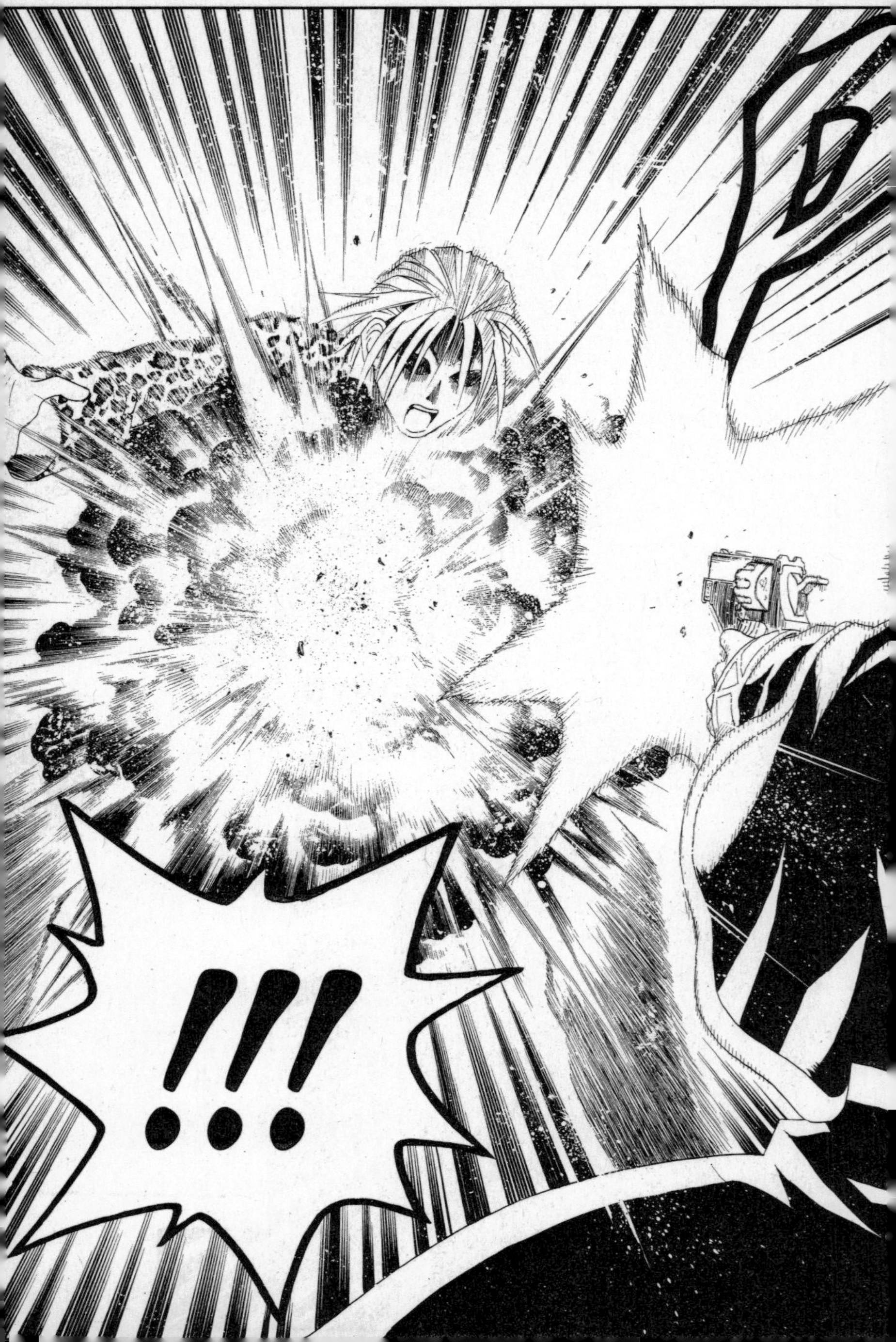
!!!

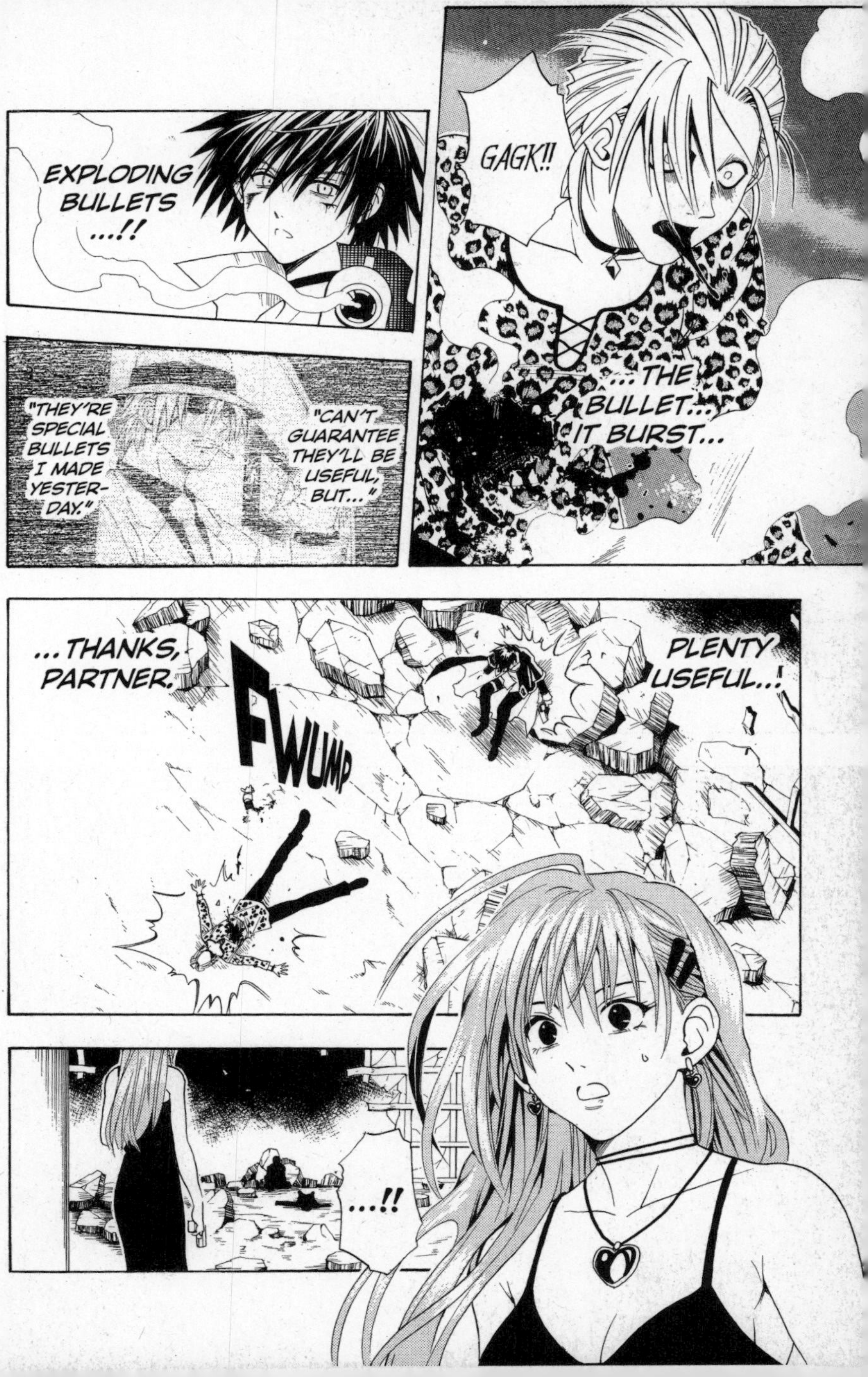
GAGK!!
...THE BULLET... IT BURST...
EXPLODING BULLETS ...!!
"CAN'T GUARANTEE THEY'LL BE USEFUL, BUT..."
"THEY'RE SPECIAL BULLETS I MADE YESTER-DAY."
PLENTY USEFUL...!
FWUMP
...THANKS, PARTNER.
...!!

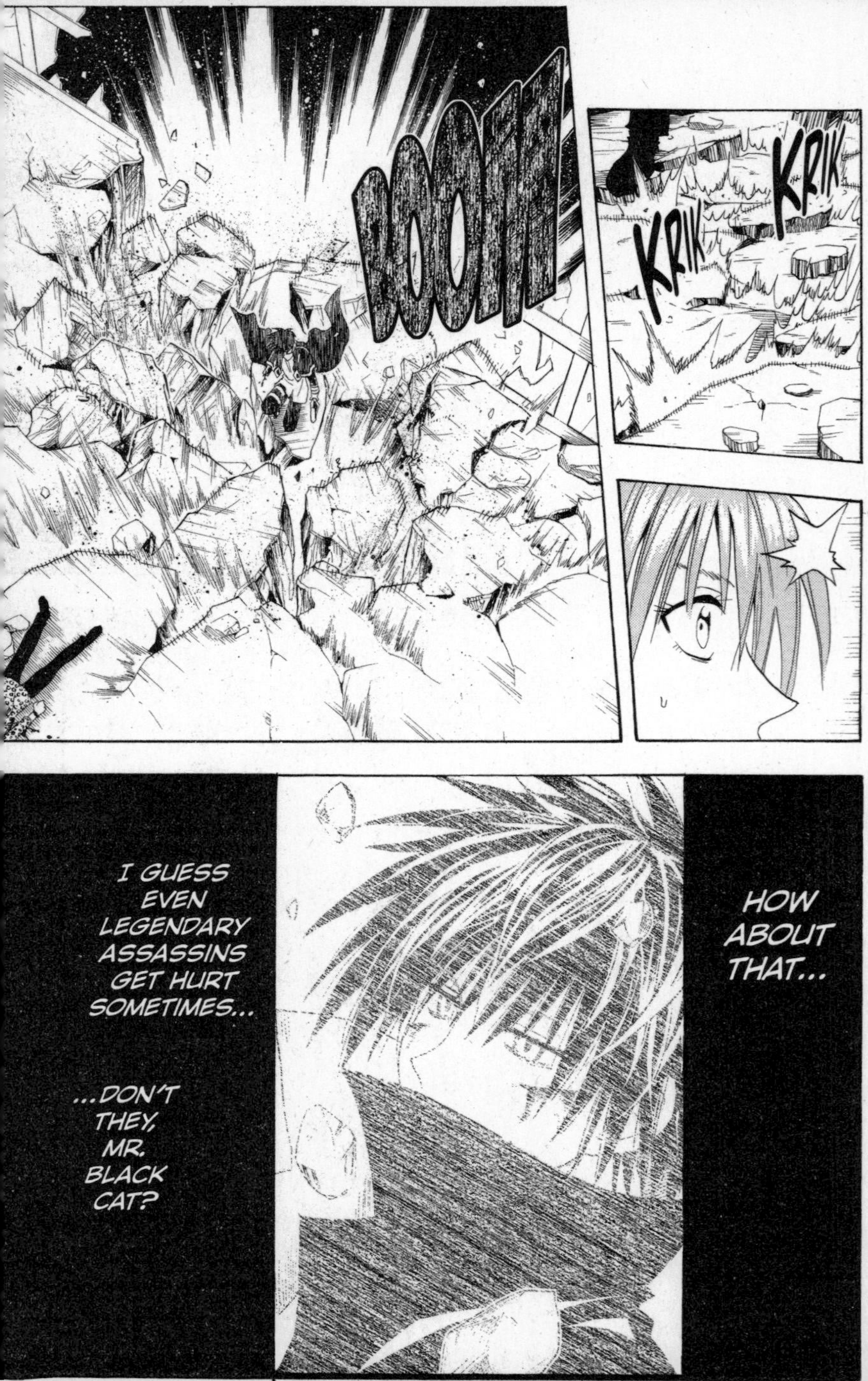
KRIK
KRIK
BOOM
HOW ABOUT THAT...
I GUESS EVEN LEGENDARY ASSASSINS GET HURT SOMETIMES...
...DON'T THEY, MR. BLACK CAT?

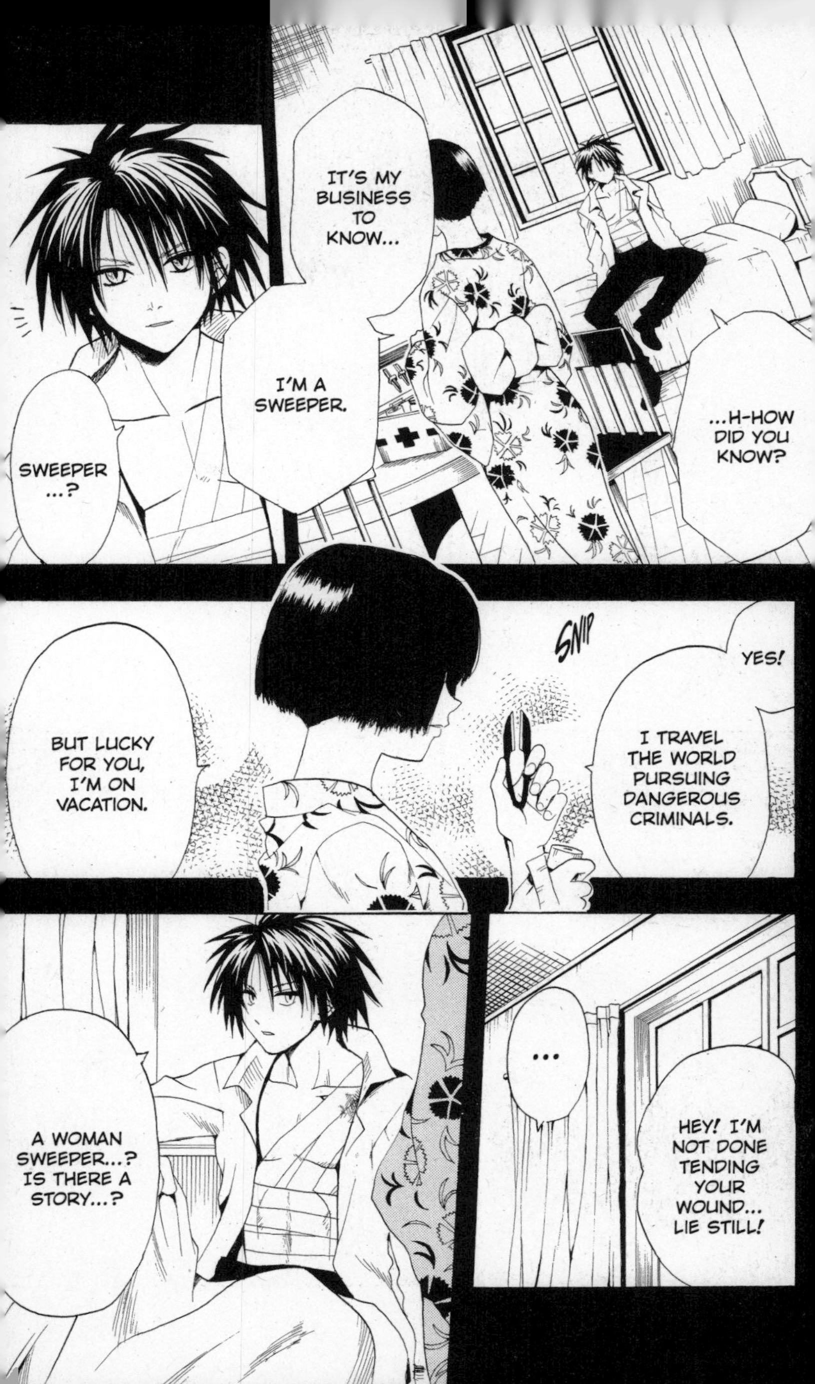
...H-HOW DID YOU KNOW?
IT'S MY BUSINESS TO KNOW...
I'M A SWEEPER.
SWEEPER ...?
YES!
I TRAVEL THE WORLD PURSUING DANGEROUS CRIMINALS.
SNIP
BUT LUCKY FOR YOU, I'M ON VACATION.
...
HEY! I'M NOT DONE TENDING YOUR WOUND... LIE STILL!
A WOMAN SWEEPER...? IS THERE A STORY...?

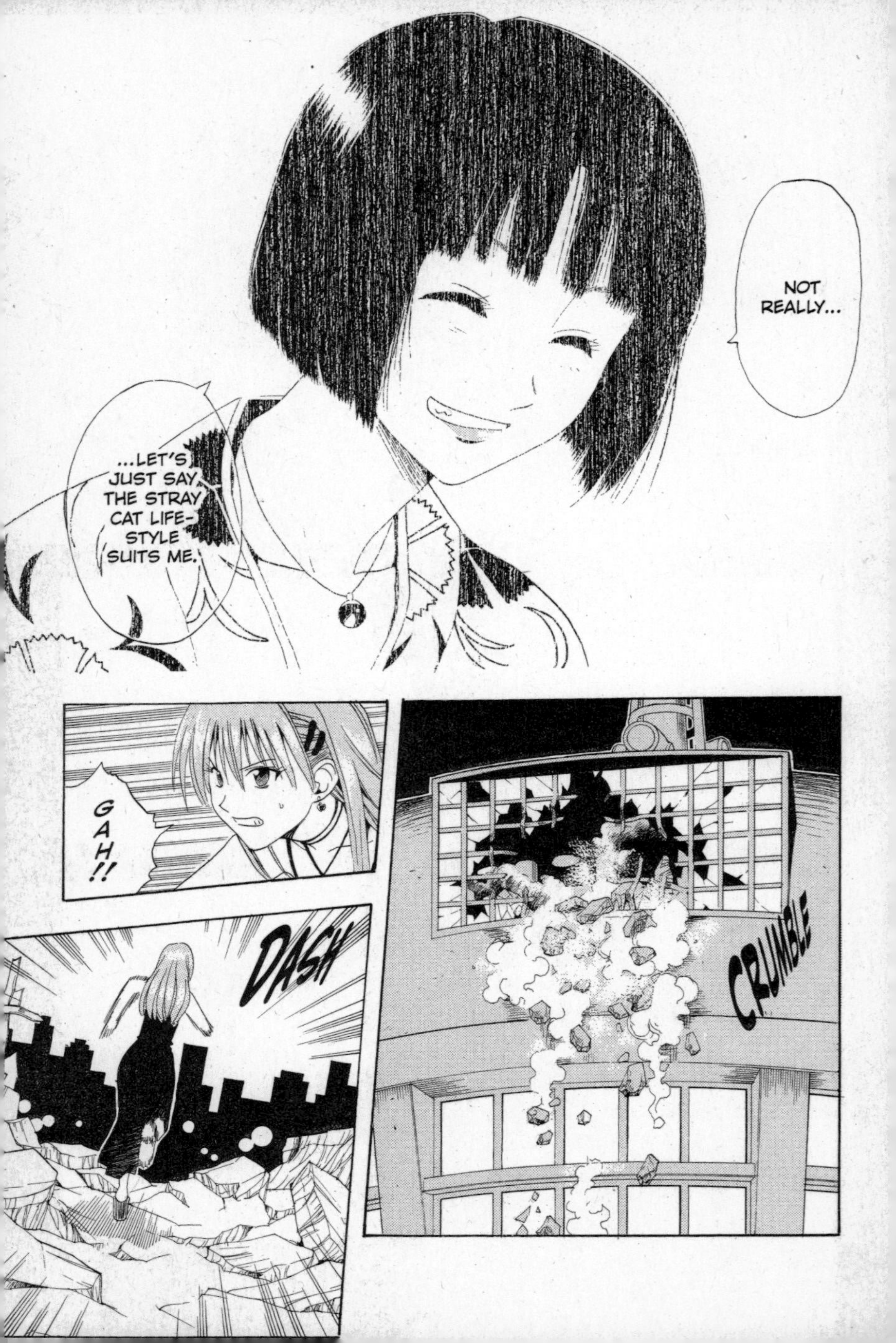

NOT REALLY...
...LET'S JUST SAY, THE STRAY CAT LIFE-STYLE SUITS ME.
CRUMBLE
GAH!!
DASH

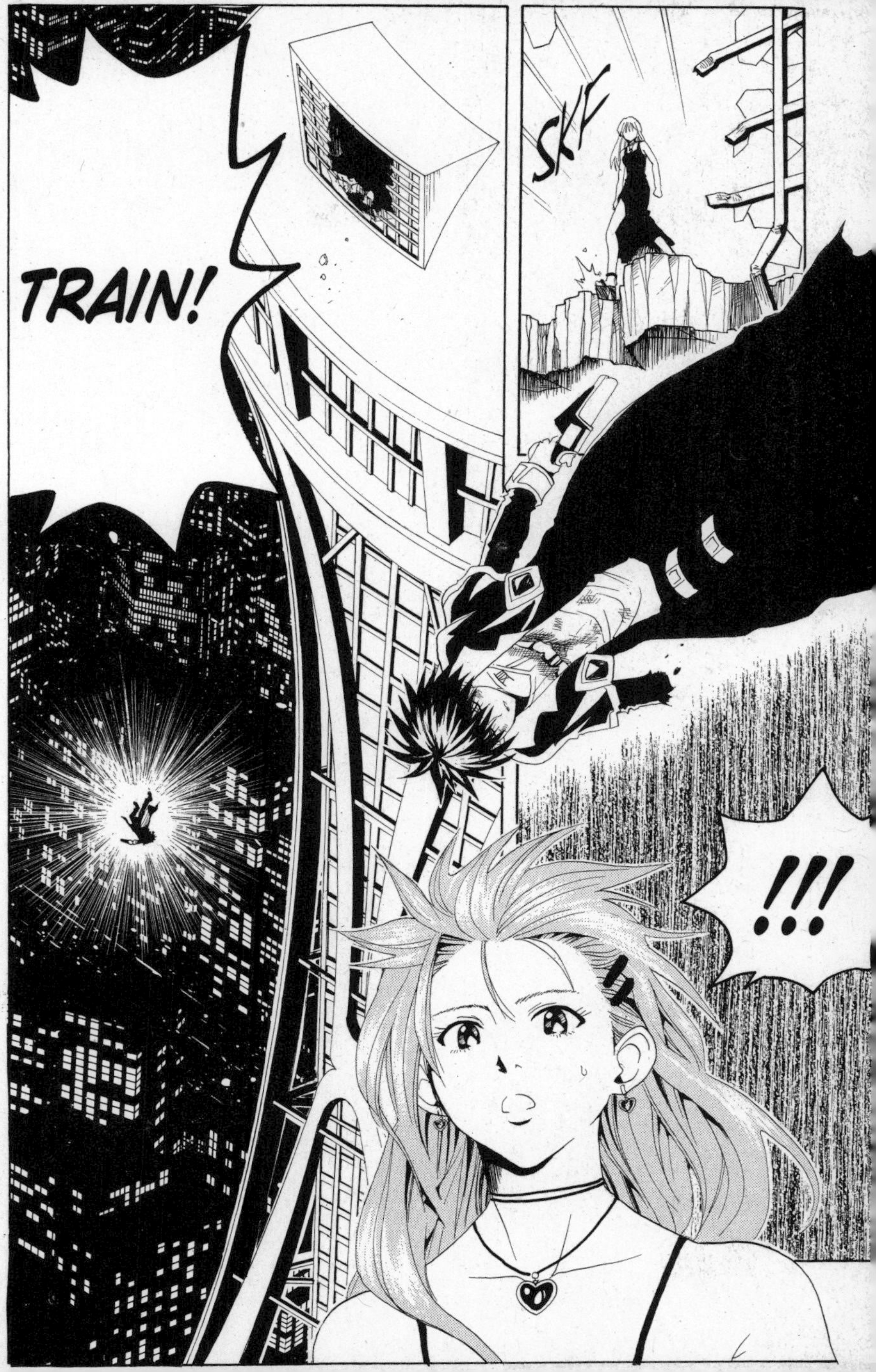
SKF
TRAIN!
!!!

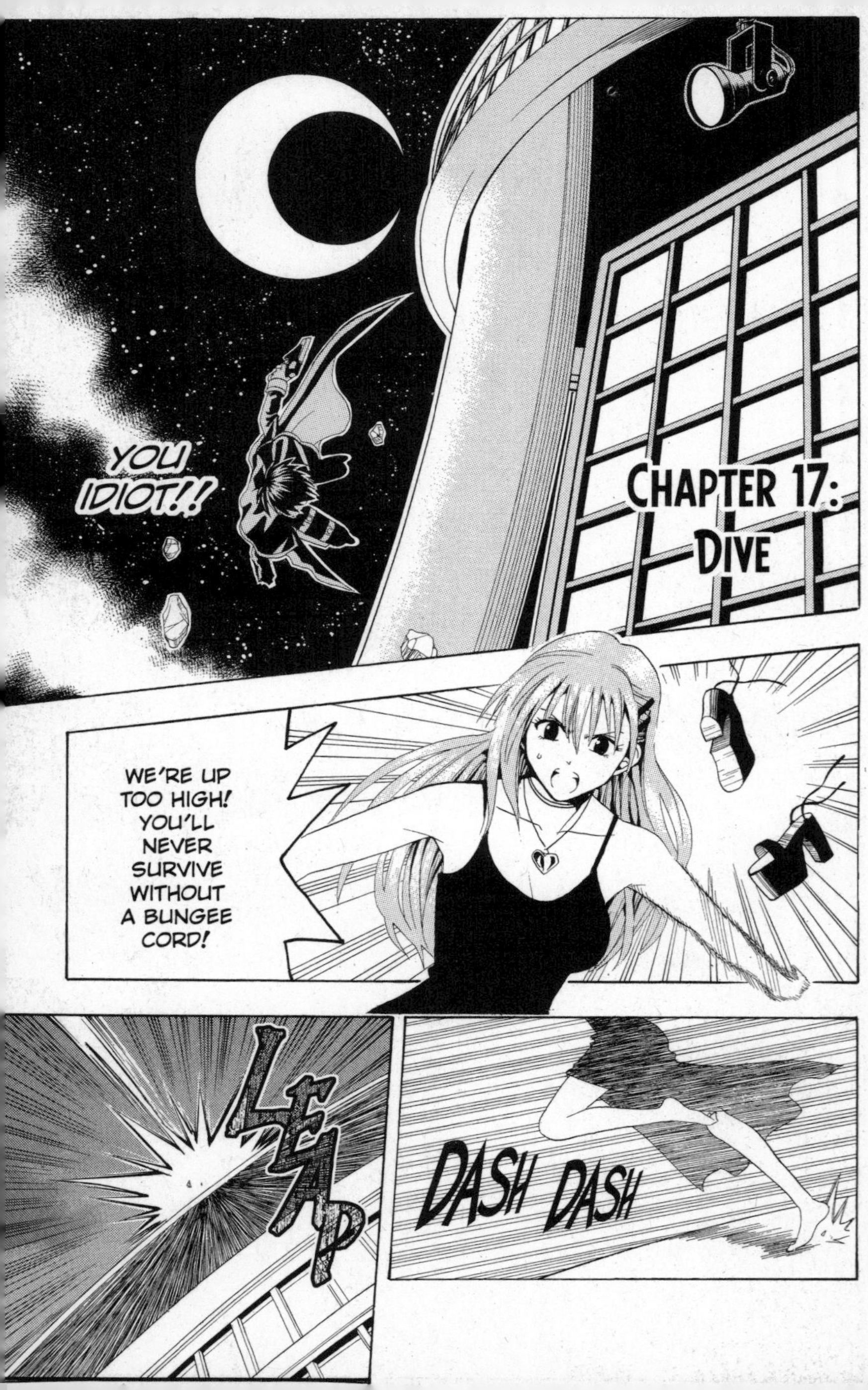
Chapter 17: Dive
YOU IDIOT!!
WE'RE UP TOO HIGH! YOU'LL NEVER SURVIVE WITHOUT A BUNGEE CORD!
DASH DASH
LEAP

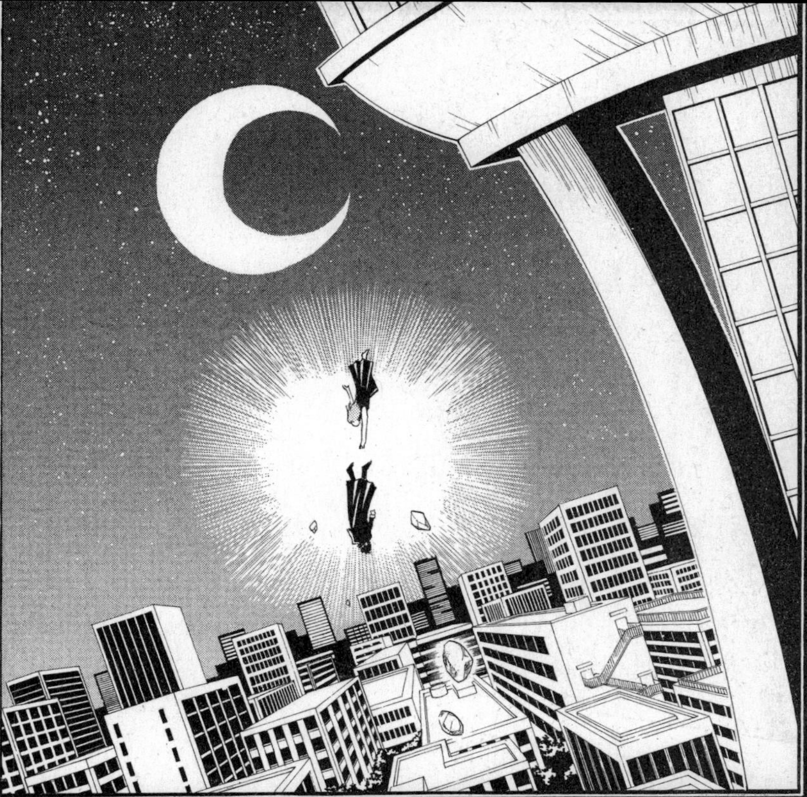

Chapter 17: Dive

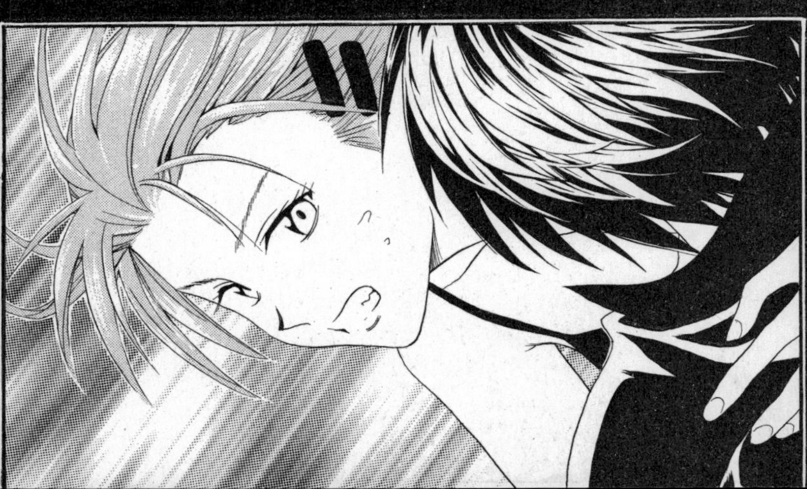

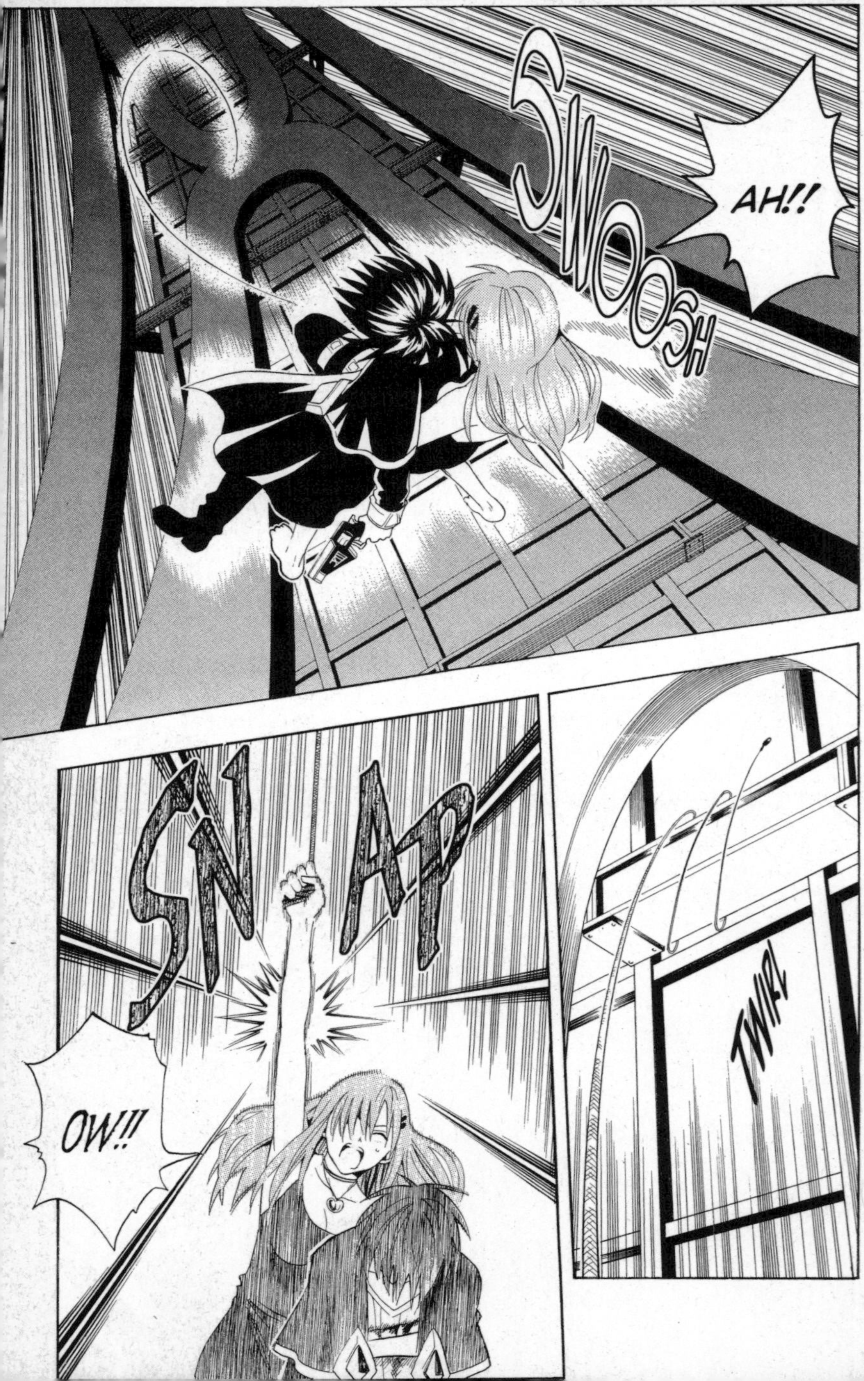
AH!!
SWOOSH
TWIRL
SNAP
OW!!

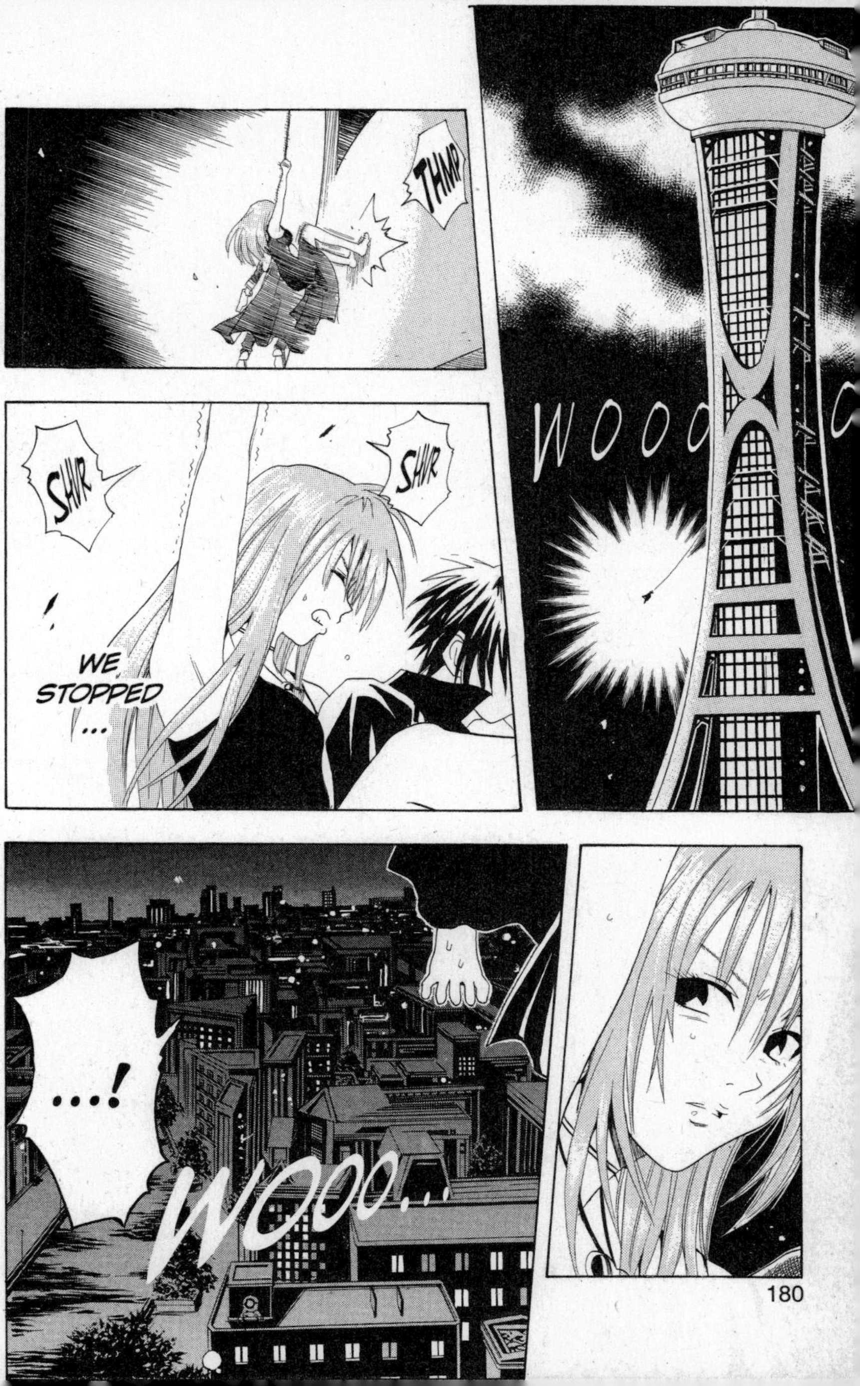
WOOO
THMP
SHIR
SHIR
WE STOPPED ...
...!
WOOO...

READ THIS WAY

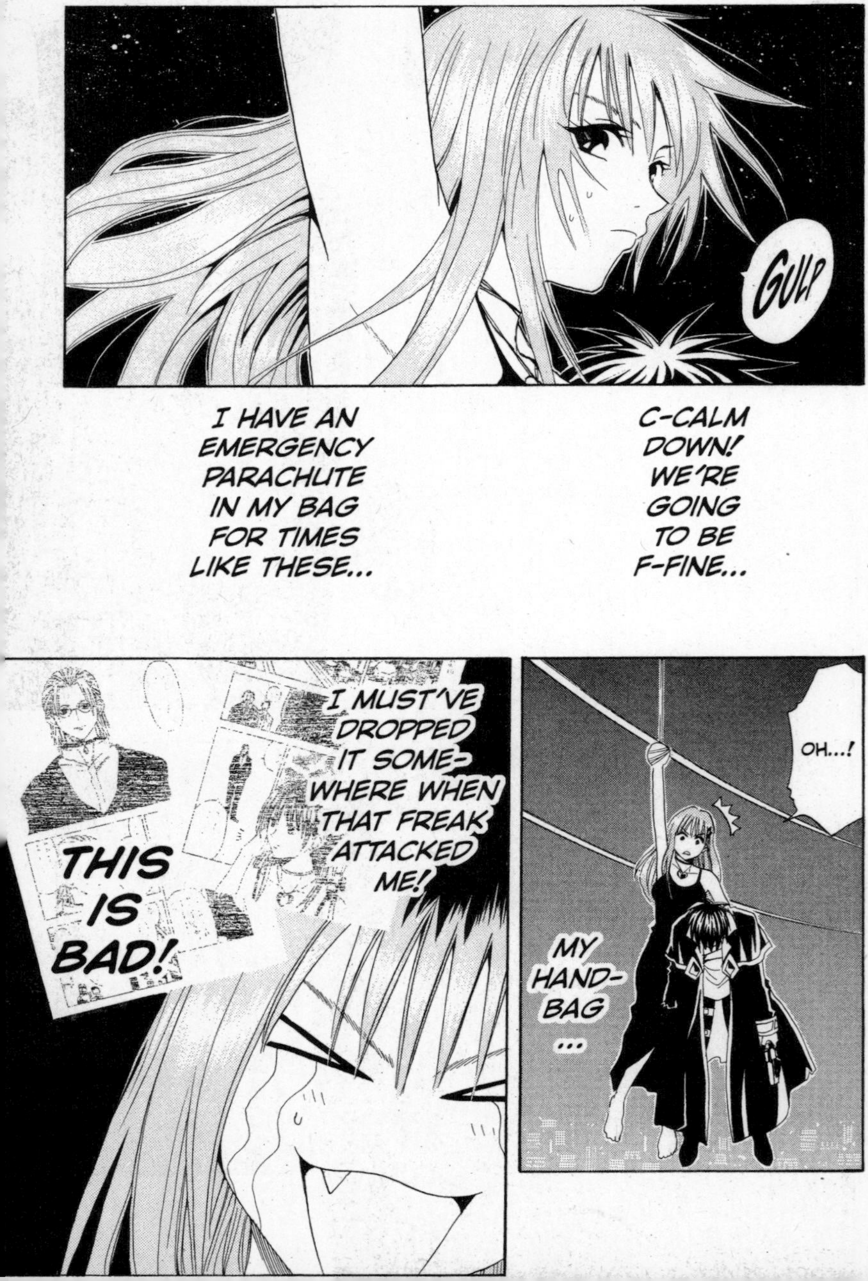
GULP
C-CALM DOWN! WE'RE GOING TO BE F-FINE...
I HAVE AN EMERGENCY PARACHUTE IN MY BAG FOR TIMES LIKE THESE...
OH...!
MY HAND-BAG ...
I MUST'VE DROPPED IT SOME-WHERE WHEN THAT FREAK ATTACKED ME!
THIS IS BAD!

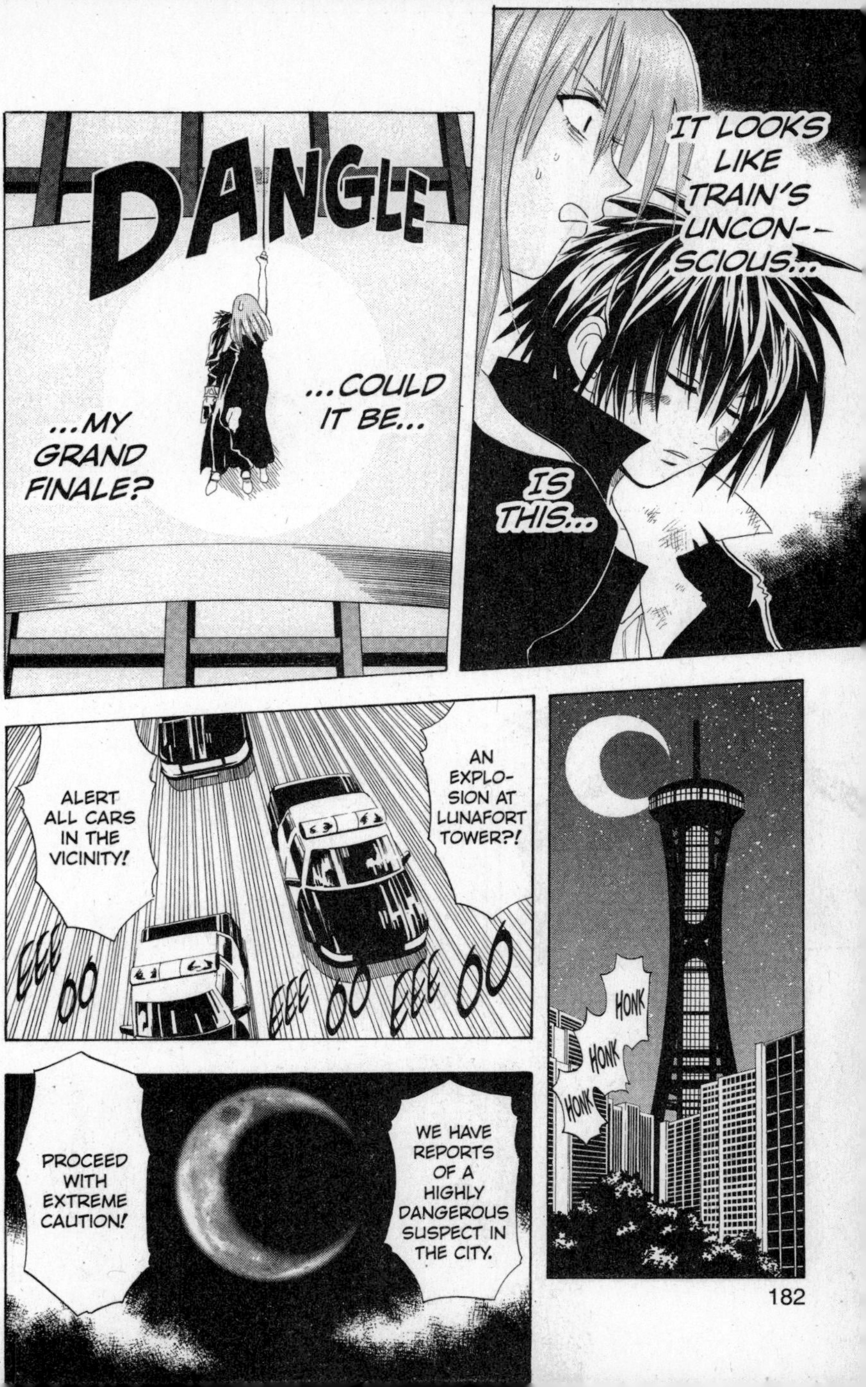
IT LOOKS LIKE TRAIN'S UNCON- -SCIOUS...
IS THIS...
DANGLE
...COULD IT BE...
...MY GRAND FINALE?
HONK
HONK
HONK
AN EXPLOSION AT LUNAFORT TOWER?!
ALERT ALL CARS IN THE VICINITY!
EEE OO
EEE OO EEE OO
WE HAVE REPORTS OF A HIGHLY DANGEROUS SUSPECT IN THE CITY.
PROCEED WITH EXTREME CAUTION!

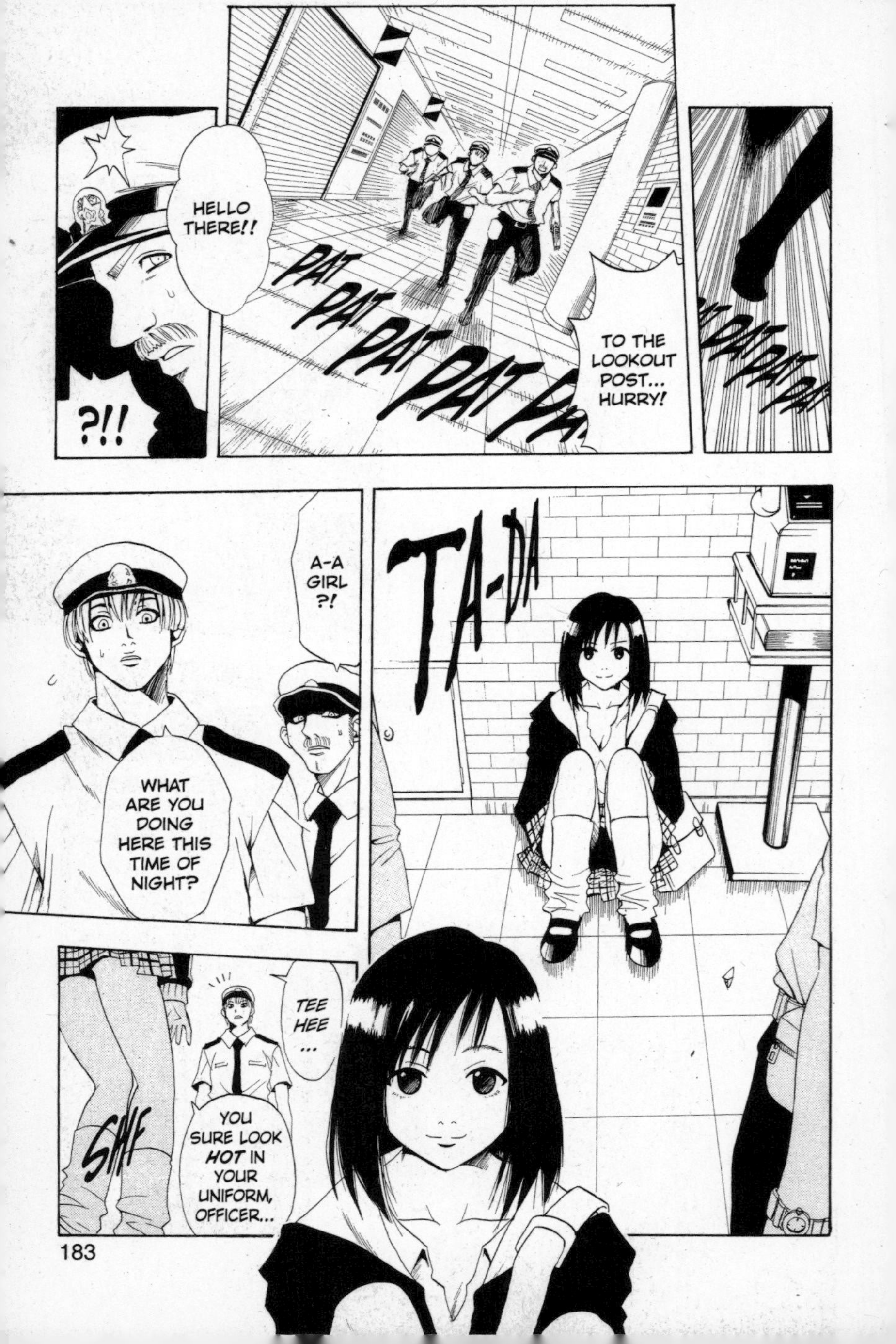
TO THE LOOKOUT POST... HURRY!
PAT PAT PAT PAT PAT
HELLO THERE!!
?!!
TA-DA
A-A GIRL ?!
WHAT ARE YOU DOING HERE THIS TIME OF NIGHT?
TEE HEE ...
YOU SURE LOOK *HOT* IN YOUR UNIFORM, OFFICER...
SHF

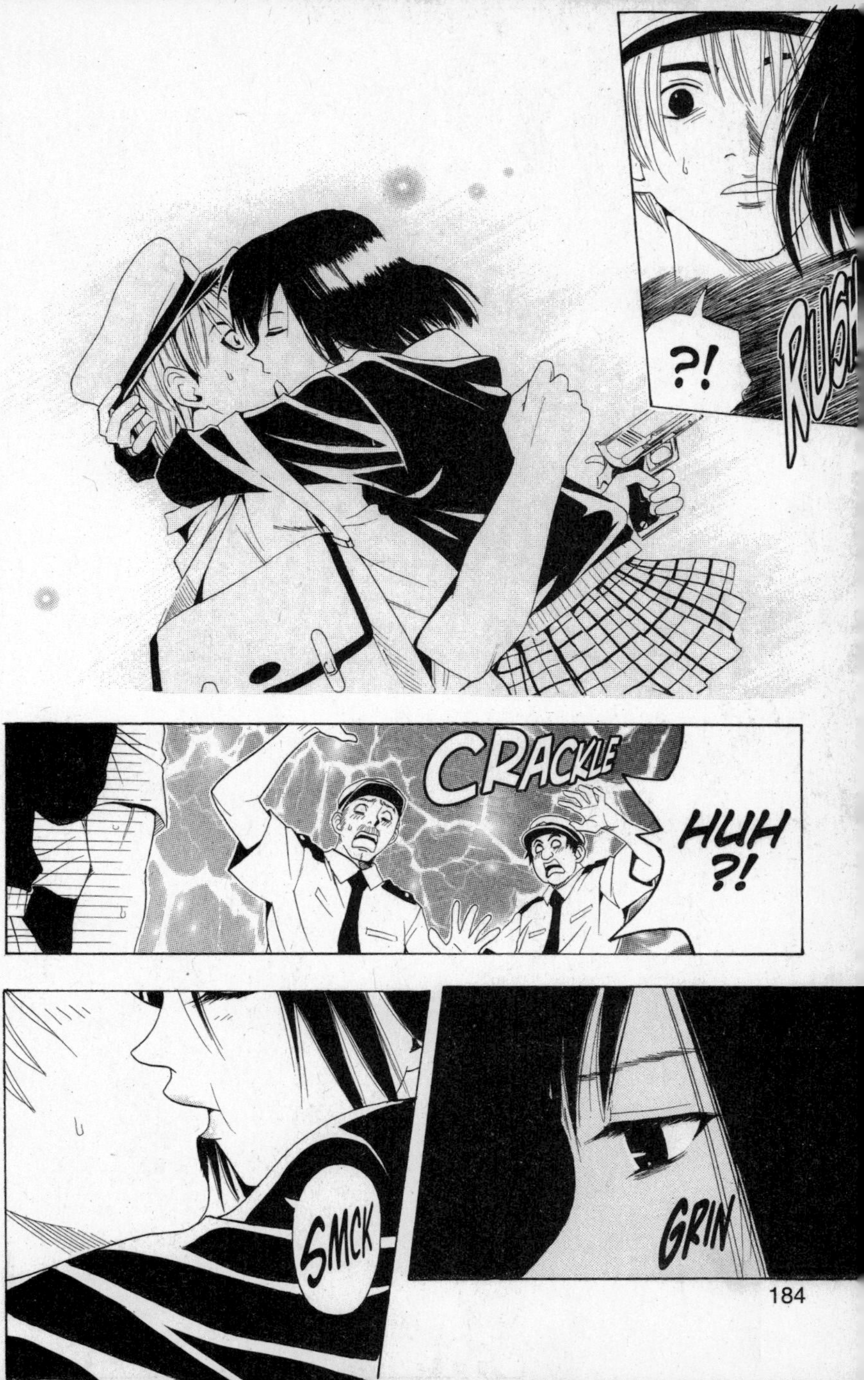
?!
RUSH
CRACKLE
HUH ?!
GRIN
SMCK

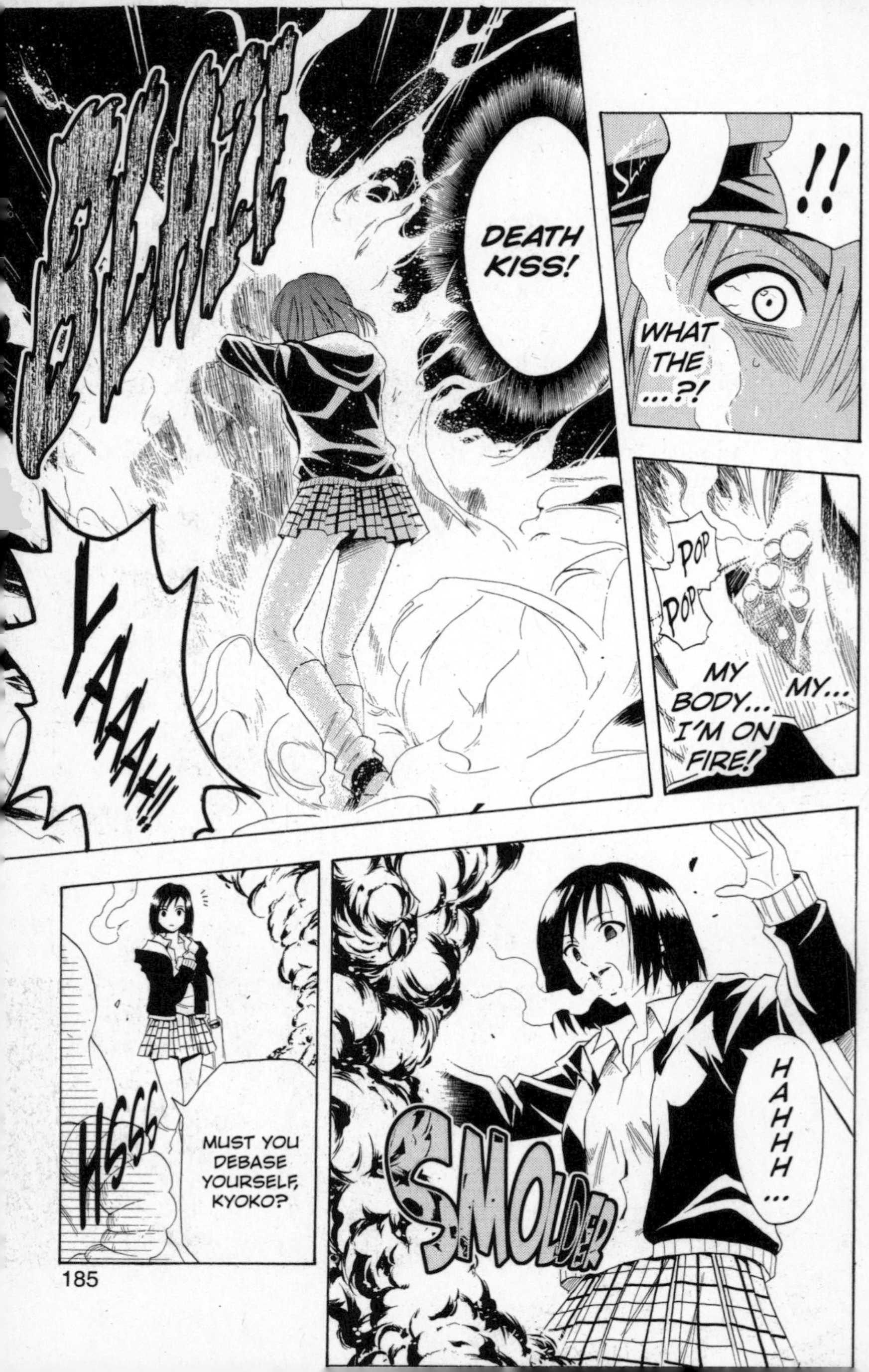
!!
WHAT THE ...?!
POP
POP
MY... MY BODY... I'M ON FIRE!
DEATH KISS!
YAAAAH!!
HAHHH ...
SMOLDER
HSSS
MUST YOU DEBASE YOURSELF, KYOKO?

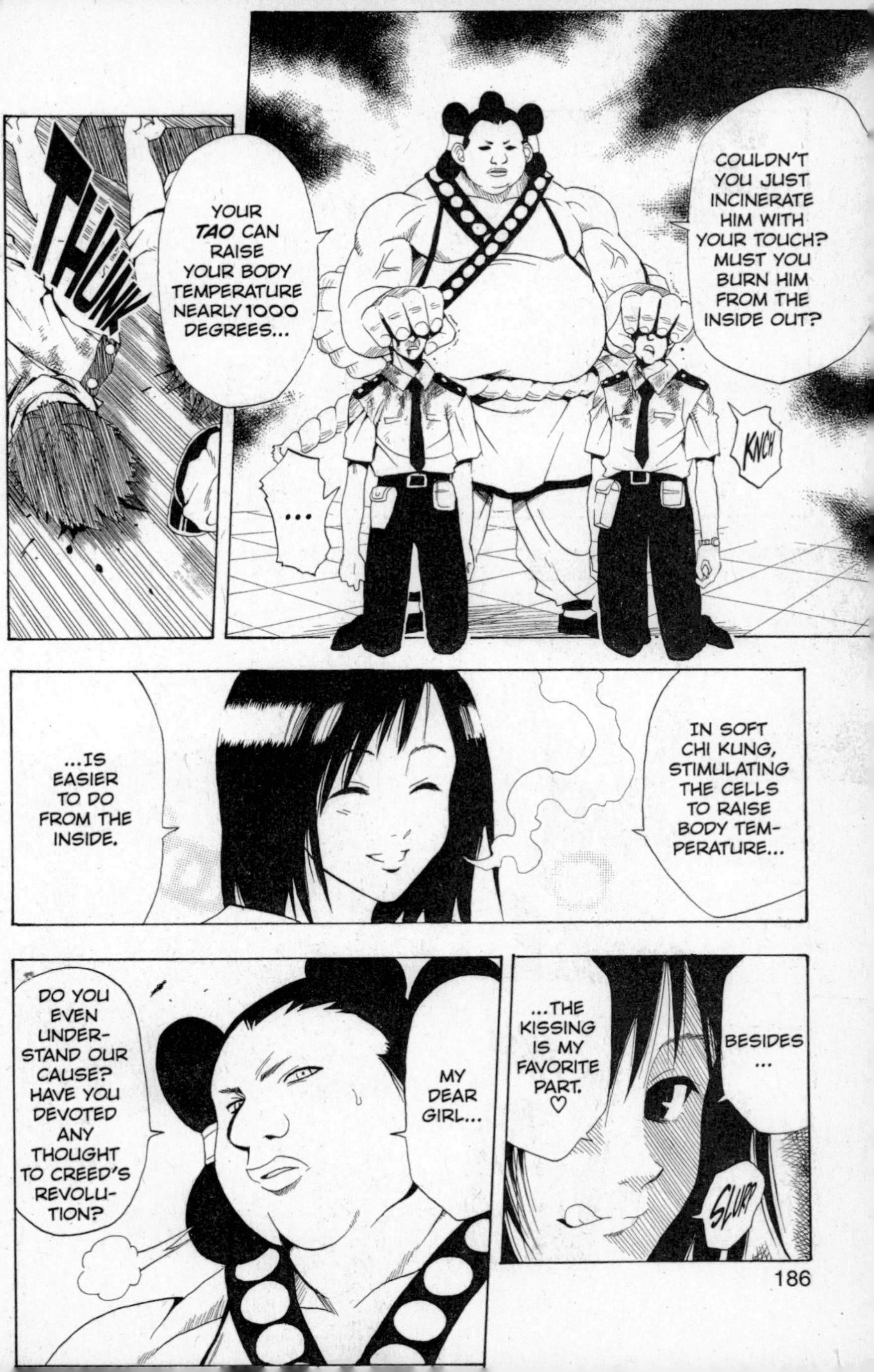
COULDN'T YOU JUST INCINERATE HIM WITH YOUR TOUCH? MUST YOU BURN HIM FROM THE INSIDE OUT?
YOUR *TAO* CAN RAISE YOUR BODY TEMPERATURE NEARLY 1000 DEGREES...
KNCH
...
THUNK
IN SOFT CHI KUNG, STIMULATING THE CELLS TO RAISE BODY TEMPERATURE...
...IS EASIER TO DO FROM THE INSIDE.
BESIDES...
...THE KISSING IS MY FAVORITE PART. ♡
SLURP
MY DEAR GIRL...
DO YOU EVEN UNDERSTAND OUR CAUSE? HAVE YOU DEVOTED ANY THOUGHT TO CREED'S REVOLUTION?

READ THIS WAY

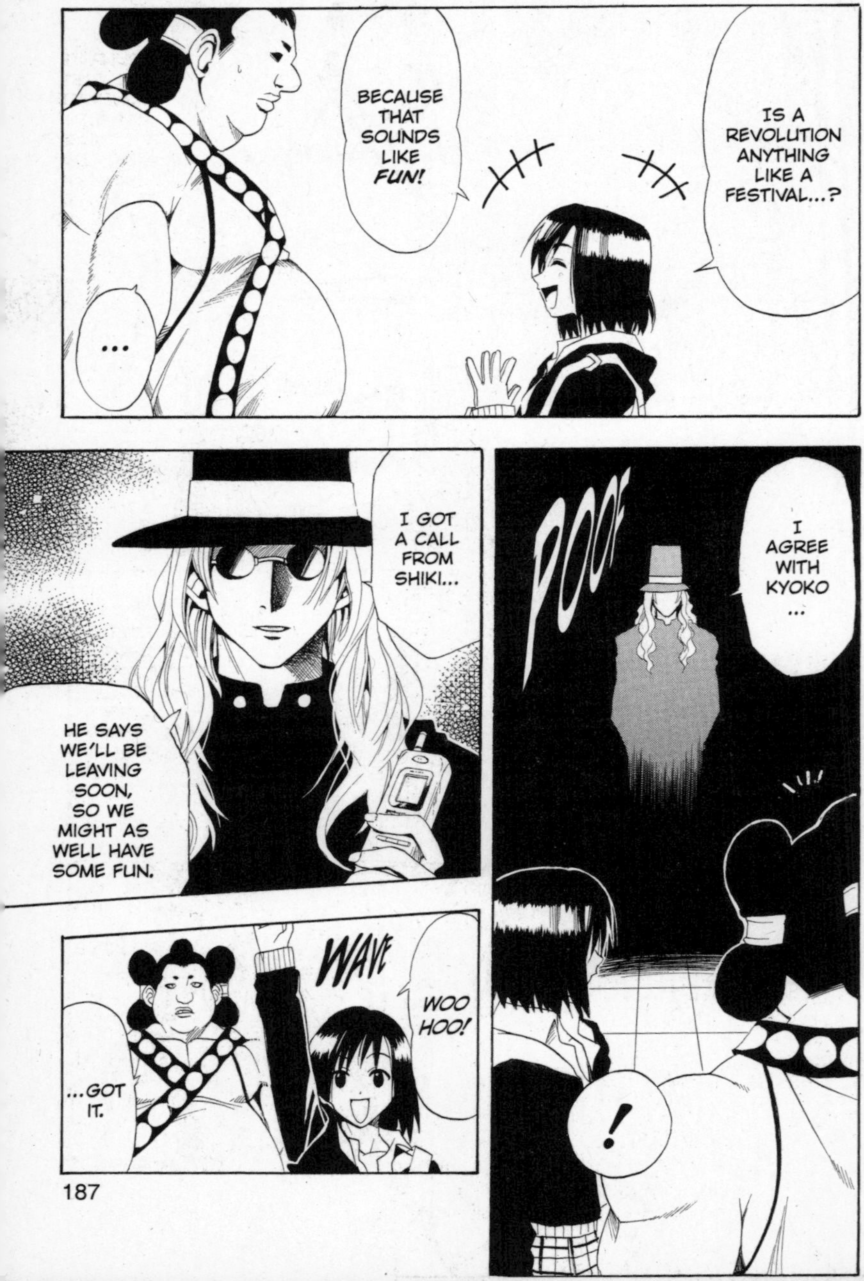

IS A REVOLUTION ANYTHING LIKE A FESTIVAL...?
BECAUSE THAT SOUNDS LIKE *FUN!*
...
POOF
I AGREE WITH KYOKO ...
!
I GOT A CALL FROM SHIKI...
HE SAYS WE'LL BE LEAVING SOON, SO WE MIGHT AS WELL HAVE SOME FUN.
WAVE
WOO HOO!
...GOT IT.

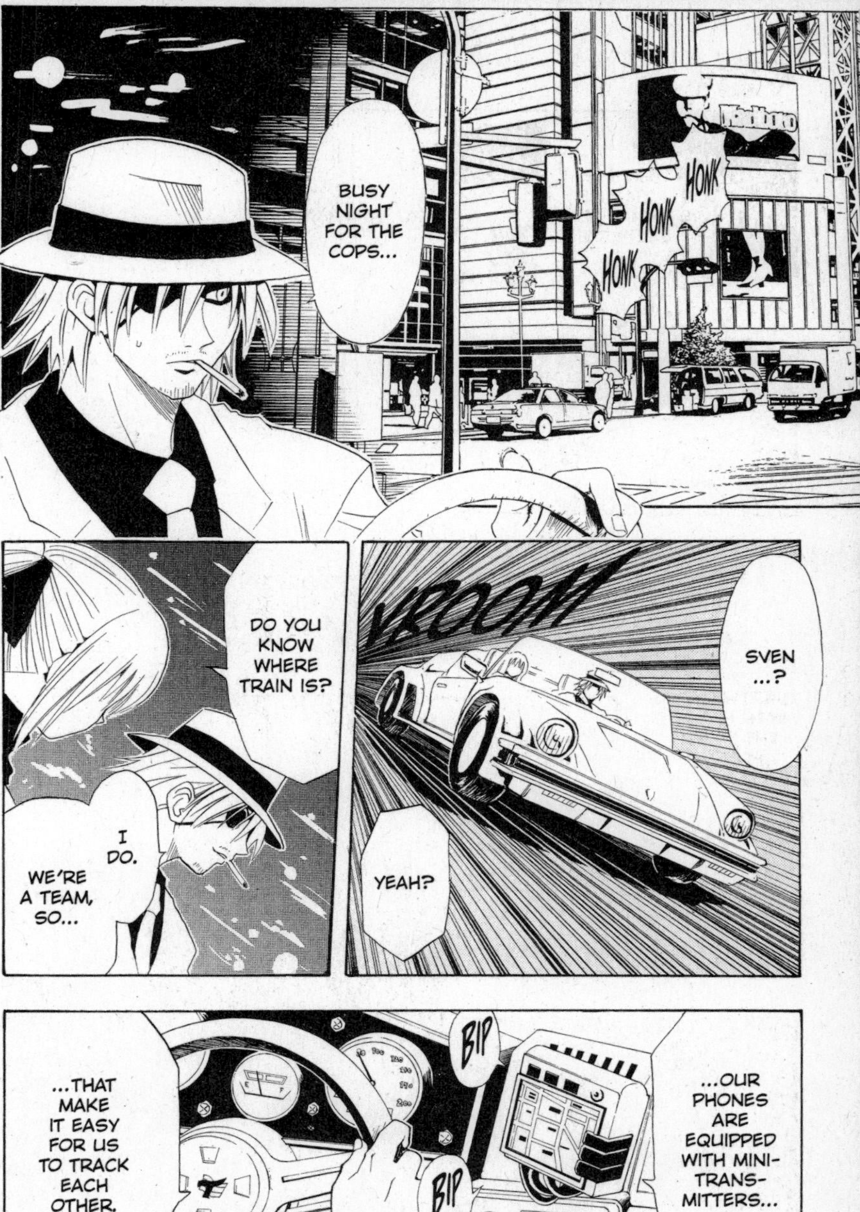
BUSY NIGHT FOR THE COPS...
HONK
HONK
HONK
SVEN ...?
VROOM
YEAH?
DO YOU KNOW WHERE TRAIN IS?
I DO.
WE'RE A TEAM, SO...
...OUR PHONES ARE EQUIPPED WITH MINI-TRANS-MITTERS...
BIP
BIP
...THAT MAKE IT EASY FOR US TO TRACK EACH OTHER.

READ THIS WAY

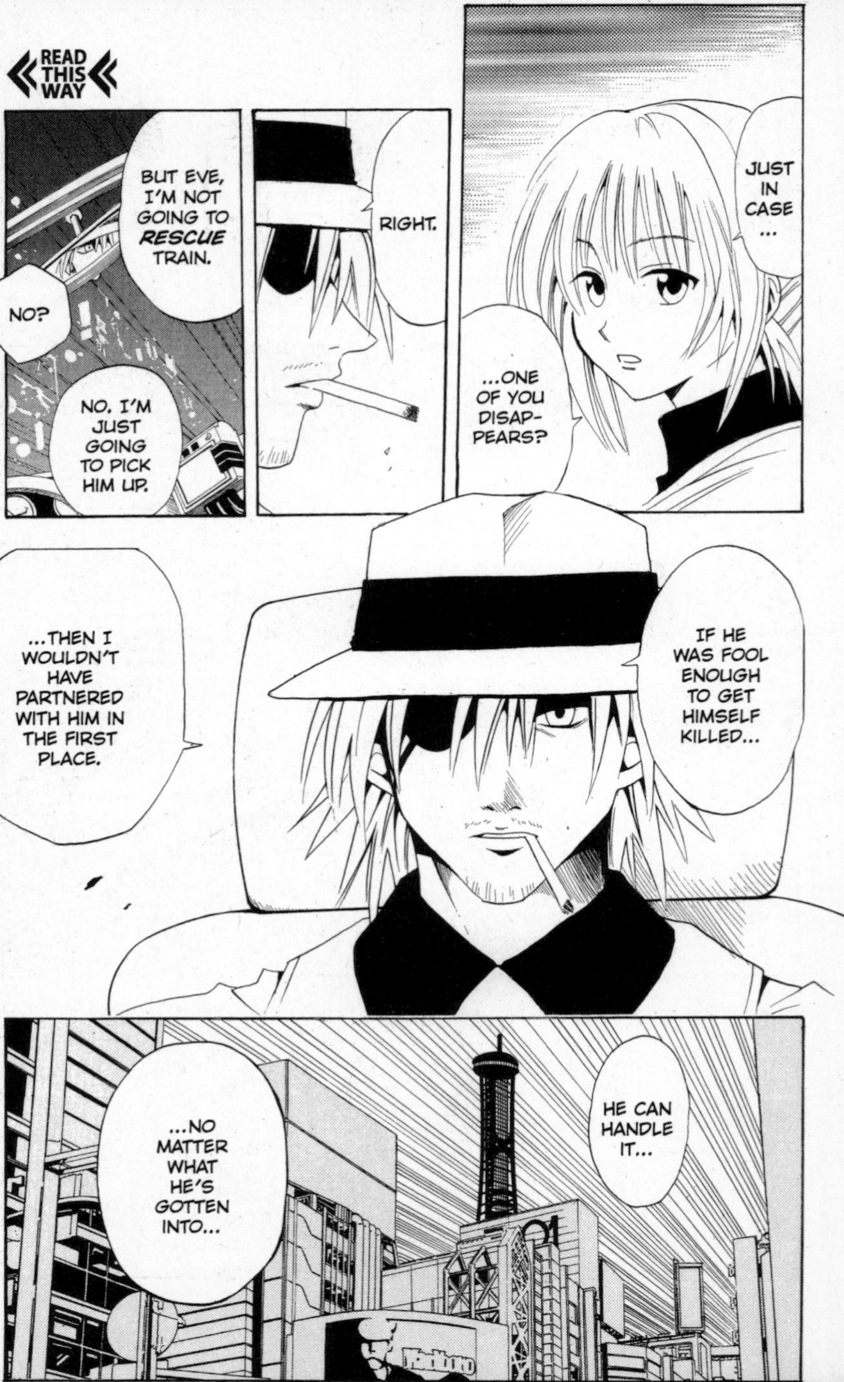
JUST IN CASE...
...ONE OF YOU DISAPPEARS?
RIGHT.
BUT EVE, I'M NOT GOING TO *RESCUE* TRAIN.
NO?
NO. I'M JUST GOING TO PICK HIM UP.
IF HE WAS FOOL ENOUGH TO GET HIMSELF KILLED...
...THEN I WOULDN'T HAVE PARTNERED WITH HIM IN THE FIRST PLACE.
HE CAN HANDLE IT...
...NO MATTER WHAT HE'S GOTTEN INTO...

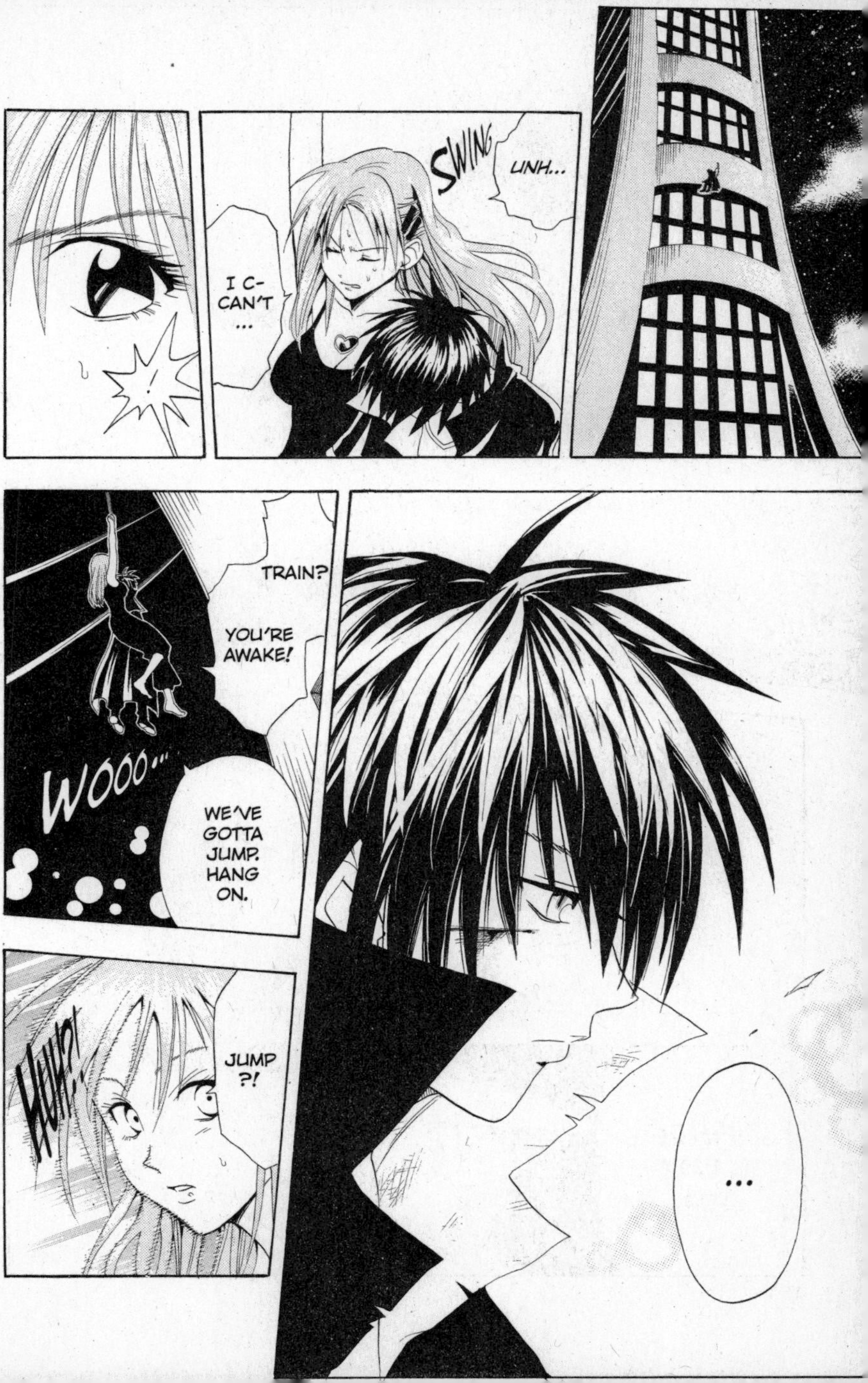
SWING
UNH...
I C-CAN'T ...
!
...
TRAIN?
YOU'RE AWAKE!
WOOO...
WE'VE GOTTA JUMP. HANG ON.
HUH?!
JUMP?!

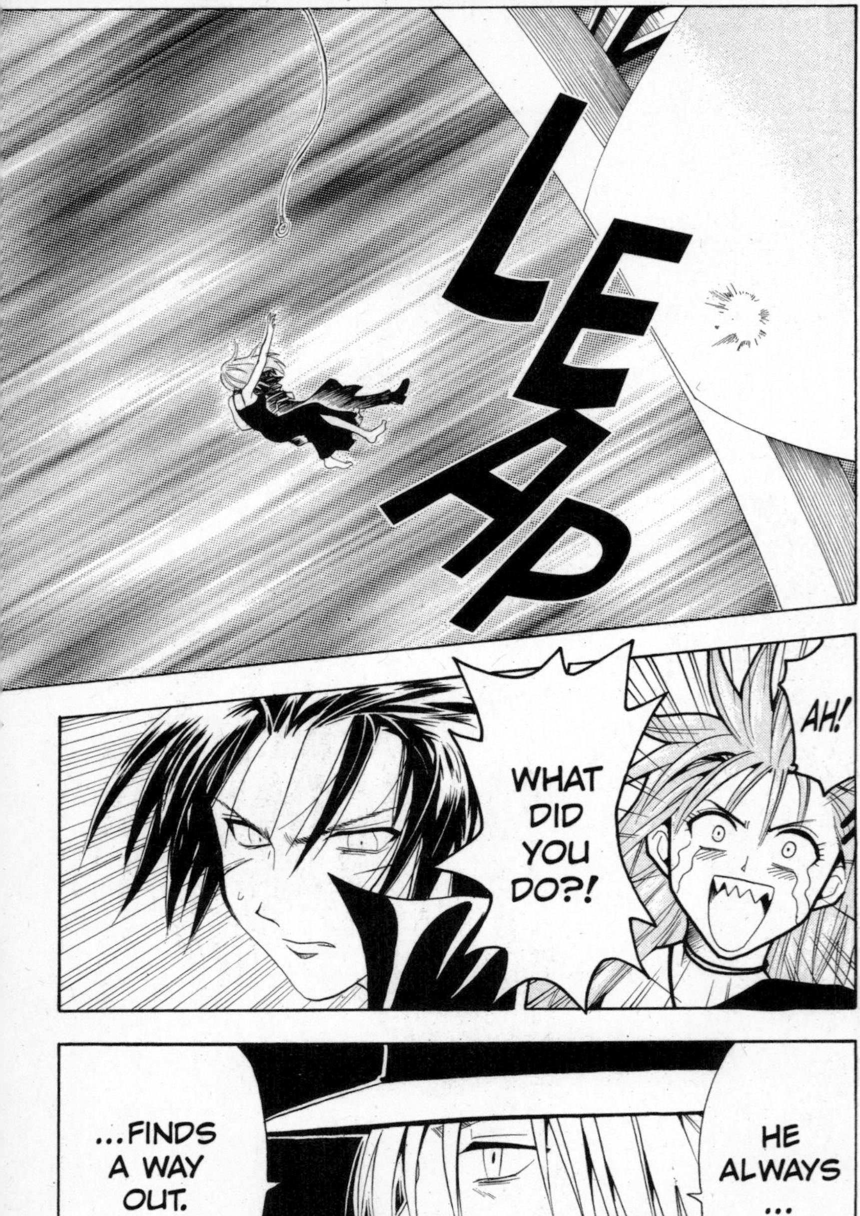
LEAP
AH!
WHAT DID YOU DO?!
HE ALWAYS ...
...FINDS A WAY OUT.

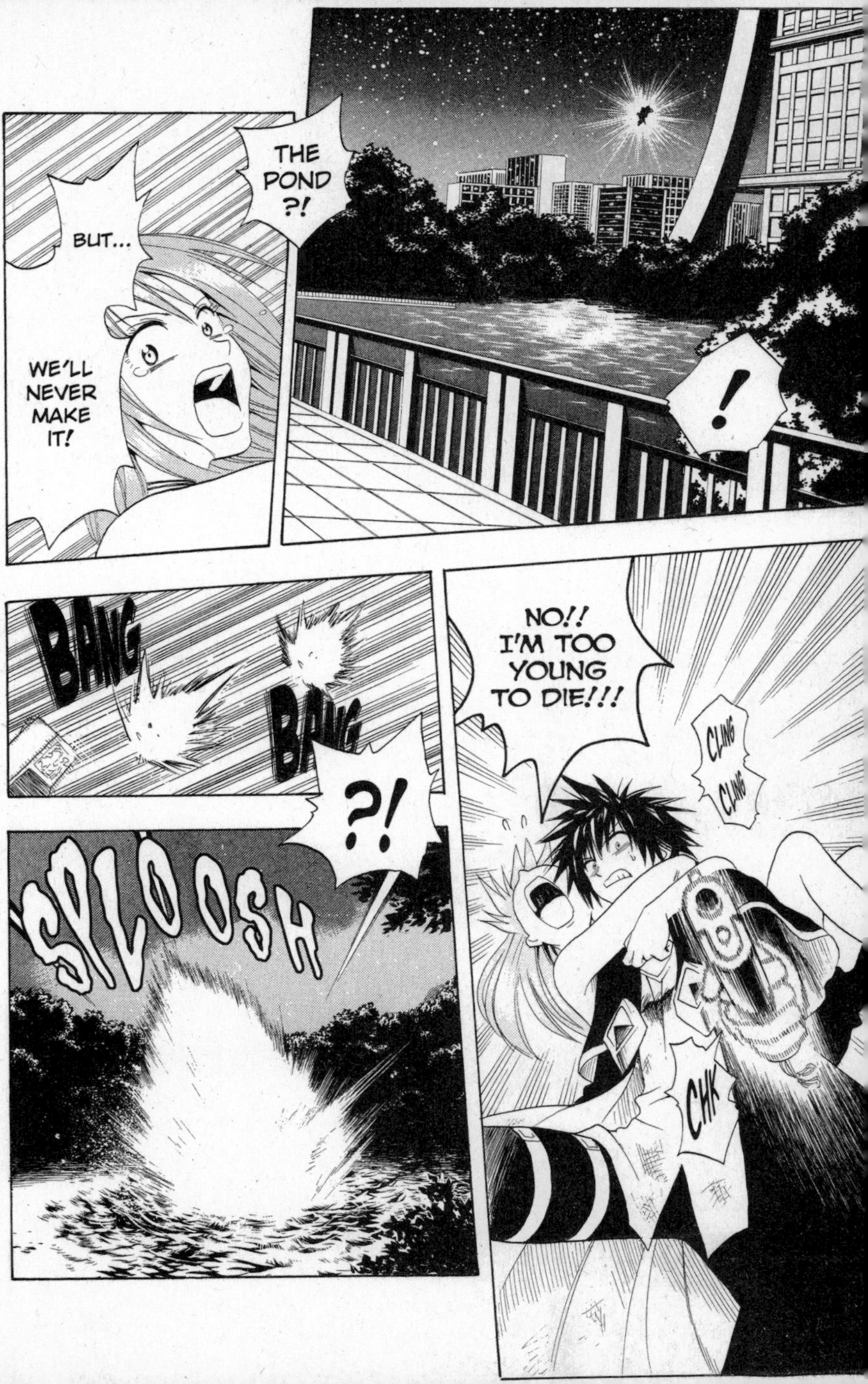
THE POND ?!
!
BUT...
WE'LL NEVER MAKE IT!
NO!! I'M TOO YOUNG TO DIE!!!
CLING
CLING
CHK
BANG
BANG
?!
SPLOOSH

READ THIS WAY

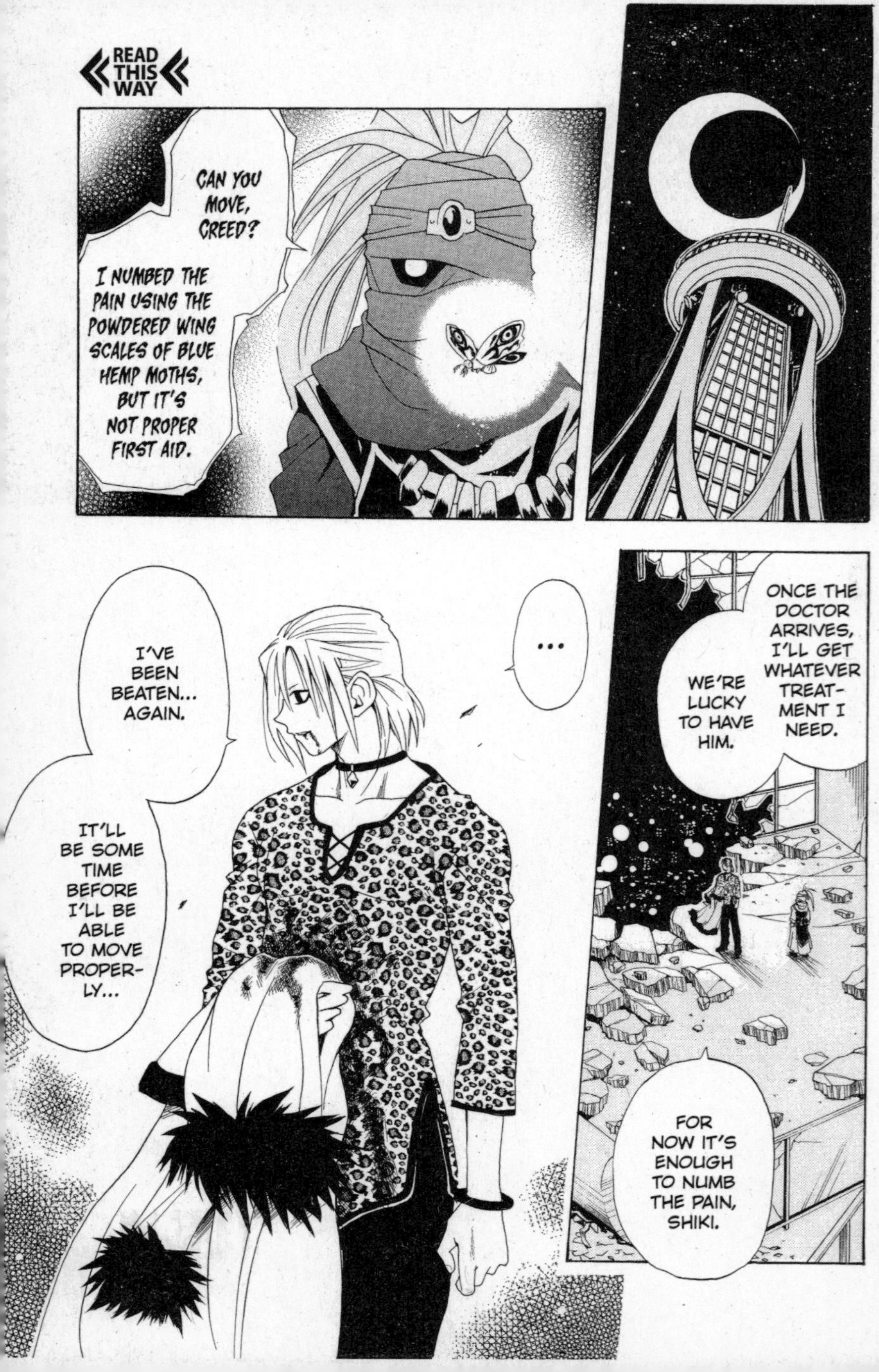
CAN YOU MOVE, CREED?
I NUMBED THE PAIN USING THE POWDERED WING SCALES OF BLUE HEMP MOTHS, BUT IT'S NOT PROPER FIRST AID.
ONCE THE DOCTOR ARRIVES, I'LL GET WHATEVER TREAT-MENT I NEED.
WE'RE LUCKY TO HAVE HIM.
FOR NOW IT'S ENOUGH TO NUMB THE PAIN, SHIKI.
...
I'VE BEEN BEATEN... AGAIN.
IT'LL BE SOME TIME BEFORE I'LL BE ABLE TO MOVE PROPER-LY...

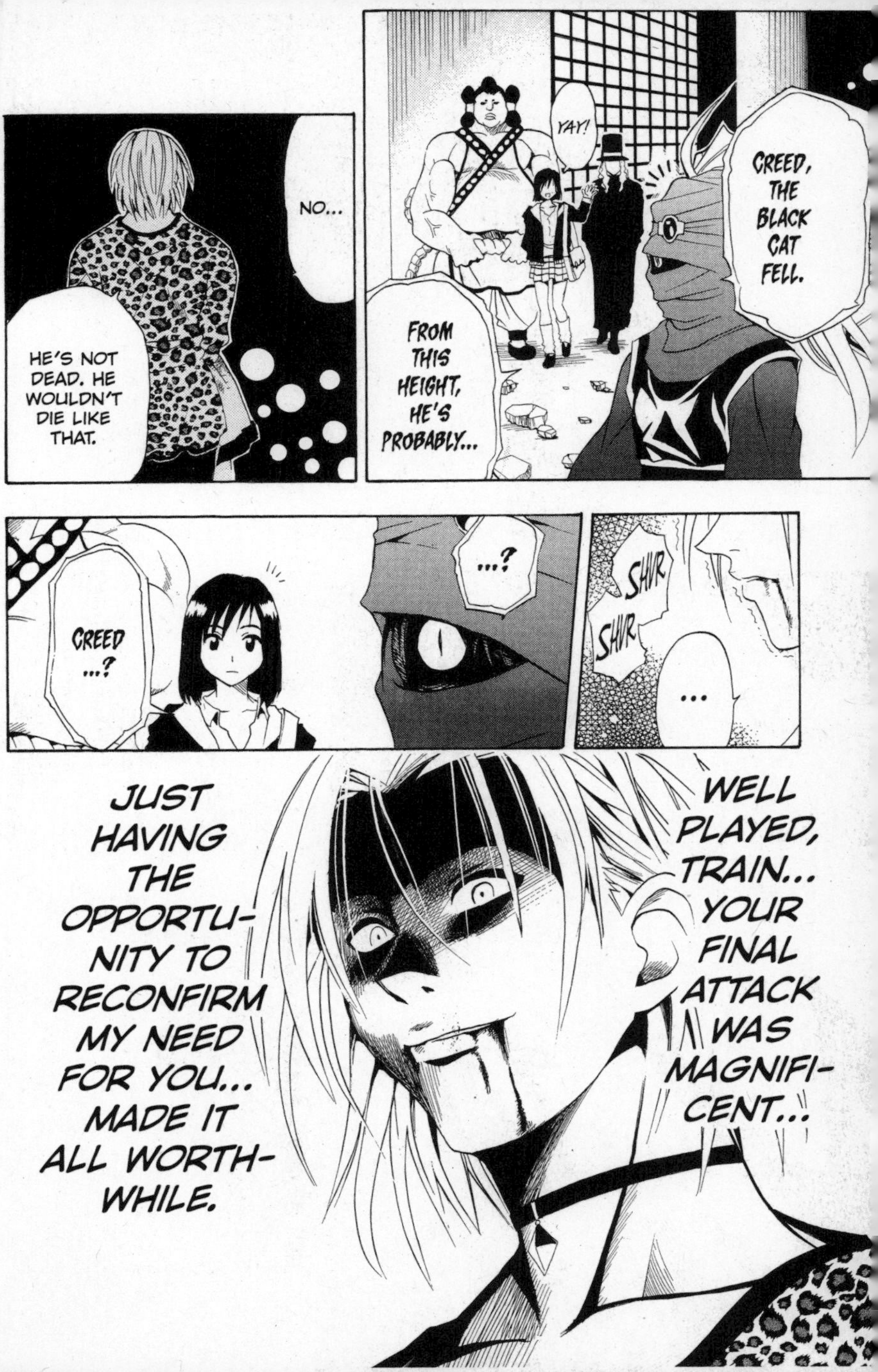

CREED, THE BLACK CAT FELL.
YAY!
FROM THIS HEIGHT, HE'S PROBABLY...
NO...
HE'S NOT DEAD. HE WOULDN'T DIE LIKE THAT.
SHVR
SHVR
...
...?
CREED ...?
WELL PLAYED, TRAIN... YOUR FINAL ATTACK WAS MAGNIFICENT...
JUST HAVING THE OPPORTUNITY TO RECONFIRM MY NEED FOR YOU... MADE IT ALL WORTHWHILE.

READ THIS WAY

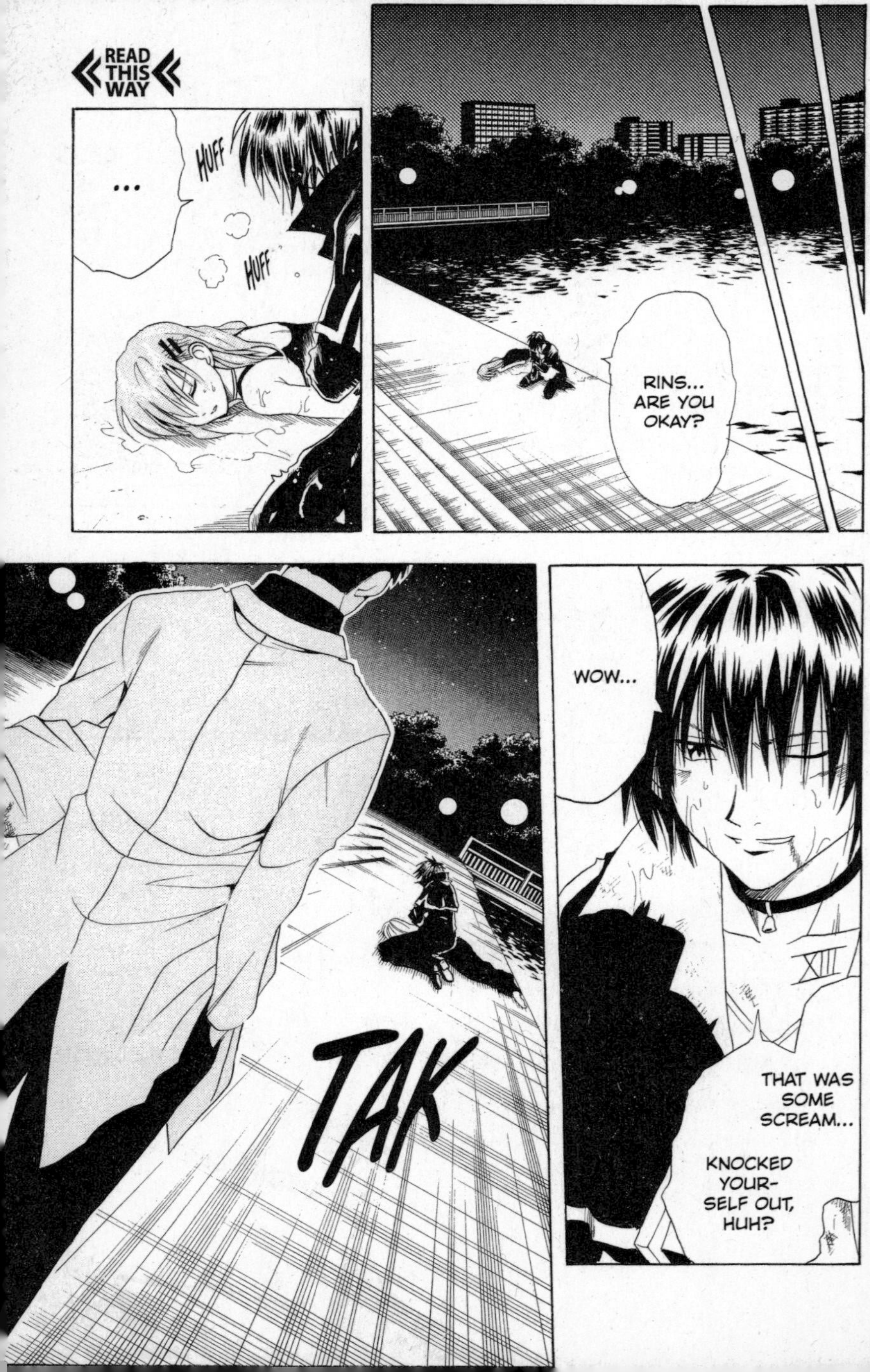
RINS... ARE YOU OKAY?
HUFF
HUFF
...
WOW...
THAT WAS SOME SCREAM...
KNOCKED YOUR-SELF OUT, HUH?
TAK

 **QUICK NOTES**

◎ **THE BLACK CAT GRENADE:**
TRAIN THOUGHT THE GRENADES SVEN
MADE WERE TOO PLAIN, SO HE DREW THAT
BLACK CAT FREEHAND. NOT BAD! TRAIN
APPARENTLY HAS A KNACK FOR DRAWING.

◎ **CREED'S NECKLACE:**
THERE'S NO SPECIAL SIGNIFICANCE TO HIS
NECKLACE. PERHAPS HE JUST WANTED TO
COPY TRAIN... WHAT A GUY.

◎ **RINSLET IN TRAIN'S CLOTHING:**
I RAN OUT OF SPACE, SO I COULDN'T
EXPLAIN IT ORIGINALLY AND A FEW READERS
WERE CONCERNED... YES, RINS IS WEARING
TRAIN'S OUTFIT. IT WASN'T SVEN WHO
CHANGED HER CLOTHES, THOUGH (EEP!).
ACTUALLY, SVEN TOOK THEM TO AN UN-
DERGROUND HOSPITAL. THAT'S HOW HE
KNOWS TO SAY, "IT'S NOT TOO SERIOUS,
BUT YOU INJURED THE TENDON IN YOUR
RIGHT ARM."

IT'S NOT TOO SERIOUS, BUT...

...YOU INJURED THE TENDON IN YOUR RIGHT ARM.

Chapter 18: When Day Breaks...

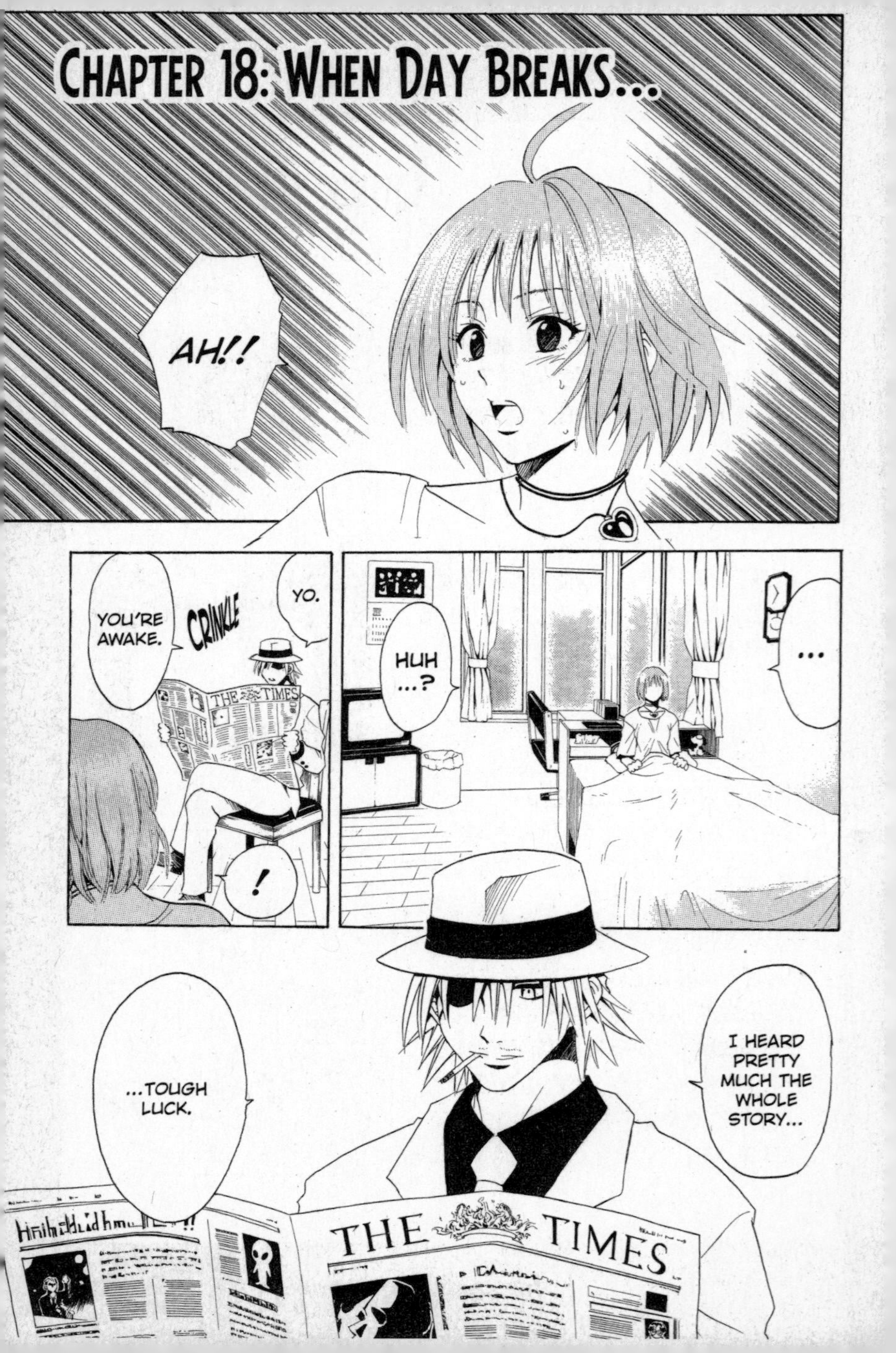
AH!!
...
HUH ...?
YO.
CRINKLE
YOU'RE AWAKE.
THE TIMES
!
I HEARD PRETTY MUCH THE WHOLE STORY...
...TOUGH LUCK.
THE TIMES

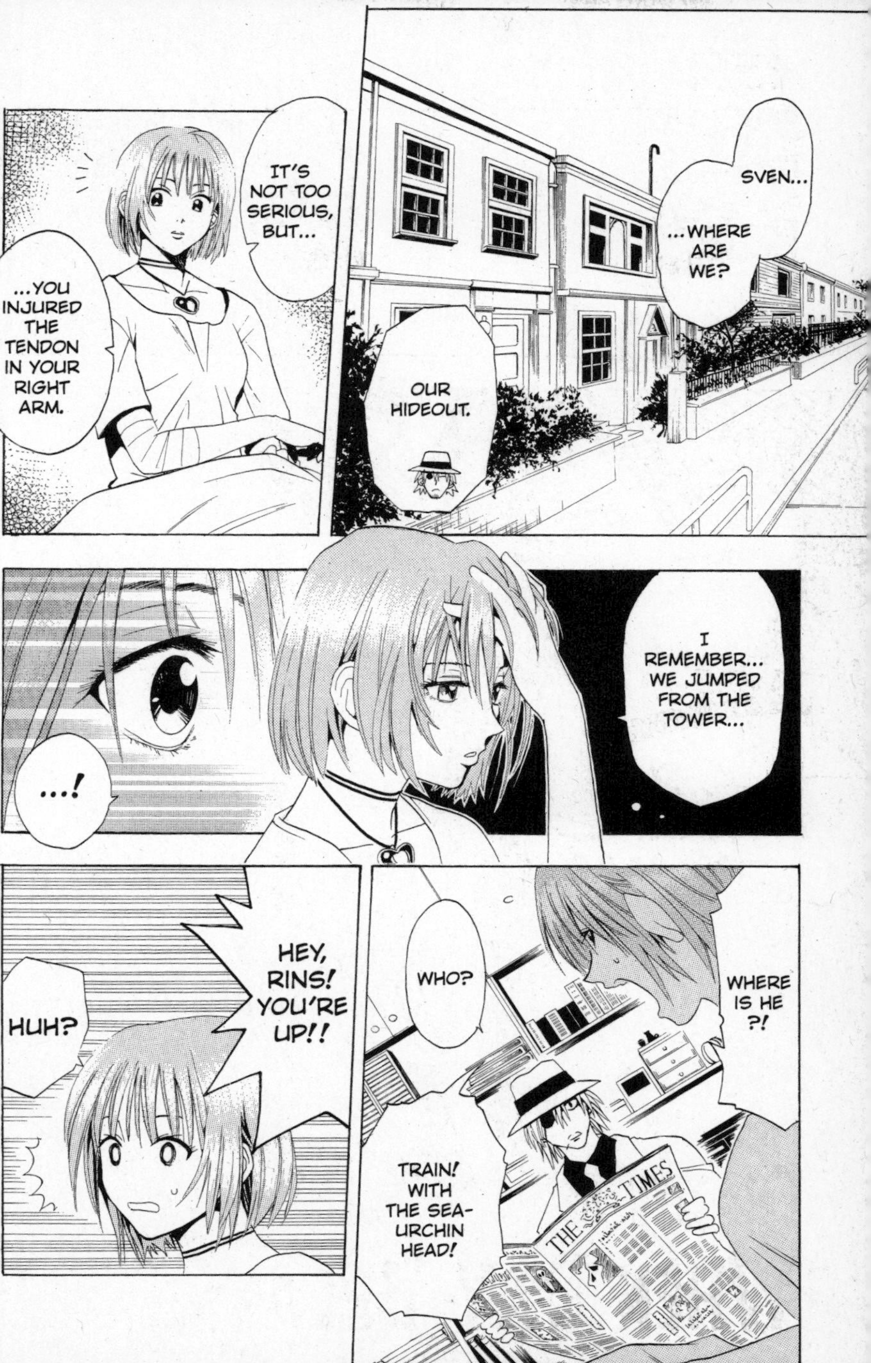

SVEN...
...WHERE ARE WE?
OUR HIDEOUT.
IT'S NOT TOO SERIOUS, BUT...
...YOU INJURED THE TENDON IN YOUR RIGHT ARM.
I REMEMBER... WE JUMPED FROM THE TOWER...
...!
WHERE IS HE ?!
WHO?
TRAIN! WITH THE SEA-URCHIN HEAD!
THE TIMES
HEY, RINS! YOU'RE UP!!
HUH?

READ THIS WAY

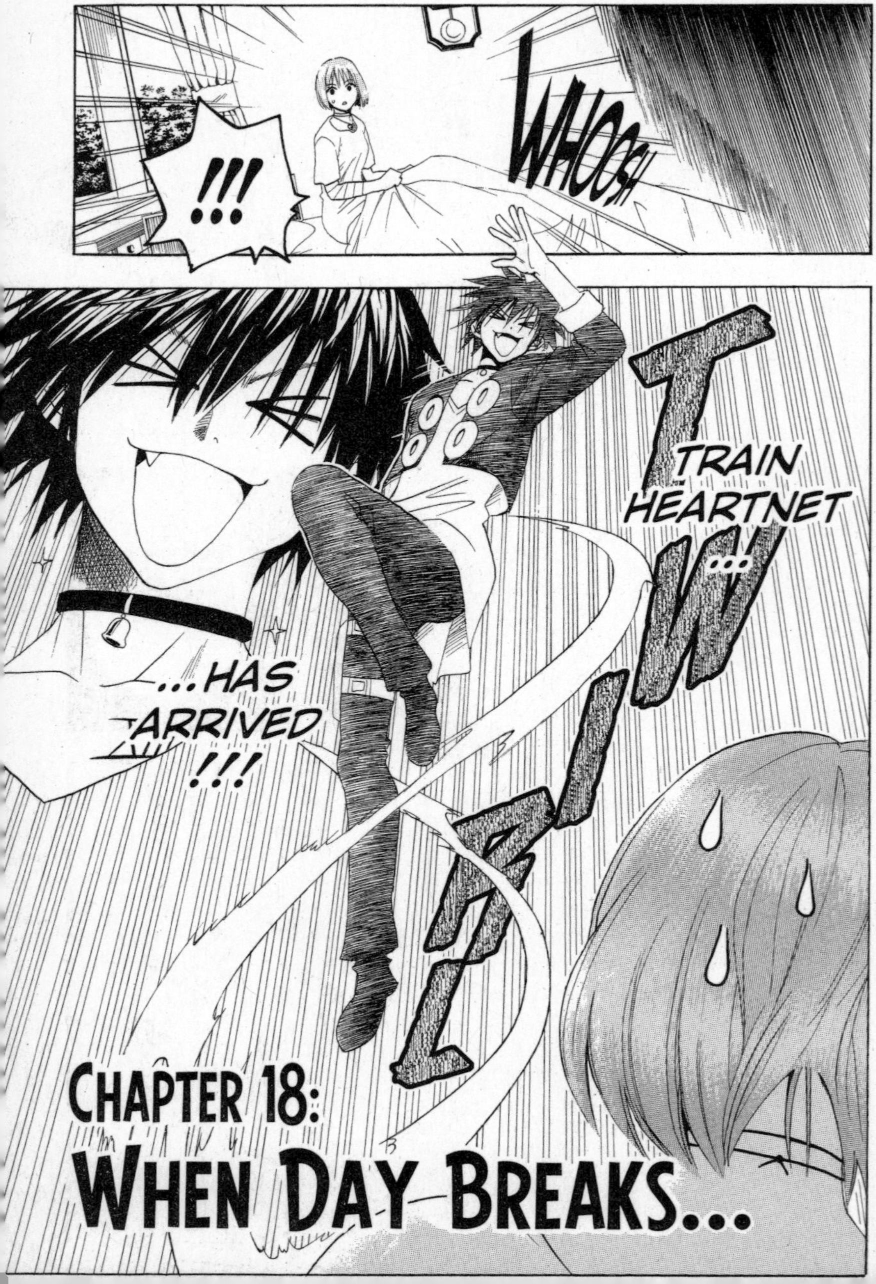
WHOOSH
!!!
TRAIN HEARTNET...
TWIRL
...HAS ARRIVED!!!
Chapter 18:
When Day Breaks...

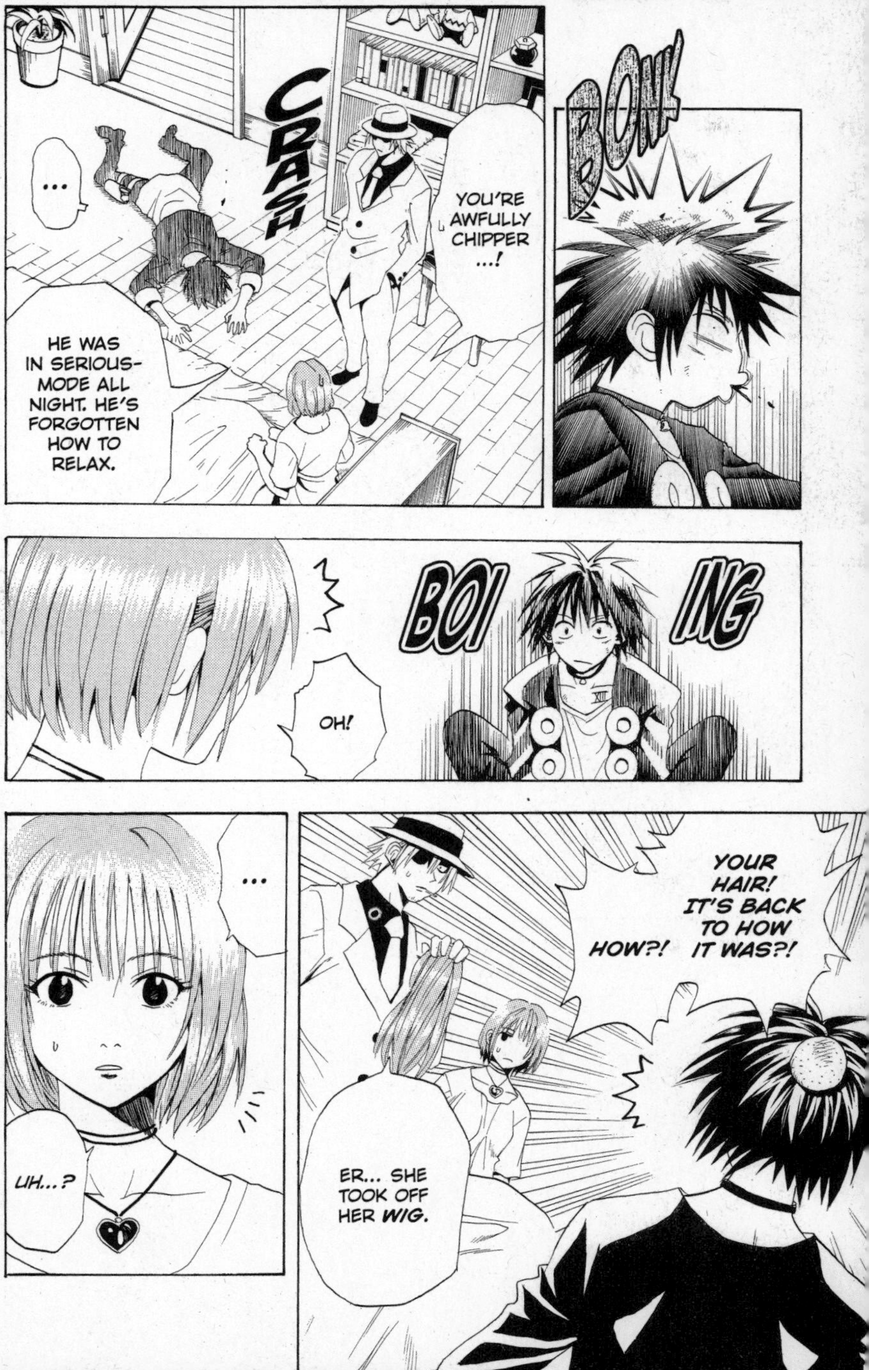
BONK
YOU'RE AWFULLY CHIPPER ...!
CRASH
...
HE WAS IN SERIOUS-MODE ALL NIGHT. HE'S FORGOTTEN HOW TO RELAX.
BOI ING
OH!
YOUR HAIR! IT'S BACK TO HOW IT WAS?!
HOW?!
ER... SHE TOOK OFF HER WIG.
...
UH...?

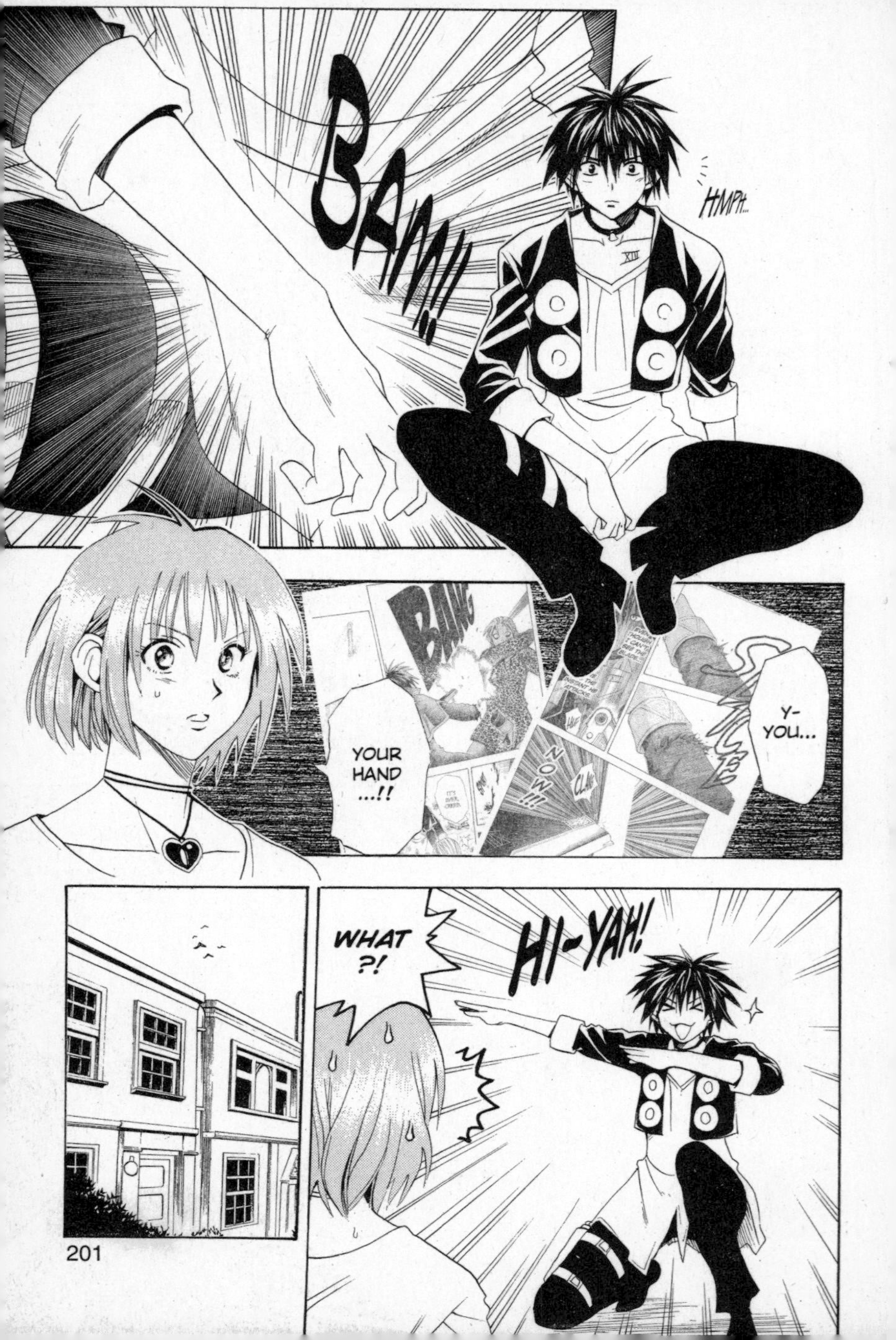
BAN!!
HMPH...
Y-YOU...
BANG
NOW!!
YOUR HAND ...!!
HI-YAH!
WHAT?!

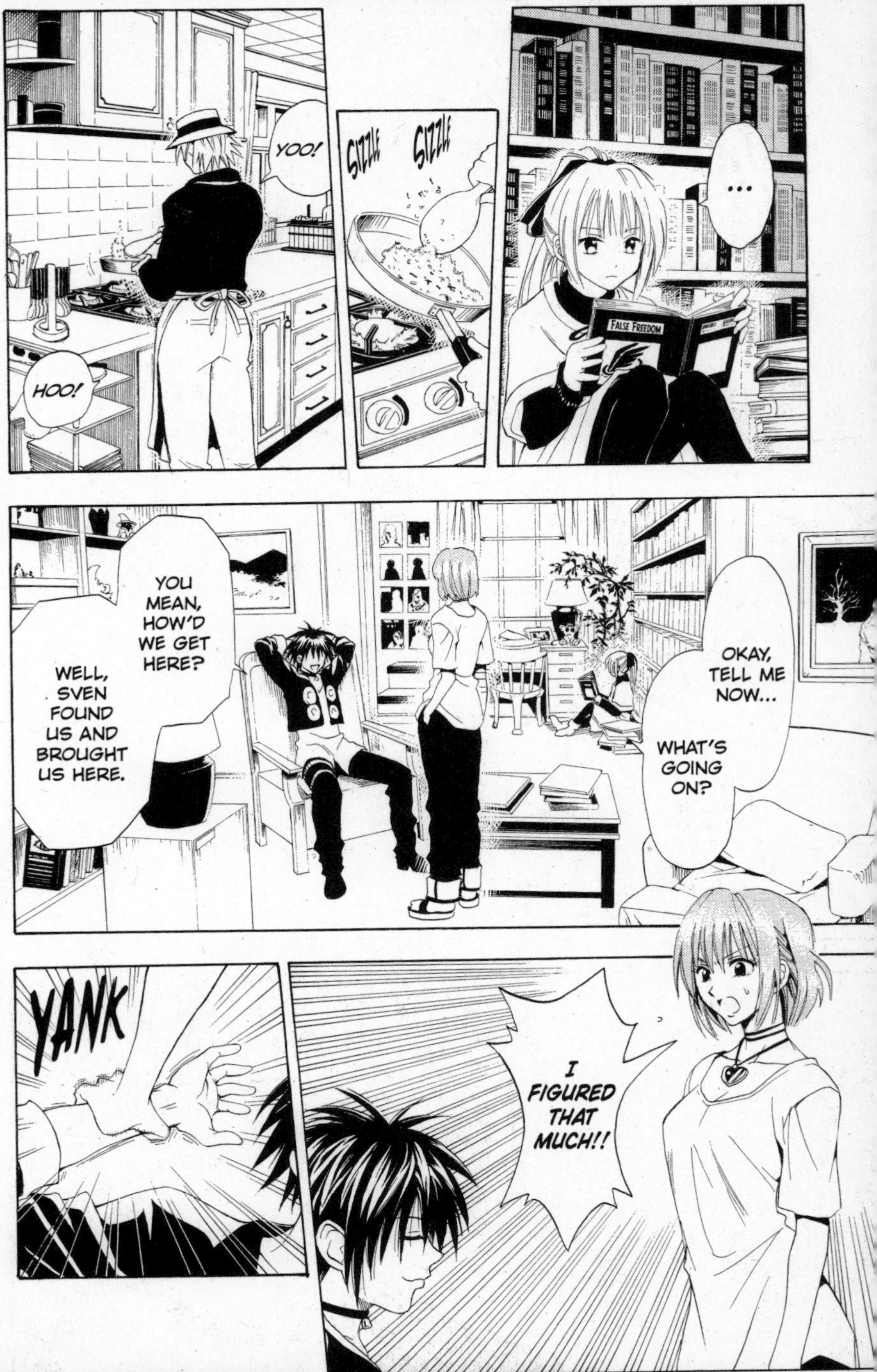
...
FALSE FREEDOM
SIZZLE SIZZLE
YOO!
HOO!
OKAY, TELL ME NOW... WHAT'S GOING ON?
YOU MEAN, HOW'D WE GET HERE?
WELL, SVEN FOUND US AND BROUGHT US HERE.
I FIGURED THAT MUCH!!
YANK

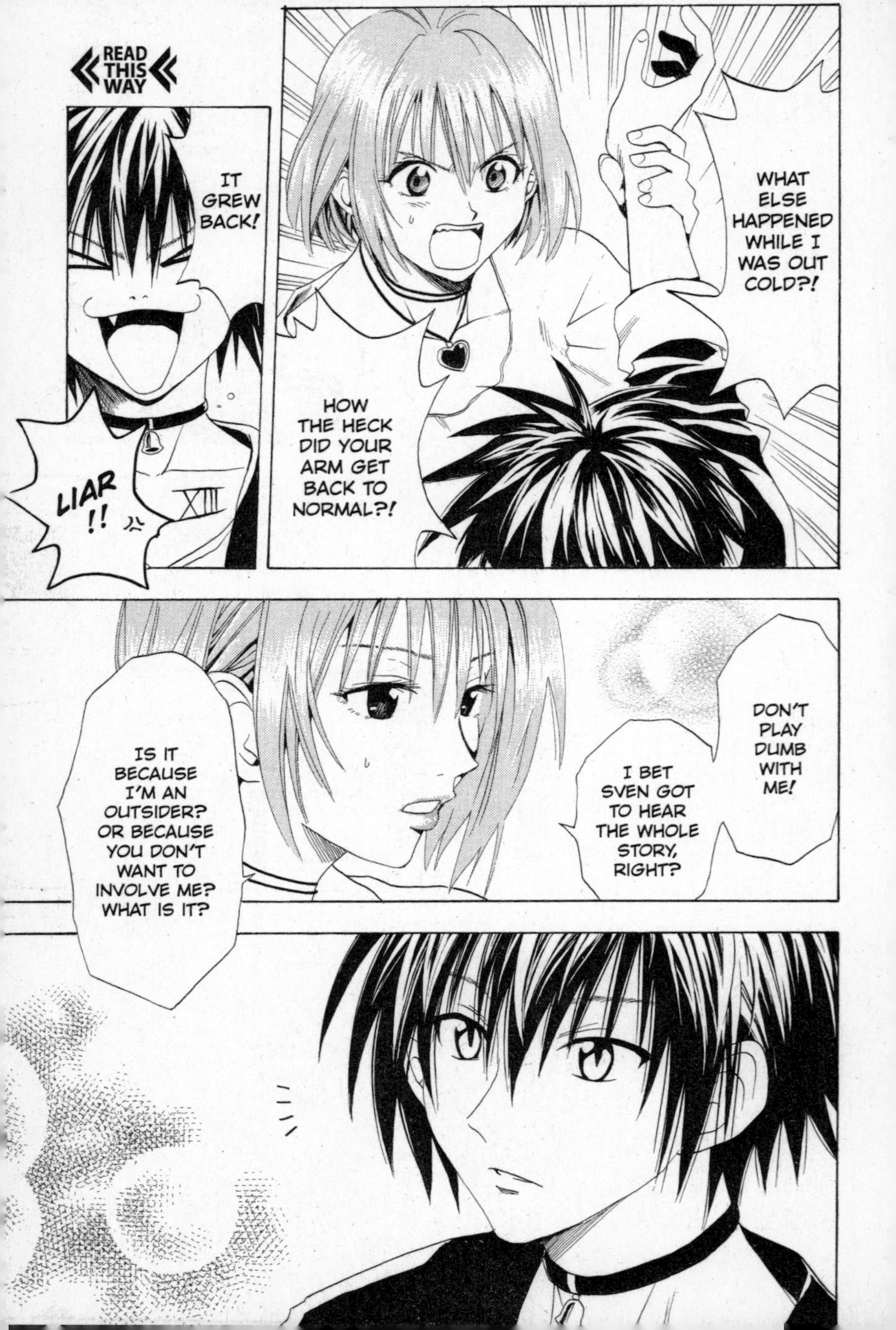
READ THIS WAY
WHAT ELSE HAPPENED WHILE I WAS OUT COLD?!
HOW THE HECK DID YOUR ARM GET BACK TO NORMAL?!
IT GREW BACK!
LIAR!!
DON'T PLAY DUMB WITH ME!
I BET SVEN GOT TO HEAR THE WHOLE STORY, RIGHT?
IS IT BECAUSE I'M AN OUTSIDER? OR BECAUSE YOU DON'T WANT TO INVOLVE ME? WHAT IS IT?

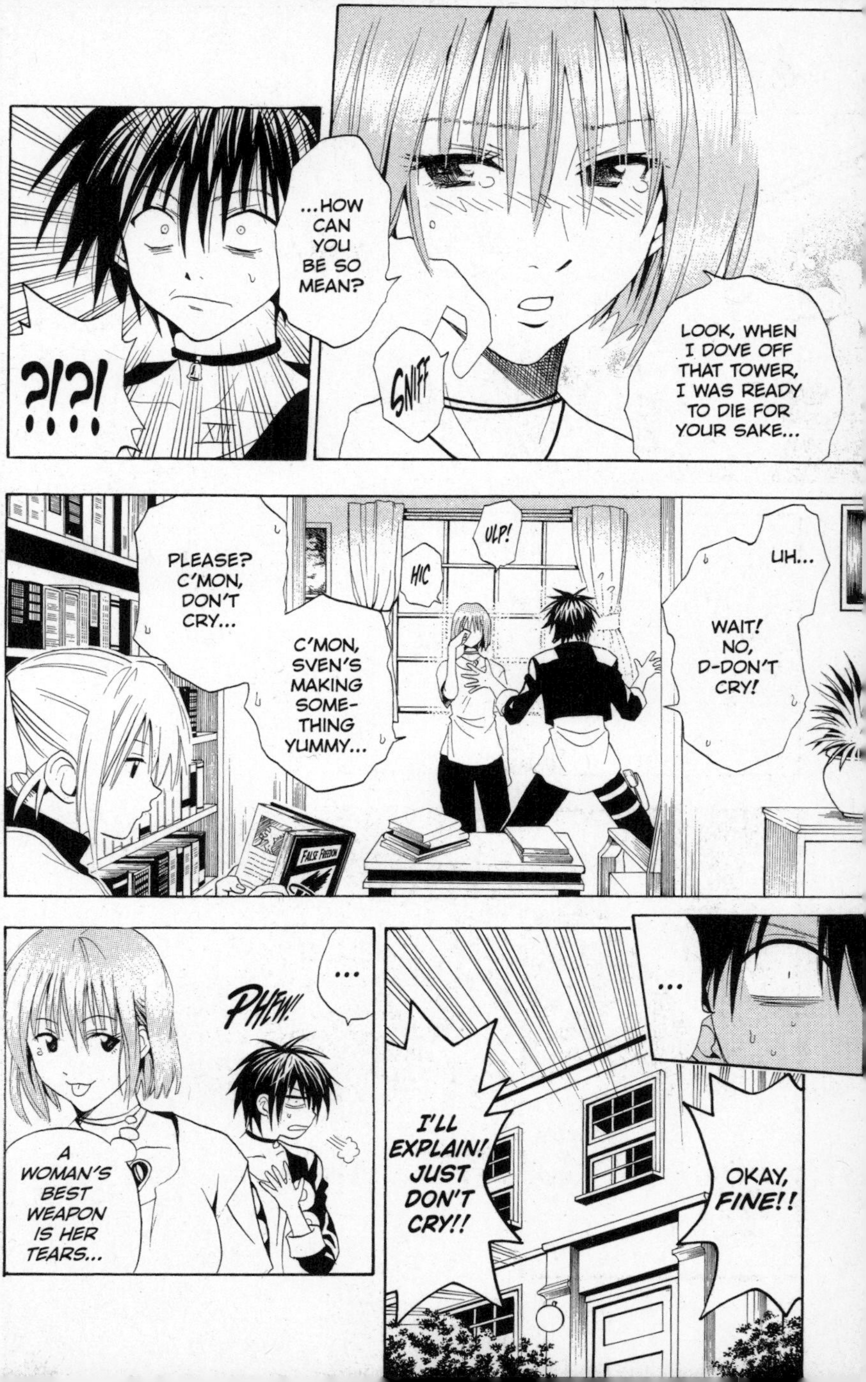
LOOK, WHEN I DOVE OFF THAT TOWER, I WAS READY TO DIE FOR YOUR SAKE...
SNIFF
...HOW CAN YOU BE SO MEAN?
?!?!
UH...
WAIT! NO, D-DON'T CRY!
ULP!
HIC
C'MON, SVEN'S MAKING SOME-THING YUMMY...
PLEASE? C'MON, DON'T CRY...
FALSE FREEDOM
...
OKAY, FINE!!
I'LL EXPLAIN! JUST DON'T CRY!!
...
PHEW!
A WOMAN'S BEST WEAPON IS HER TEARS...

READ THIS WAY

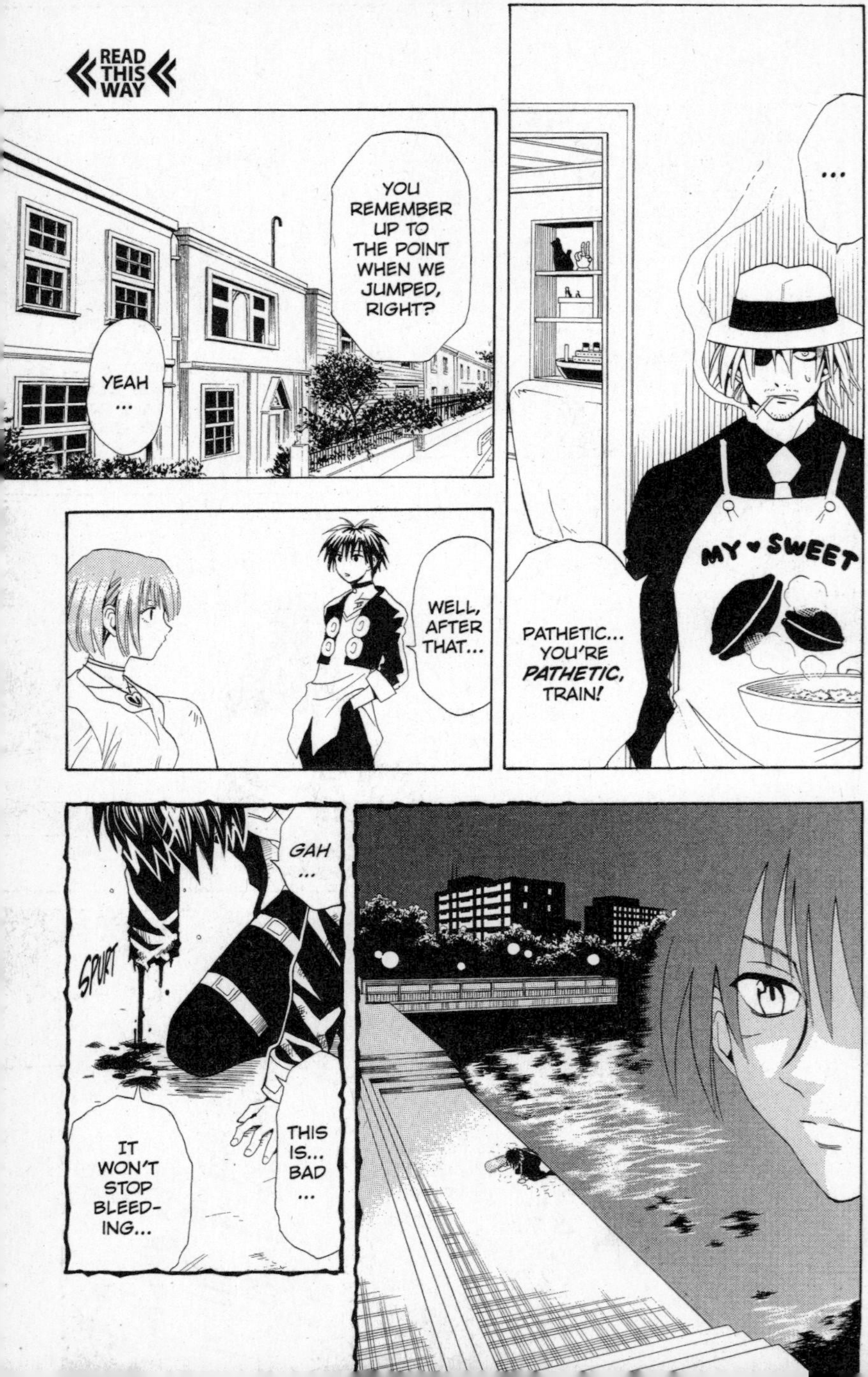
...
MY ♥ SWEET
PATHETIC... YOU'RE *PATHETIC*, TRAIN!
YOU REMEMBER UP TO THE POINT WHEN WE JUMPED, RIGHT?
YEAH ...
WELL, AFTER THAT...
GAH ...
SPURT
THIS IS... BAD ...
IT WON'T STOP BLEEDING...

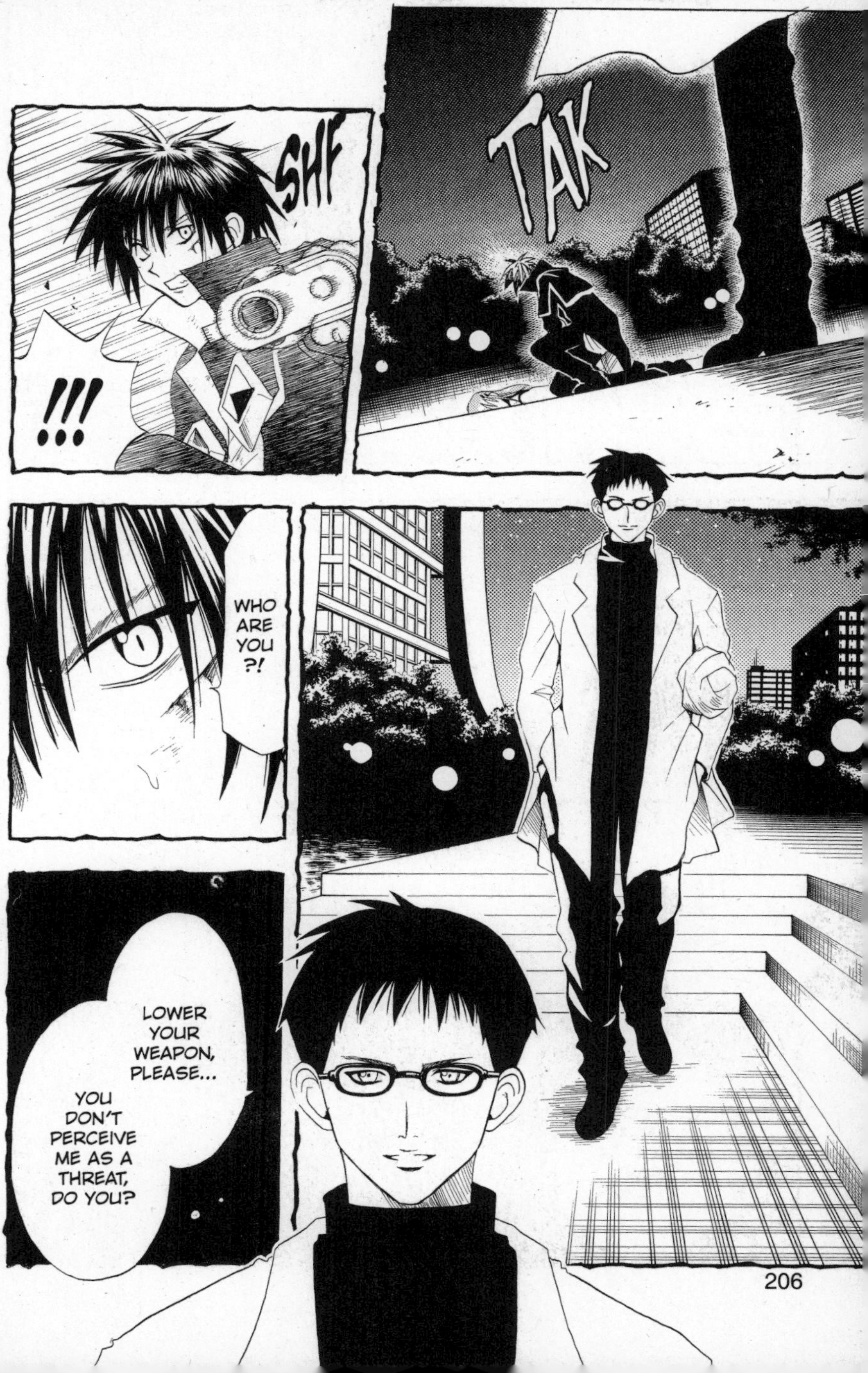
TAK
SHF
!!!
WHO ARE YOU ?!
LOWER YOUR WEAPON, PLEASE...
YOU DON'T PERCEIVE ME AS A THREAT, DO YOU?

READ THIS WAY

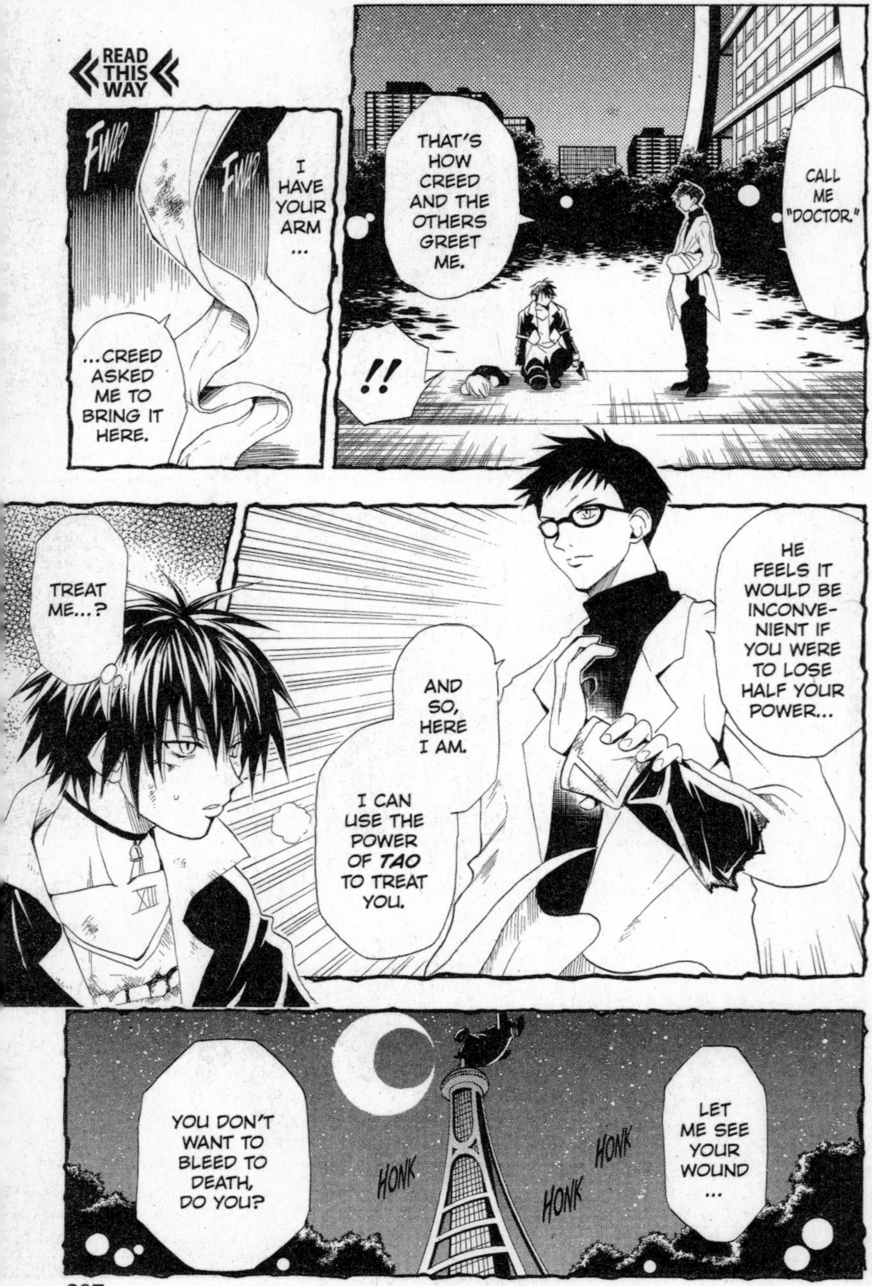
CALL ME "DOCTOR."
THAT'S HOW CREED AND THE OTHERS GREET ME.
!!
FWAP
FWAP
I HAVE YOUR ARM...
...CREED ASKED ME TO BRING IT HERE.
HE FEELS IT WOULD BE INCONVENIENT IF YOU WERE TO LOSE HALF YOUR POWER...
AND SO, HERE I AM.
I CAN USE THE POWER OF *TAO* TO TREAT YOU.
TREAT ME...?
LET ME SEE YOUR WOUND...
HONK
HONK
HONK
YOU DON'T WANT TO BLEED TO DEATH, DO YOU?

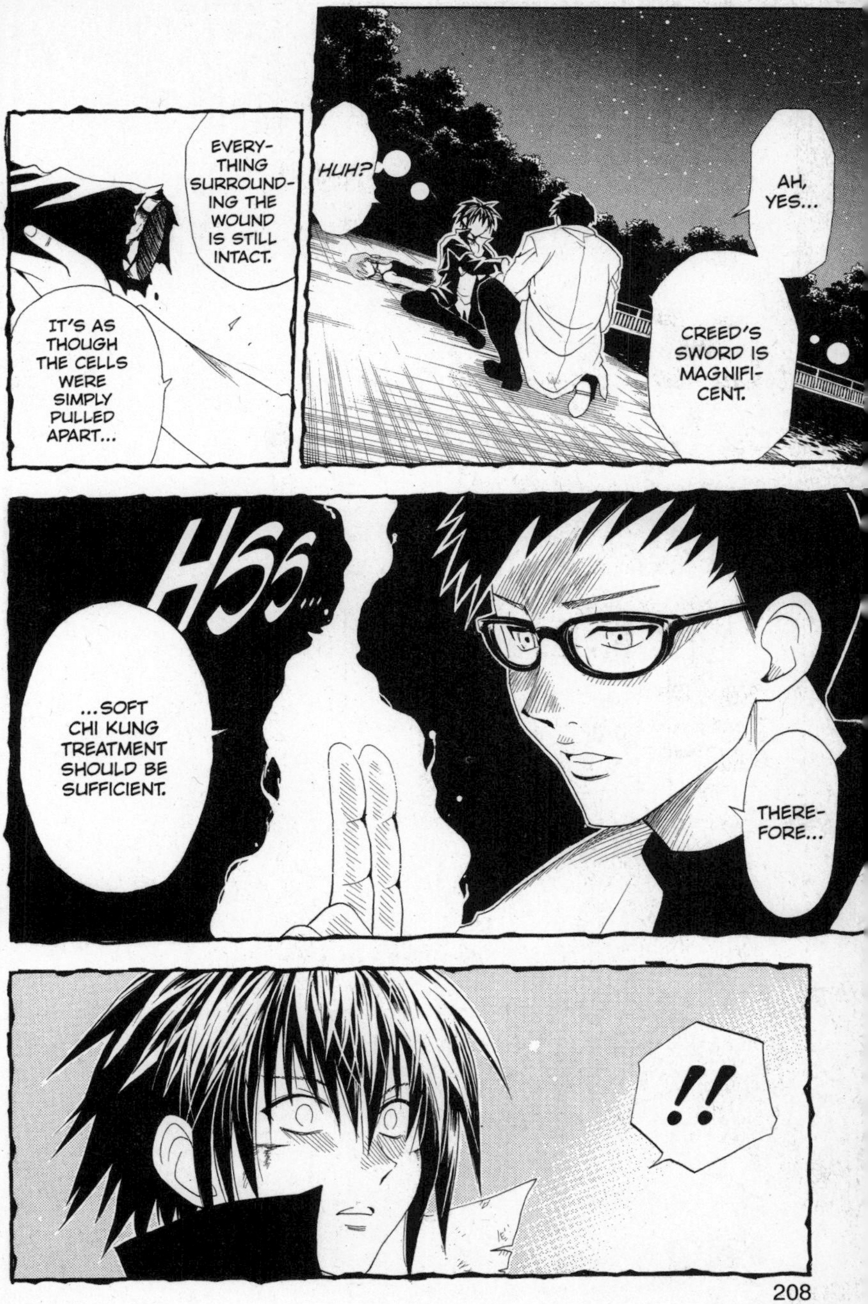
AH, YES...
CREED'S SWORD IS MAGNIFICENT.
HUH?
EVERYTHING SURROUNDING THE WOUND IS STILL INTACT.
IT'S AS THOUGH THE CELLS WERE SIMPLY PULLED APART...
THEREFORE...
HSS...
...SOFT CHI KUNG TREATMENT SHOULD BE SUFFICIENT.
!!

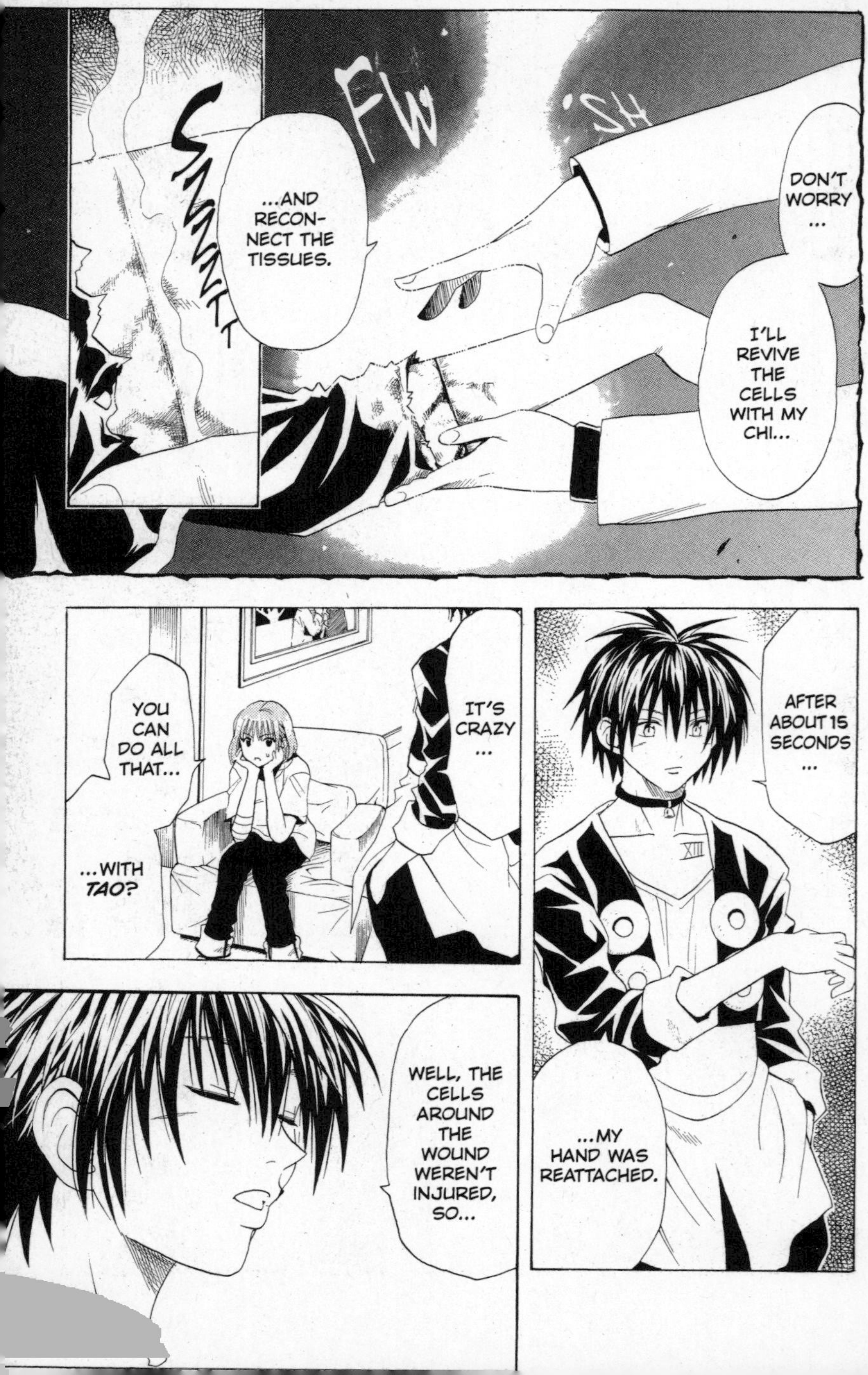
FWSH
DON'T WORRY...
I'LL REVIVE THE CELLS WITH MY CHI...
...AND RECONNECT THE TISSUES.
SZZZZZTT
AFTER ABOUT 15 SECONDS...
...MY HAND WAS REATTACHED.
IT'S CRAZY...
YOU CAN DO ALL THAT...
...WITH *TAO*?
WELL, THE CELLS AROUND THE WOUND WEREN'T INJURED, SO...

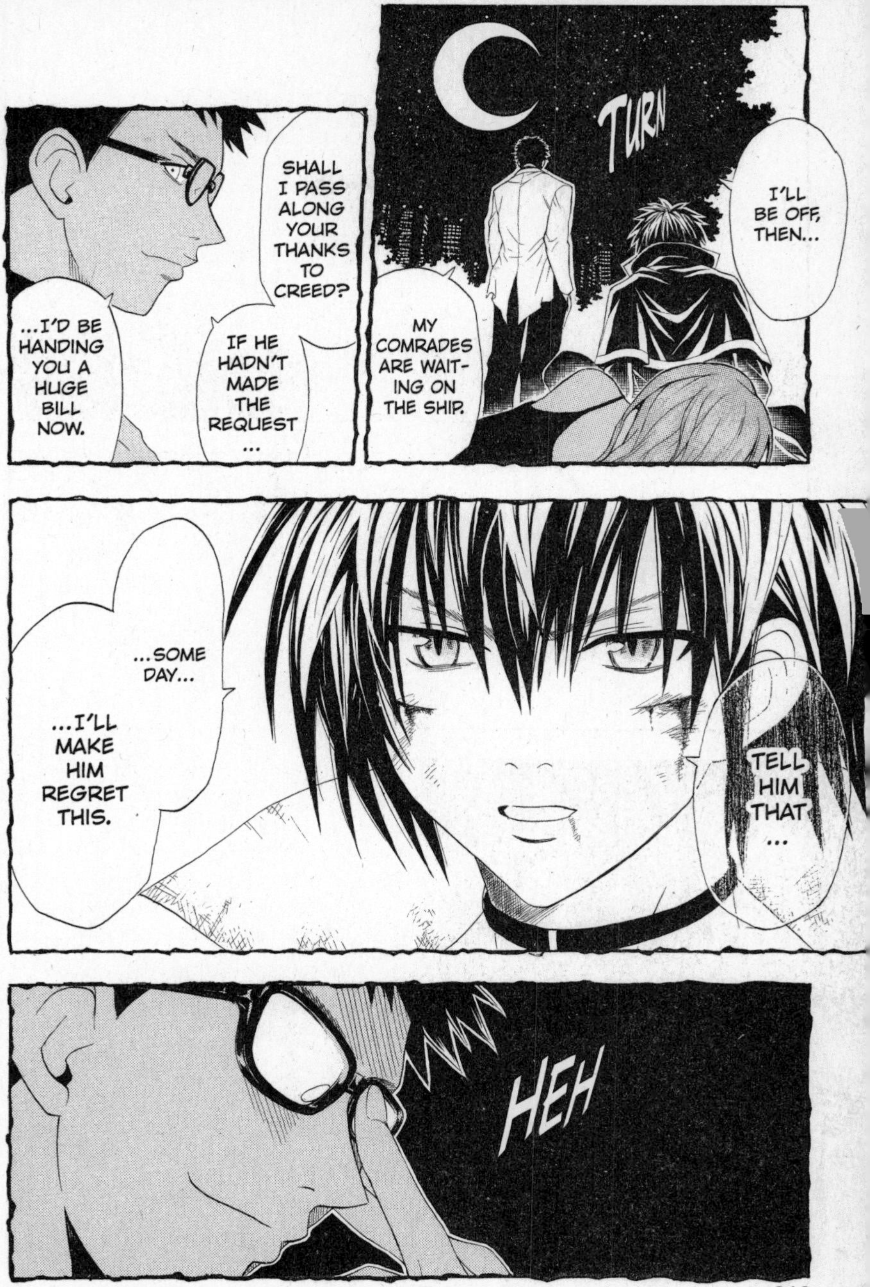
TURN
I'LL BE OFF, THEN...
MY COMRADES ARE WAIT-ING ON THE SHIP.
SHALL I PASS ALONG YOUR THANKS TO CREED?
IF HE HADN'T MADE THE REQUEST...
...I'D BE HANDING YOU A HUGE BILL NOW.
TELL HIM THAT...
...SOME DAY...
...I'LL MAKE HIM REGRET THIS.
HEH

READ THIS WAY

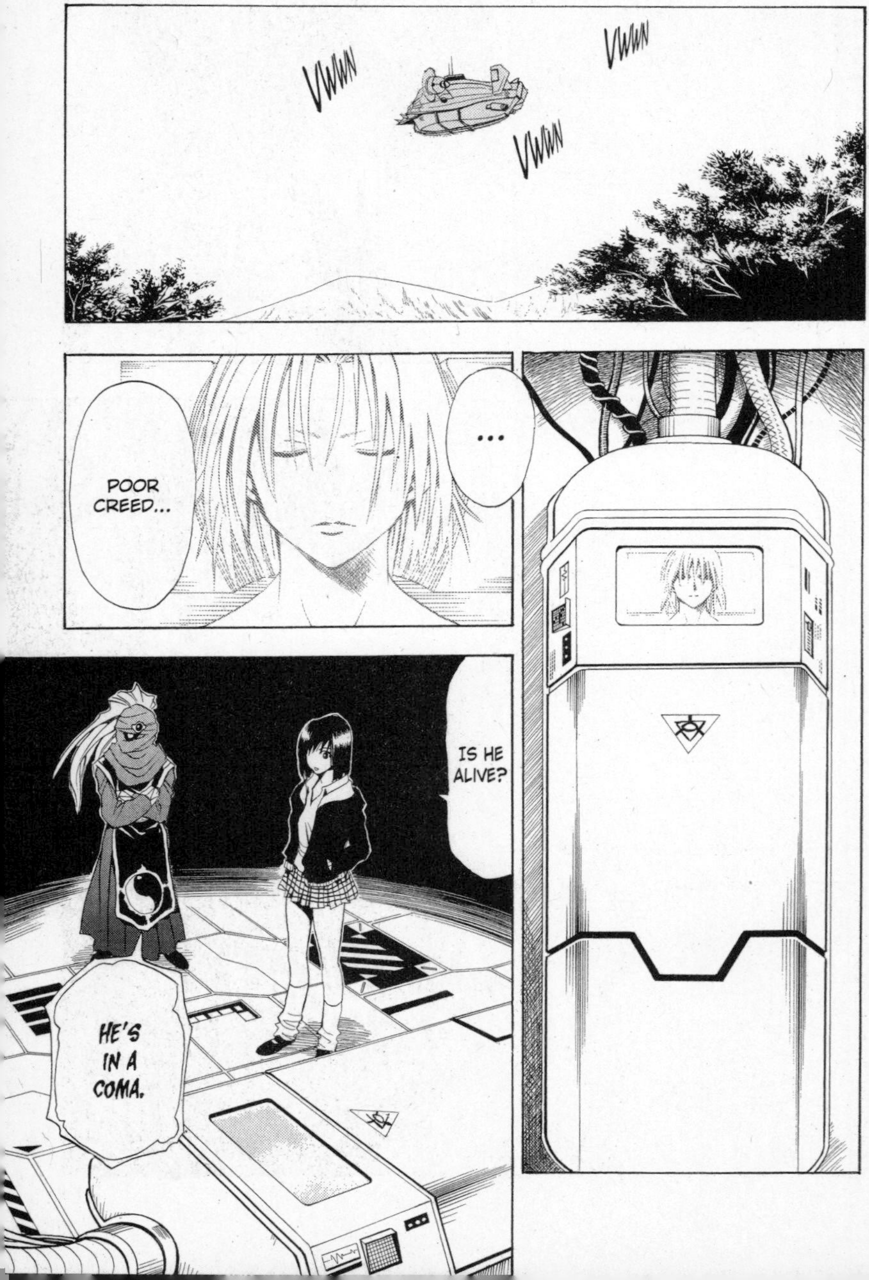
VWWN
VWWN
VWWN
...
POOR CREED...
IS HE ALIVE?
HE'S IN A COMA.

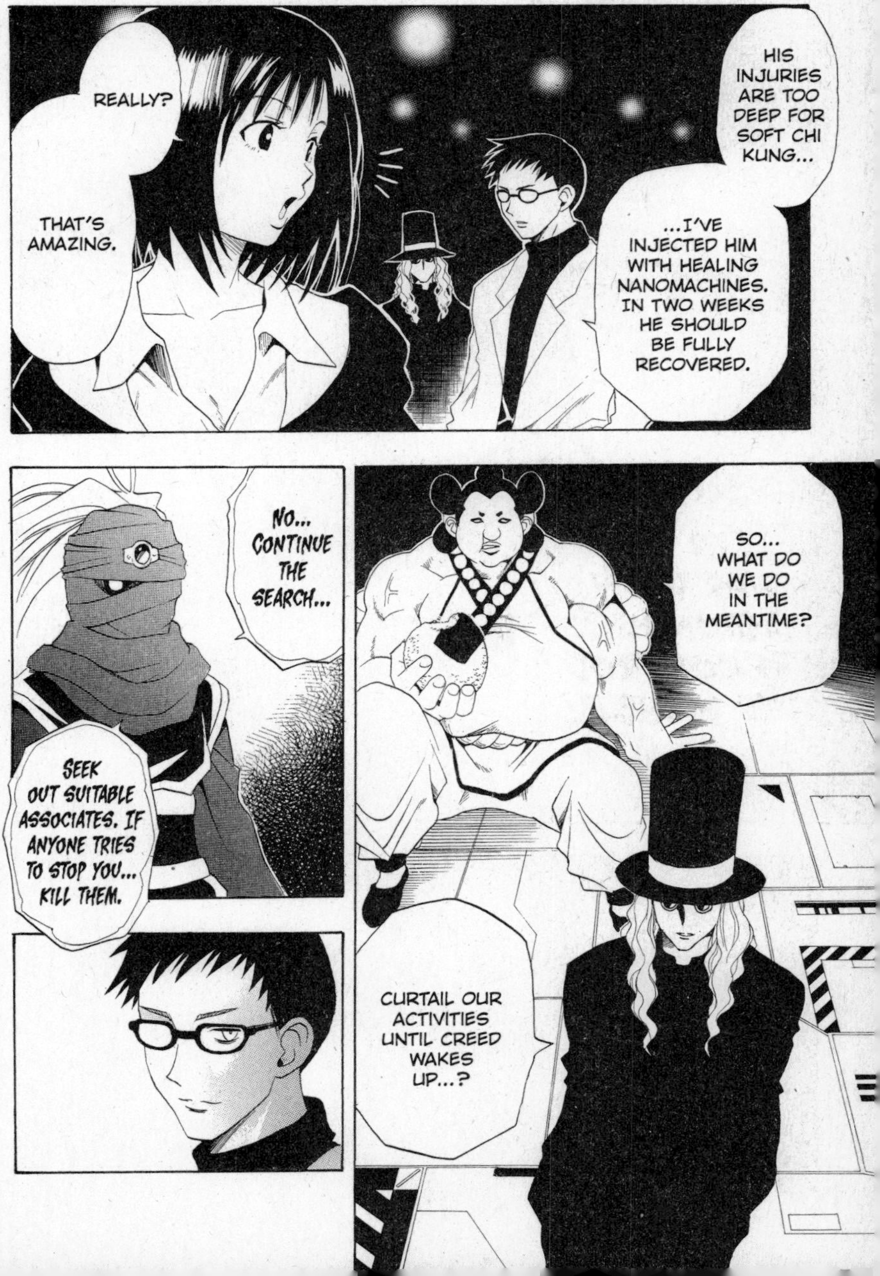
HIS INJURIES ARE TOO DEEP FOR SOFT CHI KUNG...
...I'VE INJECTED HIM WITH HEALING NANOMACHINES. IN TWO WEEKS HE SHOULD BE FULLY RECOVERED.
REALLY?
THAT'S AMAZING.
SO... WHAT DO WE DO IN THE MEANTIME?
CURTAIL OUR ACTIVITIES UNTIL CREED WAKES UP...?
NO... CONTINUE THE SEARCH...
SEEK OUT SUITABLE ASSOCIATES. IF ANYONE TRIES TO STOP YOU... KILL THEM.

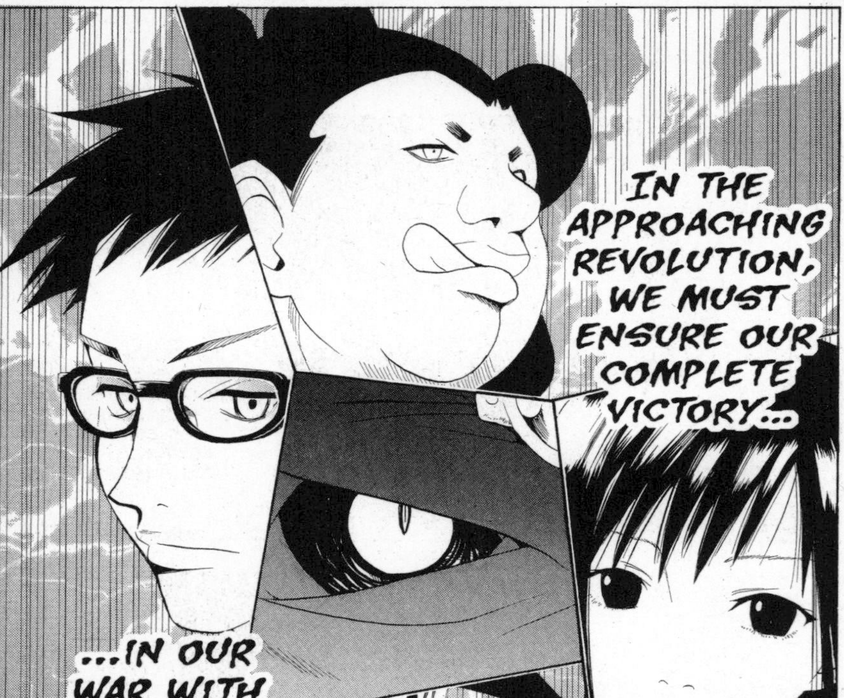
IN THE APPROACHING REVOLUTION, WE MUST ENSURE OUR COMPLETE VICTORY...
...IN OUR WAR WITH CHRONOS...! TO CONTROL THE WORLD!
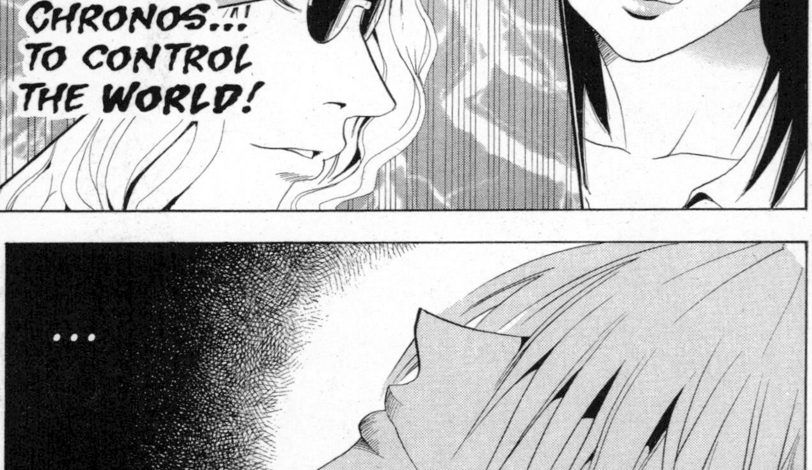
...

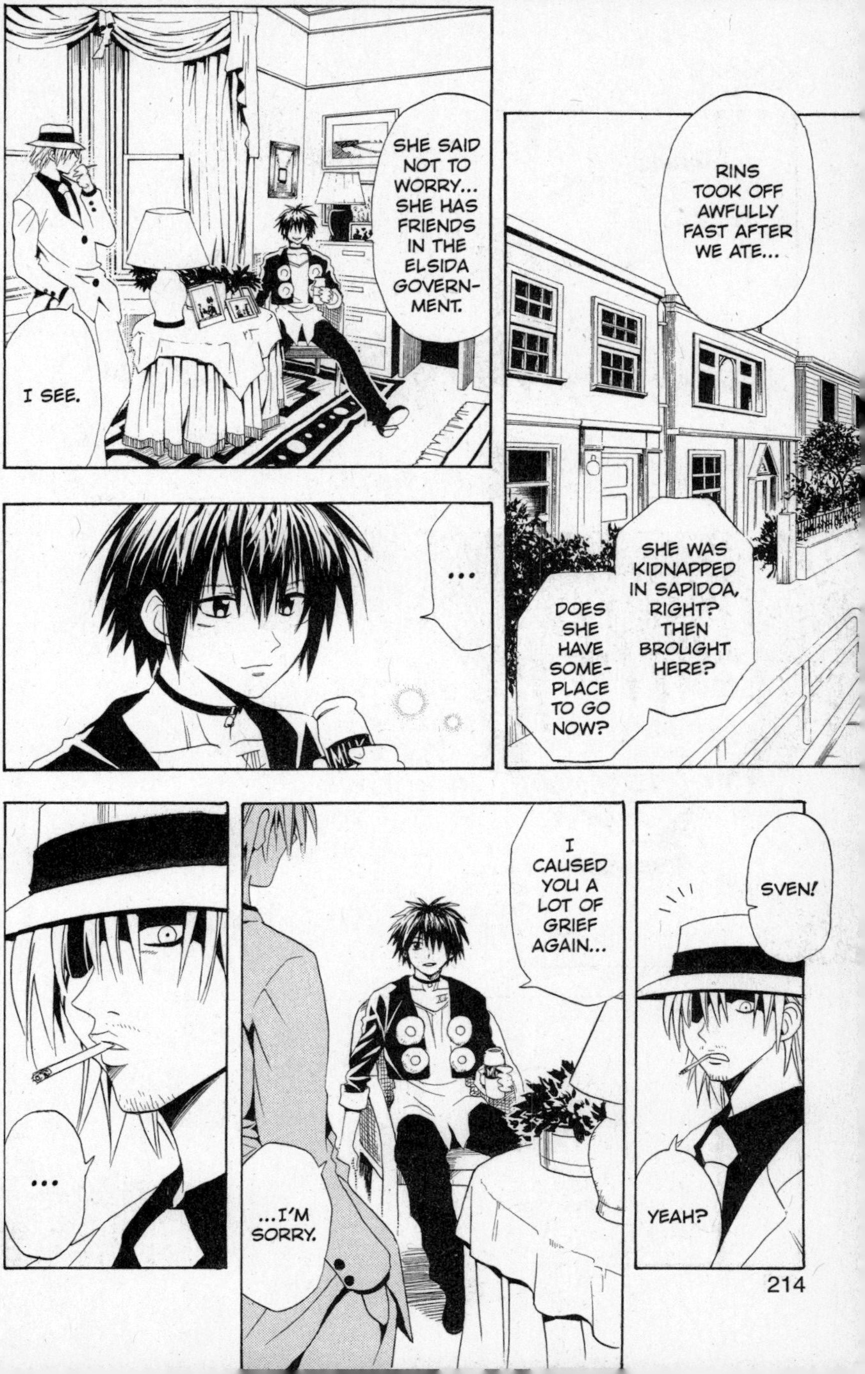
RINS TOOK OFF AWFULLY FAST AFTER WE ATE...
SHE WAS KIDNAPPED IN SAPIDOA, RIGHT? THEN BROUGHT HERE?
DOES SHE HAVE SOMEPLACE TO GO NOW?
SHE SAID NOT TO WORRY... SHE HAS FRIENDS IN THE ELSIDA GOVERN-MENT.
I SEE.
...
SVEN!
YEAH?
I CAUSED YOU A LOT OF GRIEF AGAIN...
...I'M SORRY.
...

READ THIS WAY

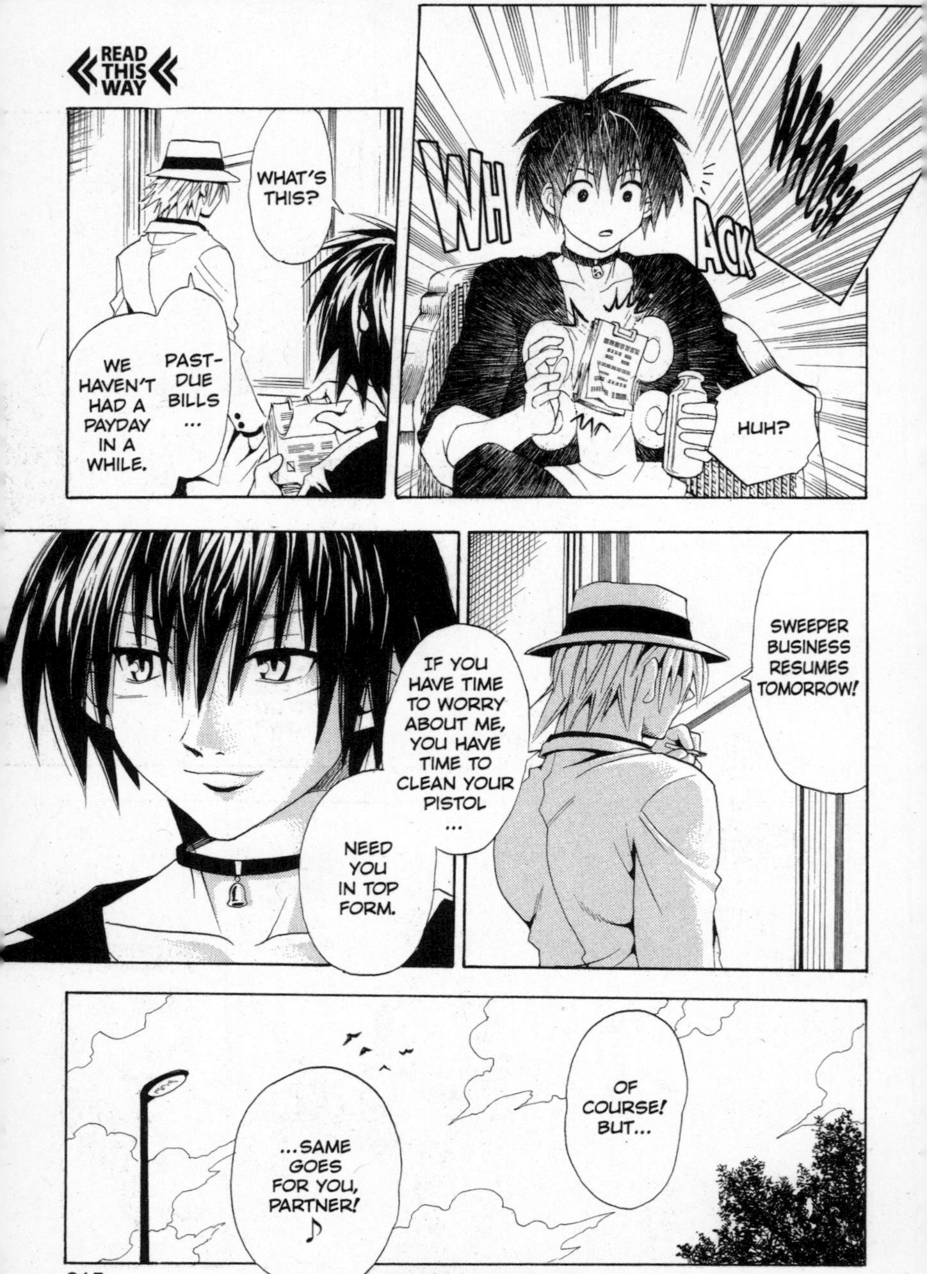
WHOOSH
WHACK
HUH?
WHAT'S THIS?
PAST-DUE BILLS...
WE HAVEN'T HAD A PAYDAY IN A WHILE.
SWEEPER BUSINESS RESUMES TOMORROW!
IF YOU HAVE TIME TO WORRY ABOUT ME, YOU HAVE TIME TO CLEAN YOUR PISTOL...
NEED YOU IN TOP FORM.
OF COURSE! BUT...
...SAME GOES FOR YOU, PARTNER! ♪

2 Creed (The End)

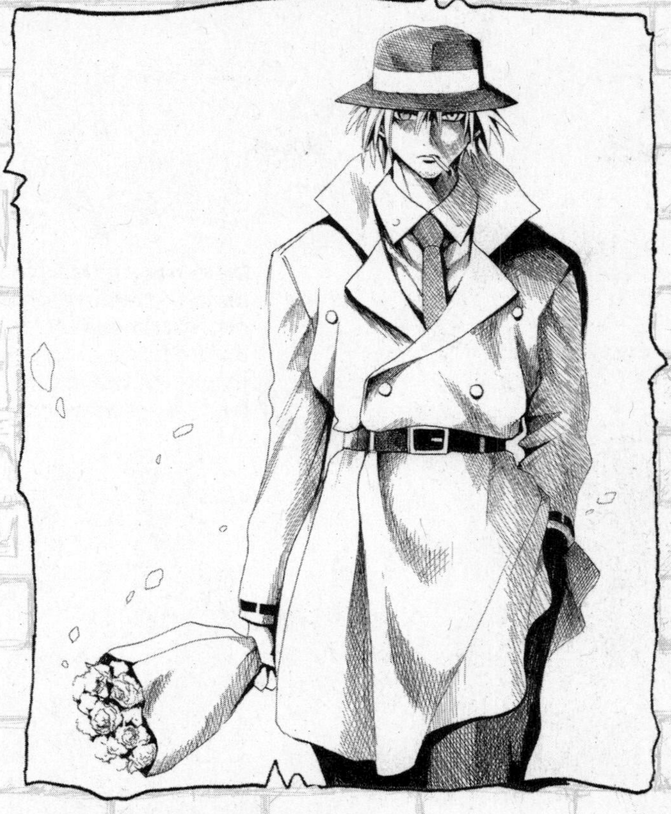

IN THE NEXT VOLUME...

When Train and Sven go after a pair of notorious jewel thieves, they find more trouble than they bargained for! Train receives a desperate plea for help from an old colleague whose town is being terrorized by a serial murderer with strange powers. Eve offers herself as bait to lure the killer out, but will she be caught in a deadly trap?!

AVAILABLE JULY 2006!

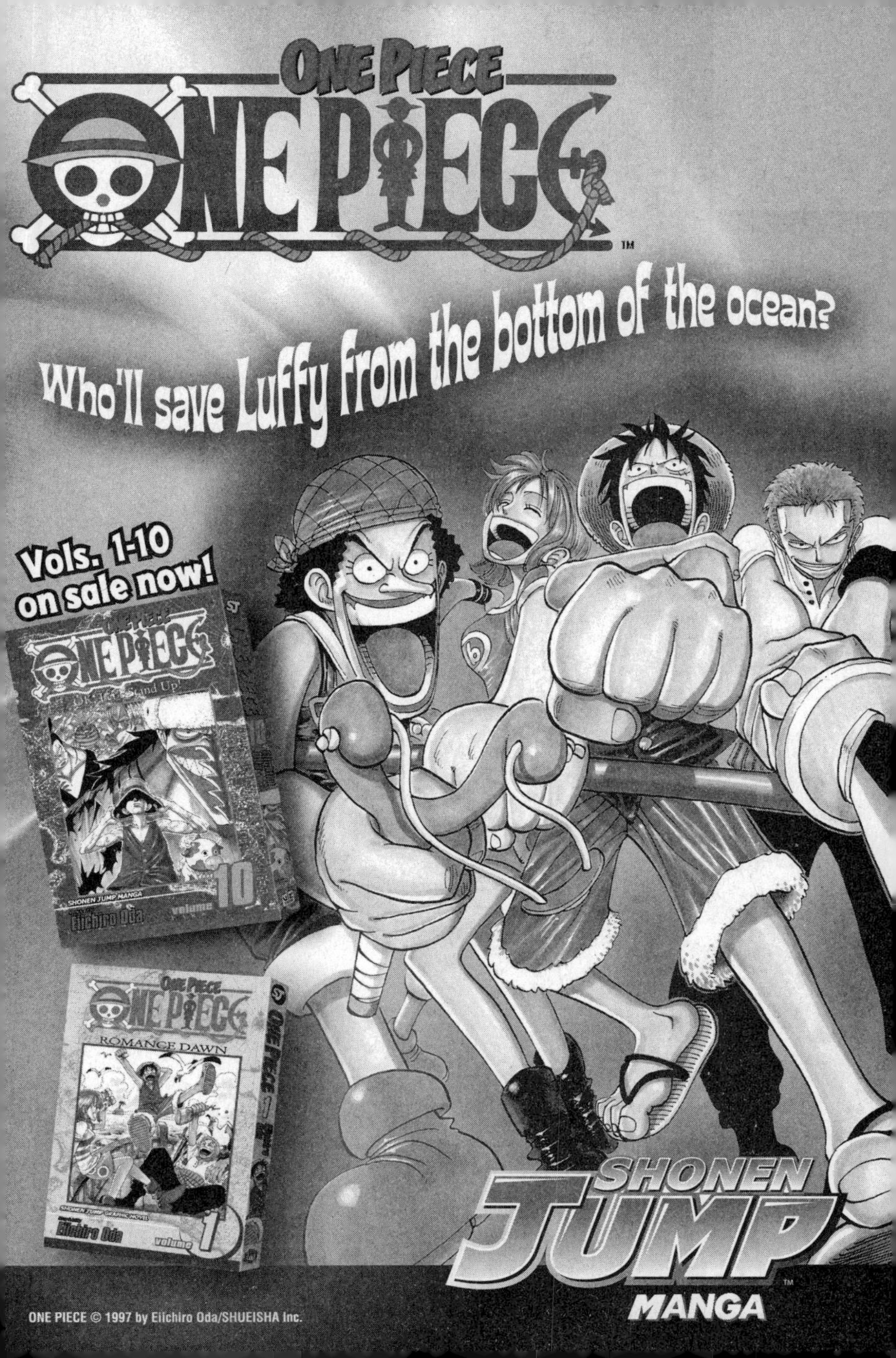
ONE PIECE
ONE PIECE
Who'll save Luffy from the bottom of the ocean?
Vols. 1-10 on sale now!
ONE PIECE
ROMANCE DAWN
Eiichiro Oda
volume 1
SHONEN JUMP MANGA
ONE PIECE © 1997 by Eiichiro Oda/SHUEISHA Inc.

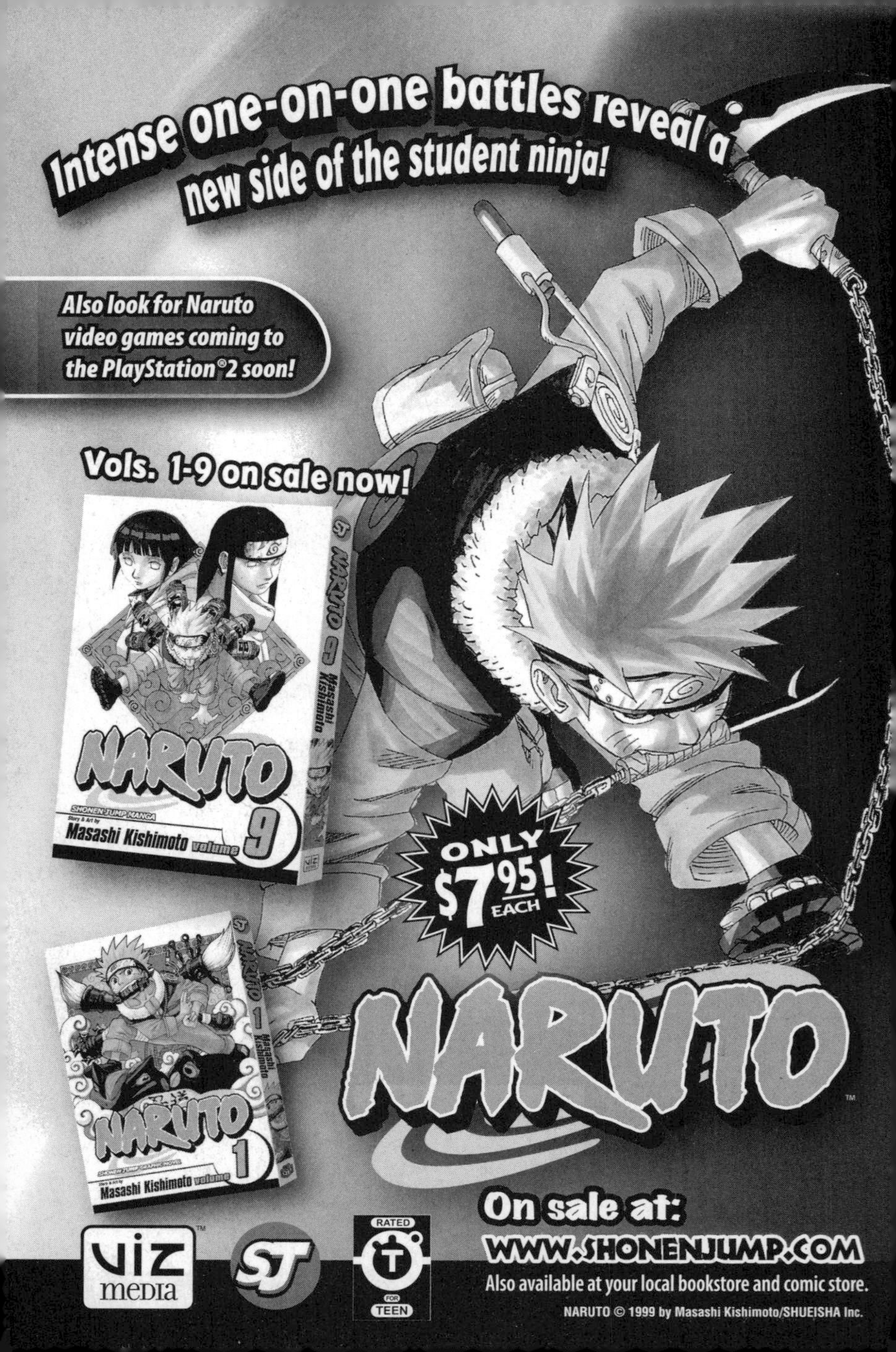
Intense one-on-one battles reveal a new side of the student ninja!
Also look for Naruto video games coming to the PlayStation®2 soon!
Vols. 1-9 on sale now!
NARUTO
SHONEN JUMP MANGA
Story & Art by
Masashi Kishimoto volume 9
NARUTO 1
Masashi Kishimoto volume 1
ONLY $7.95! EACH
NARUTO™
On sale at:
WWW.SHONENJUMP.COM
Also available at your local bookstore and comic store.
NARUTO © 1999 by Masashi Kishimoto/SHUEISHA Inc.
VIZ media
SJ
RATED T FOR TEEN

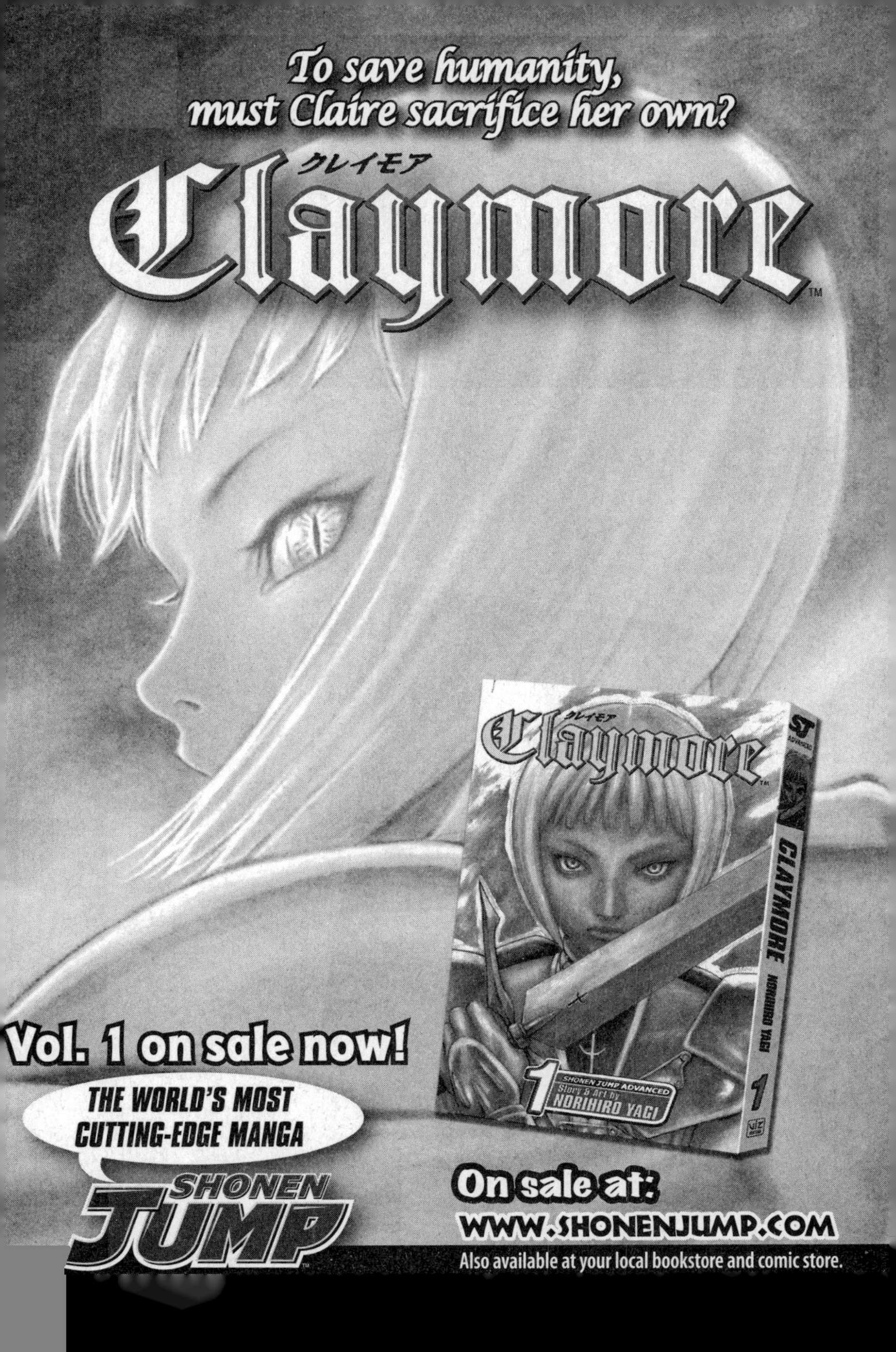

To save humanity,
must Claire sacrifice her own?
クレイモア
Claymore™
クレイモア
Claymore
SJ ADVANCED
CLAYMORE
NORIHIRO YAGI
1
1
SHONEN JUMP ADVANCED
Story & Art by
NORIHIRO YAGI
Vol. 1 on sale now!
THE WORLD'S MOST
CUTTING-EDGE MANGA
SHONEN
JUMP
On sale at:
WWW.SHONENJUMP.COM
Also available at your local bookstore and comic store.

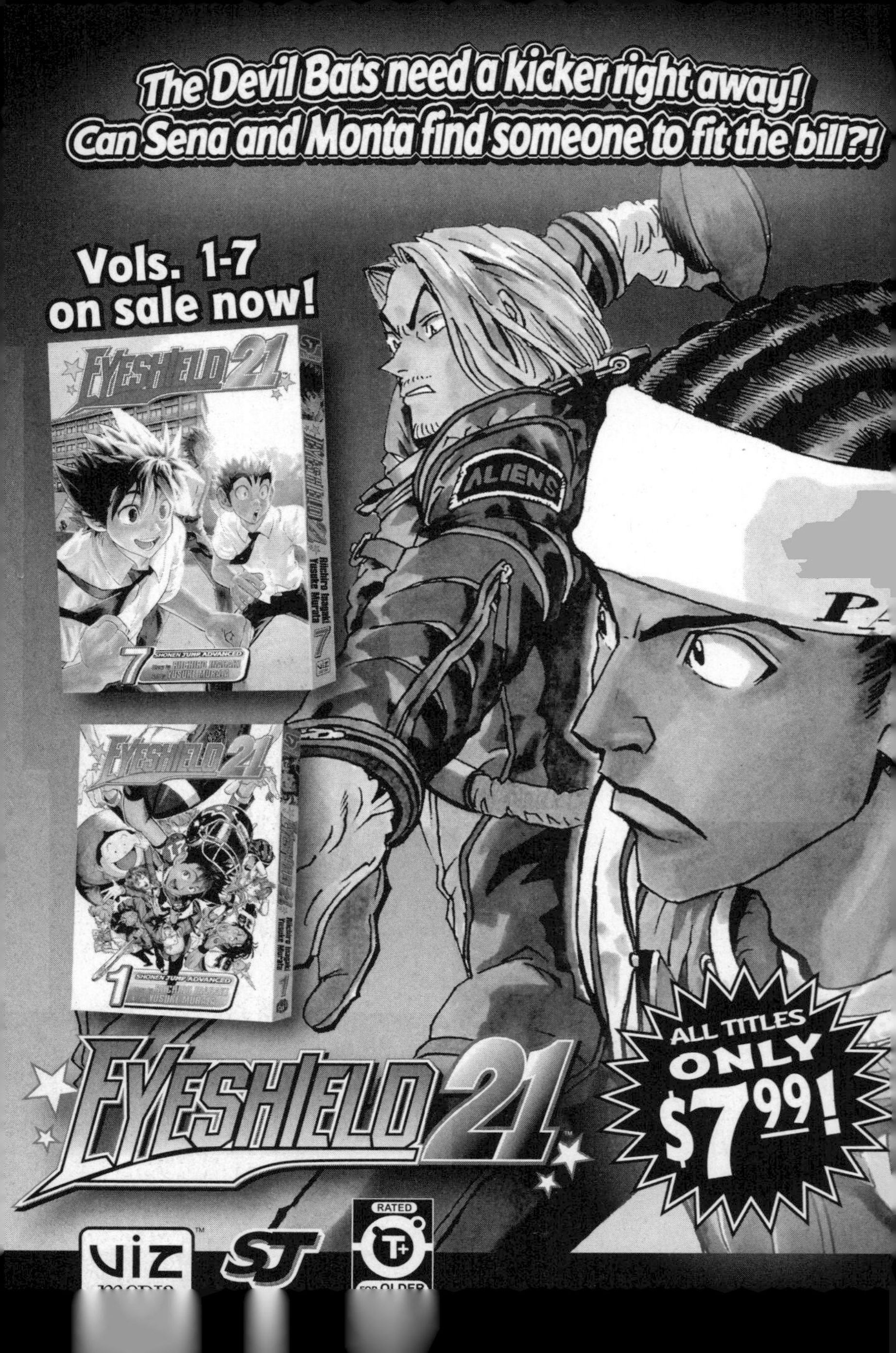

The Devil Bats need a kicker right away!
Can Sena and Monta find someone to fit the bill?!
Vols. 1-7
on sale now!
EYESHIELD 21
ALL TITLES
ONLY
$7.99!
RATED
T+

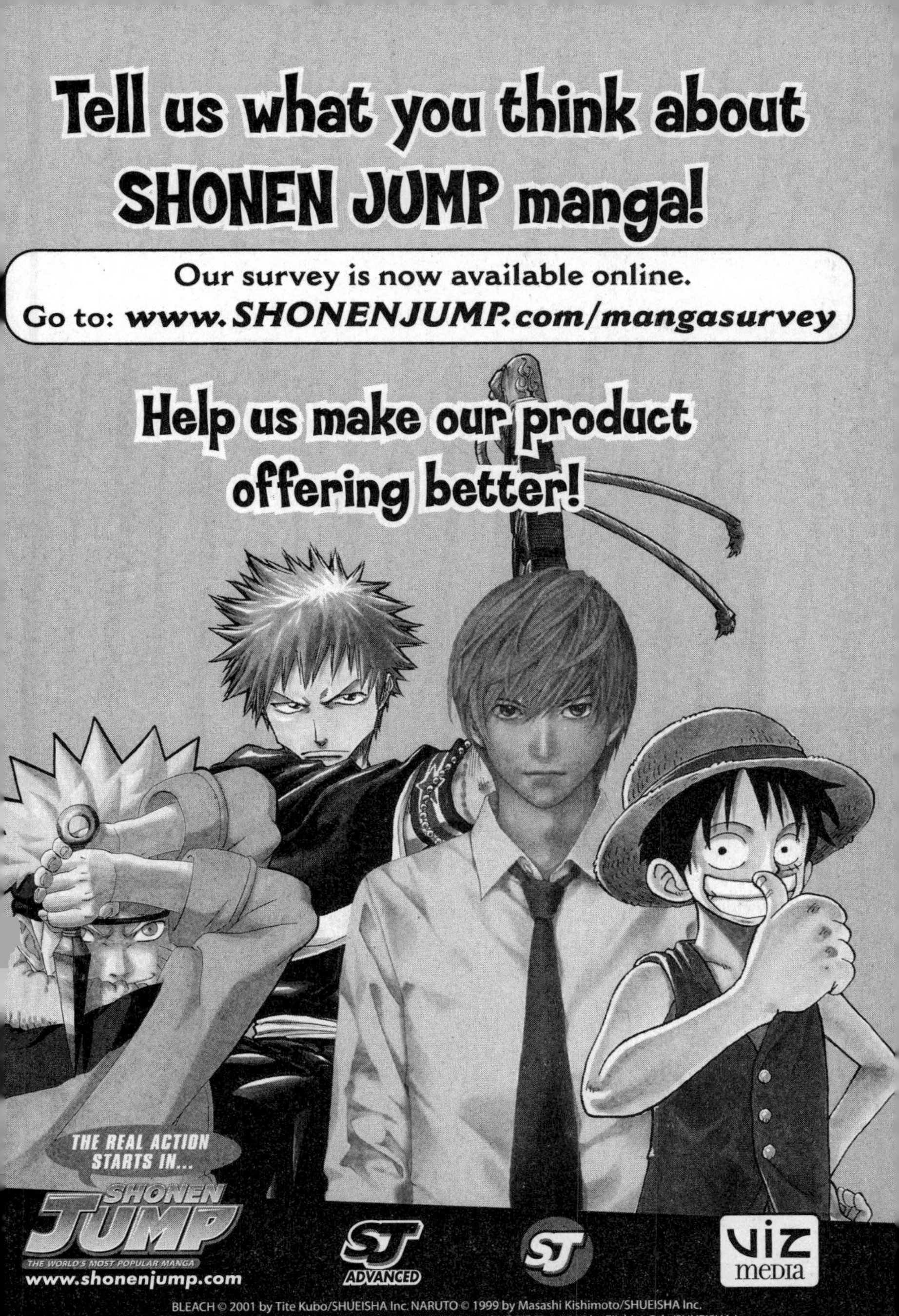
Tell us what you think about SHONEN JUMP manga!
Our survey is now available online.
Go to: www.SHONENJUMP.com/mangasurvey
Help us make our product offering better!
THE REAL ACTION STARTS IN...
SHONEN JUMP
THE WORLD'S MOST POPULAR MANGA
www.shonenjump.com
SJ ADVANCED
SJ
VIZ media
BLEACH © 2001 by Tite Kubo/SHUEISHA Inc. NARUTO © 1999 by Masashi Kishimoto/SHUEISHA Inc.

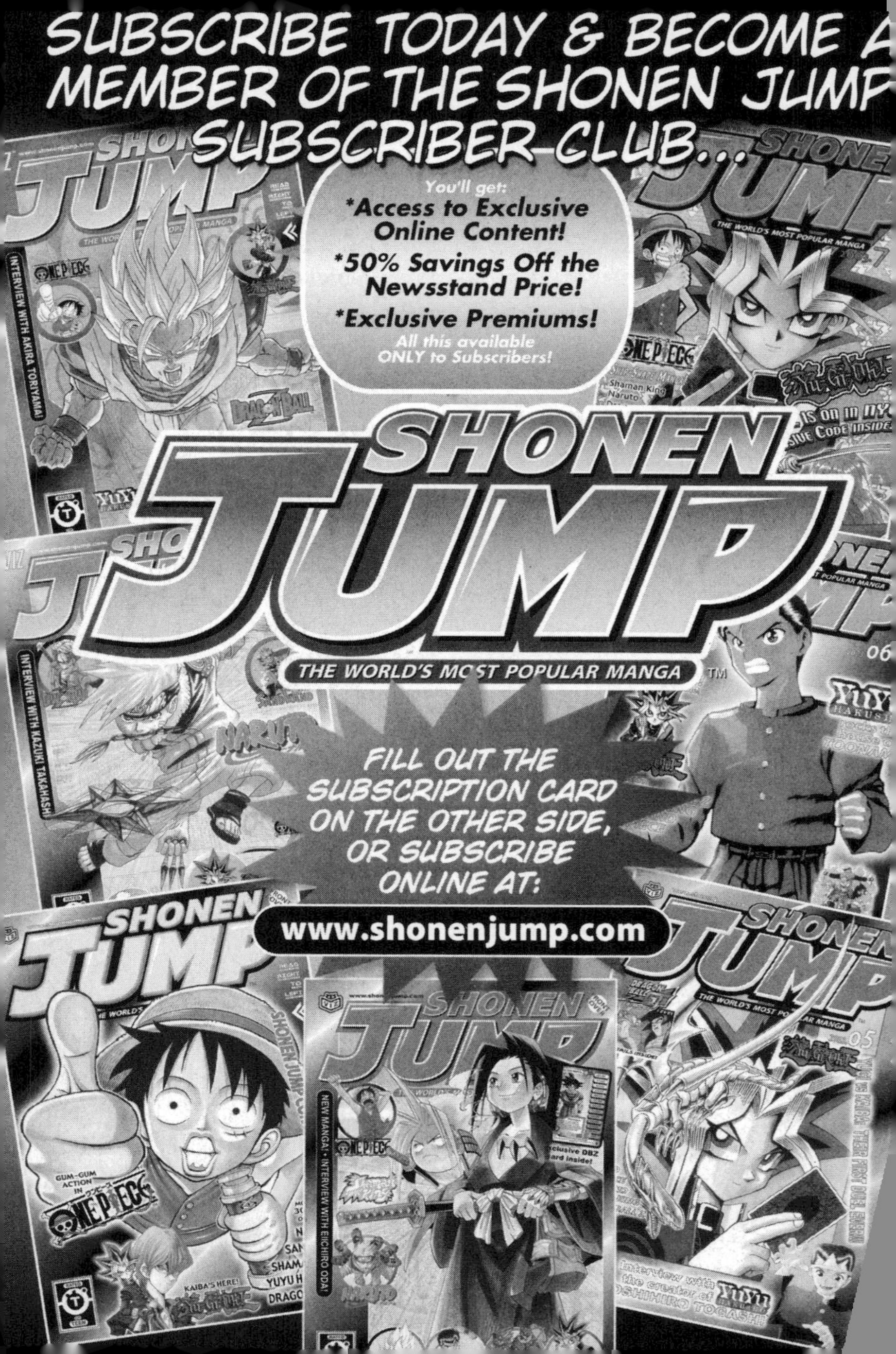

SUBSCRIBE TODAY & BECOME A MEMBER OF THE SHONEN JUMP SUBSCRIBER CLUB...
You'll get:
*Access to Exclusive Online Content!
*50% Savings Off the Newsstand Price!
*Exclusive Premiums!
All this available ONLY to Subscribers!
SHONEN JUMP
THE WORLD'S MOST POPULAR MANGA TM
FILL OUT THE SUBSCRIPTION CARD ON THE OTHER SIDE, OR SUBSCRIBE ONLINE AT:
www.shonenjump.com